D1534827

ASPECTS OF THE STUDY
OF ROMAN HISTORY

ASPECTS OF THE STUDY OF ROMAN HISTORY

BY

Thomas Spencer Jerome, M.A.

CAPRICORN BOOKS, NEW YORK
1962

Originally published in 1923
Capricorn edition, 1962

MANUFACTURED IN THE UNITED STATES OF AMERICA

CONTENTS

Contents

ASPECTS OF THE STUDY
OF ROMAN HISTORY

Aspects of the Study of Roman History

CHAPTER I

INTRODUCTION: THE VALUE OF HISTORY

"WE are learning," said a scholar, who in this spoke wisely, "that European history, from its first glimmerings to our own day, is one unbroken drama, no part of which can be rightly understood without reference to the other parts which come before and after it. We are learning that of this great drama Rome is the centre, the point to which all roads lead, and from which all roads lead no less. It is the vast lake in which all the streams of earlier history lose themselves, and from which all the streams of later history flow forth again." [1] The essential truth of Professor Freeman's metaphor has been recognized by all who have turned a large and penetrating vision upon the past of mankind. In a very real sense Rome is the eternal city; her power has been transmuted from a material to a spiritual thing, and her conquests are wider now than when an old writer coined

[1] E. A. Freeman, *Comparative Politics: The Unity of History* (London, 1874), p. 306.

the phrase *Romani gentium domini*.[1]   Anatole France has happily expressed this idea of the power and permanence of ancient Rome by saying: "Rome n'est pas morte puisqu'elle vit en nous." [2]

It is precisely because Rome still lives, and lives abundantly, in our art, our language, and our institutions, that scholars have devoted so much toil to every aspect of her history. For this reason, also, no interpretation of her past can hope to prove final, since every age, in addition to finding new data from the distant past, will develop and disclose certain lines of kinship with it. Each generation, as it comes on, will find new conditions capable of supplying it with similarities to the past, in the light of which, by analogical reasoning, it will be able to perceive certain aspects of the past in new and significant relationships. In consequence, the history of Rome possesses, and will always possess, so long as the form and content of our civilization endure, direct and serious utilities, as well as the dramatic interest inherent in the fortunes of a city whose authority once ruled the world.

What is true of Roman history is, of course, also true, in a varying degree, of all history; for without a knowledge of the past the present must remain intelligible only in part. The present is what it is, because of the character of the past which lies beyond it. To this extent, it is evident, all history possesses a direct utility, because it furnishes us a notion of relativity. It helps us to explain the origin of existing things, to elucidate the *processsus* of human development, to weigh evidence and to view social changes without dread. Whether the knowledge gained from its study can be of direct value in controlling choices in practical life, as Polybius

[1] Florus, II, 26.
[2] *Sur la Pierre Blanche* (Paris, 1910), p. 159.

asserted,[1] or whether conditions repeat themselves in
forms sufficiently similar to permit any useful conclusions
to be drawn from them, as Thucydides implied,[2] the
scientific historian will seriously doubt. The former
proposition leads substantially to the position taken by
Lord Morley: "I do not in the least want to know what
happened in the past, except as it enables me to see my
way more clearly through what is happening to-day." [3]
And acceptance of the latter leads inevitably to a belief
in what is vaguely called a "philosophy of history," a
doctrine dearer to the heart of the metaphysician than of
the historian. The exact scholar of to-day does not feel
himself compelled to accept either the one thesis or the
other in the form stated, because he realizes that the
utility of history cannot be directly equated in terms of
conduct—history is no longer a department of ethics as
it was to many of the ancients—and because he knows that
history is not "philosophy teaching by examples."

Some scholars, indeed, in their endeavor to elevate
history into an independent science, free from the bondage
of ethics, politics, and religion, have gone so far as to
assume that any value history may have apart from an
exact record of facts must be incidental. But it is obvious

[1] III, 31.
[2] I, 22.
[3] *Critical Miscellanies,* vol. II (London, 1877), p. 345. Similarly
Nietzsche, taking for his text Goethe's dictum: "I hate everything
that merely instructs me without increasing or directly quickening
my activity," roundly asserted that "antiquarian history degen-
erates from the moment that it no longer gives a soul and
inspiration to the fresh life of the present." *Thoughts Out of
Season, The Use and Abuse of History* (London, 1909, edition
of Levy), vol. II, pp. 1, 27. Langlois et Seignobos, *Introduction
aux Études historiques* (Paris, 1898), pp. 277, 278, aptly term
the doctrine *historia magistra vitæ* "une illusion surannée."

that if this position be taken in its extreme form, the labor of the historian is vain. Accumulations of facts are not entertaining, and if they lack utility as well, it is difficult to see why time should be wasted in collecting them. Professor Bury, in his *Ancient Greek Historians,* has clearly shown how the doctrine of "History for its own sake" may be reconciled with the doctrine of utility. The maxim, he points out, is " a regulative principle; it concerns only the methods and immediate aims of historians; it does not express the final purpose of their labours. . . . Human interest is its ultimate justification." [1]

But discussion of the utility of history is largely academic. In the last analysis it hinges on the question of the utility of knowledge. For it is obvious that such utility can be neither limited nor defined. It becomes didactic in so far as all knowledge is didactic, but the precise form of the lesson to be learned, and the quality of the judgment which may be pronounced, are not the historian's primary concern. The direct value of his work must necessarily vary with circumstances. The knowledge which is useful, and therefore valuable, to a statesman will not be equally so to a mechanic. In like manner it is apparent that a knowledge of the great democracies of the past, namely those of Athens and Rome, concerns modern civilization more intimately and at more points than a knowledge of ancient Egypt and Babylonia because many of our experiences and institutions have their roots in the culture of Greece and Rome. And to be ignorant of these antecedents is to remain something of a child or a barbarian all one's life long.

America, especially, owes so great a debt to ancient Rome that a knowledge of her history is the price we must pay for understanding ourselves. "The heritage of

[1] New York, 1909, pp. 245-247.

Rome," Ferrero declared to his American audiences,[1] "is, for the peoples of America still more than for those of Europe, an heredity not purely artistic and literary, but political and social, which exercises the most beneficent influence on your history. In a certain sense it might be said that America is to-day politically, more than Europe, the true heir of Rome; that the new world is nearer—by apparent paradox—to ancient Rome than is Europe. Among the most important facts, however little noticed, in the history of the nineteenth century, I should number this: that the Republic, the human state considered as the common property of all—the great political creation of ancient Rome—is reborn here in America, after having died out in Europe. The Latin seed, lying buried for so many centuries beneath the ruins of the ancient world, like the grains of wheat buried in Egyptian tombs, transported from the other side of the ocean, has sprung up in the land that Columbus discovered. If there had been no Rome; if Rome had wholly perished in the great barbarian catastrophe; if in the Renaissance there had not been found among the ruins of the ancient world, together with beautiful Greek statues and manuscripts, this great political idea, there would to-day be no Republic in North America. With the word would probably have perished also the idea and the thing; and there is no assurance that men would have been able so easily and so well to rediscover it by their own effort."

But if it is true that a knowledge of Rome serves to explain institutions and conditions of America, it is equally true that a knowledge of these will help us to understand the history of Rome. The relationship is reciprocal. "On a dit quelquefois que l'histoire nous aide

[1] *Characters and Events of Roman History* (New York, 1909), pp. 261-262.

à comprendre notre temps; il est peut-être plus vrai encore de dire que notre temps nous aide à comprendre l'histoire." [1]   For it is generally agreed that the student must know how men of to-day think and act if he is to understand the known facts of the actions of men in the past.[2]   He proceeds on the hypothesis that the acts and motives of the past are somewhat similar to like contemporaneous facts.   This is indeed the prime postulate of history; for if humanity in the past were unlike humanity in the present, all history would be unintelligible. "We cannot observe past reality, and we know it only by its resemblance to reality in the present." [3]

Historical reasoning, then, must rest on what has been called "the fundamental principle of history, the analogy between men of former times and men of to-day."   There is no logical difficulty involved in thus reasoning from past to present as well as from present to past, but the process, as results have shown, is often beset with danger.   Mistakes arise in assuming that the two groups of facts or situations have sufficient points of resemblance to justify our confidence in a similarity between other elements which exist in the one case and which we seek to establish in the other.   Historical analogies in the field of political institutions are, as a rule, of doubtful utility.   In all ages men have been prone to overestimate the importance of their institutions, to mistake their nature and origin, and to exaggerate their influence, regarding them as the creators rather than the creatures of their age.   An institution is in essence only the outward, static mani-

---

[1] G. Monod, De la Méthode dans les Sciences (Paris, 1909), p. 337.

[2] See A. B. Hart, American Historical Review, vol. XV (1910), p. 238.

[3] Langlois et Seignobos, op. cit., pp. 189, 193.

festation of some aspect of the character of a few or of many members of a community, of their average feelings and beliefs, and hence, ultimately, of their primal needs and tendencies exhibited concurrently in relation to some general and fairly permanent element of their environment. It is easy to trace in very broad lines the principal institutions of human societies back to the fundamental characteristics of the human mind; and as these do not vary much fundamentally we can find a certain rough similarity in the resultant institutions.

But while these general similarities exist, there are nevertheless very considerable differences between the institutions of societies which may resemble each other in the character of their individual members. These differences arise, in part at least, from the fact that each community has a special environment whose peculiarities give rise to manifold results. Obviously, it is bound to make a great difference whether a people inhabit a large island like Great Britain, or a small adjacent one like Ireland, or a vast plain like Russia; whether the land is fertile, like Egypt, or barren, like Arabia. The problems to be met in these different cases are not alike, and the solutions must differ even though the inhabitants were precisely the same in their original natures. Again, the life of man is short, but peoples, communities, and classes come into existence slowly and are of long duration. What may be called a class or national consciousness arises with certain ideas, memories, and modes of reaction. These characteristics are not, of course, transmitted by biological inheritance, but are handed down by imitation and education with such strength as to affect profoundly the coming generations.

When, however, the analogical reasoning is confined to the pyschology of men, it proceeds on surer and more helpful lines. While we may be puzzled by many ancient institutions, we understand easily a panic fear or a pæan of victory. These are universal; these we have ourselves known. We may not be certain how the Romans held a levy or census, but we know perfectly well how they feared Hannibal and yet stood firm; how they hated and admired Cæsar; how proud they were of their *gravitas* and probity, and yet indulged in shameless trickery. When we reach these psychological regions we feel that history and life draw very close together; and here the student cannot go very far towards understanding his material without wide experience of human nature.

There has come into existence, in recent years, a large amount of new and useful interpretative material which has made possible a clearer understanding of the history of ancient Rome. In one field, especially, the modern scholar possesses advantages far superior to those of earlier students. History, inasmuch as it deals with human conduct, has for its underlying science the general nature and working of the human mind. And since it has to do with the deeds of one or many men possessing various kinds of minds more or less divergent from the ideal average, it involves a knowledge of psychology, both normal and abnormal, as well as individual and collective. Monod, indeed, even defines history as a sort of collective psychology.[1] Now scientific psychology is a creature of yesterday, and while it is not yet a completed study, it has progressed far enough to make the branch of metaphysics which bore the name of psychology a generation or two ago seem as hopelessly worthless as the dæmonic psycopathic theories of earlier times.

One need not go far in the study of this new science to find that much of history begins to wear a different

[1] *De la Méthode dans les Sciences*, p. 350.

aspect. Relations appear between events which had previously seemed unrelated; things which had been taken to be causes now appear to be effects or symptoms; what seemed malignant crimes become conscientious acts based on delusions. Our scepticism is accordingly aroused by all suggestions that historical reasoning should be teleological, that events of the past are to be viewed as purposive in character and directed towards a certain end selected by the historian out of many possible ends. For we have learned how small a field consciousness covers, how little a man ordinarily knows of even his own motives, and how his statements on the subject are generally *ex post facto,* justificatory, and often erroneous.

Another discipline capable of assisting the historical inquirer is the law of evidence as formulated by Common Law jurists and by psychologists. For more than five hundred years there has been a body of men, the Justices of the English Common Law courts, engaged in the work of getting at the truth of serious matters, by eliminating, so far as possible, the element of falsity in the testimony of witnesses. These judges, nearly always experienced, highly skilled, and scrupulously honest, have gradually discovered and developed a system of empiric rules and doctrines based upon the actual study of the relations between testimony and veridicality, and of the best methods of determining, from the statements of various types of men, what are the real facts of the matter under consideration. The rules and doctrines so developed have been carefully transmitted from generation to generation, applied in great numbers of cases, and limited, modified, or expanded as growing wisdom and experience might suggest. They have thus developed into a system which represents a very high achievement of human sagacity. They are almost purely empiric in origin and character, and for that reason, perhaps, have not received the attention which scholars generally give to systems of thought more neatly speculative, more deductive, and more amply endowed with formal harmony. In recent years they have received a more philosophic treatment, and the principles underlying them have been more clearly brought to view.

Within recent years, too, there has sprung up, mainly among French, German, and American psychologists, a scientific study of testimony as affected by the general characteristics of the human mind. Extensive experiments have clearly shown, as Binet remarks, that no human testimony is absolutely truthful. "Cette étude, dès le début, s'est recommandée par son bel intérêt philosophique; il a paru singulièrement important d'apprendre et de démontrer à tous, aux magistrats comme aux historiens, que nul témoignage humain n'est absolument véridique." [1] It has been repeatedly proved that even trained observers can rarely describe an event as it actually occurred.[2] If the modern psychologist, trained to acute observation, is unable, even when describing an incident while it is fresh in his mind, to avoid a large percentage of error, we cannot escape the conclusion that the statements of ancient writers, less exact and less observant, must, for similar reasons, contain much that is biased and untrue.

Some acquaintance with the law of evidence and the psychology of testimony is a valuable part of the equipment of any student of history, but their application to historical studies is far from being fully effected. Those

[1] Binet, *L'Année Psychologique*, 1911, p. VII. See G. F. Arnold, *Psychology Applied to Legal Evidence* (2nd ed., London, 1913).

[2] See H. Münsterberg, *On The Witness Stand* (New York, 1908), p. 37ff.

who are familiar with the English Common Law of the trial of causes and of the rules of evidence, have not, as a rule, been versed in scientific psychology; and the psychologists, in turn, do not seem to have drawn upon English jurisprudence for the apposite illustrations and applications of their discoveries. Furthermore, neither the lawyers nor the psychologists, from the nature of their specialties, have as yet contributed greatly to the criticism of the sources of ancient history; and the professed historians, for the most part, have given to neither the empirical nor the methodical study of testimony the attention which it deserves.

The student of Roman history is forced to rely almost entirely on documents of one sort or another whose credibility is not always above suspicion. Carelessness, bias, imagination, and often downright mendacity have collaborated in the production of our materials. The sources from which we obtain our knowledge of Roman affairs under the late Republic and the early Empire especially, have been so infected with these qualities that we are forced to regard much of what has ordinarily passed for history as little more than fiction and fable. It is the task of the modern historian, utilizing all the information which the progress of scientific studies now places at his disposal, to endeavor to separate the true from the false, and to reconstruct the story, in von Ranke's memorable phrase, *wie es gewesen war*.

CHAPTER II

CLASSICAL history touches the modern world so intimately and at so many points that it often seems less ancient in reality than much of mediæval history. The Middle Ages, although not nearly so dark as they are commonly painted, are still remote from us in spirit and content. Cæsar is nearer to us than Charlemagne, and Seneca complains of social ills that are our own. The *Res Publica* of the Romans is the antecedent, politically as well as linguistically, of our own *Republic* and with the name we have also inherited certain characteristic traits. The long struggle between democracy and aristocracy, the transition from an agricultural community to an Empire, the crass materialism of a society founded on wealth, the social unrest which led to revolutions in politics and morals—all these mark the modernity of Rome.

A sketch of social development, applicable indifferently to either Rome or America, would show that this people —whichever we prefer—grew from an admixture of several similar stocks and that for many generations its members were predominantly small freehold farmers. They were not, in their early days, an urban folk, nor, it must be added, were they altogether urbane. Foreigners, coming in contact with them, remarked deficiencies in the manners and graces of social life. Indeed, they were rather hard and severe, as well as suspicious and censorious, not only towards neighboring communities but also towards one another; and a keenly intrusive and meddlesome intolerance, manifesting itself in their social relations, was directed against departures from their somewhat narrow code of approved habits and customs. Partly as a result, perhaps, of this pressure towards uniformity, they produced but few striking individualities; but competence they had, and common sense, and—so it seemed to unsympathetic observers—commonplaceness. Towards distinctive characters, perhaps even towards personal distinction, they showed a jealous distrust and even hostility which easily led, through early revolutionary movements, to a highly prized, republican form of government, to a detestation of the name "king," and eventually to elaborate counterchecked democratic institutions.

They were not eminent in the domain of pure intellect, for they were especially occupied in applying intelligence to the practical side of life. A very important part of their activities lay in the acquisition of wealth. In the field of æsthetics they were distinctly weak, not regarding the beautiful as entitled to an existence independent of the materially useful or the ethically laudable. Their literary products showed little originality and long remained relatively unimportant, while their achievements in the other arts were even more imitative and subordinate.

Their morals, tinged with asceticism, occupied a large share in their consciousness. Mere amusement and delight in life seemed to them generally to deserve some reprobation, while gravity, even to the degree of austerity, was highly esteemed. Although they probably overestimated the righteousness of their conduct, they were, no doubt, on the whole a sedate and serious people, and so actively reprehended breaches of their strict if somewhat narrow ethical code as to render a measure of moral hypocrisy inevitable. Strong volitional powers are quite as often the cause as they are the result of stern moral ideals, and it is not surprising that both the Romans and the Americans showed abundant self-reliance and self-confidence which, especially in unimportant matters and in conjunction with a limited intellectual purview, tended to degenerate into vanity and boastfulness. As a result, unsympathetic observers marked only the defects of their qualities and failed to evaluate the real excellence of their achievements.

With what appeared to outsiders a ruthless disregard of the rights of others, they continually extended their dominions, though their military exploits were probably not so glorious as their patriotic historians loved to assert. Indeed, their Capital was once easily occupied and destroyed by an invading army under circumstances not wholly creditable to the defenders. But even this event did not check their progress or diminish their self-confidence. A great war menaced the national existence of both peoples—the second Punic War that of Rome, and the Civil War that of America. By indomitable perseverance the crisis was overcome, and the national life was quickened by the victory won and the ensuing peace and prosperity. But the war brought also economic changes destined to affect profoundly the social and political character of the people. Immigration to new and fertile lands recently opened for settlement had been in progress for some time but now became accentuated. Free farms were given actual settlers and new regions grew peopled and prosperous, while complaints of depopulation were heard from some of the long-settled localities. The immigration of foreign born persons of inferior economic status was also augmented, and their notable acquisition of wealth and prominence, together with their reception into the body politic in large numbers, awakened apprehensions. At the same time a noteworthy tendency to urbanism appeared and problems incident to city life developed, with the consequent change in many of the distinctive qualities of the people.

Another very important influence in the social development of the people was the rapid growth of great private fortunes following the definite establishment of national solidity. Hence resulted an era of ostentatious luxury and the vulgar extravagances of the *nouveaux riches* with their full-blown genealogical trees—and the satires on them. The taste for luxury, without the means to satisfy it, produced parasitism among the abject and disgust among those who were unwilling to fawn. Contact with riper foreign civilizations both by travel and by the importation of works of art often produced a pseudo-culture which had neither the skill to produce nor the taste to appreciate. The art of living had lost, largely, the simple virility of the older native folk and had not yet won the refined elegance of the new models.

In the older days, the women had been remarkably competent and devoted wives and mothers. With the increase of wealth came more attention to the ornamental side of life. The tedium of a life devoid of duties and devoted to self-indulgence drove them into a restless search for some means, not always clearly apprehended, of imparting a satisfying flavor to existence. As women of the wealthier classes became progressively more decorative than useful, there became evident on the part of some men a distaste to form matrimonial connections with women of their own class or to tolerate bonds which proved irksome. This preference for celibacy on the one side, and on the other the disinclination to interrupt the pursuit of pleasure by the bearing and nurture of children, coöperated to cause a marked diminution in the birth-rate among the wealthier classes. In families with children the employment of nurses, generally springing from a more primitive or sometimes from a decadent social *milieu*, tended to abolish family discipline and to alter the traditional characteristics of the nation. This condition of affairs attracted the complaints of moralists and the censure of statesmen.

The number of those who became feverish from their sudden glut of wealth and devoted themselves to the cult of pleasure by the manifestation of "conspicuous idleness and conspicuous waste" was probably at no time very great, but they loomed large in the eyes of superficial, that is to say, of most, observers. The few who vociferate make more stir than the many who keep silent. In the eyes of onlookers they excited not so much the disapprobation due to blatant folly as the craving arising from unsatisfied desire. The aim of the rich was pleasure, and that of the poor was to be rich. When the most conspicuous class of a community seems to be making the things purchasable by money the principal end of life, those who lack money feel that there is something wrong with the cosmos. Not many are reckless enough to blame Providence, and still less are they inclined to blame themselves; hence the third possible culprit is charged with responsibility, and the many came to feel that the few in some way, by force or by guile, had elbowed them out of their place in the sun. So with the growth of class consciousness came an increase of class jealousy, exacerbated by the bitterness of a sense of injustice.

The prejudices of the many were continually stimulated

by the railing of satirists and the wailing of sentimentalists who have in all ages easily found imperfections in human affairs. The tendency of both Romans and Americans to exalt extravagantly the virtues of their ancestors gave moralists opportunities to paint moving pictures of decay. The position of the great mass of the smaller property owners was uncertain and changeable. Their dislike of the rich prevented their having plutocratic sympathies, while their detestation of the indigent kept them from any real union with the proletariat. In time, their desire for quiet and order contributed powerfully to the final pacification.

Under these conditions it is not surprising that demagogues found fertile fields for their labors. Then as now, most of them advocated in one form or another some homeopathic plan by which the evils thought to spring from the unearned and undeserved possession of property on the part of the few were to be cured by general donations to the many of equally unearned and undeserved advantages. Indiscriminate attacks and the consciousness of their own numerical inferiority drove the rich to an equally indiscriminating defense. Clever "bosses" organized and manipulated the voters. Aristocratic demagogues arose who sought to placate the people by doles, and the large gratifications bestowed upon the veterans of armed civil strife helped to spread the idea of getting something for nothing. Under a complicated framework of government, the political and social institutions came to be inharmonious with the facts of social life, and some parts of the machine, originally designed for a small homogeneous people, could hardly be kept in successful operation when the State had grown vastly larger, and the character of the people had greatly changed.

There is never much danger of the dispossession of the

wealthy unless property has passed by inheritance into the hands of weaklings or unless those who profit by the existing order fail to stand together; but both these elements of weakness began to appear. Causes for unsatisfactory conditions were discovered in the malign activities of individuals, and the result was disorder. But disorder in the long run satisfies nobody, and after this fact had finally been made clear, general rearrangements of political affairs were effected to assure at least external domestic tranquillity and to force the chronic feeling of discontent into a different channel.

But our sketch has now gone a step or two beyond the point reached by the modern parallel. Abandoning, therefore, a chronological narrative, we shall consider the general personal characteristics shown by the citizens of the late Republic and early Empire. Here we find many peculiarities which are now again manifesting themselves in the more advanced societies of Europe and America. To attempt an exhaustive survey of them is beyond our scope, but in a general way some similarities may be suggested.

One aspect of this resemblance, namely, that of religion, is noted by Sir Leslie Stephen in these words: "We should perhaps find the best guidance, in any attempt at prophesying the future of religion, from studying the history of the last great revolution of faith. The analogy between the present age and that which witnessed the introduction of Christianity is too striking to have been missed by very many observers. The most superficial acquaintance with the general facts shows how close a parallel might be drawn by a competent historian. There are none of the striking manifestations of the present day to which it would not be easy to produce an analogy, though in some respects on a smaller scale. Now, as then, we can find mystical philosophers trying to evolve a satisfactory creed by some process of logical legerdemain out of theosophical moonshine; and amiable and intelligent persons labouring hard to prove that the old mythology could be forced to accept a rationalistic interpretation —whether in regard to the inspection of entrails or prayers for fine weather; and philosophers framing systems of morality entirely apart from the ancient creeds, and sufficiently satisfactory to themselves, while hopelessly incapable of impressing the popular mind; and politicians, conscious that the basis of social order was being sapped by the decay of the faith in which it had arisen, and therefore attempting the impossible task of galvanising dead creeds into some semblance of vitality; and strange superstitions creeping out of their lurking-places, and gaining influence in a luxurious society whose intelligence was an ineffectual safeguard against the most grovelling errors; and a dogged adherence of formalists and conservatives to ancient ways, and much empty profession of barren orthodoxy; and, beneath all, a vague disquiet, a breaking-up of ancient social and natural bonds, and a blind groping toward some more cosmopolitan creed and some deeper satisfaction for the emotional needs of mankind." [1]

Perhaps the most fundamental characteristic which in protean forms manifested itself in all the aspects of Roman life during the years under consideration, was a general unrest and a dissatisfaction with existing conditions. The world had acquired a great capacity for *ennui,* and many travelled from place to place, blind to the truth of Horace's sage line: *caelum non animum mutant qui trans mare currunt.* [2] Various psycho-neuroses

[1] Sir Leslie Stephen, *An Agnostic's Apology* (London, 1893), pp. 353, 354.

[2] *Epistulæ* I, 11, 27.

seem to have been increasing, or at least to have been attracting more attention. Seneca, especially, was much occupied in giving advice regarding conditions of mind and nerves which we can now recognize as distinctly pathological. For it is now known that a feeling of un-rest and *malaise* is the result of a generally disordered coenesthesis. Similarly, many, if not most, commentators on modern life refer to our restless superficiality, our incapacity for simple repose of mind and body: we are easily bored and we fidget. We seem to be losing a capacity for calm leisure, and if we may judge from imaginative literature, we are prone to manifest a heart-ache about—it is not always very clear what it is about, but we feel none the less distressed over the matter.

To what degree the gentle melancholy of Virgil and Marcus Aurelius, the timorous despair of Seneca, the shrill railing of Juvenal, and the lurid horror which casts a baleful glare over Tacitus's writings present a correct picture of Roman conditions, is not our present concern. We are now observing merely the fact of the similarity of Roman and modern societies and one of the similarities is that we have similar accounts of them. "Taking account of these various groups of undoubted facts," says Alfred Russel Wallace, "many of which are so gross, so ter-rible, that they cannot be overstated, it is not too much to say that our whole system of society is rotten from top to bottom, and the Social Environment as a whole, in rela-tion to our possibilities and our claims, is the worst that the world has ever seen." [1] Such indictments are a prom-inent and not altogether trustworthy characteristic of both civilizations, and are much alike whether we have them in the literary form of Roman satire or the cruder shape

[1] *Social Environment and Moral Progress* (New York, 1913), p. 169.

of modern "muck-raking." From the point of view of the psychiatrist, these manifestations of morbid emotivity are easily referable to pathological, psychic states. Feelings of this nature tend naturally to establish congruent beliefs, and to find persons or personified abstractions, either malignant dæmons, or Society, Capitalism and Vested Interests, against whom the disordered emotions discharge themselves.

Other indications of similar general psychological states in the men of old times and of the present may be found in an efflorescence of pity, philanthropy and kindred feelings which evidence the consciousness of certain defects in organized society. The lot of the poor, especially, then as now, attracted increasing attention. While the direct gift of food to the Roman poor was carried further, although not primarily for charitable reasons, than is the case in any modern state, yet we spend, no doubt, a sum relatively as large in the relief—and manufacture—of poverty. With the slackening of individual effort, the humbler classes of Roman society seemed to become less able to care for their own needs, and after generations of peace, and in fertile parts of Italy, the emperors felt called upon to enter into large schemes of loaning money to freehold farmers. "Rural credits," it will appear, are not altogether a modern economic measure. Again, we are trying, rather fitfully, to be sure, to readjust society in the interests of the weak. Enormous charitable gifts, some wise and some foolish, were made, then as now, with the vague idea of buying popularity and mental peace. That the gifts were sometimes looked upon as "tainted money" is clear from Lucian.[1]

It would be easy to extend almost indefinitely these

[1] Lucian, *Phalaris,* I, II; see also S. Dill, *Roman Society from Nero to Marcus Aurelius* (London, 1905), pp. 192ff., 223, 245.

suggestions of similar conditions in the societies of ancient Rome and the modern world. Some of them have been noted by Ferrero in his *Characters and Events of Roman History.*[1] But there are, of course, many and obvious differences between Roman and contemporary civilizations. Foremost among these is the great unlikeness in political organization. The Roman theory of government suggested by the word *imperium* is something unfamiliar to us. The Romans' failure to develop a system of representative institutions; their notion of the intimate relation between the soldier and his general; their idea of the tribunicial power; their easy acceptance of the exercise of a magistracy by two or more persons possessing full power, everyone, and not acting as a board; their failure to utilize the power that seems to us to be inherent in the control of the public purse; their conception of judicial authority; their legal theory of the family with its *patria potestas;* their institution of slavery with the ensuing bond between patron and freedman; and, above all, the fact that Rome as a city state at a relatively early time so decisively transcended all possible rivals in power as to become overlord of an awe-struck world—all these and many more differences make it clear that there are very important dissimilarities between the two societies, especially in structure, form, and function. But these differences, it will be observed, lie in the domain of institutions, where historical analogy, from the very nature of things, can be neither close nor convincing.

Quite apart from them, Rome, with her great social problems of proletariat and patricians, of wealth and

[1] Putnam's (New York, 1909), p. 243ff. The subject is treated with greater detail in Ferrero's *Ancient Rome and Modern America,* Putnam's (New York, 1914), a work which appeared after Mr. Jerome's death.—*Editor.*

poverty, of urbanism and the decline of agriculture, has a message for the modern world. The Middle Ages, with their monasticism, their feudal wars, and their conception of the individual, are infinitely more remote from us than the City of the Seven Hills. In a very real sense, she is for us the synthesis of human life. Embracing a larger variety of men, politics, and conditions, all brought into direct relations with a focal point than is the case with any other country of the past, and including in simple, well-defined lines all the important aspects of human societies, Rome has this further advantage, that while her influence continues potent in the world, her career as a political organism is finished. And we may learn from her; to quote Eduard Meyer,[1] it is "just because here (*i.e.*, antiquity) the development has come to an end, because ancient history is finished and gone, and lies before our eye complete and entire, that we may put questions to it and derive lessons from it such as are possible in no other part of history." We can see what happened. We can observe Rome emerging, as it were, from the inane, simple in government and in social life; we can follow, almost step by step, her evolution into a fully developed, complex coherent heterogeneity, and then we can witness the long decline, while the complicated social and political structure slowly disintegrates and finally disappears, leaving mankind to readjust itself in the Ages called Dark, but which never quite lost the saving memory of Rome.

This is the greatest backward step in the life of humanity of which history affords any clear record. That a civilization so like our own in many respects should fail to endure, should, in fact, succumb to a barbarism which camped among its ruins, is a reflection likely to give rise, at times, to a vague fear that our boasted

[1] *Kleine Schriften* (Halle, 1910), p. 217.

modern society may further resemble the ancient in the manner of its dissolution. The incredible has once happened, and the history of the past does not justify a facile optimism.

CHAPTER III

THE CREDIBILITY OF TESTIMONY

THE student of Roman history is confronted at the outset by the general problem of the degree of confidence which may justly be felt regarding information based on human testimony. There have been many indeed who have gloomily questioned the extent of our knowledge of the past of human societies. Motley asserted that "the record of our race is essentially unwritten. What we call history is but made up of a few scattered fragments, while it is scarcely given to human intelligence to comprehend the great whole." [1] And Froude, with what some scholars would call his own method in mind, declared that "it often seems to me as if History was like a child's box of letters, with which we can spell any word we please. We have only to pick out such letters as we want, arrange them as we like, and say nothing about those which do not suit our purpose." [2]

The scholar is bound to weigh his evidence with the utmost care, for the testimony may be either deliberately or unconsciously falsified. It is evident, for example, that Weems, the Plutarch-like biographer of Washington, invented out of whole cloth the tale of the cherry tree, and that, being animated by the same exalted principles

[1] *The United Netherlands* (New York, 1868), vol. III, p. 477.
[2] J. A. Froude, *Short Studies on Great Subjects* (*The Science of History*), vol. I (New York, 1876), p. 1.

as his amiable Greek predecessor, his intention was not "to give information about George Washington but to suggest virtuous conduct to young Americans." [1] The president of the American Historical Association in 1909 devoted a considerable part of his annual address to certain striking cases of fraudulent evidence deliberately manufactured to support various historical theses, with results that may well produce dismay in the moralist and caution in the student. He refers to the men of the Middle Ages and Renaissance busily and joyously engaged in fabricating books which purported to come from the ancients; to that master of imaginative historians, George Psalmanazar, who in 1704 evolved from his inner consciousness a *Historical and Geographical Description of Formosa;* to Lucas, the nineteenth century jobber in spurious letters, who palmed off on avid customers 27,000 autograph epistles, among which were those of Sir Isaac Newton, Shakespeare, Rabelais, Strabo, Plato, Lazarus, and Judas Iscariot; to Ingulf's *History of the Abbey of Croyland,* and Simonides's *History of Egypt* by Uranius; to the so-called *Letters of Montcalm,* the *Travels* of Jonathan Carver, Gordon's *History of the Revolution,* and to Buell's recent life of John Paul Jones, with its entertaining but spurious "original documents." [2]

In addition to evidence thus deliberately manufactured, there is also testimony which has been unconsciously falsified through defects of observation, imagination, and memory. For instance, in 1911 there appeared in a small English magazine, which shall remain unnamed, a description by an eye-witness of the eruption of Vesuvius in 1906. The most interesting feature of this article was

[1] A. B. Hart, *American Historical Review,* vol. XV (1910), p. 242.

[2] A. B. Hart, *op. cit.,* pp. 227-251.

that it contained, with the exception of the eruption and of the writer's presence in Capri, practically not a single correct statement of the events observed; and the defect extended to very simple matters of fact about which there ought to have been no question of interpretation. It was said, for example, that just before the eruption the volcano seemed on the point of extinction, whereas the "smoke" had been gradually increasing for three years; that the sea became too rough to permit crossing to Naples, and that for over a week no mail or news was received from the mainland. As a matter of fact, no day passed without at least one mail boat, and the weather was continuously calm. Capri, the writer of the article went on to say, was buried under the volcanic ash; "our roof and garden were covered to the depth of half a metre;" whereas the fall of ash would have been considerably overestimated if put at half an inch. And yet the article, I have reason to believe, was written by a young man whose good faith was not open to question. If the memory could thus go wrong in five years, we cannot wholly avoid the suspicion that the famous letters of Pliny the Younger, written some twenty-five or thirty years after the catastrophe which overwhelmed Pompeii, may contain elements due to a similar defective recollection.

But selected episodes, however valuable they may be as illustrations of an established proposition, possess little probative force; at most they serve to indicate merely that many false stories obtain currency—a matter of common knowledge. What is needed for our purposes is a class of cases obtained under strict control from identical objective data, and sufficiently numerous to furnish us with averages and percentages, so that we may see, not simply that human minds are sometimes inaccurate—everyone knows that—but rather in what proportion such inaccuracies exist, and how profound they are. Such cases should also have the characteristic of relation to minds which for the time being had no motive to misstate and presumably were endeavoring to bear true testimony as to simple objective facts.

For material of this sort recourse must be taken to the researches of certain scholars, chiefly Continental, who of late years have made careful investigations into the psychology of testimony. A glance at the results obtained in a few cases will furnish some idea of the difficulties which beset a student whose material is derived from human testimony.

One of the simplest experiments was that carried out by M. Binet with children.[1] A new reddish-brown French two centimes stamp together with some other simple objects—we confine our attention to the stamp—was pasted on a piece of cardboard and shown to twenty-four children for a space of twelve seconds, and they were then separately interrogated about what had been exhibited. Four questions were asked about the stamp. All but three of the children said it was a French and not a foreign stamp. Only nine, however, stated its color correctly, although either red or brown was taken as a correct answer. The false answers were with one exception given positively. The blue of the fifteen centimes stamp was perhaps most familiar to the children, and

[1] *L'Année Psychologique,* vol. XII (1906), p. 161ff; XI (1905), p. 128ff. Dr. Gross, after a careful examination of the subject, reached the conclusion that a healthy child, at least a boy, is one of the best witnesses to simple events, and that the errors of children, while different from those of adults, are neither more gross nor more frequent than those of their elders. See H. Gross, *Zur Frage der Zeugenaussage, Archiv für Kriminal-Anthropologie und Kriminalistik,* vol. XXXVI (1910), pp. 372-382.

six of them declared this stamp was blue; three said green; four said rose, and even white had its witness. Nine out of the twenty-four gave the correct denomination of the stamp, which was plainly marked on it. There was noticed a correlation between mistakes of color and of denomination. Thirteen answered correctly that the stamp was an unused one. One intelligent boy declared it was a used stamp; and being asked how he had reached this opinion, said that he saw that the gum had been removed; yet the stamp was pasted upon a card. Four asserted positively that it had been used, alleging that they were able to see distinctly the cancelling stamp, and they described its location. One of the older pupils even saw the letters "RIS"—the last letters of the word Paris —in the cancelling mark. The experimenter calls attention to the precision of these false memories as showing that a very positive statement given without the least hesitation can be entirely false. So also the descriptions were generally exact on one point and false on another: few were erroneous in all particulars. When experiments of this sort were carried on by means of leading questions, the percentage of errors was much greater, and similar results were obtained with students from sixteen to nineteen years of age. Where a written description of an object seen was required, only one-sixth of the observers made no mistakes. It was abundantly shown in all these cases that positiveness on the part of the witness and presence of detail in his answers gave no assurances whatever of their correctness.

One of Stern's tests was slightly more complicated.[1] He had three simple pictures in black and white, which he exhibited for forty-five seconds each to about thirty cultivated adults who immediately wrote down what they

[1] Compare *L'Année Psychologique*, vol. XII (1906), p. 168ff.

had seen in each picture, and thereafter at certain intervals of time again submitted written statements. Such parts of their depositions as they were willing to take oath upon were indicated by underlining. Without going into details, it may be said that the results were not of a nature calculated to give one great confidence in the value of testimony. Error was not the exception, but the rule. Out of two hundred and eighty-two depositions only seventeen were entirely correct; and of these seventeen, fifteen were among the statements written down immediately. By the fifth day even, the proportion of mis-statements reached about a quarter of all the details submitted. In the depositions containing indications of matters on which the observer was willing to take an oath, only thirteen out of sixty-three failed to contain false statements, to all of which however the witnesses were prepared to swear. Many of these were cases of the introduction of elements which were absolutely absent from the picture. So one student wrote three weeks after the event: "The picture shows an old man seated on a wooden bench. A small boy is standing at his left. *He is looking at the old man who is feeding a pigeon. On the roof is perched another pigeon which is preparing to fly to the ground to get its share of the food.*" The italicized statements were wholly incorrect: there were no pigeons in the picture. Perhaps the figure of a cat in the scene may have suggested the idea of a bird to the observer. In this, as in other cases, the testimony of women revealed more, but less exact, remembrance than that of men.

A third class of experiments is that of a representation before spectators who do not suspect the fictitious character of the scene, of a short but striking event carefully prepared beforehand. For instance, at a Psychological Congress at Göttingen before witnesses who were psychologists, jurists, and physicians, and therefore presumably more skilled in observation and statement than ordinary persons, the following carefully prepared experiment was tried:

"Not far from the hall of meeting of the Congress, a public festival and masquerade ball were in progress. Suddenly the door of the hall opened and a clown rushed madly in, pursued by a negro with a revolver in his hand. They stopped in the middle of the hall, reviled one another; the clown fell, the negro leaped upon him, fired, and then suddenly both ran out of the room. The whole affair had lasted barely twenty seconds. The presiding officer requested the members present to write out, severally, statements of the affair, since doubtless there would be a judicial investigation. Forty reports were made out. Only one had less than twenty per cent of errors, fourteen had from twenty to forty per cent of errors, twelve from forty to fifty per cent, and thirteen more than fifty per cent. Furthermore, in twenty-four reports, ten per cent of the details were pure inventions, and the proportion of inventions surpassed that figure in ten other reports. . . . It goes without saying that the entire scene had been arranged and even photographed in advance. The ten false reports are then to be put in the category of fables and legends, the twenty-four are semi-legendary, and six only can be regarded as having approximately the value of exact testimony. But with an ordinary public, the proportions are different, and one may estimate the percentage of pure inventions at fifty per cent at least."[1]

It will appear from these and similar experiments that erroneous testimony was given in simple matters of direct, personal observation by witnesses who were not influenced by any conscious preëxisting emotion or prepossession,

[1] A. van Gennep, *La Formation des Légendes* (Paris, 1910), pp. 158-159.

and who were actuated by a desire to give an exact and truthful narrative. Yet the results were not encouraging. It is evident, as scholars who have conducted or studied such experiments have shown, that good faith, the desire to tell the truth, and the certainty that the testimony is true, as well as the opportunity to secure correct information, and the absence of prepossessions, are far from affording adequate guarantees that the truth will be told. The most honest witness may misstate; the worst may tell the truth. Entirely faithful testimony is not the rule but rather a rare exception. If such then are the distortions which appear in testimony when there is a desire to give a precise and accurate narrative, we cannot be surprised at any result where the feelings are less scientific in character, as is the case with most of Roman historical material.

The fact is that the human mind considered as an instrument for the attainment and enunciation of correct knowledge of the external world leaves much to be desired. The average mind remains essentially primitive. And inasmuch as most of our historical information regarding the later Republic and the early Empire has come down to us through several minds and presumably been affected in the process, it is worth while, before scrutinizing the evidence in detail, to gain some general idea of the defects of the agents whereby the evidence has been transmitted.

In the first place we are forced to recognize the fact that in their general mental characteristics, most people are and always have been not very far removed from their earliest ancestors.[1] Sir Henry Maine declares that even after the ages of change which separate the civilized

[1] See review of L. Lévy-Bruhl, *Les fonctions mentales dans les sociétés inférieures* (Paris, 1910), in *Revue Philosophique*, vol. LXX (1910), pp. 279-291.

man from the savage or barbarian, the difference between them is not so great as the vulgar opinion would have it. There is much of the savage in our contemporaries. Many occupations, pursuits, and tastes are common to them and their primitive ancestors. "Like the savage, the Englishman, Frenchman, or American makes war; like the savage, he hunts; like the savage, he dances; like the savage, he indulges in endless deliberation; like the savage, he sets an extravagant value on rhetoric; like the savage, he is a man of party, with a newspaper for a totem, instead of a mark on his forehead or arm; and, like a savage, he is apt to make of his totem, his God." [1]

All this will appear perfectly natural if it be remembered that biologically speaking the mental attainments of one generation do not pass on to the next by inheritance. Each infant comes into the world quite as ignorant as every other of his contemporaries, or of his predecessors. What we ordinarily call his education is mainly devoted to teaching him a few things received by him on authority —many of them far from true—and to giving him some ability to read and write so that he may come in touch with other minds, most of which are not more advanced than his own. An ocean of knowledge lies before him, but it is bitter to his taste. The necessities of remunerative employment force him to learn more or less, sometimes a good deal, about some one limited field of human achievement. If it be farming, he may come to know the succession, coördination, and inevitability of a certain class of natural phenomena; he knows that he must sow to reap. But when he gets away from his farm, the first confidence man can persuade him that he can reap in some unfamiliar field without sowing.

[1] Sir Henry Maine, *Popular Government* (New York, 1886), p. 144.

It is necessary, then, to examine the nature of this common mind, which has shown itself *semper ubique et ab omnibus idem*, in order to ascertain in what ways it is an imperfectly and inaccurately functioning machine, and how these imperfections and inaccuracies manifest themselves in matters which are of special concern to students of history.

The unity of the human mind renders all schemes of classification of psychological phenomena particularly misleading. As a matter of mere convenience in orderly exposition, we may find it possible to distinguish difficulties in obtaining truthful and accurate evidence into those arising out of :

(1) The general inherent imperfections in the thinking mechanism. (2) The effects of the general principle apparent in all manifestations of force, which may be called "the law of least effort." The forms assumed by this principle bear different names as it is related to different sorts of dynamics ; in human action it is often termed indolence.[1] (3) The controlling influence of the primary organic and affective life of the organism on the secondary and derivative activities of thought, belief, and expression.

In an analytical treatise, in which mental phenomena could be viewed at some particular angle, split up into their elements, and segregated, such a classification might answer ; but we are dealing with actual, complex manifestations resulting in most cases from these three causes acting together in various combinations. Consequently a less neat division is preferable. Starting, then, from the

---

[1] Compare Th. Ribot, *Le Moindre Effort en Psychologie*, in *Revue Philosophique*, vol. LXX (1910), pp. 361-386; *ibid.*, LXXI (1911), pp. 164-167; Sir Leslie Stephen, *An Agnostic's Apology*, p. 324.

proposition that there is an affective element in all thinking, we may first examine those mental imperfections
which may coexist with any sort of desire or feeling,
and hence may impair testimony even when there is a
wish and intention to give a simple, straightforward, and
truthful narrative; and secondly, the conscious or subconscious perturbations caused by a desire on the part
of the narrator to please, annoy, persuade, or otherwise
affect the auditor in a way not calculated to give him
correct and complete information.

The mental imperfections referred to under the first
head may be separated, to some extent, into those inherent
in the mechanism and those due to its defective operation
under "the law of least effort," although no sharp line
of demarcation is possible between the two. In considering the perturbation caused by a desire to affect the
auditor in a special, but improper, way, we shall have
occasion to observe the power of the feelings to produce
not only mendacious assertions but also honest, although
erroneous, beliefs supporting the dominant sentiment;
beliefs which give rise to judgments of fact probative
of the beliefs and justificatory of the primary, emotional
state.

Viewed in a general way, the main and perhaps the only
function played by the neural and cerebral organism is
to put man in touch with his environment as a basis for
adaptive reactions on his part. The various forms of
activity of the nerves and brain are parts of the mechanism
by which this end is accomplished. This function, the
last human power to be developed in evolution and the
first to disappear in involution may be termed "the function of the real," which "consists in the apprehension of
reality in all its forms," in that "attention to the present
life, of which M. Bergson speaks in a metaphysical work

which often seems to foresee the results of psychological observations." [1]

In its simplest form the matter may be stated thus: the physiological process which is expressed on the psychological side as a thought or an idea may be initiated by a stimulus coming either from the organs of sense directly or by revivals in memory, or originating in some other brain cell; as if, let us say, a bell had several bell-pulls attached to it. In case of a complete mistake as to the source of the stimulus, the result is an hallucination. The well-developed mind is able to discriminate promptly and surely as to the source, but in a primitive mind this power is very feeble. A child up to about his seventh year at least does not clearly distinguish between the real and the imaginary. [2] He may in play begin by pretending that a well-known skin before the fireplace is a bear, and suddenly become frightened by the purely imaginary qualities which he has just given it. A savage constructs a fetich in much the same way. A metaphysician hypostasizes concepts, until the Platonic Idea of Chair seems to become more real to him than the chair in which he sits. In sleep it is not the emotions, the memory, the imagination, or the reasoning that ceases activity, but it is the synthetic function of the real. In those suffering from psychopathies, the most characteristic symptom is that their feelings, thoughts, and acts become unrelated to reality.

The most difficult mental synthesis to make, that requiring what has been called the "highest mental tension," and

[1] P. Janet, *Les Obsessions et la Psychasthénie* (Paris, 1908), vol. I, p. 477. The reference to Bergson is *Matière et Mémoire* (Paris, 1896), p. 190. See further Janet, *op. cit.*, vol. I, p. 443ff; 470ff; II, p. 29ff; 461.

[2] See *Revue Philosophique*, vol. LXVII (1909), p. 658.

possessing the greatest richness of content of thought, is a *real* situation. Imagining or reasoning about unreal things is far simpler: it is easier, as M. Bergson has remarked, to read a novel than a history. Utopian dreams and idealistic speculations are well within the powers of a psychasthenic, even of a lunatic: it is only the fully developed man, however, who can grasp the world as it is, and because he can, dares grasp it. But minds of even fair general precision are instruments which few possess, and one who cannot see things as they are, cannot, *a fortiori*, narrate them as they are.

It is not to be supposed that a fundamental human characteristic like the "function of the real" has been reserved for modern scholars to discover. The ability of a living organism to make a wide and accurate synthesis of the facts of its environment, correctly perceived and remembered and put into proper relation with one another, and then to react upon it in such a way as to promote the welfare of the organism, is nothing more than sound common sense. In civil or military affairs we call it a genius for statesmanship or generalship; in biology we know it is the power of adaptation; in historiography it means clear vision, critical acumen, fearless independence and complete veracity.

The basis of all right knowledge about anything is accuracy and completeness of observation. A highly developed power of ratiocination, if not based on precise and correct data, is simply an additional cause of error, since it is more misleading to take the wrong path and follow it rigorously than to keep on making errors which may, and sometimes do, cancel one another, and eventually bring one out into the right path. But precision and accuracy require a mental effort which fatigues and pains one unaccustomed to it. "It is," as Spencer says, "impos-

sible to get accuracy from undeveloped minds; and undeveloped minds dislike prescribed ways of obtaining accuracy. Cooks hate weights and scales—prefer handfuls
and pinches; and consider it an imputation on their skill
if you suggest that definite measures would be better.
There are uneducated men who trust their own sensations
rather than the scale of a thermometer—will even sometimes say that the thermometer is wrong, because it does
not agree with their sensations. The like holds with language. You cannot get uncultivated people, or indeed
the great mass of people called cultivated, to tell you
neither more nor less than the fact. Always they either
overstate or understate, and regard criticism or qualification of their strong words as rude or perverse." [1]

These qualities of vagueness and inaccuracy are pain-
fully frequent in most of our authorities.[2] Polybius and
Livy present rather full statements regarding Hannibal's
route across the Alps, but it is impossible to identify with
any certainty the pass which was actually used; and nearly
all ancient geographical information is equally unsatisfactory. The Romans had available a great mass of sta-
tistical material in their census lists, but with rare exceptions they carefully kept away from it when they wrote
books. Cassius Dio seems to apologize for making an
exact statement of an important date, as if precision were
a blemish.[3] We should never suspect from literary sources
that much of the agricultural land of Italy was cut up
into small holdings, as the inscriptions indicate; while the
sources from which we endeavor to solve questions of

[1] Herbert Spencer, *The Principles of Psychology*, section 416,
Appleton edition (New York, vol. II, 1910), p. 388.
[2] See Langlois et Seignobos, *Introduction aux Études Historiques*, pp. 48ff; 102ff.
[3] Cassius Dio, LI, 1.

population, commerce, or finance seem to be perversely deficient in breadth, depth, and precision. A great part of our material bears about the same relation to fact as do old maps or plans to the real topography, or old prints to the landscape which they purport to represent.[1]

These are some of the difficulties in the way of obtaining trustworthy reports from the promptly written narratives of eye-witnesses; but only a very small part of our historical material was set down forthwith from personal observation. Even when participants in events composed descriptions of them, it was frequently after the lapse of many years, and, as the experiments described have shown, testimony rapidly becomes more defective with the passing of time.

For memory, as is well known, is a common source of error. There are extensive *lacunæ* in it which are filled in by subconscious imagination. "We meet with a blank or a chaos in traversing the particular field of remembrance from which the events have lapsed; but this will often be filled with some conjectural events which rapidly become attached to the adjacent parts, and form, in conjunction with them, a consolidated but fallacious fragment in memory;" or it "may be that the edges of the *lacunæ* close up—events originally separated by a considerable interval are now *remembered* vividly in immediate juxtaposition, and there is no trace of the piecing."[2] If one has wide general intelligence and sound common sense, and if the subject matter is familiar, this completion and reconstruction of the memory may be done with substan-

---

[1] Compare James Thomson Shotwell, article *History* in *Encyclopædia Britannica,* 11th edition, vol. XIII, p. 532.

[2] Dr. R. Hodgson quoted by F. Podmore, *Studies in Psychical Research* (London, 1897), p. 99.

tial accuracy; but otherwise it is not so. In any case, the reconstruction is purposive and selective.

Another significant factor in impairing the validity of testimony is that of language. The failure on the part of a writer to interpret correctly events of another age and sometimes of another *milieu,* frequently rests upon the imprecision of language. Words often change their meaning with the lapse of years, and expressions which are figurative or symbolic may mislead the commentator of a later day.[1] It is evident that later writers on religion went astray in their interpretations of earlier religious thought,[2] and it is probable that in the controversy between Gaius and the Jews each party misinterpreted the other's language.[3] We should know more than we do now about the Roman census, if we were quite sure of the exact meaning of such expressions as *capite censi.* Beloch, indeed, bases his discussion of the population of ancient Italy on the theory that the phrase *civium capita* quite changed its meaning between the years 70 and 28 B.C.[4] Ferrero has pointed out that what a Roman writer calls corruption, we generally call progress.[5] Again, had the word *tyrant* possessed a distinct and unchanging significance, certain pages of ancient history would have been less misunderstood. Language, indeed, often obscures rather than elucidates the facts lying back of it; for, as Hobbes says: "words are wise men's counters, they do but reckon by them: but they are the mony of fooles."[6]

[1] See E. B. Tylor, *Primitive Culture,* vol. II (5th edit., London, 1913), p. 445ff; Langlois et Seignobos, *op. cit.,* pp. 122ff., 190, 230; Le Bon, *Les Opinions et les Croyances* (Paris, 1911), p. 145ff.
[2] See below, p. 167.   [3] See below, p. 417.
[4] J. Beloch, *Die Bevölkerung der griechisch-römischen Welt* (Leipzig, 1886), p. 374ff.
[5] Ferrero, *Characters and Events in Roman History,* pp. 3-35.
[6] T. Hobbes, *Leviathan,* I, 4.

The credulous acceptance of statements made by others, due to a tendency to shirk mental effort, is another serious defect in many historical sources. Livy, for example, frequently accepted on authority of the older annalists statements which he could easily have corrected by consulting official documents extant in his day. Especially slavish is such credulity when the statement reported harmonizes with one's emotional prepossessions. One readily accepts scandal about a person whom one dislikes.[1] But credulity does not stop at accepting statements of fact. The "law of least effort" leads most men to avoid all mental exercise necessary to form an opinion about any matter, and to accept *in toto* the statements of others in regard to beliefs and judgments. To the mind of a primitive type every mental presentation, whether of internal or external origin, appears to be true unless the mind is already possessed by some contradictory idea. Where the contradiction between two ideas cannot be ignored, it is explained by some fanciful theory, such as a metamorphosis. It is so much easier to admit than to deny, for the act of criticism essential to denial involves an effort. Many shirk this effort to such an extent that a bold assertion often prevails in the face of its obvious absurdity, even in the face of clear evidence of the senses. In its extreme form, this process leads to hypnosis.

So feeble was the critical spirit in Roman times, so relatively unimportant was it to many of our authorities whether a thing was true or not, so little interested were they in independent, scientific research, that unmitigated credulity as to the most incredible assertions was their commonest as well as perhaps their most blighting defect. What exacerbates the situation is the fact that they seldom mention their sources, or even indicate that they

[1] See Tacitus, *Histories,* I, 34: *et facilius de odio creditur.*

have any. As a result, we are left quite uncertain whether the writer from whom a statement is derived was capable of affording honest information.

The foregoing are some of the difficulties which beset the mind in the correct ascertainment of facts; but there are further difficulties to be encountered before a truthful narrative emerges. The mind is not a phonograph which repeats in testimony what it takes in from the senses; and in the manipulation and transformation which experience undergoes before it reappears in evidence, there participates a whole brood of sophistries and fallacies, blunders and botches of intellection, which play their part in distorting and confusing the original facts. In much of what commonly passes for reasoning there is less logic than dreaming.[1] Careful reflection and close reasoning require too much effort. Men "guess at results," said Spencer. "They will not deliberately examine premises and conclusion . . . . Just in proportion as their ability to reason is small, they resent any attempt to bring their conclusion, or any part of their argument, to the test." [2] The trouble with a slovenly reasoner is not primarily intellectual; it is rather volitional and affective. He does not care enough about perfecting himself to take the trouble and make the effort involved in rigorous mental processes. It is much easier to argue from extreme facts than to weigh carefully and to avoid hasty generalizations. This is a sturdy and shameless fallacy, much esteemed by controversialists, and ancient writers afford some striking instances of it. Many of them were prone to confuse judgments of facts with judgments of value, and to present what were really only expressions of per-

---

[1] See J. Jastrow, *The Subconscious* (Boston, 1906), p. 85.
[2] Herbert Spencer, *The Principles of Psychology*, section 416, vol. II, p. 388.

sonal tastes, ideals, or interests, in the guise of objective facts.[1]

We are thus led to consider the second point involved in the falsification of evidence, namely, the conscious or sub-conscious perturbations caused by the narrator's desire to affect the reader or auditor in some special way.

It is necessary to bear in mind from the outset that there is "no thinking without desire, intention, or purpose. 'The one thing that stands out,' says, for instance, Professor Dewey, is 'that thinking is inquiry, and knowledge as science is the outcome of systematically directed inquiry.' Thought absolutely undirected would be not even a dream—mere meaningless, chaotic atoms of thought. It is *the intention, the purpose,* which makes thought what it is; that is to say, significant. We think because we will. Thought does not exist for itself; it is the instrument of desire. To discover ways and means of gratifying proximate or distant desires, needs, cravings, is the function of intelligence." [2]

"Every pulse of consciousness is psychically compounded of will, feeling, and thought." No one of these elements can be absent, although at successive stages of consciousness they differ in relative intensity. "The unit of conscious life is neither thought, nor feeling, nor will, but all three in movement towards an object." [3]

Thinking, then, has for its sole function that of assisting the organism to adjust itself to the exigencies of the social or physical environment in such a way, if possible, as to bring about results agreeable to its feelings and

[1] For judgments of value, compare G. Fonsegrive, *Revue Philosophique,* vol. LXIX (1910), p. 553ff; vol. LXX (1910), p. 44ff.

[2] J. H. Leuba, *The Psychological Origin and the Nature of Religion* (London, 1909), p. 6.   [3] *Ibid.,* pp. 7, 8.

corresponding to its desires. It is a bit of mechanism to accomplish our wishes, to gratify our sentiments, as well as may be in view of its defects.[1]

Without attempting an analytical sketch of the thinking process, we may say that after the mind has been directed to a subject, and some progress has been made in choosing, congruent to the directing impulse, the various images, memories, and ideas that have swarmed into consciousness, a sort of auto-criticism comes into play and a judgment of the present results of thinking is made.[2] This is not primarily a judging of the results of our thinking with reference to the objective world, but with reference to the relation of the results to the initial and continuing stimulus of thinking, that is, the feeling of desire. If the result of the thinking appears to accord with the desire, and if the action based upon it seems to satisfy the feelings, the point at which most men stop thinking has been reached. But in a complete thinking out of a problem the mind necessarily takes a broader survey of the situation. The conclusion arrived at will then be developed in imagination and its projected results will be held up for comparison with two groups of things, one subjective and the other objective.

In the first place the conclusion with its probable results is scrutinized with reference to the elements of the affective and volitional life other than the particular feeling and desire which have hitherto been directing the operation; since the conclusion, while congruous to one feeling and desire, may be incongruous to others which are stronger, or to a complexus whose aggregate is stronger.

[1] See W. McDougall, *An Introduction to Social Psychology* (London, 1908), p. 44.

[2] For a fuller discussion of this process, compare A. Binet and Th. Simon, *L'Année Psychologique*, vol. XV (1909), p. 128ff.

It may be realized, for instance, that the conclusion arrived at by the thinking will gratify our hate but compromise our safety. In such a case the thinking process is repeated in the search for a result which will be more generally satisfactory.

But in the second place, when the mind has accumulated a stock of experiences, it has learned that the arrangement and order of thoughts do not always correspond to the arrangement and order of objective things. It is at this point that the desire of the bard to please the assembled warriors by singing of their extraordinary prowess, or of the historian to inculcate virtue by glorifying the records of his race, or of the witness in the box to save his case, leads to what may fairly be called mendacity. Indeed, so ingrained is the practice of gratifying the feeling and desire which initiate thinking that conventional fictions are apt to be less misleading than scrupulously exact statements. We may imagine the misunderstandings which would be caused by a refusal to adopt the common mendacities of polite society. In the more serious field of statecraft, Bismarck is said to have found that nothing so deceived his adversaries as to tell them the truth.

In conclusion, the matter comes down to this, that the human mind is not primarily an organ by which man determines the real objective truth of things and gives utterance to it, but is rather a tool by which one accomplishes one's desires. As this intelligence grows, man comes to know to a greater or less degree that inanimate nature, as well as the lower animals, has uniform modes of reaction, and that his desires in regard to them can be effected only by real knowledge; hence he abandons magic for science when dealing with them and tries to think clearly and accurately. But his fellow men he finds more complex problems. They can be deceived to his profit;

they can be entertained by fictions to his profit; they can be coerced by threats to his profit; and in these various ways of extracting profit from them, his language will be guided by dominating principles other than a desire to give them truthful information.   He finds furthermore that there are various sorts of obligations laid upon him to refrain from truth-telling under divers penalties.   He is a member of a state, a church, a party, a class, a clique, a family, and in all these relations he is virtually obliged to see things as they are not, and to speak that which is false, under penalties varying from execution down to mere inarticulate unpopularity, most difficult to be borne. Acting in these various capacities he is constantly trained in juggling testimony, in judicious blindness, in expressing opinions he does not feel, in bringing his words and actions and thoughts, if possible, into conformity with something other than real facts; and all the while he sees those who are most completely and skilfully disingenuous reaping rewards, or what he has been taught to regard as such, in private and public life.   Apart from certain occupations where he is brought into contact with something other than human nature, he finds little to encourage resolute veracity of thought and speech; and many forms of declension from this ideal he is taught to hold as very precious virtues—many aspects of loyalty and patriotism, or of orthodoxy, much of conventional morality, politeness, tact, *savoir faire,* and the like.   He started with a cerebro-neural system which was far from perfect, and his training is usually not of a kind to lead him to struggle against its defects, or to seek after an ideal of veracity.

So when he comes to write a letter or a book which deals with his human relations, he is not only confronted with the facts which he must judge, but also with an abundance of interests, likes, dislikes, and beliefs relating to the facts.

Towards his reader he is possessed by a desire to interest, entertain, to persuade, or to dissuade; and his autocriticism is directed toward one or more of these ends rather than toward the end of giving accurate and unbiased instruction. The sentiments of those whom he is addressing are satisfied by his supporting and stimulating them, not by his putting them to confusion and forcing them to fight for their beliefs.

Enough of these perturbations arise about the threshold of consciousness, but many more lurk beneath and affect what is said and written, even when there is a desire to tell the simple truth. Fortunately, mixed up with them is a great measure of truth which, hostile to dominant prepossessions, has been thrust into the background, but which nevertheless frequently crops out to give the lie to mendacity itself. It is the problem of the historical student to identify these unconscious fidelities to fact, and to extract them from the mass of conscious or unconscious perversions, clear them up, link them together, and establish the real situation. And the first principle to be observed is that when a document from the distant past is under consideration, we have not made the first step towards its interpretation until we have recognized that although it is in a learned tongue, it is none the less a human document. Only so can we dismiss from our minds the powerful prepossession of man's childhood—a blind reverence for the written word.

CHAPTER IV

THE USE OF INVECTIVE

THE preceding chapter has made it clear that human testimony is rarely an accurate, complete, and uncolored transcript of reality. Imprecision of language, no less than that of thought, distorts the real situation and therefore operates as the personal equation in any attempt to analyze and evaluate the facts with which the testimony purports to deal.

It is not difficult to recognize in daily life the failure of people to limit themselves habitually in speech to precise meanings and careful discriminations, and we therefore take the personal equation into consideration: we apply the necessary corrective in forming our judgments of men and events. But the same corrective is, unfortunately, not always applied to those more distant, but not less fallible, fellow-men from whom we gain our historical material. There is error in assuming that the lapse of years has introduced into their written words an element of accuracy and trustworthiness which is foreign to records of contemporary events. Nor does the fact that the statements were originally penned in a classic tongue justify the unreserved credence which a blind reverence, based, it would seem, on the principle *omne ignotum pro magnifico,* has sometimes given them. A lie is a lie, even in Latin.

The determination of the nature and extent of the personal equations which should be applied to the exegesis of historical sources is a matter of such extreme delicacy and difficulty as to render vain any expectation of agreement among students. Yet the task, in some form or other, is an indispensable preliminary to fruitful historical labor. There is no reason to believe that the minds of the ancients functioned more accurately than the minds of the moderns do, and what the limitations of the latter are is clear from the preceding chapter. We may safely assume that a group of Roman scholars would scarcely be more exact in reporting an occurrence to which they were witnesses than were the psychologists assembled at Göttingen.[1]

One of the prime requisites of a historian, it will generally be conceded, is a thorough knowledge of the intellectual habits of the people and age whose life he seeks to reconstruct. He will recognize the fact that language is an unfailing index of intellectual capacity and moral attainment; that it is never a static thing; that there are always particular modes or fashions of expression which, if widely spread and long continued, are embodied in literature, and that a period becomes distinctive by the use and abuse of certain words and phrases as surely as it does by dress. To be ignorant of the language of the literary remains of an age is no greater disqualification for one who seeks to interpret them correctly than to be ignorant of how that language was used—what the public sentiment of the times tolerated, expected or approved as mere *façons de parler;* what expressions were recognized as being no more than figurative and not to be understood literally; what touches were simply established conventions; what allowances contemporary readers were

[1] See p. 33.

prepared to make; what differences in form of composition, if any, there were between a positive, honest assertion of fact, and a bit of badinage or politeness or general abuse.

All these things are so perfectly understood by any educated and experienced person as to his own epoch and people, that they often remain almost subconscious; and he sometimes forgets, when he reads the writings of another age, that there were then perhaps different fashions, conventions, and tacit understandings regarding the use of language. The way is full of pitfalls to a student who fails to appreciate the kind of allowance he must be prepared to make, and inasmuch as this error has been rampant in the field under discussion, it is necessary to obtain a clear idea of the conditions in Roman life which bore on their habits in literary expression.

At all times in their history so far as we have any knowledge of it, there prevailed among the Romans, not only in controversial but in other forms of expression, the habit of a reckless use of invective, vituperation, and scandalous scurrility. These statements, unfortunately, have frequently been accepted at their face value and have given rise to wildly distorted ideas of social and moral conditions in ancient Rome.

This indulgence in violent and abusive language appears in the early rustic merrymakings of the Romans, and the unrefined tastes of the crowd were delighted with the coarse jokes and taunts of the farces and Fescennine verses.[1] Horace speaks of the early predilection for rustic taunts, cutting jests, and undisguised abuse which spared no one, and which had to be restrained by law.[2]

[1] M. Schanz, *Geschichte der röm. Lit.* (*Erster Teil*, München, 1907), section 9.

[2] Horace, *Epist.*, II, 1, 139ff.

The only form of literature in which the Romans achieved originality was the Satire, which, in the hands of very early writers, abounded in malice and invective. This spirit displayed itself at festivals as well as at funerals; and on occasion of the triumphs of distinguished generals, the soldiers sang facetious songs regarding even their most beloved leaders, often containing the most atrocious slanders, but which were really intended to express only their high spirits and genuine, if coarse, affection.[1] The chaffing songs of the unquestionably devoted soldiers of Cæsar would, if sung to-day, hardly be taken to indicate good-humored regard.[2] It is not improbable, as Fowler suggests, that this friendly abuse had its *raison d'être* in the notion that evil was likely to befall the man whose good fortune and felicity were too conspicuous, and that by means of this pseudo-vituperation the malevolence of Nemesis would be averted. "The history of this vituperation," Fowler remarks in speaking of Cicero, "is a curious one; it was a traditional method of hostile oratory, and sprang from an old Roman root, the tendency to defamation and satire, which may itself be attributed in part to the Italian custom of levelling abuse at a public man (e.g., at his triumph) in order to avert evil from him."[3]

Whether this explanation be sound or not, there can be no doubt as to the fact that a free resort to the adornments of scurrilous excoriation was a settled literary as well as conversational fashion among the Romans. They cultivated a freedom of speech in their observations upon one another which frequently partook of the nature of caustic and sardonic reviling. As these characteristics

[1] See Schanz, *op. cit.*, section 9a, and the passages cited.
[2] See Suetonius, *Julius*, 49, 51, 80.
[3] W. Warde Fowler, *Social Life at Rome* (New York, 1913), p. 107.

were commonly present where the occasion was not serious and where, indeed, friendly and complimentary comment was intended, it was natural that, where feelings became strong and anger was excited, the intensity and extravagance of recrimination rose to an extraordinary pitch. Frequently, when difference of opinion developed between advocates or statesmen, there seems to have been not much real argument about the matter in controversy; instead, the opponents devoted themselves to slander and castigation of one another, which may have been amusing to the judicial or comitial gatherings, but which doubtless tended more and more to alienate the auditors from oratory less highly spiced.

Even among those who were capable of expressing noble thought in perfect form, there appears an occasional disregard of conventions which modern standards of taste impose. The exquisite urbanity of Horace did not prevent him from penning *Epodes* marked by unseemly invective,[1] and Virgil's gentle spirit, full of the sense of life's sadness, resorted in his youth to common abuse.[2] Catullus, too, justly famed for the polish and elegance of his verse, sometimes sank into scurrilous anger of almost incredible violence. The charges against a certain Gellius, for example, are utterly obscene, but a measure of their essential unreality may perhaps be found in the fact that the poet had been endeavoring, in vain, to conciliate his victim.[3] His vile attacks on Cæsar and Mamurra, probably growing out of a personal grievance

[1] *Epodes,* V, VI, VIII, X, XII, XVII.
[2] *Catalepton,* 6, 12, 13. It should be added that the authenticity of the *Catalepton* is not beyond question. The work is accepted as Virgil's by Theodor Birt, *Jugendverse und Heimatpoesie Vergils* (Leipzig, 1910).
[3] *Catullus,* 74, 80, 88, 89, 90, 91, 116.

against the latter, were not regarded seriously by the former who, according to Suetonius, continued his intimacy with the poet's family, freely accepted his apology, and invited him to dinner.[1]

Ovid, in spite of the grievous trick fortune played on him, was a man of entire sanity; his poems of exile indicate no loss of mind, and yet when he came to denounce a man whom he regarded as his enemy, his tirade borders on the ravings of the madhouse.[2] So also Apuleius, in repelling a criminal accusation brought against him, seemed to consider it an aid to his defence to charge his opponent with every infamy that a depraved imagination could conjure up, even extending his invective to cover the man's wife, daughter, father and son with delirious imputations.[3]

Abuse of this sort pervaded every form of literature, even moral, philosophical and religious. The greater one's prominence, the more savage the vituperation. The emperors were naturally shining marks and hardly one of them escaped charges whose very extravagance prove their puerility.[4] If we may trust Suetonius[5] one at least of the emperors, Augustus, was a fair match for his traducers. The reader of Suetonius is left with the feeling that the Romans were not over-sensitive to such vilification, which was probably the reason why it was necessary to exaggerate it to so inconceivable a degree. But what is especially significant is the fact that the subject was treated in manuals on composition; Quin-

[1] Suet., *Jul.*, 73.

[2] See *Ibis.*

[3] Apuleius, *Apologia*, 74ff.

[4] See Suet., *Augustus*, 68ff; *Tiberius*, 43-45; Seneca, *Apokolokyntosis.*

[5] Suet., *ibid.*; Martial, XI, 20.

tilian, indeed, feels it necessary to deprecate its excessive use against those who merely happen to dissent from the orator in opinion.[1]

A good illustration of this merely rhetorical use of invective may be found in the case of Cicero, who in this as in other respects, seems not below the general moral standards of his age; who was from the nature of his occupations and activities exceptionally familiar with the public taste and the most effective methods of persuasive speaking and writing; and the amplitude and variety of whose literary productions make him the most satisfactory exemplar of the subject under discussion.

In the case of not a few of us, the earliest memories of Cicero centre about his orations against Catiline, in which the consul's powers of invective appear in striking form. There are extant also the fragments of an electoral speech in which Catiline is charged with a shocking series of crimes; with many murders committed some years before, including the decapitation of Gratidianus; with plundering his province; with bribery, corruption, and shameful licentiousness. The associates in the conspiracy are said to be thieves, swindlers, assassins, parricides, debauchees, and their plot is said to involve the murder of all decent men and the burning of Rome.[2]

Sallust, who can scarcely be accused of favoring Catiline, implies that some of the charges were not based on evidence.[3] In a letter from Cicero to his friend

---

[1] Compare Quintilian, *Institutiones,* VI, 3; A. E. Chaignet, *La Rhétorique et son Histoire* (Paris, 1888), p. 103.

[2] Cic., *in Cat. II; in Toga Candida; cf.* Asconius (Clark), p. 84.

[3] *Cat.* 14: *scio fuisse non nullos qui ita existumarent, iuventutem, quae domum Catilinae frequentabat, parum honeste pudicitiam habuisse; sed ex aliis rebus magis, quam quod cuiquam id compertum foret, haec fama valebat.* 22: *non nulli ficta et haec et*

Atticus,[1] written shortly before his consulate, reference is made to some prosecution of Catiline, possibly for extortion in his province. "At present I am thinking of undertaking the defence of my fellow candidate Catiline. We have a jury to our mind—with the full consent of the prosecutor. I hope that if he is acquitted he will be more closely united with me in the conduct of our canvass: but if the result should be otherwise, I shall bear it with resignation." Some light on this "consent" is found in a later oration in which Cicero charges Clodius, the accuser, with having been bribed by Catiline;[2] and in another letter to Atticus he regards the condemnation of Catiline on the matters involved in this prosecution as certain if the jury decide correctly.[3] It is not clear whether or not Cicero actually helped to secure Catiline's acquittal on this trial—Fenestella says he did, while Asconius argues that he could not have done so—but it appears that the coalition with Catiline was not arranged.[4]

A few years later we find Cicero[5] giving a very different account of the associates of Catiline. He then says that many virtuous men, young and old, espoused his cause; that Catiline's character had many marks of eminent virtue; that he had the friendship of many and illustrious men; that he seemed to Cicero and to many other good men a worthy citizen, desirous of the regard

---

multa praeterea existumabant ab eis, qui Ciceronis invidiam, quae postea orta est, leniri credebant atrocitate sceleris eorum, qui poenas dederant. nobis ea res pro magnitudine parum comperta est.

[1] *Epist. ad Att.*, I, 2 (B.C. 65).

[2] *De Har. Resp.*, 20: *a Catilina pecuniam accepit, ut turpissime praevaricaretur.*

[3] *Ad Att.*, I, 1.

[4] Asconius, p. 76 (Clark, p. 85).

[5] *Pro Cael.*, 4-6.

of every good man, a firm and trustworthy friend; and that it was only at the last, when it became necessary to act against him by force, that Cicero's suspicions were awakened and he found he had been deceived. Yet many of the savage charges which Cicero had made against Catiline concerned matters which, if true, must have been of public notoriety, and which were alleged to have happened years before the period when Cicero claims he deemed Catiline a virtuous citizen. Indeed, the time when Cicero suddenly awoke to the fact that Catiline was an utter villain comes suspiciously soon after his plans for a coalition between them had fallen through, and his opponent—now become a blood-stained scoundrel —had entered into a political combination against the orator. His enlightenment as to the virtue and high-mindedness of Catiline's friends also follows in due course after his banishment may have suggested to him the wisdom of more discriminating denunciation. Cassius Dio [1] states, with some probability, that Cicero at the time of his return from exile composed secretly an invective against Crassus and Cæsar,—whom he regarded as most to blame for his banishment—in which he assembled charges of utmost violence against them; but warned by the unpleasant results of his unbridled speech, he sealed the book and delivered it to his son [2] with the injunction not to open it until his death. Catiline, in all probability, was in point of morals no better and no worse than the young nobles of his day. What is certain is that he had been treated most unfairly by the senate in his first candidacy, and that he has suffered the supreme misfor-

[1] XXXIX, 10. Cf. Cic. ad Att., II, 6.
[2] The Greek is τῷ παιδί. The reference may be to Cicero's slave.

tune of having had a man of literary genius for his enemy.[1]
In general, it is sufficient to observe that the inveterate
duplicity of character which Cicero found it convenient
to attribute to Catiline was in harmony with his general
theory of pleading.[2]

No better illustration can be found of how easily
Cicero's statements as to a person's character varied with
his changing regard for that person, than is afforded by
his expressions concerning his son-in-law Dolabella. This
young man must have been well known to Cicero, for
he had defended Dolabella in two serious prosecutions
prior to his engagement to Tullia.[3] The "defects," at
which Cicero vaguely hints, were certainly not unknown
to Caelius who, in a congratulatory letter written in 50
B.C., expresses hope that time and matrimony will have
a salutary effect upon one who *sibi parum utilis fuit.* The
passage reads: *Gratulor tibi adfinitate viri medius fidius
optimi; nam hoc ego de illo existimo. Cetera porro, quibus
adhuc ille sibi parum utilis fuit, et aetate iam sunt de-
cussa, et consuetudine atque auctoritate tua, pudore
Tulliae, si qua restabunt, confido celeriter sublatum iri;
non est enim pugnax in vitiis neque hebes ad id quod
melius sit intellegendum. Deinde, quod maximum est, ego*

[1] Cf. E. S. Beesly, *Catiline, Clodius, and Tiberius* (London,
1878), p. 36.

[2] Cf. *de Oratore*, II, 59: *Perspicitis genus hoc quam sit facetum,
quam elegans, quam oratorium, sive habeas vere quod narrare
possis, quod tamen est mendaciunculis aspergendum, sive fingas.*

[3] *Ad Fam.* III, 10, 5 (written in the year 50 B.C.): *Illud vero
mihi permirum accidit, tantam temeritatem fuisse in eo adolescente,
cuius ego salutem in duobus capitis iudiciis summa contentione
defendi, ut tuis inimicitiis suscipiendis oblivisceretur prope
omnium fortunarum ac rationum suarum, praesertim cum tu
omnibus vel ornamentis vel praesidiis redundares, ipsi, ut le-
vissime dicam, multa dessent. Cf. ad Att., VII, 3, 12.*

illum valde amo.[1] In writing to Caelius the following year Cicero characterizes Dolabella as "a most excellent young man, and very dear to me." [2] Even after the divorce between Dolabella and Tullia in 46 B.C., Cicero's relations with him continue to be marked by intimacy and apparent affection; [3] and upon the death of Tullia (45 B.C.) Cicero writes that he could have borne the loss more easily had Dolabella been by his side, for, he says, "your wise discourse and your marked affection for me would have been a great support." [4] After Dolabella had taken violent measures against those who mourned the murdered Cæsar, Cicero's affection becomes enthusiastic and finds expression in the phrase "wonderful Dolabella." [5] The judgment of Atticus, it may be remarked, was more reserved.[6]

Later, in the year 44 B.C., he comments with heat on Antony's daring to make the outrageous suggestion that there had been an intrigue between Antonia and Dolabella.[7] But by March 43 B.C. news came that this excellent young man had joined the avengers of Cæsar's

[1] *Ad Fam.*, VIII, 13, 1. *Cf.* VIII, 4, 1.

[2] *Ad Fam.*, II, 16, 5. *Cf.* VII, 32, 3; II, 15, 2; *ad Att.*, VII, 13, 3.

[3] *Cf. Ad Fam.*, VII, 33, 2; IX, 10, 13, 16, 7; XII, 1, 1; *ad Att.*, X, 4, 11; XIII, 9; 52, 2; 47.

[4] *Ad Fam.*, IX, 11: *quem ferrem certe moderatius, si te haberem; nam et oratio tua prudens et amor erga me singularis multum levaret.*

[5] *Ad Att.*, XIV, 15, 1 (May, 44): *O mirificum Dolabellam meum! iam enim dico meum; antea, crede mihi, subdubitabam. Magnam ἀναθεώρησιν res habet, de saxo, in crucem, columnam tollere, locum illum sternendum locare! Quid quaeris? heroica. Cf.* XIV, 16, 2.

[6] *Ad Att.*, XIV, 18, 1. *Cf.* 19. 1.

[7] *Phil.*, II, 38, 99: *probri insimulasti pudicissimam feminam. Quid est quod addi possit? Contentus eo non fuisti: frequentissimo senatu Kalendis Ianuariis sedente patruo hanc tibi esse cum*

assassination, and had killed Trebonius, one of the tyrannicides. Dolabella's real character seemed suddenly and
darkly revealed, if we may trust the eleventh Philippic.
The swan had become a very black goose indeed. The
man whom it were monstrous for Antony to charge with
crime now shares with Antony the distinction of being
the blackest scoundrel that ever lived. The two are
united, we now learn, in a special intimacy by the remarkable similitude of their wicked natures and unclean lives.[1]
After lavishing adjectives like *infamis, impurus,* and
incestus upon Dolabella, Cicero gives a brief but shocking
review of his life. From childhood he has delighted in
cruelty, and so shameful has been the nature of his lusts
that he has always revelled in acts which a modest person may not mention: in view of what Cicero finds it
possible to mention in moments of annoyance, this remark
is not without its grim humor.[2] In explaining his long
and intimate friendship with this monster, Cicero offers
a lame defence, somewhat reminiscent of his experience
with Catiline. We are urged to believe that Cicero, the
experienced statesman, was completely deluded by the
innate duplicity and deceit of Dolabella's character. He
declares that perhaps even now he would not have dis-

Dolabella causam odi dicere ausus es, quod ab eo sorori et uxori
tuae stuprum esse oblatum comperisses. Quis interpretari potest, im-
pudentiorne, qui in senatu, an improbior, qui in Dolabellam, an
impurior, qui patre audiente, an crudelior, qui in illam miseram
tam spurce, tam impie dixeris?

[1] *Phil.,* XI, 1, 1: *Nam duo haec capita nata sunt post homines*
natos taeterrima et spurcissima, Dolabella et Antonius.

[2] *Phil.,* XI, 4, 9: *alteri (i.e., Dolabella) a puero pro deliciis*
crudelitas fuit; deinde ea libidinum turpitudo, ut in hoc sit
semper ipse laetatus, quod ea faceret, quae sibi obici ne ab
inimico quidem possent verecundo

covered Dolabella's turpitude and have been alienated
from him, had it not been for the revelation afforded by
his political acts.[1] Here indeed the orator incautiously
lets the truth slip forth. It is clear that he had known
Dolabella intimately for years and had not found him
unfit to be the husband of the dearly loved Tullia and a
close friend, even after the marriage had proved a failure.
And there can be no doubt that this new moral judgment
would never have occurred to Cicero but for the change
in Dolabella's political affiliations. Whatever may be the
real facts as to Dolabella's private life—apparently black
enough in all conscience—yet it is evident that in this case,
as often elsewhere, the supposed exigencies of legal and
political pleading served to impair seriously the value of
Cicero's testimony.[2] For Cicero, as for many another,
belief created its proofs, and considerations of truth and
consistency interposed no barriers to the will to believe.

This is indeed abundant evidence that neither Cicero
nor, in general, those whom he attacked took his vituperation too seriously. He was annoyed at Vatinius, for instance, for appearing as a witness against Sextius, his
client, and proceeded, as he boasts to his brother, "to cut
him up" to the applause of gods and men. The infamy

[1] *Phil.*, XI, 4, 10: *et hic, di immortales! aliquando fuit meus.
Occulta enim erant vitia non inquirenti. Neque nunc fortasse
alienus ab eo essem, nisi ille nobis, nisi moenibus patriae, nisi
huic urbi, nisi dis penatibus, nisi aris et focis omnium nostrum,
nisi denique naturae et humanitati inventus esset inimicus.*

[2] Cass. Dio (XLVI, 29; cf. XXXVII, 29; XXXVIII, 12)
remarks that Cicero habitually spoke his mind intemperately
and immoderately, sometimes forgetting all public interest while
indulging in general abuse of an opponent; that he alienated
more people by his unbridled tongue than he attached to himself by benefits conferred; and that his invective was thought
to be based rather on personal enmity than on justice and truth.

of his life, says Cicero, renders his testimony worthless;
he is a perjurer, he springs from his hole like a serpent
with eyes starting from his head, neck inflated and throat
swelling to give utterance to his lies; he hates all good
men and craves for pillage and slaughter; he is a man
of scandalous character, disgraced by all manner of
foulness and infamy. In his youth he stole from his
neighbors and beat his mother; in his public service he
was a swindler and robber; and he appeased the Infernal
Gods with the entrails of murdered boys. Bribery, corruption, extortion, rapine and murder—these had been his
constant companions and delight.[1] But two years later,
having been reconciled to Vatinius, the orator undertook
his defence in a criminal prosecution; testified to his good
character, and obtained his acquittal. Their later association, if we can judge from Cicero's letters, was one
of cordial and intimate friendship.[2] In short, "public
vituperation," as Professor Fowler remarks,[3] "in senate
or law-courts, was a fact of every day, and the wealth
of violent personal abuse which a gentleman like Cicero
could expend on one whom for the time he hated, or
who had done him some wrong, passes all belief. . . . To
single out a man's personal ugliness, to calumniate his
ancestry in the vilest terms,—these were little more than
traditional practices, oratorical devices, which the rhetorical education of the day encouraged, and which no
one took very seriously."

The unreality of such abusive speech is indeed acknowledged by Cicero himself in a significant passage. To
charge a person with sexual immorality, we are told,[4]

[1] *Epist. ad Q. Frat.* II, 4; *in Vatin., passim.*
[2] *Epist. ad Fam.*, I, 9; V, 9; 10a, 11; *ad Att.*, XI, 5.
[3] *Social Life at Rome*, pp. 106-107.
[4] *Pro Caelio*, 3, 6.

is a common practice among prosecutors. Such reproaches are merely oratorical commonplaces habitually
heaped upon everyone who in youth was of attractive
appearance. To vituperate is one thing; to accuse is
another. The latter requires a charge of some definite
act and detailed proof, witnesses, and legal argument.
Vituperation has no settled object except insult. If one
be attacked with ill-temper, it is called abuse; but if it
be done facetiously it is called chaffing—*urbanitas*. To
call a man an adulterer, a rake, a pimp—this is reviling,
not accusing. Such expressions are mere vituperation
recklessly poured forth by an angry enemy, not a regular
charge of criminal misconduct.[1]

In leaving the subject of this aspect of Cicero's imper-
fection as an historical source, we must not forget that
it may seem to us the more striking because we have such
an exceptionally intimate revelation of his private opinion
in his letters. There is truth, and perhaps a partial
explanation of his defects, in the remark attributed to
Augustus when in his later years he came upon one of
his grandsons reading a book of Cicero's writings. The
youth sought to conceal it; but the emperor saw it; picked
it up; read it a while, and then handed it back to the
boy, saying: "He was a learned and eloquent man, my
boy, and a lover of his country." [2]   Eloquence and
patriotism are admirable qualities, but in an historical
source they have the defects of their qualities.

The free resort to vituperation was far too thoroughly
established in ancient habits of expression to be deeply
affected by the change which Christianity wrought in
the national life. Even the Fathers of the Church reviled
their opponents with an open directness and disregard

[1] *Ibid.*, 13, 30. Compare Quintilian, III, 7, 1 and 19.
[2] Plutarch, *Cicero*, 49: λόγιος ἀνήρ, ὦ παῖ, λόγιος καὶ φιλόπατρις.

of truth abhorrent to modern standards of taste. So, for example, Gregory Nazianzen delivered two fierce invectives against the memory of the emperor Julian "whose private life," according to Lecky,[1] "was a model of purity, who carried to the throne the manners, tastes, and friendships of a philosophic life, and who proclaimed and, with very slight exceptions, acted with the largest and most generous toleration." He had, however, openly abandoned the new religion, and "all the vocabulary of invective was in consequence habitually lavished upon him." So, too, St. Jerome kept alive the guiding rules of ancient controversial debate in his violent strictures upon the conduct and character of Vigilantius who had objected, wisely, it would now be held, to the stupid adoration of relics and images and the excessive alms to the poor in Jerusalem. Both Gregory and Jerome were men of high repute and yet it is apparent to the critical student that their testimony concerning their enemies is worthless, for neither Julian nor Vigilantius, we certainly know, was the foul monster of villainy imagined by the Saints. Christian historiography, in these instances, obviously continued the pagan tradition.

[1] *History of European Morals* (3rd ed., New York, 1891), vol. II, p. 262.

CHAPTER V

IT is apparent from the foregoing chapter with what careless freedom the Romans frequently made their statements harmonize less with the reality of things than with the design of promoting some predetermined object, or with the satisfaction of some preëxisting sentiment. The examples there given were chiefly cases growing out of personal enmity, either genuine and deep-seated, or fictitious and superficial, but marked by abusive speech in either instance. Similar results followed from the more general and impersonal, but not less powerful, sentiments; that is, from the various biases, bigotries and prejudices which the Romans share with all peoples who have played a great part in the world. With most of these the modern world is sufficiently familiar: we recognize their existence, their effects; and we make the necessary allowances for them. We observe easily how political prejudices warp a neighbor's views on public affairs; we remember that George Washington was called a tyrant, and that Abraham Lincoln was denounced as a "Tiberius" on the floor of the Senate at a time when no doubts as to the inerrancy of Tacitus had penetrated America.[1]

[1] See James Ford Rhodes, *History of the United States* (New York, vol. IV, 1899), p. 531; J. A. Logan, *The Great Conspiracy* (New York, 1886), p. 578: "This modern Emperor, this

But there are certain respects in which we share the biases of the Romans so completely that it is difficult for us to dissociate ourselves from their states of mind and to view their controversies with entire detachment. Where the bias is the same in the source and in the student cool consideration of the matter at issue is rendered doubly difficult. There is then the danger of treading *de novo* the same path of error.

The respects in which we so far resemble the Romans as to share in their emotional perturbations are certain social discontents and moral biases. In these matters there is not simply that similarity which exists in general political situations, where, however, there are differences of detail sufficient to enable us to view their controversies calmly; but there is to a considerable extent identity of detail, since so many of our social aspirations and moral prejudices are the same. Nor is this surprising, since we, like them, have to reconcile the fact of great social differentiation with the theory of political equality; and since, on the moral side, so great a part of our ethical principles has come to us from Stoicism,—a philosophy modified, it is true, in its metaphysical outlook by adoption into Christianity, but in its ethical character changed little or not at all. It is for these reasons that the moderns have been especially misled by those Roman social critics who, as moralizing satirists or philosophical moralists, appealed to social and moral prepossessions which we share.

To maintain a critical attitude toward those with whose general principles we sympathize is not easy. Their congruity to us in their general professions predisposes us to

---

Tiberius, a sort of Tiberius, and his Sejanus, a sort of a Sejanus, the head of the War Department, are organizing daily their Military Courts to try civilians." The speech was delivered in the Senate by Garret Davis.

credit their assertions of details which explain and justify the position occupied by them—and by us. They please us, we incline towards them, and since we have, in theory at least, elevated veracity into a high virtue, we find it especially difficult to refrain from attributing the possession of it to those whom we regard as "good" men, especially where they vehemently claim the right to it. The "law of least effort," indeed, by eliminating the exertion of an independent judgment serves to inspire confidence in moralists.

The general attitude of the Romans toward censoriousness is well illustrated by Plutarch's comment on the censorship in his *Life of Cato:* "They thought that neither a man's marriage, nor his rearing of children, nor his mode of life, nor even his banquet ought to be free from criticism and control, managed according to the individual's choice and desire." [1] Naturally enough this characteristic found concrete form in one of their governmental institutions, for institutions are but the expression of a people's character. The crown of a Roman's public career, as Plutarch says, was the censorship. The office carried with it the legal right to examine the public and private life of every citizen, to denounce and to punish, if need be, harshly and inexorably. When censor attacked censor, as sometimes happened, the ensuing scandal caused the Senate no little embarrassment.[2]

The practice of electing periodically two old men who, after lives spent in giving and receiving vituperation, were granted full legal power to discharge their accumulated prejudices, became obsolescent in the last century of the Republic, reviving only fitfully thereafter. In fact, men whose long public service qualified them for the honor had,

[1] Chap. XVI.
[2] Livy, XXVII, 11; XXIX, 37; *cf.* XL, 45-46.

as Cassius Dio[1] remarks, grown wise enough not to desire it. But so inveterate a characteristic as censoriousness, so long established and, we may say, so consecrated by the Roman constitution, and one, likewise, so congruous to the national taste could not be obliterated easily. The intelligent few might see its futility and feel a distaste for its invidious power; but the more primitive and passionate people, devoid of the quiet sanity and broad vision which come with the intellectual life, naturally continued to delight in the personal exercise of unbridled criticism of society and morals.

So harmonious was all this to the general character and customs of the people that not a few seriously devoted themselves to its literary expression and more listened with delight to their productions. The satirist and militant moralist took the place of the censor. It is worth remarking in this connection that while the Romans were imitators of the Greeks in most branches of letters, in the domain of satire they were original and powerful. Several causes contributed to determine the character of satire as a literary type. The formal study of rhetoric and the consequent gain in facile expression; a tendency toward ethical reflection and speculation as active careers were closed under the Principate; and a *fin de siècle* weariness expressing itself in fretful discontent and gloomy forebodings, gave rise to a species of writing which, while preserving the old qualities of vituperation and reckless mendacity, was further marked by brilliant but hopeless moralizing, and *per contra,* by an ascetic ideal of life under primitive nature.

There were many of these satirists and some of them have come down to us, but Juvenal so far surpasses the other survivors that an examination of him will include

[1] XL, 57.

the others; for the subjects of complaint touched on by
them are practically all to be found in his castigations.
He is perhaps the most illustrious example in letters of the
satirical critic of social conditions—a class of writers
which has received of late from those who are unsympathetic toward them the appellation of "muckrakers."

To understand Juvenal's point of view, it is necessary
to know what manner of man he was; unfortunately, the
extant *Vitae* afford little information that cannot be inferred from the satires. D. Junius Juvenal (*ca.* 60-140
A.D.) seems to have been the son or the *alumnus* of a
well-to-do freedman, and to have received a careful
rhetorical training. Many years of his life were spent
in the practice of declamation before he devoted himself
to composing satires which were published, it is generally believed, in the times of Trajan and Hadrian.[1]   A
votive inscription from the temple of Ceres in his native
town of Aquinum, commonly accepted as referring to
the satirist, records the fact that he held the office of
duumvir quinquennalis and was a *flamen* of the deified
Vespasian.[2] We may fairly regard him as a man obscure
in social rank and not very successful in gaining prominence by his literary labors: such at least would seem to be
the inference from the failure of his name to appear in the
letters of Pliny the younger,[3] who touches on most of the

[1] Compare W. S. Teuffel, *Geschichte der röm. Literatur,* section 331, 2. Juvenal himself admits that his victims were beyond
the reach of his venom: *experiar quid concedatur in illos | quorum
Flaminia tegitur cinis atque Latina.* II, 170f.

[2] C. I. L., X, 5382: *C(ere) ri sacrum [. . Iu] nius Iuvenalis,
[trib.] coh(ortis) [I??] Delmatarum, II [vir] quinq (uennalis),
flamen divi Vespasiani, vovit dedicav[itq]ue sua pec (unia).*

[3] In the course of the first three centuries, Martial is the only
Latin writer who mentions Juvenal. See Martial, *Epigrams,*
VII, 24; VII, 91; XII, 18.

contemporary writers, as well as from the tone of bitterness and jealousy so characteristic of the satirist in referring to those who have achieved success.[1] Martial's epigram suggests the picture of a rather uncouth, nervous man, who, wearied by his eager but fruitless search for patronage, proceeded to depict the evils of society from the point of view, and with the prejudices and notions concerning the great, of one of that unhappy crowd of educated, sensitive, ambitious and disappointed poets and rhetoricians who besieged the antechambers of the nobles by day, and at night exchanged with their fellows observations on the sourness of the grapes.[2]

An analysis of Juvenal's satires shows that a considerable part of his stock in trade consists of the solemn and emphatic assertion of ethical commonplaces, such as have been uttered *semper, ubique et ab omnibus,* but which he brings forth almost as if they were new discoveries. That virtue is the only true nobility, that pride goeth before a fall and a haughty spirit before destruction, that the path of glory leads but to the grave, that a sound mind in a sound body is a desirable possession, are valuable

[1] Compare, for example, VII, 188, 197ff; II, 38-41.
[2] Martial, XII, 18, compares his own felicity in Spain with Juvenal's weary round of things in Rome:

> *Dum tu forsitan inquietus erras*
> *clamosa, Iuvenalis, in Subura*
> *aut collem dominae teris Dianae;*
> *dum per limina te potentiorum*
> *sudatrix toga ventilat vagumque*
> *maior Caelius et minor fatigant:*
> *me multos repetita post Decembres*
> *accepit mea rusticumque fecit*
> *auro Bilbilis et superba ferro.*

Martial, in all probability knew Juvenal, however, only as a rhetorician.

moral maxims rather than illuminating historical material. So, too, that one should know one's self, that revenge is the pleasure of weak souls, that conscience punishes the sinner, that he who meditates a crime incurs the guilt thereof, are more or less true but not fruitful for our purpose.[1] These precepts, so earnestly laid down by Juvenal throw no especial light upon the characteristics of his age, unless to indicate that it possessed much the same substratum of moral ideas as our own. Much of this portion of his work, and the same might be said of other parts as well, bears on its face indications of unreality— signs that it is rhetoric rather than real feeling which speaks. So, for example, in a satire (XIV, 107ff) devoted to our duty to set a good example to the young, we find some two hundred lines urging that avarice be discouraged in them. But this is surely not a vice to which youth is prone.[2]

Nor can we properly assign much greater value to another large class of Juvenal's utterances, namely, the general denunciations of his times. Rhetoricians were fond of these things : Seneca the elder tells us that Fabianus inserted them in his orations whenever he had a chance.[3] Juvenal starts with the assumption of a golden age when vice was a prodigy and even breaches of etiquette were punished by death; but now everything is the worst possible : the earth brings forth only evil, virtue is the prodigy; the wicked prosper, there are even religious sceptics; Rome is no place for honest men but only for

[1] Compare Juvenal, *Satires,* VII, 20; X, *passim;* XI, 27; XIII, 189ff, 209, etc.

[2] The poet indeed comes very near to denouncing industrious habits and legitimate business. Compare Persius, *Satires,* V, 132ff.

[3] Seneca, *Controversiae,* II, *Praef.* 2.

liars, wizards, bawds, thieves, hooligans, and Greeks.[1]
There are fires and accidents, and poets spouting in the
month of August; there are noises and crowds, one is
jostled and stepped on.[2] All this throws more light on the
character of the satirist than on that of the great city.

The rich of course are a bad lot. They owe their
wealth to fraud and crime.[3] Poverty is scorned and cannot even aspire to the hand of a rich bride. Especially
bitter are the strictures on the failure of the wealthy to
subsidize literary men. The *sportula* is inadequate, and is
given only after insulting precautions against fraudulent
impersonation: a sudden death from indigestion is the
proper fate for such meanness.[4] They live luxuriously
and extravagantly; they keep stables; they gamble, and,
worse than all, they even indulge in gladiatorial sports.[5]
The satirist regales himself with the thought of their dread
of poverty and of senile decrepitude, "more to be feared
than death." [6]

Few satirists in any age have refrained from flings at
women, whose peculiarities seem to drive a certain class
of irritable men into veritable frenzy. Juvenal was undoubtedly irritable, and his famous sixth satire, the
longest, is a perfect orgy of vituperation. "All the world
of woman is represented as stained by one or other of the
offences which in the second Satire are treated as ex-
ceptional." It is not so much that he disliked "women
because the sex in his time was corrupt," but rather that

---

[1] *Sat.*, XV, 70ff; I, 75ff; 147; XIII, 23ff; 53ff; 86ff; 105ff; III,
passim.

[2] *Sat.*, III, 7ff; 190ff. etc; XIII, *passim*.

[3] *Sat.*, I, 74-76; 112; III, *passim*.

[4] *Sat.*, I, 95-146.

[5] *Sat.*, I, 22ff; 60ff; II, 143; VIII, 10; XI, *passim*.

[6] *Sat.*, XI, 38-45.

"his dislike to the sex makes him keen to detect and eloquent to dilate upon all the instances of corruption which society supplied."[1] Inasmuch as it is in regard to this matter of the relations of the sexes that ancient society is supposed to have gone especially wrong, it may be of interest to examine in some detail just what its most savage critic has to say.

In the first place the great majority of charges he brings are trivial almost to the point of silliness. They are in the main complaints against certain manifestations of *das Ewig-Weibliches,* which are no doubt rather perplexing to the average man, which he would gladly see changed, or thinks he would; but which, having existed from all time, are regarded by an even-tempered man as a part of the established order of nature, and of which he complains no more than of the weather. Only the immature or the unbalanced cry because it rains, or because a woman acts like a woman.

So we cannot become heated when Juvenal laments that Roman women affected Greek styles and even interlarded their conversation with Greek phrases. Nor is it fatal that a wife should at times be a bit irritating in letting her husband know very plainly her own good qualities, though the poet exclaims that these things are "not to be borne by husbands."[2] We detect the Thackerayan note in the complaint that a wife tyrannizes over a loving husband, that she does not wish him to make presents without her approval, that she turns the cold shoulder on his friends.[3] Many a man, even in modern days, has observed the same thing—in the wives of his friends.

[1] G. A. Simcox, *History of Latin Literature,* vol. II (London, 1883), p. 117.
[2] *Sat.,* VI, 178ff.
[3] *Ibid.,* 206-214.

Mr. Caudle would have sympathized with Juvenal's moving description of a curtain lecture and consequent loss of sleep, the upbraiding about an imaginary rival, and the "tyranny of tears," finally kissed away by the unfortunate husband.[1] Ogulnia, that she may go in due style to the shows, hires a dress and attendants, also a sedan chair, pillows, female friends and a yellow-haired maid to whom she may give her commands; all of which is ridiculous extravagance considering her moderate means, but some women seem to lack the *pudorem paupertatis* and refuse to let their outward show be measured by their *res angusta domi*. [2]

Another serious cause of offense to our satirist is the sempiternal "New Woman," who matches and compares the poets, weighs Virgil in one scale and Homer in another, and pours forth a torrent of words silencing the company about her; who is familiar with history, who is precise on points of grammar, quotes books unknown to her husband, and corrects the phrases of an old-fashioned friend—things a well-bred man would never notice—and who does not allow her husband to commit a solecism. She also converses unabashed with great generals, and knows all that is going on from international politics to the latest scandals, and what she does not know she invents. She has a liking for athletic exercises, delights in sweating with heavy dumb-bells, and then flushed and heated tosses off a flagon or two before she eats, sometimes with unfortunate results.[3]

The various artifices of the feminine toilet perplexed Juvenal, as they have perplexed other men before and since his time. Few husbands have easily appreciated why

[1] *Ibid.,* 268-277.
[2] *Ibid.,* 352ff.
[3] *Sat.,* VI, 252ff; 398ff; 434ff; 456.

wives should disfigure themselves with pastes and face-washes at home, in order that they may appear beautiful to their admirers abroad.   When our poet complains of the woman who punished her servants because she was angry with her husband, he forgets that, according to masculine tradition, logic was never a woman's strong point.   Her conduct in dressing her hair aloft and wearing high-heeled shoes to give herself a fictitious appearance of tallness, even her proneness to encircle her neck with emeralds and insert great jewels in her ears, seems hardly adequate to justify the poet's wail: "Nothing is more intolerable than a rich woman." [1]

Credulous and superstitious he declares women to be, and prone to be imposed upon by priests.[2]   Rich and poor are alike in this regard, and she who has no necklace of gold to display inquires of the fortune-teller whether she shall jilt the tapster and marry the old-clothes man.   Yet the poor, when circumstances require, are ready to encounter the perils of child-birth and endure all the toils of nursing; but rarely does a confinement take place in a gilded bed, so potent are the arts and drugs which ensure barrenness.[3]

As might be expected, Juvenal deems all women to be unchaste.   'I believe that when Saturn was king,' he begins the sixth satire, called by Mackail his "Legend of Bad Women," [4] 'chastity dwelt upon earth, and was long seen there,' but this was when men dwelt in caves and lived on acorns.   'Perhaps many traces of chastity remained—a few at least—even under Jupiter, but this was before his beard was grown.'   Then it fled to Olympus, and now

---

[1] *Ibid.*, 457ff.

[2] *Ibid.*, 511ff.

[3] *Ibid.*, 588ff; *cf.* 596-600.

[4] J. W. Mackail, *Latin Literature* (New York, 1895), p. 223.

violation of marriage is an old custom. 'Are you thinking of marriage, Postumus? You once were sane; what snakes are driving you mad? Can you submit to be the slave of any woman when so many means of suicide are open to you?' Farther on he advises his friend to fall prostrate at the temple and offer to Juno a heifer with gilded horns if he finds a chaste woman, for few are those whose kisses their own fathers might not dread. Luxury broods over Rome, and no deed of lust is wanting since Roman poverty has disappeared. Enervating riches sap the sinews of the age with foul excess.[1]

Even should a woman be that black swan, a chaste wife, the situation of the husband is hardly improved, since such a rare bird is bound to be haughty and vain; and all chance of domestic happiness is hopeless while the wife's mother is alive.[2] We are not surprised to learn that Roman women disliked the offspring of a husband's mistress, though we may question the poet's flourish that it was allowable to kill such children;[3] and we suspect that the credulity of an unscientific age is at the bottom of his assertion that women disturb their husband's reason and render them slavishly submissive by drugs, and even poison them, preferring the life of a lap-dog to that of a husband.[4] In view of such conditions we do not see why Juvenal did not congratulate the husband on Eppia's elopement with a gladiator.[5]

In curious contrast to the universal sinfulness at which Juvenal frantically rails is the fact that in this very era there is abundant evidence testifying to the charm and purity of family life of his contemporaries, whether it be the imperial household of Trajan and Plotina—where she and the other women of the family were honest, right-

---

[1] *Sat.*, VI, 1-51; 292-8.   [2] *Ibid.*, 161ff; 231ff.
[3] *Ibid.*, 627ff.   [4] *Ibid.*, 610ff; 652ff.   [5] *Ibid.*, 104ff.

minded, and affectionate, modest in their toilettes, simple
in their manners, and devoted to the domestic virtues—or
the families of nobles like Agricola, Tacitus, and Pliny,
and the many others of whom we catch glimpses in the
latter's Epistles,[1] or the host of obscure folk of whom we
hear so little in literature but so much in inscriptions.[2]
Viewed with this perspective, it is abundantly evident that
Juvenal's gloomy canvass is vivid but unreal.   By skilfully omitting the good and sedulously seizing on the evil
elements present in every highly organized society, the
brilliant but morbid rhetorician constructed a distorted
and consequently untruthful picture of his age.

[1] See, for example, Tac., *Hist.*, II, 64; *Ann.*, XV, 63, 64; XVI,
10; *Agricola*, 6 (*vixeruntque mira concordia, per mutuam carita-
tem et in vicem se anteponendo*); Pliny, *Epist.*, III, 16; IV, 19;
VI, 4, 7; VII, 5; Martial, *Epigrams*, XI, 104; XII, 21; Seneca,
ad Helviam, 14; Cass. Dio, LXVIII, 5.

[2] Compare the interesting chapter, *Les Classes inférieures et
les associations populaires* in G. Boissier's *La Religion romaine*
(*quatrième édition,* Paris, 1892), II, pp. 238-304.

CHAPTER VI

THE PHILOSOPHICAL MORALISTS

UNDERLYING Roman satire and vituperation, and giving to these manifestations their hardihood and confident audacity in venturing to stalk naked and unashamed through an admiring community, was the strengthening spirit of Roman moral principles. They formed a major premise so imposing and paralyzing to thought as to support by their sheer prestige the most flimsy minor premises and the most fallacious conclusions, which are too often credulously accepted by those moderns who are awed by their own privilege of basking in a similar splendor. No men were ever more profoundly convinced than were the Romans that conduct was at least, as Matthew Arnold estimated, three-fourths of life, unless perhaps we except the ancient Hebrews and ourselves. That this laudable conviction did not always result in a righteousness of action congruous to the rectitude of principle is one of those disharmonies of life whose explanation may, from the abundance of contemporaneous material, profitably engage the attention of modern students.

Whether or not this confidence in the strength of their moral ideals made the rationalizing of their ethical principles seem a negligible matter to the Romans, the fact remains that they were distinctly weak on the side of ethical theory. It was perhaps this weakness and the resultant difficulty, so easily comprehensible by us, of seeing the incongruity of two contradictory lines of action which afford the key to the correct understanding of a character like Seneca, to whom we may be tempted to apply the phrase used to characterize an eminent English statesman of the last century,—"a good man in the very worst sense of the word." [1] Seneca was a far better man than Juvenal and had at least a love for the truth, if not a passion for it. He may be fairly taken as the best representative of the moralists, and the information to be gathered from his works contains, when discreetly used, much that is valuable for the student of social conditions.

It is hardly worth while to repeat his general complaints: they are much the same as men of his kind have uttered at all times of human history, the psychological explanation of which will be considered later. In less savage tones than Juvenal's he frequently condemns the sins of the world—its luxury, gluttony, and covetousness; decency and righteousness have forsaken us; crimes go unpunished; murder and robbery are rampant; men are given over to lust and avarice: the times are out of joint.[2]

Denunciations of women were of course part of the stock in trade of all moral writers, and Seneca must have his fling at them. They are declared to be tainted with all the vices of men,[3] although the gravamen of the accusation is lightened by the fact that the women of his own family

[1] For criticism of Seneca, see Tac. *Ann.*, XIII, 42; XIV, 11, 52-54: Cass. Dio, LIX, 19; LXI, 10; S. Dill, *Roman Society from Nero to Marcus Aurelius*, p. 294ff; Havet, *Le Christianisme et ses origines* (Paris, 3rd ed., 1880), vol. II, p. 261ff.

[2] Among other passages may be cited: *Epist.*, LX; LXXIV; LXXXVII, 23; XCVII; CXV; *de Ben.*, I, 9; III, 16; VII, 27; *de Ira*, II, 8; III, 33; *de Tranq.*, 15ff.

[3] Compare *Epist.*, XCV, 20, 21; *ad Helviam*, 16; *de Ben.*, I, 9; VI, 32; *de Constantia*, 14; *de Ira*, II, 9.

and nearly all of his intimate acquaintances, as appears from his own writings, were modest, high-minded, and blameless. His mother Helvia was a matron of the best Roman type, pure in her domestic life, courageous in her misfortunes, and simple in her prosperity. His aunt, though occupying a high station, lived with such modesty and quiet devotion to her family as to escape even the tongue of Roman gossip.[1] Of Paulina, his wife, he writes that as her life depends on his, he is the more careful of his own because it is useful to her and conduces to her happiness. "What is more delightful," he remarks, "than to be so dear to your wife that by reason thereof you become dearer to yourself?" Her life was in harmony with his praise of her, and at his death she sought to share his lot.[2]

Apart from his preachments as an ascetic moralist, as a Stoic of the Schools, Seneca seems, in fact, to have had a genuine regard for women;[3] it is only when he assumes the rôle of the philosophic director that the hollow conventional criticisms form a part of his scheme of things.[4] Throughout all his moralizing indeed, Seneca shows himself less exacting, more humane, than his Stoic principles would seem to demand.[5] Were it quite certain that we could rely on the trustworthiness of some reports regard-

[1] *Ad Helviam*, 15-19.

[2] *Epist.*, CIV, 5; Tac. *Ann.*, XV, 63-64; Cass. Dio, LXII, 25.

[3] Compare *Epist.*, CIV; *ad Helviam*, 15; *ad Marciam*, 16; *de Vita beata*, 17; *Epist.*, LXIII, 14.

[4] For the usual Stoic logic, *cf. de Ben.*, IV, 27; for women see *Naturales Quaestiones*, I, 17, 8-12; VII, 32, 3; *de Const.*, XIV, 1; *ad Marciam*, XXIV, 3; *ad Helviam*, XVI, 3-4; *Epist.*, XCV, 20-21; *de Ben.*, I, 9, 3-4; III, 16, 2-4.

[5] Compare *Epist.*, XXIV, 15: *hoc enim turpissimum est, quod nobis obici solet, verba nos philosophiae, non opera tractare.* See further G. Boissier, *La Religion romaine*, vol. II, pp. 34-45.

ing his intimacy with a lady of the imperial family, resulting in his exile,[1] we might be tempted to urge that discovered irregularities together with failing health sometimes act as powerful moralizing agents. But independently of any question of this sort, Seneca was not—like Juvenal—a real misogynist.

Seneca's gloom was doubtless due to invalidism. The undertone of his writings, as Dr. Dill has justly observed, is one of "horror which hardly ever takes definite shape, a thick stifling air, as it were, charged with lightning. Again and again, you feel a dim terror closing in silently and stealthily, with sudden glimpses of unutterable torture, of cord and rack and flaming tunic." [2] Too often this has been taken to be the legitimate reaction of a good and wise man against an environment of unparalleled baseness. But the general color of our thoughts comes from within; we shall never understand Seneca's gloom unless we take into account his physical condition, and this was a state of almost life-long invalidism.[3] When a youth he had long periods of illness; when a young man he practised many forms of abstinence, became extremely emaciated and was so depressed on several occasions as to contemplate suicide.[4] For some years his health became better, but his later years were full of the pains of chronic illness. Even the heat of summer, he writes [5]—and at this time he was not much over sixty—can scarcely keep him warm, so that he spends most of his time bundled up in bed. The least moving about, even washing his hands, exhausts

---

[1] Cass. Dio, LX, 8; LXI, 10; Tac. *Ann.*, XIII, 42.
[2] Dill, *op. cit.*, p. 13. Compare *Epist.*, LXX; XC; XCIV, 70ff; *ad Marciam*, 20, 22; *de Tranq.*, 10, 15; *de Brev.*, 16.
[3] See *Epist.*, LXVII; LXXVIII; LXXXIII, 1-7; CVIII, 13-23; *ad Helviam*, 17.
[4] *Epist.*, LXXVIII, 1-4.   [5] *Ibid.*, LXVII, 1-2.

him; he has lost his teeth; he sleeps and eats very little, and he feels his memory to be failing.[1]

During all his life he was tormented with fears. The world seemed to him to be full of objects of dread. At one time he was going by boat close to the shore of the bay of Naples; in a panic of fright and seasickness he induced the pilot to head shoreward and when near it, he leaped from the boat to escape the perils of the sea.[2] Going through the tunnel between Baiae and Naples he became panic-stricken,[3] and gave evidence of claustrophobia. He sees dangers everywhere; he thinks of fires, shipwrecks, and other accidents—which however, he says, may not happen—but some human enemy may be preparing secretly to destroy you, so much pleasure does man take in ruining man. Be careful, his advice runs, to annoy no one; rejoice with men, grieve with them, serve them, and distrust them, so that they may be less dangerous to you; go with the crowd, do not offend people, do not reject current customs, be cautious, avoid awakening envy, do not boast, do not excite resentment or fear, do not talk much, and do not mingle much with others.[4] The letters of this timid, sickly, worried old man, afraid of nature, afraid of the dark, afraid of his fellow men, longing for a sense of safety and security, seeking anxiously a refuge in the brave doctrines of Stoicism against the terrifying fancies of his morbid imagination, penning maxims which he had learned to repeat but not to feel, cautiously counselling his friend Lucilius, equally a victim of psychasthenia—these furnish a spectacle deeply instructive

---

[1] *Ibid.*, LXXXIII, 3-7.
[2] *Ibid.*, LIII, 1-4. See Aulus Gellius, XIX, 1, for a picture of a Stoic frightened by a storm.
[3] *Ibid.*, LVII, 1-3.
[4] See *Epist.*, XIV, 10; CIII; CV, 1, 5, CX.

and profoundly pathetic. But it is not from a timid child lost in the woods at night that one gets a complete and accurate description of what is round about.

Seneca's abilities had brought him into relation with some dangerous members of the neurotic imperial family, the high-tempered Agrippina and the paranoiac Nero; and in this eddying, turbulent stream the philosopher's little earthen pot was ill-suited for jostling with those brazen jars,—but he could not withdraw to safer waters. So Seneca, sick in body and mind, shivered on through what was to him a confused and lurid haze in which loomed menacing and awful forms. We may easily imagine that his condition of chronic nightmare finally got on Nero's nerves, and Seneca received—and perhaps heard with relief—the curt order to take himself off.

But Seneca's gloom was not permanent: he was sometimes in relatively good health and consequently less pessimistic and terror-stricken. We get indications now and then of a sturdier condition of mind; for as the general condition of the world was probably reasonably constant, different language about it may fairly be attributed to different subjective states of the observer. In one of these periods of *euphoria,* he writes Lucilius that there are more things which frighten us than which actually damage us, that we suffer more from imagination than from realities. Do not worry prematurely, he tells him, do not cry out before you are hurt. Out of mere uncertainties we often create phantom dangers; the imagined future troubles rarely arrive. From the close of this letter it appears that Seneca had been reading some of the sane counsels of the calm Epicurus.[1]

At times he doubts his own pessimism, pulls himself up in his extravagances of moralizing, opens his eyes and

[1] *Epist.,* XIII, 4, 5.

sees that he has been indulging in rhetorical nonsense. So after one very purple description of the moral dissolution of the times he pauses to remark: "but excited by my subject, my ardor has carried me too far." Then, in calmer tones, he proceeds to point out that vice is not peculiar to any one time, that our ancestors before us have lamented the ruin of morality and that our children after us will no doubt do the same. On the whole, virtue and vice keep about the same balance. Sometimes one vice is more prominent, sometimes another; but man in general does not change greatly. What he has been, he is, and always will be.[1] Again, Seneca himself suggests that there is more or less posing in this moral sermonizing, and that seriousness can be too greatly stressed.[2] Indeed, he goes farther in a suggestive passage and intimates that many complaints against the evils of the times arise from the dissatisfaction with self caused by idleness, and that this state of mind expresses itself in jealousy and bitterness against those who have forged ahead while we have been slothfully standing still; wherefore our discontented and despairing minds seek solace in declaring that world to be evil in which we have failed.[3] We are sometimes unreasonable in our condemnations of our age, he warns Lucilius; human misconduct is no new thing. In fact, Seneca expresses himself as inclined to think that there has been a moral improvement in the last hundred years, that certainly our youth are more decent now than were those of the past.[4] This is a view which forms an interesting exception to the prevailing *laudatio temporis acti* of the moralists.

[1] *De Ben.*, I, 10.
[2] See *de Tranq.*, 15; *de Ira*, II, 10.
[3] Compare *de Tranq.*, 2, 15; *cf.* 2, 11.
[4] *Epist.*, XCVII.

The tendency of writers to complain of a decay among their contemporaries from the supposed excellence of their ancestors is so general a feature of every age that it is easily given its proper evaluation by the judicious observer. The reason is obvious. The elderly man often gets into a moral rut, and the passions which in earlier years suggested revolt from traditional morality have weakened. As he lacked the instigation to break out, it is difficult for him to grasp the fact that he ever felt differently, for the affective memory, as La Bruyère points out, is weak and men with difficulty represent to themselves those youthful feelings and follies which they no longer enjoy. The old man sees around him passionate, turbulent, rebellious youth rushing stormily along. Really, did he but know it, his crabbed age is viewing his own earlier days—but it seems different. In most cases the accuracy of his memory yields to the exigencies of his present self-esteem. He could not have done so; hence he did not do so. These young men are a new type, the world is degenerating. Then, too, the various novelties annoy him. Old mental habits are formed and harden into an obstinate conservatism, for mental habits like other things resist destruction. The very presence of the new ways angers him and he invents reasons *ex post facto* for "the pain of the new idea." He resents them, so he says, because they are foolish and sinful; but really his resentment is due to the effort involved in making new cerebral adjustments, and he becomes

> *Dilator, spe longus, iners, avidusque futuri,*
>
> *Difficilis, querulus, laudator temporis acti*
>
> *Se puero, castigator censorque minorum.*[1]

[1] Horace, *Ars Poetica*, 173ff. Compare Martial, V, 10; Tac. *Ann.*, II, 88: *dum vetera extollimus recentium incuriosi; Dialogus*, 18; Pliny, *Epist.*, I, 16.

The examination of what we may call general vituperation of Roman society by the most eminent writers among
the satirists and moralists has seemed to suggest that the
acceptance thereof as sound material for a sketch of moral
conditions needs to be done cautiously and with reservations. It will probably assist us in interpreting them if
we take up some particular subject treated by writers im-
bued with the spirit of ethical criticism, in order that we
may determine in greater detail the precise nature and
extent of these cautions and reservations.

It would be easy to present a collection of statements
from extant authors, which would support the belief
formerly universal of the wildly extravagant excesses of
Roman luxury.[1] Seneca never wearies of returning to
lavish invective against this mania for boundless self-
indulgence and pampered voluptuousness.[2] But it has
become gradually clearer to modern scholars that luxury
as viewed by a moralist is not always just what the
ordinary mind understands by that word, and some have
even suspected that the fall of the Romans into this great
sin was something very much akin to what we generally
call "progress in civilization."[3] The word luxury in Eng-

[1] Compare *e.g.*, Sallust, *Cat.*, 2-16, 52; Diodorus Siculus,
XXXVII, frag. 2; Livy, *praef.*, XXXIX, 6; Valerius Maximus,
IX; Pliny, *Nat. Hist.*, IX, 67; 104ff; XXII, 14; XXXIII, 148ff;
Lucan, *Pharsalia*, I, 158ff. It is of course a stock theme of all
the professed satirists and moralists.

[2] See among other passages, *de Ben.*, VII, 9; *Epist.*, LVI, 10;
CXIV, 2; XCV, 19, where occurs the graphic phrase: *luxuria,
terrarum marisque vastatrix;* C, 10; LI, 3-13; LXXXVI, 5-13;
LXXXVII, 1-11; LXXXIX, 19-23; XCV, 13-32; CX, 12-20;
CXIV; CXIX; CXXII; CXXIII; *Nat. Quaest.*, III, 17; IV,
13; VII, 31, 32.

[3] See G. Ferrero, *Characters and Events of Roman History*,
pp. 13ff; 22ff; *idem, The Greatness and Decline of Rome*, Eng.
ed., vol. I (London, 1907), p, 309ff; L. Friedländer, *Roman Life*

lish retains some color from the meaning of indulgence in
the sins of the flesh, which it acquired in the Middle Ages;
and even if it be taken in its broadest extent as including
those personal pleasures which are in a certain sense socially useless,[1] our association of the good and the unpleasant tends to prejudice us against things or acts regarded as
luxurious, and against persons guilty of enjoyment of
them.   The personal indulgence in socially valueless emotions or sentiments, such as anti-social forms of religiosity,
is not however stigmatized as luxury, unless the feeling
be unpleasant, when we speak of the "luxury of grief."
Here no doubt the dolorous character of the emotion gives
it an ethical merit sufficient to outweigh the culpability involved in its social inutility.   But the endeavor to elucidate
historical questions by playing with definitions is out of
date, and we shall be better employed in ascertaining just
what the moral critics were talking about when they pronounced their fervid denunciations of luxury, and whether
we may safely take the word as connoting the idea of
debilitating or damaging the person who indulges in it.

---

and Manners under the Early Empire, Eng. ed. by Freese and
Magnus, vol. II, p. 131ff; S. Dill, Roman Society from Nero
to Marcus Aurelius, p. 66ff; idem, Roman Society in the Last
Century of the Empire (London, 1899), p. 115ff; F. Nietzsche,
Beyond Good and Evil, English ed. by Levy, vol. XII (London,
1914), sec. 9; H. Baudrillart, Histoire du luxe, privé et public
depuis l'antiquité jusqu'à nos jours, vol. II (Paris, 1881), p. 373ff.

[1] Compare Fr. Paulhan, La morale de l'ironie (Paris, 1909),
p. 136ff: "Il semble bien que le 'luxe,' ce soit essentiellement,
non point ce qui coûte cher, mais ce qui est inutile à la société
dans les plaisirs que se donne un individu.   Il y a un luxe d'art,
un luxe de bijoux, un luxe de sentiments même, ou d'intellectua-
lité, c'est un luxe que de se griser de mauvais vin, c'est un luxe
aussi de passer son temps en études stériles, ou d'errer dans des
musées, de se complaire à des jeux d'amour ou de collectionner
des diamants."

Coming to this detailed examination, we shall find that the word as used by the moralists included many things which we do not generally regard as directly harmful to the possessor, or obnoxious to a fair amount of virtue on his part. For instance, we find Seneca and others reprehending the building of spacious houses in sightly places upon the hills, or by the seashore, especially denouncing an intrusion upon the sea by building rooms over it, and the use of hot springs. The ideal habitation is declared to be a cave, or at the most a hut, made of branches, leaves, and clay.[1] Varro, one of whose residences seems to have been of very ample dimensions, feels constrained to deprecate the erection of large villas; while Cicero, who had several large houses in town and country, cites as one of the bad examples set to the Roman people by Lucullus, his fine country seat at Tusculum.[2] Pliny the Elder, indeed, thinks that conflagrations are punishments inflicted upon the Romans for their vice in erecting great buildings;[3] but, as in the Messina earthquake and other catastrophes which have been interpreted as manifestations of the disapprobation of Providence, the just were at least as much afflicted as the unjust, since the great fires at Rome were mostly in the poorer quarters.

With exception of a few imperial residences, easily

[1] Compare *Epist.*, LXXXIX, 20ff; CXXII, 8; XC, 15ff; Tac. *Ann.*, III, 53; and the idealized *Germania*, 16, 17; Lucan, *Pharsalia*, I, 160ff. Horace, too, not over-seriously, intimates the moral excellence of the turf-hut, *Odes*, II, 15. We may compare the similar cult of Lincoln's log cabin.

[2] Varro, *de Re Rustica*, I, 13; II, 1-3; III, 5; Cicero, *de Legibus*, III, 13. *Arpinas* in Arpinum, was Cicero's lodestar; others were *Formianum* at Formiae; *Tusculanum* at Tusculum, *Puteolanum* at Puteoli, *Pompeianum* at Pompeii, and *Cumanum* on Lacus Lucrinus.

[3] *Nat. Hist.*, XXXVI, 110; *cf.* the entire chapter (24).

surpassed in size by modern palaces, none of the remains of Roman town or country houses are very prodigious. The so-called House of Livia on the Palatine and the Villa of Pollius Felix near Sorrento, which Statius describes in glowing terms, must have been modest enough buildings. Even the supposed residence of Tiberius on Capri is far from enormous, while the remains as well as the amount of space available at Baiae do not render possible any remarkable magnitude for the numerous structures. The area of ancient Rome is inconsistent with the ascription of a very great size to the many palaces of the luxurious nobles.[1] It is evident that to understand the language about the immensity and luxury of Roman dwellings we must not forget that the standard of comparison is the hut.

The use of marble in building is shocking to Seneca;[2] and Pliny, apparently on philosophical grounds, stigmatizes it as an especial madness. Nature, he says, put the rocks where she wanted them, and to quarry them interferes with the natural order of things. Marble columns were first used in public buildings, for "how do vices more insidiously creep upon us than under the plea of serving the public?"[3] But Nature does not approximate the

---

[1] See L. Friedländer, *Roman Life and Manners* (ed. cit.), vol. II, p. 185ff; Statius, *Silvae*, II, 2, describes the villa near Sorrento. At a rough calculation, the great Villa of Hadrian near Tivoli—probably the largest of Roman residences—aggregating all the detached buildings, seems to be considerably smaller than the palace built by Charles IV at Caserta.

[2] *Epist.*, XVI, 8; LXXXVI, 6; XC, 25; C, 6; CXIV, 9; *de Ben.*, IV, 6, 2.

[3] *Nat. Hist.*, XXXVI, 1-8. Compare Valerius Maximus, IX, 1, 4. This argument about the impiety of interfering with the way nature has arranged the earth was strongly pressed by the Nez Perces Indians in 1876 as constraining the tribe to refuse

moral principles of the learned Roman, for, so he regrets to state, marble grows again in the quarries from which it is extracted; hence luxury will never be at a loss for it.[1]

Such things as window glass, water pipes, locks, keys, and the like were naturally offensive luxuries to these strict censors, and Seneca hotly repudiates the slander that philosophers are responsible for any of the so-called useful inventions. Warming a house by furnaces is of course sternly condemned.[2] Hot baths are a flat violation of those Laws of Nature to which appeals are made so frequently and confidently, notwithstanding Nature's recreancy in the matter of marble, and Seneca devotes much space to eulogizing Scipio for his simple habits. In his bath, so the Philosophic Director informs his friend, there were no mosaic pavements, no glass windows, no silver taps, no constant renewal of water, nor any meticulous care for its limpidity. And furthermore the great man did not bathe every day, it was enough for him if he did so on market days. To the natural objection *olim liquet mihi immundissimos fuisse,* there is the reply of the doctrinaire: *quid putas illos oluisse? militiam, laborem, virum.*[3]

Seneca's argument is too elliptical to be followed easily, but its apparent conclusion that personal cleanliness exercises a deleterious influence on manly character certainly seems to suggest a flaw somewhere. The Duke of Wellington is said to have remarked the fighting abilities of dandies and neither the modern English gentleman nor the

---

to till the ground or to build roads. *Cf.* Gen. O. O. Howard, *Nez Perce Joseph, His Pursuit and Capture* (Boston, 1881), pp. 32, 64.

[1] *Nat. Hist.,* XXXVI, 125.
[2] *Epist.,* LXXXVI, 6; XC, 8; 25; *de Prov.,* 4, 9.
[3] *Epist.,* LXXXVI, 12. *Cf.* 8-10, XCV, 22.

Japanese peasant has found the bath fatal to virile energy; lacking these examples, Seneca might have remembered that Sulla and Cæsar were clean yet vigorous enough. The real fact is that we are here coming in sight of that curious attribution of ethical merit to personal squalor, that exaltation of foulness which forms so remarkable an element in the ascetic morality soon to dominate the world. The mysterious miasma was stealing over the world and a few keenly sensitive souls like Seneca already felt it. He had many of the instincts confusedly seeking expression, which at a later age would have found the due environment for a full efflorescence, when his emotional and intellectual characteristics would have made him a great and glorious saint for the admiration and adoration of mankind;[1] instead of which, born too soon, he could be no more than a peevish critic of a dying world.

All the other conveniences and comforts of civilized life fall likewise under the philosopher's ban. It is shameful effeminacy to use feather pillows, and there are groans at the progress of luxury indicated by the fact that in the time of Gaius, senators began to sit on cushions instead of on the wooden seats, and to wear hats at the theatre to protect themselves from the sun's rays.[2] The iniquity of improving on nature appears again in Seneca's

[1] The number of ideas in Seneca's writings of the character called Christian has been noticed by most writers who have dealt with him. *Cf. Epist.*, XLI, 2; LXXIII, 15; XCIII; XCV, 2, 10, 11, 52; CXVI, 6ff; *de Prov.*, 1; *de Ira*, I, 14; II, 27; *de Ben.*, III, 18. The similarity of general feeling is even more striking than that of ideas. *Cf.* Tertullian, *de Anima*, 20; *Seneca saepe noster;* Augustine, *Epist.*, 153, 14: *cuius etiam quaedam ad Paulum apostolum leguntur epistulae.* On the supposed Pauline influence see G. Boissier, *La Religion romaine* (ed. cit.), vol. II, pp. 46-92.

[2] Compare Pliny, *Nat. Hist.*, X, 54; Cass. Dio, LIX, 7.

disapprobation of hothouse flowers, or roses out of season, or potted plants on the roof.[1] It is disgraceful, he declares, to make frozen water an object of expense and luxury. His reasoning on this point is rather vague, but perhaps he reaches firmer ground when he claims that it is bad for the stomach.[2] Pliny is indignant at the affront to nature involved in boiling water and then chilling it again with ice or snow.[3] As these moral views seem to have had no rational basis, we can well understand that they might vary with the feelings of the moment.

All forms of æsthetics were of course repugnant to the growing asceticism of the moral systems which were soon to dominate the world. An eminently practical people like the Romans had of course always looked somewhat askance at beauty as consuming time, thought, and money which might be devoted to more "useful ends." Furthermore the person who lacks a capacity to produce, appreciate, or even understand works of art, is generally distrustful of something so foreign to himself, as a dull person is suspicious as well as half-consciously envious of wit and cleverness. The traditional Roman attitude, while not at all really ascetic, was still strictly unæsthetic; and the later ascetic ethical teachings may be regarded as making explicit what was substantially implicit in these earlier prejudices, while in addition the later theories fortified the old bigotries by giving them a new basis of justification in the doctrine of the sinfulness attached to the pleasures of the senses. Thus the ancient, customary moral feelings regarding beauty and the later speculative ethics came to coincide in many respects touching their practical applications.

We get glimpses of the older position in Sallust's state-

[1] *Epist.*, CXXII, 8.   [2] *Nat. Quaest.*, IV, 13; *Epist.*, XCV, 21.
[3] *Nat. Hist.*, XIX, 55.

ment referring to the period when "The armies of the
Roman people first became habituated to licentiousness
and intemperance, and"—the order of gravity of the vices
acquired is striking—"began to admire statues, pictures,
and sculptured vases." Polybius undoubtedly reproduces
conservative feelings in declaring that the works of art
carried from Syracuse to Rome were damaging to character, and Cicero speaks as a *vir vere Romanus* in complain-
ing that, but for the bad example of Lucullus, knights and
even freedmen would not have been permitted to fill their
houses with statues and paintings.   Even so late as the
time of Trajan, Frontinus voices his contempt for the
useless though renowned works of the Greeks as compared with the aqueducts of the Romans.[1] Virgil in a
famous passage expresses exactly the traditional sentiment
of his countrymen in his proud boast that Rome's glorious
task in the world was other than to shine in art:

"Others will mould their bronzes to breathe with a tenderer
    grace,
  Draw, I doubt not, from marble a vivid life to the face,
  Plead at the bar more deftly, with sapient wands of the
    wise,
  Trace heaven's courses and changes, predict us stars to
    arise.
  Thine, O Roman, remember, to reign over every race!
  These be thine arts, thy glories, the ways of peace to
    proclaim,
  Mercy to show to the fallen, the proud with battle to
    tame!" [2]

It is indeed not always easy to determine in a Seneca
or a Pliny whether the moralist is proceeding in his critique

[1] Sallust, *Cat.*, 9; Polybius, IX, 10; Cic., *de Leg.*, III, 13;
Frontinus, *de aqueductis*, 16. *Cf.* Livy, XXXIX, 6; Tac. *Ann.*,
III, 53.
[2] *Aeneid*, VI, 847-853 (Bowen's translation).

of luxury on grounds which Cato, for instance, would have understood and approved, or on speculative principles which he would have jeered at if he had been able to understand them.   But it is probable that Cato and Seneca would have been in agreement in most cases of their condemnations, by however different paths of reasoning they might have reached them.

Interest in works of art they would all agree in deprecating.   Seneca speaks contemptuously of those who fill their houses with objects of beauty.[1]   The mania for beautiful wooden tables is denounced by him, as well as by Pliny, and they doubt not that veneering partakes of the nature of sin. It seems indeed that Seneca had an enormous number of these artistic tables, but the lot of an ascetic millionaire is very perplexing when one of his principles is that he must not awaken hostility by refusing to follow the fashion.[2]

The use of mirrors awakens his wrath, apparently because they reflect wicked acts, but they have become very common: "corruption has made immense progress," he exclaims.[3]   The use of woven cloth for clothing is also sinful—skins and feathers are more in accord with Nature.   Pliny agrees, finding dyed stuffs especially offensive, and adds a word on the use of chaplets of leaves or of silks as painful examples of evil luxury.[4]   "The

---

[1] Seneca, *de Ben.*, VII, 9.

[2] *De Ben.*, VII, 9; *Epist.*, CIII; Pliny, *Nat. Hist.*, XIII, 91; XVI, 233.

[3] Seneca, *Nat. Quaest.*, I, 16-17.

[4] *Epist.*, XC, 17-19; *de Ben.*, VII, 9: Pliny, *Nat. Hist.*, VIII, 194ff; IX, 124ff; XI, 75ff; XXI, 12ff; XXII, 3ff; XXXVII, 18ff; Lucan, *Pharsalia*, I, 160ff; Tac. *Ann.*, II, 33; Cass. Dio, LVII, 15.   The Romans seem to have regarded it as a scandal not to wear the conventional woolen toga.   *Cf.* Cic., *Phil.*, II, 30; Suet., *Aug.*, 40.

worst crime against mankind," says Pliny, "was committed by him who first put a ring on his finger"[1]—the next being the coining of money.[2] Even a single seal ring on the little finger was reprobated as an ostentatious announcement of the possession of precious property kept under seal. Of a piece with the foregoing is the enumeration of Roman iniquities in the Apocalypse, consisting largely of purchases of jewelry, fine clothes, furniture, and food.[3]

That branch of æsthetics concerned with the adornment of the female body has of course always been a sore point with moralists and, like all the rest, the Roman writers tilted at it with the same universal failure to produce any effect. Women have been obstinate, and even in ages when asceticism was most rampant and women most submissive, this was the thing on which they displayed an unconquerable resistance, most exasperating to their spiritual directors. The detachment of philosophers from the facts of life has prevented them from seeing that the toilette is for women not a mere indulgence in some socially useless pleasure, but an immensely practical and indispensable economic expedient for all save the few supremely beautiful, whereby the many may draw the comparing and appraising eye of men from the natural attractions in which most women are relatively deficient, and direct it toward those artificial embellishments of which money can give them the possession, and, with the possession, the desired better chance to compete with their sisters more gener-

---

[1] *Nat. Hist.*, XXXIII, 42ff.

[2] *Ibid.*, 8ff; 17ff; 39ff; Seneca, *Nat. Quaest.*, VII, 31. For the condemnation of precious stones see Pliny, *op. cit.*, XXXVII, 1ff; IX, 106ff; of plate, XXXIII, 4ff; 48ff; 139; of amber, XXXVII, 30ff.

[3] Chapter XVIII, 11ff.

ously endowed by nature. But the Roman social critics, as well as those of other times, ignorantly and unjustly persisted in clamoring against what they deemed women's special sinfulness in this regard; and failed, then as ever, to devote due attention to that fundamental, though probably unattainable, prerequisite of their desired reform, namely the development in men of a more discriminating vision as to women and a less hasty reliance on the immediate dictates of blind sexual impulse toward superficial pulchritude. These characteristics of men and women, and of moralists, have been so unchanging through all ages as to render it hardly necessary to examine their manifestations in the period under consideration.

In addition to things of beauty, most of the other elements of civilized life were involved in a grotesquely sweeping condemnation. Seneca deplores man's avarice in digging metals out of the earth; iron he views as the instrument of murder, and gold and silver as its rewards. Nature brings forth on the surface everything of use to men but has hidden deep and rested her whole weight on these substances, so pernicious to virtue. The whole "unnatural" process of mining and smelting appears to him vile and hideous, staining the soul even more than the body, soiling the possessor even more than the miner.[1] In Pliny's view, our sacred parent, the earth, expresses by earthquakes her indignation at our intrusion into her entrails. Gold was discovered only for the ruin of mankind—would that it could be banished and the happy age of barter return! With the crime of the invention of money came a new development of the vice of avarice by lending money at interest. Nature has, however, done better in the case of metal than of marble, for she benevolently limits the dangerous power of iron, that useful but

[1] *De Ben.*, VII, 10; *Nat Quaest.*, V, 15.

fatal instrument of man, by inflicting upon it the punishment of rust.[1]

Commerce, too, is highly objectionable to our moralists, for it is in the interest of some vice. Pliny denounces with heat the criminal perversity of those who go to the sea in ships, and finds no execrations equal to the demerit of him who first invented sails. This excitement over what hardly seems a very vicious employment suggests a clue; perhaps the agitation is due to timidity. Like Horace and Juvenal, Seneca is much concerned over the perils of the sea.[2] But there was a less intelligible sentiment at least coöperating, since the more recondite methods of commerce are equally objectionable to Seneca. Letters of credit, bills of exchange, and promissory notes are declared to be mere deluding phantoms by which our minds are deceived into rejoicing over unrealities. What are interest and books of account but the names of unnatural developments of human covetousness—mere dreams, "ghosts of anxious avarice?"[3]

In the production of much of this sorry moralizing there is evidently some factor other than rationality in operation. Some of the judgments are obviously the cant *dicta* of the Stoic schools. Still others might be explained as due to error, incorrect observation, and false logic; but after allowing a wide margin for charitable interpretation, there remains much which can be accounted for only on physi-

[1] Pliny, *Nat. Hist.*, XXXIII, 1ff; 39ff; 95ff; XXXIV, 138ff.

[2] Horace, *Odes*, I, 3; Juvenal, *Sat.*, XIV, 267ff; Seneca, *Nat. Quaest.*, V, 18; Pliny, *Nat. Hist.*, XIX, 1, 6: *nulla exsecratio sufficit contra inventorem dictum suo loco a nobis, cui satis non fuit hominem in terra mori, nisi periret et insepultus.* Cf. II, 125. For an attempt to cloak ignorance and terror of the sea under the pretense of religious awe compare Tac., *Germania*, 34.

[3] Sen., *de Ben.*, VII, 10.

ological grounds.   Running through the criticism of
things indifferent in themselves is an element of sourness
against all the innocent ameliorations of life, which suggests a person in a chronic state of discomfort who, finding no relief in ordinary physical pleasures, feels bitter
toward those who enjoy them.   Seneca regards the body
as a prison, a burden, and a cause of suffering; contempt
for it is the true liberty.   To care for the body is a mistake: let it be ugly—beauty of soul is sufficient.   Misfortune is the opportunity for virtue.   It is a mark of
divine favor to have ill health and trouble, for it shows
that "God has thought us worthy subjects on whom to
try how much suffering human nature can endure."
Misery is a proof of goodness, comfort is the enemy, the
more the discomfort, the more the virtue.[1]

Sentiments of this character are not those of a sound,
healthy man who feels a natural pervading sense of
physical well-being.   It is conceivable, of course, that they
might be uttered by such a man because of his having
received them from some revered teacher, and this would
remit the inquiry to that diseased source.   But in the
case of Seneca, as we have seen, we know that he was in
fact a sufferer from chronic ill health nearly all his life,
though with some intervals of apparent improvement—
an ill health which interfered with his nutrition, since he
speaks of the extreme emaciation that enfeebled him at
an unduly early age, but did go on rapidly to a fatal issue,
for he died by suicide when nearly seventy;[2] his attitude
towards life, as expressed by his writings, suggests that
he was the victim of some chronic digestive disorder, perhaps gastric neurasthenia, a malady whose effects upon

[1] Compare, for example, *Epist.*, LXV, 20ff; LXVI; LXXVIII;
CII; *ad Helviam*, 11, 7; *de Prov.*, 4.
[2] See p. 84.

the mind, according to modern science, are such as appear in his case; and this hypothesis seems to receive abundant confirmation from his utterances regarding gastronomic matters.

It has been a well-recognized custom of moralists in all ages to convert their digestive insufficiency into moral worth, and to view gastric potency as tainted with vice. So we need not be surprised to find Seneca frequently denouncing those gourmands whose immoderate and insatiable voracity lays waste land and sea, leaving no animal in peace—Seneca being constrained to vegetarianism. At the horrid spectacle of the consumption of mushrooms, oysters, and garum sauce, he becomes almost nauseated.[1] Dinners where the guests tarry long at the table and where there is much eating and drinking cannot, of course, be called anything but disgusting gluttony, though the horrors of a banquet which he describes to his sympathetic friend Lucilius appear to be nothing very serious; and one seems to find occasionally a veritable gastralgic nightmare rising to the point of delirium.[2]

In the case of Pliny, whose moral judgments on so many matters closely resemble those of Seneca, we have less explicit evidence on which to base a similar hypothesis, but the conclusion to be drawn from his references to dietetics seems to point the same way. He denounces the "abominable mania for devouring fattened birds," an enormity which he rejoices to state has been forbidden by many sumptuary laws, and he thinks that "no greater inroads have been made upon our morals" than those effected by the consumption of shellfish.[3] The importation of

[1] *Epist.*, LXXXIX, 22ff; XCV, 18-19, 25; CXXII, 3; *Nat. Quaest.*, III, 17-18; *ad Helviam*, 10.

[2] *Epist.*, CXXII, 18, 19; CX, 12, 13; *ad Helviam*, 10.

[3] *Nat. Hist.*, X, 139, 140; IX, 104, 105; XIX, 52ff.

oysters and game moves him to outbursts of ascetic indignation, and he goes even farther than Seneca in deploring the confection of specially delectable breads, as well as the cultivation of particularly fine cabbages, asparagus, and artichokes, "which Nature intended to grow wild. Alas for the monstrous excesses of gluttony!" [1]

But perhaps the strongest indication of some considerable physical disorder, which both Seneca and Pliny display, is their disgust at the whole alimentary process. Excess of food seems to the latter the most pernicious of things, and he describes the pains of digestion in a way to suggest personal experience.[2] But they become even more morbid when they devote their hyperæsthetic attention to the character of the unsubservient residuum of the comestibles ingested. Moral edification by scatoscopy [3] suggests a state of mind not far removed, if at all, from the psychopathic.

The human mind, as we have seen, keeps continually busy in furnishing to us explanations and justifications of our states of feeling, and that activity is the greater and more elaborate, the more intensely and continuously the affective state appears in consciousness. Furthermore, the opinions, beliefs, and judgments thus formed in our attempts to interpret and rationalize our emotions tend to get farther away from soundness and sanity as these emotions become more strange and abnormal and thus seem to demand more unusual and peculiar explanations. When the disorder of the feelings reaches a sufficient degree, they are reflected in the thought by delirious ideas which we recognize as clearly unsound.

But before this point is reached, we get the phenomena

---

[1] *Idem*, XIX, 54; *cf*. chapter 8 (43).
[2] *Idem*, XI, 284; XXVI, 43-45.
[3] Sen., *Epist.*, CX, 13; Pliny, *Nat. Hist.*, XXVI, 43.

manifested by many satirists and moralists such as those
authorities on Roman social conditions whom we have
been examining. Moral judgments fully as much as those
of any other kind arise out of the process just mentioned.
Men deceive themselves when they think that certain acts
are offensive and certain others are acceptable to them
because the former are bad and the latter good. The
actual course of events is that we call good those acts
which are congruous to our deepest desires, and stigma-
tize as wicked those which would produce in us confusion
and pain were we to perform them. But so many, especially of our profounder, sentiments or inclinations appear in consciousness but dimly if at all, that they become
manifest to our understanding only after the thoughts
which they have originated give them a certain definiteness. Hence we mistake the order of the causal relation,
and think that the unperceived antecedent emotion is the
result of the recognized consequent idea.[1]

In the case of a man like Seneca, the fact of fundamental importance is that he was a prey during most of his
life to organic distress, by reason of which the general
tone of his thought was gloomy and apprehensive. This
lifelong rasping of his nerves produced a morbid sensi-
tivity keenly alive to the disharmonies of life but incompetent to dominate them. Dread, worry, and misery
naturally flowed from distrust of his power to stand the
environment, control it, or adequately adapt himself to it.
Perhaps past defects in adaptation gave rise to regret and

---

[1] This process has been analyzed by modern psychologists.
See, for example: C. Read, *Natural and Social Morals* (London,
1909); W. McDougall, *Introduction to Social Psychology* (London, 1908); Fr. Paulhan, *La morale de l'ironie* (Paris, 1909);
P. M. F. Janet, *Les Obsessions et la Psychasthénie*, vol. I (Paris,
1903). Significant too is the discussion in Sen., *de Tranq.*, 2ff.

remorse. Having this feeling of dissatisfaction, he failed to realize that what he was really dissatisfied with was himself; and the search for a cause to explain his melancholy was almost certain to result in the conclusion that the trouble lay with the external world.

Nothing is more irritating to a sensitive person than to see another indulge in acts which he never could or can no longer commit, and it is an almost inevitable tendency for him to solace his self-esteem by reprehending the deed as unseemly and the doer as culpable, whereby his own abstention may appear to result not from inability but rather from disinclination, and his physical weakness may be masked as moral strength.[1] It is necessary for a person of feeble condition to simplify his life, to reduce its diversity of manifestation, to avoid strain and excess, so as to conserve his strength by lessening the demands on it. The thoroughly sound man does not worry much over vices of excess, for he has reserve power; but when excess makes one ill, then it is regarded as a serious matter. A strong man, also, feeling able to endure his environment, is not seriously perturbed by the acts or opinions of others which do not directly affect him; but when a man has only a narrow margin of strength he is disinclined to allow any of it to be wasted in meeting unwelcome, unexpected, or discouraging ideas; he is impatient of divergences of opinion which compel him to think; he becomes intolerant of anything which introduces complexity and a need of effort into his mental operations. His ideal tends towards a life of extreme simplicity in

---

[1] Macaulay speaks of Laud as "prone to the error, common in superstitious men, of mistaking his own peevish and malignant moods for emotions of pious zeal." *Hist. of England*, vol. I (New York, 1856), pp. 82-83. *Cf.* his characterization of Sir Philip Francis in *Essay on Warren Hastings*.

every respect, as far removed as possible from the fatiguing complications of civilized existence with its differentiation of function and diversity of thought and action. A primitive environment in which individuals are too much alike for envy or dispute, and are blissfully untroubled by the burdens of housekeeping or the cares of the toilette; where virtue is easily practised by reason of an absence of possibilities of excess or of opportunities for misconduct so richly open to the unfortunate dwellers in a highly developed society; where there is a happy freedom from differences of opinion, need for economic activity, difficult problems, or disturbing situations requiring a painful expenditure of thought; and especially where that great, perplexing perturbation of sex is reduced to the lowest terms compatible with the survival of the race—such a society, such a life was the ideal of the psychasthenic philosopher; and into this highly artificial "state of Nature" he read all his dislikes, prejudices, and timidities. He felt that he could endure such a *milieu* without the exhaustion, pain, and dread incident to the complicated turmoil of sin and danger seething around him. His estimate of the actual society before his eyes was made with reference to that ideal, and his judgments on it increased in severity proportionately to the degree of its declension in any of its aspects from his Utopian paradise of poverty, uniformity, ignorance, and asceticism. It is the departures from this ideal which are the sins and vices denounced by him and his fellows with such grotesque misplacing of emphasis.

Unless we understand the point of view of these writers, we shall never be able to restate their curious notions in accurate language, or to know what are the things really covered by their fervid words. There is one excess, says Seneca, "which is the most harmful of all; it affects the brain; it leads men's minds into vain imaginings; it spreads a thick cloud over the boundaries of truth and falsehood."[1] This, he says, is happiness, or, as the context perhaps suggests, comfort, of which he had so little experience. So it may be of men as conceived by a moralist; but from the standpoint of the scientific student, an excess more damaging in a historical source is that of ascetic moral antipathies on the part of a dyspeptic.

It might be supposed that there was little danger of carrying away a misleading impression from the extravagances of those who are lashing themselves into a fury over such vices as the indulgence in fattened fowls, boiled water, hats, cushions, woven cloth, seal rings, or bills of exchange; and no doubt in many cases the absurdity is sufficiently apparent.   But this confidence does not take adequately into account the natural and unconscious tendency of the student to attribute his own good faith and sobriety to the classical authors he is reading,—a tendency reinforced by the proneness of man, indolent and uncritical as he is, to accept any statement made unless his mind is already occupied by a contradictory belief.   This inclination is especially strong when the general nature of the statement is congruous to the pervading affective tone of his own mind, as is so often the case in the matter under discussion, owing to the similarity of fundamental moral principles or prejudices.   We can see three ways in which undue weight comes to be given to exaggerations such as have been considered.   In the first place, the ancient writer often fails to follow up his general invective by any exact specification of what he has in mind, and we carelessly

---

[1] Sen., *de Prov.*, 4: *cum omnia quae excesserunt modum noceant, periculosissima felicitatis intemperantia est: movet cerebrum, in vanas mentes imagines evocat, multum inter falsum ac verum mediae caliginis fundit.*

assume that this is as serious a matter as the solemnity of his language seems to suggest. In another class of cases, while his fervid generalization is accompanied by tame particulars, the glow of the former attaches to the latter and suffuses them with a baleful light not their own. The broad statement is conspicuous and dominates the field of memory, like a mountain peak, while the flat and unimpressive character of the circumjacent part fails to catch the attention or remain in mind. Lastly, and this is perhaps the most far-reaching effect, the continual, earnest repetition of a general charge, even though each particular can be not beyond the reader's critical powers to limit or discredit, almost inevitably succeeds at last in tinting his mind with a color harmonious to that existing in the writer. This having once become established, then the bias produced goes on unconsciously to do all the necessary work of selecting from the facts adduced those which contribute to fortify the bias, dismissing or forgetting those which make against it.[1]

When such a predisposition is once established, then indeed the work is done, and the mind continues to feed itself on the most inadequate scraps. Debauchery and dissoluteness worthy of moral reprehension are found in culinary improvements, good clothes, a taste for horses, hunting dogs, and philosopher's marble columns, and the paying of a stiff price for imported salt fish.[2] One reads sympathetically that Varro indignantly reproved such vices

[1] In a later chapter, on Tiberius, we shall have occasion to examine more in detail how this mode of producing a powerful effect out of most inadequate and rebellious material is done by a master of the art.

[2] Polybius, XXXI, 24, records the price of 300 drachmae (about $60.00) for a jar of Pontic salt fish. *Cf.* Valerius Maximus, IX, 1; Livy, XXXIX, 6.

as the consumption of imported sea foods and nuts, and does not find ridiculous the repetition of Euripides's praise of bread and water as the diet of virtue.[1] Perhaps one even fails to laugh off the criminality of that noble whose conduct in driving his own chariot on the public road made Juvenal shudder, or the charge against Apuleius that he had written in favor of toothpowder, or even the grave assertion of Cassius Dio that Caracalla "was steeped in the licentiousness of Antioch even to the point of having his chin completely shaved." [2] But when this state of mind is reached, one must have quite lost the saving grace of humor and with it all sense of values, and have become prepared to receive respectfully the vagaries of the later moralists.

[1] Aulus Gellius, VI, 16.
[2] Juvenal, *Sat.*, VIII, 146ff; Apuleius, *Apologia,* 6ff; Cass. Dio, LXXVII, 20.

CHAPTER VII

THE LATER MORALISTS

THE examination of the writings of Seneca and Pliny the Elder who, from the exceptionally large number of their surviving works, are in the first rank of sources for the study of Roman moral conditions, seems to indicate the need of considerable reserve in accepting their general declarations. As their command of the inductive process leaves much to be desired, and as they attribute the character of vice and crime to acts which we class differently, we are constrained to treat many of their statements with the caution and scepticism proper under such circumstances. The defects in their mental outlook, prepossessions, and methods, while sufficient to justify this attitude, do not however indicate such a departure from the degree of rationality possessed by the average man as to be inconsistent with sanity, nor to result in their being so incomprehensible as to deprive them, when judiciously used, of considerable value for the student. We may not unjustly regard their inconsistencies and absurdities as a not unpleasing comedy for the scholar's delectation.

But though they may be taken as a kind of moralist comedians, so light a phrase cannot be applied to the ethical writers of the various theological schools who, a century or more later, began to express the ideals then coming to dominate the world. Here, indeed, we might use the word tragedy to indicate the melancholy of the spectacle, were it not that this word connotes too much intelligence and lucidity to make it a suitable appellation for such a frantic nightmare. The grave words of Lecky are too fitting a characterization of the culmination of this period to be out of place at this point:

> There is, perhaps, [he says] no phase in the moral history of mankind of a deeper or more painful interest than this ascetic epidemic. A hideous, sordid, and emaciated maniac, without knowledge, without patriotism, without natural affection, passing his life in a long routine of useless and atrocious self-torture, and quailing before the ghastly phantoms of his delirious brain, had become the ideal of the nations which had known the writings of Plato and Cicero and the lives of Socrates and Cato.[1]

That this picture of the new ideal may not seem overdrawn it will be worth while to glance at a single episode in the life of one who typified it. St. Simeon Stylites, who spent a great part of his life on top of a pillar, continually bending his body in prayer, or standing on one leg, while his biographer picked up the worms which fell from his body and replaced them in the sores of the holy man who said: "Eat what God has given you"—this saint had begun his career by abandoning his parents who loved him passionately. His father died; after many years, when he had become famous, his mother heard for the first time of her son's whereabouts and hastened to see him again. The old woman's effort was unavailing; she was a woman, and hence, being a source of danger to the purity of a saint, could not be admitted within the precincts of his dwelling. By reason of his special holiness, he refused to permit her even to look upon his face.

[1] W. E. H. Lecky, *History of European Morals* (New York, 1891), vol. II, p. 107.

Her entreaties and prayers, her reproaches and tears, were useless against the austerity of his virtue. Three days and nights she wept and begged in vain, and at last, worn out with grief and age, she died before her son's door. "Then for the first time the saint, accompanied by his followers, came out. He shed some pious tears over the corpse of his murdered mother, and offered up a prayer consigning her soul to heaven." [1] But a slight tremor passed over her body, perhaps life was not wholly extinct; the son, however, refrained from any investigation: he "once more commended her soul to heaven, and then, amid the admiring murmurs of his disciples, the saintly matricide returned to his devotions." [2] As the writer from whose narrative this account is summarized well says:

> The glaring mendacity that characterises the Lives of the Catholic Saints, probably to a greater extent than any other important branch of existing literature, makes it not unreasonable to hope that many of the foregoing anecdotes represent much less events that actually took place than ideal pictures generated by the enthusiasm of the chroniclers. They are not, however, on that account the less significant of the moral conceptions which the ascetic period had created. [3]
> To break by his ingratitude the heart of the mother who had borne him, to persuade the wife who adored him that it was her duty to separate from him for ever, to abandon his children, uncared for and beggars, to the mercies of the world, was regarded by the true hermit as the most acceptable offering he could make to his God. His business was to save his own soul. [4]

We may well hesitate before crediting so vile an infamy as that related of St. Simeon; but if it be false, what shall

[1] Lecky, op. cit., vol. II, p. 130-131.
[2] Ibid.   [3] Ibid.   [4] Ibid. p. 125.

we think of the ideals of an age when admiring friends and devotees invented such an atrocious tale in the spirit of eulogy—and the writings of that epoch teem with laudatory anecdotes hardly less base? And if it be true, or was believed to be true, what shall be our estimate of this saint's contemporaries when we learn that "from every quarter pilgrims of every degree thronged to do him homage. A crowd of prelates followed him to the grave. A brilliant star is said to have shone miraculously over his pillar; the general voice of mankind pronounced him to be the highest model of a Christian saint." [1]

We can understand the earlier times. Nero was reputed to have caused his mother's death. If this be true, at any rate he had motives or pretexts which are not incomprehensible to us; the writers who tell us of it, tell us also of hesitations, horror, remorse, disgust, detestation, punishment, and infamy. Nero may have been a paranoiac, but his contemporaries had moral natures which we can recognize. They may have been tainted with vices and crimes but they were not imbecile or insane. But when we come to examine the moralists of the later age, whatever else we may think of them, at any rate one opinion must be that when they talk of morals their standards of judgment are so unlike our own as to make their language probably meaningless to us but certainly entitled to our most cautious and sceptical scrutiny.

In that strange period of the decay and dissolution of civilized society, if we can suppose that most of its writings give a fair picture of it, we find a curious transposition of all those moral values on which sane and healthy

---

[1] *Ibid.* p. 112. See the life of St. Simeon Stylites by his disciple Antonius in *Vitae Patrum* (Migne, *Patrologia Latina*, vol. 73, pp. 326-334); *cf.* Theodoret, *Philotheus* (*Ibid.* vol. 74), chapter XXVI.

men of every other known period of history have been in susbstantial agreement. Health and happiness have ordinarily been esteemed blessings, but then men declared a preference for sickness and gloom. A clear and strong intelligence has been desired, save in those days when cloudy, mystical meditation or a capacity to believe the absurd or the frankly impossible was proclaimed the true virtue. It was not more and fuller life that men then seemed to wish, but less life and emptier; indeed it was not life at all, but death[1] and after death the highest conceivable felicity was to consist in doing nothing. Men have at most times thought pleasures were to be desired, save when their effects brought ultimate pains, but in this queer topsy-turvy world all desires and pleasures were held essentially evil.[2] St. Augustine, one of the sanest as well as one of the most eminent men of his times, holds that the objectionable feature of connubial relations is the pleasure which it gives the participants, and that this is the penalty which was attached to propagation on account of Adam's sin. Before the fall of man, this sinful element did not exist, and a good man would now prefer to be without it; indeed, glum polygamy was more virtuous than happy monogamy.[3] This is the saint who signalized his moral regeneration by dismissing the mother of his son, a loving and beloved woman with whom he had for fourteen years maintained matrimonial relations of the inferior order known as

---

[1] Plotinus, *Enneades*, I, 4.

[2] Compare C. Guignebert, *Tertullien* (Paris, 1901), pp. 550-572, who cites a wealth of references in his interesting chapter. *Cf.* Hermas, *Shepherd, Similitudes*, VI, 5: "Every act which a man performs with pleasure is luxury."

[3] *De Civitate Dei*, XIV, 16-26; *de Doc. Christ.*, III, 18 (27); *cf. de bono conjugali*.

concubinatus, but who seemed an impediment to his courtship of a very young girl higher in social position.[1]

The curiously meticulous scrupulosity of the writers of those times seems to remove them from our easy comprehension. The sight of their own bodies was perilous, and the stricter moralists abstained from baths and denounced any concern for physical cleanliness.[2] The most eminent Neo-Platonists were shocked at the idea of generation and Plotinus's delicacy forbade him to refer to the existence of his parents, guilty as they were of a stain in this respect. The ascetic sentiment regarded women as the gateway to hell, and one prudent monk wrapped his hands in cloths so that he might not receive damage from touching his mother, explaining to his surprised parent that her body was fire and that contact with her might impair the purity of his mind.[3] Participation in family, social, or political life was deprecated and frequently shunned as almost certain to involve moral shipwreck. Deprived thus of any real knowledge of the world, their active minds were busy constructing an ideal one, filled in many cases with the creations of a debased fancy. Avoiding the society of living women, many of

[1] *Confessions,* VI, 15.

[2] *Cf.* Jerome, *Epist.,* CXVII.

[3] The story is of a monk who, while journeying with his mother, came to a stream and carried her across. *Frater quidam iter agens, habebat secum matrem suam, jam senem. Qui cum venissent ad quendam fluvium, non poterat vetula illa transire. Et tulit filius eius pallium suum, et involvit exinde manus suas, ne aliquo modo contingeret corpus matris suae, et ita portans eam transposuit fluvium. Dixit autem ei mater sua: Ut quid sic operuisti manus tuas, fili? Ille autem dixit: Quia corpus mulieris ignis est. Et ex eo ipso quo te contingebam, veniebat mihi commemoratio aliarum feminarum in animo. Verba Seniorum (Vitae Patrum, II, Migne, Patrologia Latina, vol. 73, p. 874), lib. IV, 68.*

them passed their sleeping, and often their waking hours in the contemplation of obscene visions whose unreality they had neither the power nor the desire to discover[1]; and their imaginations were often too preoccupied with such pictures to pay much attention to the realities of life about them.

Men whose activities were largely devoted to prayer, fasting, bodily macerations, or other extraordinary ascetic exercises, or hairbreadth escapes from the perilous propinquity of real women; who revelled in minute, abtruse, and prolix metaphysical disputations, and bitterly denounced as the deadliest of sins the slightest variations from their own almost incomprehensible doctrines on these subjects; who associated habitually with dæmons, angels, talking animals, hallucinations, and men similar to themselves; who saw phantasms and miracles everywhere, a glittering Apragopolis in the sky and a boiling Pit beneath; whose conception of life was a routine of useless self-torture varied by periods of ecstatic contemplation of the ineffable; men whose lives were partly or wholly of this sort, or others whose ideals of life and conduct were moulded on the views of such men and colored by their opinions and methods—these composed moral exhortations for those whom they dominated, and moral vituperation against those whom they hated. These writings have a great value for us as bearing upon the history of speculative thought and upon the psychopathic state of the times, but they can be utilized as contributing to a picture of the moral life of the community only with extreme care.[2]

---

[1] Compare Guignebert, *op. cit.*, p. 281ff; Lecky, *op. cit.*, II, p. 116ff; Anatole France, *Thais*.

[2] On this period in general there is much of value in Isaac Taylor's *Ancient Christianity* as well as in the works of Lecky

The mode of proceeding adopted by social critics in all ages has differed but little, and in all ages have their products been accepted and enjoyed. There is always a mixture of good and bad in every society and a writer can, merely by judicious selection, paint the picture he wishes of the moral condition of his people. And the more complex a society is, the greater is the opportunity to distort the picture by ingenuity of selection. Furthermore, an increasing severity of moral tone in social criticism is rather a sign of increasingly scrupulous public sentiment than of a deterioration of conduct. As a judicious historian has remarked:

> Each generation has its censors who pronounce it to be altogether extraordinary in its depravity, and these denunciations are sometimes even a sign of progress, for they merely show that men are more conscious of the evils around them; have raised their standard of excellence, and have learned to lay an increased stress upon moral improvement.[1]

The really new characteristic is not the misconduct, but the moral sensitiveness.

A survey of contemporary life will show that the

---

and Guignebert already cited (and the latter's *Manuel d'histoire ancienne du Christianisme*, Paris, 1906). The well known works of Boissier, Bury, Dill, Finlay, Harnack, Hodgkin, Holmes (Justinian) and Negri (Julian) and many more are accessible to the general reader. But in this, more than in most fields of history, there are so many conflicting judgments by modern writers, and the facts are so incredible, that nothing will take the place of direct recourse to the contemporaneous writings, Neo-Platonic as well as Christian.

[1] Lecky, *History of England in the Eighteenth Century* (3rd edition, London, 1891), vol. VI, p. 269. *Cf.* Boissier, *La Religion romaine*, vol. II, p. 155; *La Fin du Paganisme*, vol. II, p. 418.

loudest railing is against those evils which are most rapidly being ameliorated, and in fact a rough general rule might be laid down that pessimism in moral writings justifies optimistic conclusions as to the matter involved. The removal of grievances seems by no means to ensure the cessation of the complaints.

The sort of work produced by Juvenal, Seneca, and other Roman writers has been done in all ages and in all societies, and if we accept such statements as historical material we shall get some queer views of the past. In the full flood of the heroic period of English literature, three years after the defeat of the Spanish Armada, Edmund Spenser was bewailing England's decadence, for amid the "bad dooings, or base slothfulnesse" of his contemporaries, there is "nothing worthie to be writ, or told." [1]

> "Ah, wretched world! the den of wickednesse,
>   Deformd with filth and fowle iniquitie;
> Ah, wretched world! the house of heavinesse,
>   Fild with the wreaks of mortall miserie;
> Ah, wretched world! and all that is therein,
>   The vassals of Gods wrath, and slaves to sin." [2]

Poetry is in a hopeless state and English literature seems to the poet to be nearing its end. So the *Teares of the Muses,* published in 1591; two years later Shakespeare's first work appeared.

Under a thin disguise, Swift satirizes the people of England as "discoverers, witnesses, informers, accusers. prosecutors, evidence-swearers, together with their several subservient and subaltern instruments," all busily engaged in ruining one another. The noble families of England, he continues, are full of cruelty, falsehood, and cowardice, owing to the unchastity of women, which has led to the

[1] *The Teares of the Muses,* 99, 100.   [2] *Ibid.,* 121ff.

interruption of legitimate descent by the intrusion of pages, lackeys, coachmen, gamesters, fiddlers, players, captains, and pickpockets. Innocent and excellent persons are corruptly condemned to death; villains exalted to the highest place of dignity and power, and governments are largely controlled by rakes, parasites, and buffoons.[1] One might easily suppose all this to be a description of Rome as viewed by Juvenal.

Cowper, too, thought England in a bad way. Her sad case is examined in detail in *Expostulation*. The catalogue of her vices is too long for transcription—none seems to be overlooked.[2] In somewhat gentler measures Goldsmith beholds :

> "Each wanton judge new penal statutes draw,
>   Laws grind the poor, and rich men rule the law;
>   The wealth of climes, where savage nations roam,
>   Pilleg'd from slaves to purchase slaves at home." [3]

and again :

> "Opulence, her grandeur to maintain,
>   Lead stern depopulation in her train."

One "sink of level Avarice" seems to engulf everything. The *Deserted Village,* made up of elements selected from several localities and combined in one picture, was written, so the poet explains in his dedication, to combat the depopulation of England and the scourge of luxury. Its complaints are the stock themes of Juvenal: the "freaks of wanton wealth" and "shouting Folly" do not conceal

[1] Gulliver's Travels, *Laputa,* Chap. vi, viii.
[2] See also the poems *Truth, Progress of Error, The Task,* books IV, V, *Review of Schools.*
[3] *The Traveller.*

England's ruin, where "wealth accumulates, and men decay,"

> "While thus the land, adorn'd for pleasure all,
> In barren splendour feebly waits the fall."

The history of England for the century and a half since the poem was written indicates that the death agony of a nation perishing from luxury and avarice is distinguishable from a condition of robust health only by the eye of a moralist.

When we reach the nineteenth century and the amelioration of social conditions in England is proceeding rapidly, the mass of critical material becomes too overwhelming to handle. Some characteristic bits have already been cited and we need do no more than note a late observer's declaration that "a social system which produces such villainies as that of contemporary England is proven vicious, and it is an obligation on those who see that to do what they can politically to change it." [1]

Modern America, according to moralists of this mood, is, of course, visibly given over to the powers of darkness, but even in the days when Saturn was king, or at any rate when Jupiter's beard was not grown, as Juvenal would say, there was no want of complaint. In the literature of the period "language has been practically exhausted in depicting the sad state of morals and religion." [2] Evidently if Puritan New England were in this state, while old England feebly waited its fall, we should not be too much shocked at Juvenal's Rome.

[1] G. S. Street, *English Review*, vol. VI (1910), p. 50.
[2] F. M. Davenport, *Primitive Traits in Religious Revivals* (New York, 1905), p. 101ff.

CHAPTER VIII

THE ROMAN RELIGION IN RELATION TO MENDACITY

WITHOUT a knowledge of the various religious ideas and sentiments which existed in ancient Rome, it would be difficult to understand much of its history, and impossible to appraise justly many of its historical authorities. Of late years many highly competent scholars have devoted much attention to the religion of the Romans, and have presented the results of their studies in erudite treatises; but it is the very amplitude and elaboration of these works which make it not altogether useless to devote a little space to one aspect of the matter, in hopes that, stripped of other elements, it may stand forth more clearly.

In entering on an examination of this subject we may find it useful to recall that, as has been suggested in another connection,[1] an institution such as an established religion, is an outward manifestation of some aspect of the average character of the members of the community, and the institution tends, as it is passed on by the operation of education and imitation, to impress upon the members of new generations the psychological characteristics which are, so to speak, embodied in it. Thus, by a kind of social heredity which is often mistakenly thought to be biological in character, a certain permanence appears in national peculiarities.

[1] Compare p. 9.

Now long established religious beliefs and practices
are, it would seem, the best institutional expression of a
people's general character; in the first place because, affecting as they are thought to do the welfare of the entire
personality of the believers, they are related to more
numerous aspects of man's life than is the case with other
institutions; and in the second place, because in the case
of secular institutions various elements of the environment
—the geographical location of the national territory, the
sort of neighbors whose presence raises problems, the
nature of the products and trade of the people, and other
like elements—have a direct effect.   But in the case of
religion, concerned as it is with the relations between
mankind and cosmic, or at least superhuman, powers, the
two component parties are men and the objects of their
cult; and the mundane environment is not thought, at least
in the religion with which we are concerned, to be a determining factor.   Either the personage towards whom
worship is directed is a true deity whose character is
regarded as fixed, indelible, and lasting, so that the distinguishing alterable features of the religion, as compared
with others or with itself at different times, must be due
to differences in the moral or intellectual characters of
mortal members; or the religion is false, and its supposed
divinities or dæmons have in fact no existence outside
the imaginations of misguided men, but are merely creations of the believers' minds.   In this case the qualities
attributed to such creations illuminate, as does any other
intellectual product, the characters of those who have
created and accepted them.[1]

[1] "La caractère de la religion d'un peuple est l'image la plus
exacte du tempérament et des facultés de ce peuple; c'est, pour
ainsi dire, le fruit de ses entrailles, le résumé de ses espérances et
de ses terreurs, l'histoire de son âme écrite sous l'influence du

These created gods, possessing nothing save what the general consensus of a people's opinion has given them, represent, if of the beneficent sort, an imaginary social self, a highly charged portrait of what the worshippers in moments of optimism consider themselves to be capable of if they were not hampered, or at least a portrait of what they would approve, in short, the Ideal or some part of it. When these constructions are maleficent, to them are attributed such conduct as is especially offensive to their creators. All this indicates the national proclivities and gives to these works of the creative imagination their value to one who seeks to know the characters of different peoples.[1]

Even in the case of Christianity one is compelled to admit that however adequate the revelation may be as to the nature and attributes of the deity and the kind of conduct toward God and toward man on the part of the faithful most pleasing in his sight, yet nevertheless the interpretation of the celestial message has not been the same *semper, ubique et ab omnibus*. So considerable have been the divergences of opinion among such eminent Christians as, for instance, Hildebrand, St. Francis, Loyola, Calvin, Luther, Wesley, Channing, and Newman, to mention but a few, in regard to a subject which they would perhaps all have agreed in considering to be in itself the same yesterday, to-day, and forever, as to make it evident that the history of even this religion throws as much light on the various temperaments of men as on the changeless nature of God.

---

sentiment qui s'empare le plus complètement de la nature humaine." Bouché-Leclercq, *Les Pontifes de l'ancienne Rome* (Paris, 1871), p. 24.

[1] Compare W. James, *Principles of Psychology* (New York, 1893), vol. I, pp. 315-316; E. B. Tylor, *Primitive Culture* (London, 5th ed., 1913), vol. I, p. 416.

In order that a religion may serve this purpose of illustrating, by embodying, the character of a people, should be one that has grown up as a natural institution of the community; or, if it has reached them from without, then it must have been accepted by them long enough to have received those inevitable modifications which make it a fairly complete and adequate expression of those needs and elements of character with which it harmonized and hence came to be adopted in its new home, as well as of those other features, less important, perhaps, but yet distinctive, which it took from the people among whom it originated but which are incongruous with the qualities of its new adherents. Such modifications often fail to appear clearly in the formal professions of a borrowed faith. There is a strong conservative tendency regarding the public statements of religious doctrines. Hence we get, for example, the strange cases of bloodthirsty tribes of pirates and murderers whose robber barons and militant ecclesiastics are but imperfectly distinguishable from one another, but who profess allegiance to precepts of humility and altruism. In such a case, it is evident that caution is needed in arguing from a people's religious professions. The borrowed faith has never been completely assimilated.

Besides serving as an index of the general character of its votaries, so that we are enabled to comprehend and interpret their thoughts and conduct, religion, as embodied in the activities of religious teachers and propagandists, is a powerful agent in producing and moulding the character of each new generation. So abundantly recognized, however, is this function that it needs only to be mentioned.

There is another matter, however, which is not quite so obvious and to which so ready an assent cannot be expected. This relates to the extension of the conclusions reached from an examination of the modes of feeling, thinking, and acting in religious matters to the secular side of human life. Save in certain pathological cases, the mind is not split up into compartments. The

> body of habits of thought which makes up the character of any individual is in some sense an organic whole. . . . A habit formed in response to a given stimulus will necessarily affect the character of the response made to other stimuli. A modification of human nature at any one point is a modification of human nature as a whole.[1]

An eminent scholar has shown that men's general sentiments are considerably impaired by religious conceptions which may at first view seem isolated. He finds that the belief in hell blunted human affections and pity, and produced a general indifference or insensibility to pain, and that the general indulgence in cruelty thus engendered extended beyond the sphere of religious offenses and was reflected in the whole penal system of the times.[2] To attribute to God the infliction of eternal agony, says he, will produce a degree of callousness towards suffering as absolute as it is possible for human nature to attain[3]; while the softening of theological views is associated with a general development of candor and toleration towards our fellow men.[4] In the Middle Ages, Lecky observes elsewhere, the indifference to truth ac-

---

[1] T. Veblen, *The Theory of the Leisure Class* (New York, 1899), p. 289.

[2] W. E. H. Lecky, *History of Rationalism in Europe* (rev. ed., New York, 1889), vol. I, p. 324ff. Compare *id., History of European Morals*, vol. I, p. 97.

[3] *History of Rationalism* (ed. cit.), vol. I, p. 150.

[4] *Ibid.*, p. 201.

quired in the theological controversy was very naturally
carried into all other fields.

> All their writings, and more especially their histories,
> became tissues of the wildest fables, so grotesque and
> at the same time so audacious, that they were the wonder
> of succeeding ages.[1]
> For the different elements of our knowledge are so
> closely united that it is impossible to divide them into
> separate compartments, and to make a spirit of credulity
> preside over one compartment while a spirit of enquiry
> is animating the others.[2]

Instead of saying that the religious ideas overflowed
the confines of religiosity and affected the mediæval minds
in other ways, becoming the cause of the secular phenomena mentioned, it would no doubt be more accurate
psychology to say that two similar conditions existed,
one on the religious and the other on the secular side,
which were both aspects of one general effect arising from
a common cause. But whether the relation be that of
cause and effect, or of two aspects of one effect, it is nevertheless true that they are not isolated, and that the existence and character of one set of manifestations throw
light on the other. Viewing the matter either way, we
can see the interrelation of all mental activities and the
extreme difficulty of isolating any particular mental habit
and confining it to any special class of ideas. Where
there seems to be a peculiar "theological estimate of justice and mercy" it may generally be accounted for by
the fact, to be considered later,[3] that men often use words
in a technical and unnatural sense, or sometimes with no
definite sense at all—a practice not uncommon in the
field of religion. In what, to borrow a legal phrase, may

[1] *Ibid.*, p. 395.   [2] *Ibid.*, p. 404.   [3] *Infra*, p. 361.

be called the adjective as distinguished from the substantive side of the operations of the mind, that is to say, in such general forms of functioning as the various modes of expression, whether with such clarity as the degree of knowledge possessed by the speaker renders possible, or with clumsiness and confusion, whether with honesty and an attempt at truthfulness and accuracy, or with a design primarily to entertain or mislead the hearer; we find that the habitual indulgence in one mode of procedure in regard to certain subjects has its effect in other fields. Where a person has a tendency to account for certain classes of facts by other methods than examination of evidence and application of the principles of strict causation, his general intellectual processes are almost certain to suffer.[1] No one can believe in miracles, spirits, immaterial agencies, and the like, and still believe in the fundamental principles of science without mental confusion, because the two sets of ideas are contradictory. If a man tampers with his feeling for truth, if he cultivates conformity to a certain class of prevalent opinions without believing in them, then the habit of insincerity will hardly be confined to the special class of phenomena for whose solace this psychological opium was first employed. In one of Plutarch's colloquies it is suggested—though the doctrine is inconsistent with some of his other ideas—that recourse to superstition, inasmuch as it disaccustoms man to the effort of guiding his life by the exercise of reason, delivers him to all the fantasies and hazards of irrationality.[2] Sir Leslie Stephen, in a similar vein, finds that the tendency which manifests itself in a disingenuous attachment to discredited but agreeable religious beliefs is the same as that which generates in other fields an in-

[1] T. Veblen, *op. cit.*, pp. 282-290.
[2] *De Genio Socratis*, 9.

difference to truth for its own sake and an inclination to asperse the motives of those who happen to possess a bias in favor of veracity.[1]

That the extent of guile and mendacity in connection with religious matters is of direct bearing on our extant authorities so far as they deal with that phase of Roman life is of course obvious, and that it is likewise of great importance in estimating the general trustworthiness of the statements of writers living in such an environment seems highly probable. If we should find that in relation to religion there appeared in all periods of Roman history an habitual and unblushing resort to nearly every form of exaggeration and deception; that fraud and falsehood were tolerated by many of the better class, and were practised not only upon the people in relation to religion, but even upon the gods themselves; and that the objects of divine worship were so far from reprobating these departures from sincerity in word and act as to indulge in such expedients themselves;—if we reach these conclusions then we are entitled to regard such conditions as imposing a special caution in scrutinizing assertions of fact emanating from such a society. The misgivings thus arising should extend to writings on every subject where, as in the case of religion, advantage might have been thought to result from the establishment of falsities and the crediting of inexact or fictitious statements put forth as veracious chronicles. .

In entering upon an examination of the trustworthiness of the Roman moralists as historical authorities, attention was directed to the special difficulty experienced by moderns in reaching a sound judgment because of the similarity of their moral prejudices and our own, and our consequent sympathy with their writings, whereby we some-

[1] *An Agnostic's Apology*, pp. 124-125.

times permit our hearty approval of their ethics to involve us in a hasty acceptance of their pretended data. But in approaching the subject of manifestations of the religious sentiments, a difficulty of another sort confronts us.

So great is the difference between the Romans and us in this respect, that if we translate such words *e.g.,* as *religio, pietas, pius, divinus, daemon, sacer,* or *virtus* by the modern words which most closely resemble them in form, we are in great danger of falling into the error of false analogy and of acquiring inaccurate notions. Yet such is the indigence of our vocabulary that without wearisome circumlocutions we find it difficult to avoid this slovenly practice. Hence it is especially necessary to keep in mind the nature and extent of the divergence between past and present use of these words, and their analogues.[1] By most moderns, religion is more and more fully identified with general morality, or is considered its handmaid. More and more relative stress is laid on sacred texts that identify good moral conduct toward our fellow men with true piety towards the Deity, with "religion pure and undefiled;" while the possession of technical, legal or ceremonious righteousness and sacramental purification is not regarded with the favor once bestowed upon it. And, indeed, unless accompanied by a specially high degree of social virtue, such righteousness is coming to be generally pronounced offensively irreligious.

God is thought, in the more progressive modern countries, to lack interest in parades and pageants, and only among the ignorant and the opulent is He deemed to be more than mildly gratified by correctness of vestments, exactness of ritual, or elaboration of ceremonial.

[1] *Cf.* W. Ihne, *History of Rome* (Eng. ed., London, 1882), vol. IV, p. 252.

While merit is acquired by religious gifts, they are not supposed to reach the Deity otherwise than mediately through the satisfaction accruing from their application to the needs of the clergy or the indigent; and it is by alms rather than by oblations that celestial favor is felt to be most certainly obtained.

Besides our confident and unhesitating attribution to the Deity of every ethical quality in the highest imaginable degree, we assign with equal positiveness so much intelligence to God that an open attempt to deceive him, at any rate as to anything but our inmost thoughts, would seem an act of insanity; and as to these secret thoughts it is probable that in most cases we have succeeded in deceiving ourselves. The most advanced modern religious sentiment estimates the divine discrimination as to means, and scrupulosity as to ends, too highly to suppose that God is gratified with the worship of devotees won by wiles. Indeed the use of chicanery of any sort to sustain religion is beginning to offend not only against our conceptions of the divine majesty, but also against the sense of decorum and good taste which we are slowly acquiring for ourselves and which we are ascribing to our celestial moral ideal.

So far has this moralization of the religious feeling proceeded in the case of some moderns, so confident are they of the essential unity of piety and good faith, that they seem reluctant to recognize the earlier separateness of these two mental states, and endeavor to bolster up the ingenuousness of those who at any time have professed a zeal for a spiritual and religious cause. Thus we find what a cruder mind might have stigmatized as a fraudulent interpolation in the Gospels softly passed over by Dr. Percy Gardner with such comments as: "one may suspect that in this case the words of John have been somewhat expanded by the Christian consciousness," or "this Gospel, in spite of its wonderful inspiration, obviously does not lie so near to historic fact as do the others." [1] Another writer suggests as to the same Gospel that the Evangelist "may care little to separate his narrative from his soliloquy." [2] This, in effect, must be the same sort of truth as that which yet another writer finds persisting wonderfully among Christians throughout the centuries and receiving their devotion, " 'veracity' in the larger sense of the term." [3]

Whether because of a novel development of charity, or of a recognition that it is inexpedient for an apologist to admit that fraud is ever associated with any religious faith, we find the surprising phenomenon of a willingness on the part of many to take for granted all earlier sacerdotal and propagandist good faith, and to scout the assumption of fraud and the hypothesis of "priestcraft," even in the case of false and dead religious systems. [4] Yet this benevolent spirit would be carried too far were it to be applied to the subject now under consideration. And indeed all our confident assumptions of the intimate association or even fusion of religion and morality in all its branches, and especially in its aspects of straightforwardness of action and truthfulness of word, must be laid aside in approaching a consideration of the perturba-

---

[1] P. Gardner, *The Growth of Christianity* (London, 1907), pp. 80, 30.

[2] C. F. Nolloth, *The Life and Words of Christ and Modern Criticism.* (Quoted from the *Spectator,* Sept. 24, 1910, p. 470.)

[3] *Hibbert Journal,* vol. VIII (Jan., 1910), p. 445.

[4] J. M. Robertson, *A Short History of Free Thought* (2nd ed., London, 1906), vol. I, pp. 26-28. The author argues that "it belongs, further, to the very nature of the priestly function, in its earlier forms, to develop in a special degree the normal bias of the undisciplined mind to intellectual fraud."

tions in our historical material caused by the religious sentiments prevailing in ancient Rome.

Yet it is but just to remark in passing that however much lower than our own we may find Roman moral and religious principles to have been, we cannot safely assume that this defect is a true measure of their inferiority in actual conduct. One of the compensations for their religious destitution was that they were able more easily and more often than are the moderns to attain that state of serene equanimity which forms so pleasing an aspect of their spiritual life. From this state the modern is sometimes debarred by an uneasy consciousness of the inadequacy of his behavior to form a harmonious accompaniment to the melody of his celestial ideals.

That the Romans were indeed more easily satisfied with their spiritual achievements than a more scrupulous religious sentiment might have felt becoming, appears in their conviction that they were the most pious and religious of men. They seemed to think that to their habitual piety were due the benefits showered upon Rome as a mark of divine satisfaction; and the same idea occurs frequently in the writings of their Greek admirers. Polybius is struck by their extraordinary religiosity,[1] and his praise of them for this virtue is not affected by his conviction that their religion is a humbug consciously practised to deceive the ignorant. Sallust and Livy concur in their view of former times [2] and Cicero, who believes this characteristic persisted to later days, feels assured that the success and preservation of Rome are due to the notable superiority of the Romans over other peoples in religion

---

[1] Polybius, VI, 56. *Cf.* Dionysius Halic., I, 5; II, 18ff; Posidonius in Athenaeus, VI, 274a; G. Wissowa, *Religion u. Kultus der Römer* (2nd. ed., München, 1912), p. 386.

[2] Sal., *Cat.* 12; Livy, XLIV, 1; VI, 41; Val. Max., I, 1, 8.

and in their recognition of the divine government of the world.[1] Aulus Gellius does not shrink from applying to them the superlatives *castissimi cautissimique*.[2] When Tertullian, not an altogether sympathetic critic, refers to this Roman boast, he does so only to scout it, and declares that their greatness was due not to the amplitude but rather to the meagreness of their religiosity.[3] Much evidently turns on the meanings attached to *religio* and *pietas*.

Most of us can remember with interest our early excursions as children into some of the less obvious fields of scientific knowledge. For instance, we may recall when we found that in a certain condition of the air, which we later discovered to be that of dryness, we were able, by scuffling briskly over a carpet—certain kinds of carpet worked better than others—and then approximating a finger to the gas fixture, to produce a palpable, visible, and audible spark of electricity, which we afterwards learned to identify with that resulting from the operation of a frictional electrical machine in the school laboratory, and which we were told was a minute simulacrum of the imposing natural manifestations of thunder and lightning, as the genial Benjamin Franklin had established by his more or less mythical experiments. If we possessed the normal amount of experimental curiosity, we became aware that to obtain the spark there were necessary only a strict observance of certain conditions and the execution of certain movements, and that if these were correctly done, the desired effect followed, whether we sought innocently to interest and please our fellows or mischie-

---

[1] *De nat. Deor.*, II, 3; *de Har. Resp.*, 9; *cf.* W. W. Fowler, *The Religious Experience of the Roman People* (London, 1911), p. 249ff.

[2] Aul. Gell., II, 28.

[3] *Apol.* 25; *cf. id., ad Nat.*, II, 17.

vously to surprise our elders. In a form of expression with which we were not then familiar, we might have said that the spark came not *ex opere operantis* but strictly *ex opere operato.*

Now the early Roman notion about the divine objects of their cult was something not very dissimilar in essence to that which we might have held regarding the spark. The gods in general were conceived vaguely and indistinctly. They were impersonal *numina,* and only at a later date and under the influence of localization of cult, or foreign ideas, and of organized priesthoods did they assume sufficient definiteness and independence to be fairly entitled to the attribute of personality and emerge as *dei.*[1] At an earlier time the *numen* was in theory a manifestation arising *ad hoc* for the performance of some function out of the general undifferentiated mass of cosmic divinity; and then, until there was another call upon its particular function, sinking back into the homogeneous substratum of potentiality, as a special wave sinks back and disappears in the ocean of which it is a part.[2] It came forth when occasion demanded—and for that particular occasion—somewhat as the electric spark was evoked out of the undifferentiated electricity of the universe, and like it the *numen* was known and knowable only as manifested in its activities; for between these occasions it could hardly be said to have a separate existence. The titles applied to these manifestations were originally more in the nature of adjectives referring to several forms

---

[1] See in general, W. W. Fowler, *The Religious Experience of the Roman People,* Lect. VI, VII; J. B. Carter, *Religious Life of Ancient Rome* (Boston, 1911), p. 9ff; *Cf.* G. Boissier, *La Religion romaine,* vol. I, pp. 2-9. "Jusqu' à la fin ils ont mis dans le ciel plutôt des abstractions que des êtres vivants."

[2] W. Ihne, *History of Rome* (ed. cit.), vol. I, p. 118.

of functioning than of substantive names.[1] It was no easy matter to address them rightly when application was made to one of them for a boon, and most carefully guarded language was used on such occasions, with cautious additions such as "whether thou art god or goddess," or "by whatever name thou dost wish to be addressed."

The indistinctness of this conception of the divine naturally tended to prevent any great development of intimacy and affection between the gods and men. There was an abundance of narrow and cautious formality, for the Romans were profoundly superstitious, and the dimly envisaged apparitions imposed a feeling of awe because of their vague power; but little warmth, enthusiasm or devotion could arise towards divinized abstractions or momentarily manifested powers or functions. As has been said by an eminent scholar:

> There was never, perhaps, a religion so cold and prosaic as that of the Romans. Being subordinated to politics it sought, above all, to secure the protection of the gods for the state or to avert the effect of their malevolence by the strict execution of appropriate practices. It entered into reciprocal contracts with the celestial powers, from which mutual obligations arose; sacrifices on the one side, favors on the other. . . . This religion looked suspiciously at the abandonment of the soul to the ecstasies of devotion. It repressed, by force if necessary, the exuberant manifestations of too ardent a faith.[2]

[1] *Cf.* W. W. Fowler, *op. cit.*, pp. 118-119.
[2] F. Cumont, *Les Religions orientales dans le paganisme romain* (Paris, 1906), p. 36. Fowler, *op. cit.*, p. 2, expresses a general agreement in the justice of this opinion though he regards it as somewhat too sweeping. The suggestions of the latter, as well as those of Dr. Carter, in favor of a milder judgment on this

The piety felt to be incumbent on an adherent seems to have been hardly more than a determination to pay justly the obligations which had been voluntarily incurred towards the gods for value received. So Cicero asks:

> What piety is due to a being from whom you receive nothing? How can you be indebted to one who merits nothing? For piety is justice towards the gods . . . sanctity is the knowledge of how we ought to worship them; but I do not understand why they are to be worshipped if nothing is received from them, nor any benefit expected.[1]

The modes of approach used by the Romans to their gods were such as might naturally be expected to follow from piety of this sort. In the language of Dr. Dill:

> The old Roman worship was businesslike and utilitarian. The gods were partners in a contract with their worshippers, and the ritual was characterised by all the hard and literal formalism of the legal system of Rome. The worshipper performed his part to the letter with the

---

matter are not altogether convincing. Ihne seems sounder in his general conclusions (*op. cit.*, vol. I, pp. 118ff, 556; IV, p. 252ff).

[1] *De Nat. Deor.*, I, 41. A similar conception is said to prevail among some of the Southern Italians to-day. Dr. Fowler (*op. cit.*, p. 203) says "there is no trace in early Roman religious history of any tendency to abuse or degrade the divine beings if they did not perform their part" such as is observable in modern China and South Italy, but he recognizes that the attitude towards the gods was not always respectful in later times; although in saying 'the farthest the Romans *ever* went in condemning their gods was to neglect them,' he seems to have overlooked Suetonius's statements regarding the statue of Neptune degraded by Augustus (*Aug.* 16) and the popular excitement at the death of Germanicus (*Calig.* 5). Perhaps he disbelieves the statements—which would not be surprising.

scrupulous exactness required in pleadings before the praetor.[1]

Notwithstanding the scholarly marshaling of evidence by Mr. Fowler in favor of a more sympathetic attitude towards the piety displayed in Roman religious practices,[2] it is difficult to dissent seriously from the other opinions quoted. Or if we suppose that at an early period there was in existence a religious spirit somewhat more pious according to the modern sense of the word, yet, in the generations from which most of our historical sources emanate, there was, as we shall see, a general lack of deep-felt respect and devoutness towards the gods, and often indeed a lack of mere belief in them, still more profound than the foregoing statements would indicate.

In such a religion we can hardly expect to find much prominence given to the inculcation of general morality. Doubtless the strict discipline of its rigid formalism may have done something to strengthen men's characters, and the family cults may have enforced domestic dutifulness, but it was never a source of ethical endeavor or enthusiasm, and in fact it had very little effect on the moral condition of men. The concern of religion was not with social misconduct but rather with placating more or less irrational and inexplicable divine irritations.[3] Its func-

---

[1] S. Dill, *Roman Society in the Last Century of the Western Empire,* p. 75. *Cf.* Ihne, *op. cit.,* vol. I, p. 556: "the gods were entitled to certain stipulated services, and man, in his turn, duly discharging these duties, was considered equally entitled to the consideration and protection of the gods." *Cf.* pp. 116, 120; IV, p. 253ff.

[2] Compare *op. cit.,* Lect. VIII, IX.

[3] Compare T. R. Glover, *Conflict of Religions in the Early Empire* (3rd ed., London, 1909), p. 19; Lecky, *History of European Morals,* vol. II, p. 2.

tions were to obtain for the state or the individual certain material advantages and to avert certain calamities, and to this end to discover the designs of the gods and to act upon them by various rites.[1] Westermarck, following Renan, says that

> in the Roman, as in the majority of old Italian cults, prayer is a magic formula, producing its effect by its own inherent quality. . . . They wanted to compel the gods rather than to be compelled by them.[2]

The religious acts and ceremonials were designed in theory not so much to please and persuade the divine powers by means of attractive ritual gratifications, gifts, or sacrifices as to bring about some certain manifestation of divinity by the intrinsic magical force of invocation, sacrifice, liturgy, sacrament, or other duly performed observance, and then to exercise upon the manifestation thus evoked [3] some coercion or constraint whereby it was forced to assist in forwarding an end coveted by the worshipper; or at least to get for him the opportunity to bargain with it in technical legal form for its coöperation upon due compensation given or promised.[4]

[1] Lecky, *op. cit.*, vol. I, p. 398.

[2] E. Westermarck, *Origin and Development of Moral Ideas* (London, 1908), vol. II, pp. 585, 657.

[3] In time, of course, some *numina* became almost permanently manifest and acquired a more or less distinct personality; this *deus* would then be constrained or bargained with.

[4] Examples may be found in Livy, V, 21; XXII, 10; Macrobius, *Sat.*, III, 9. Compare G. Wissowa, *Religion u. Kultus*, p. 394ff. The views set forth in the text are not quite those of Fowler (*op. cit.*, pp. 185ff; 300ff) but it does not appear that his conclusions are essentially different in view of the language used by him, pp. 189-190. "The faith is, indeed, thus founded upon man's devices rather than the god's good-will as such; it is a belief in

Such was the general theory of the Roman religion—so far as a religion which had no formal theology and imposed no beliefs on its adherents can be said to have a theory—which can be discerned as underlying and informing its practices: and such we may suppose was implicit in its cult and explicit in the minds of those few who cared to attempt to rationalize their religious worship. But in the centuries and among the classes whose writings form our historical material, it is difficult to say how much there was of even this extent of religious creed. It is no part of the design of this work to trace a history of Roman religion, nor indeed to deal with it at all except in so far as it bears on the confidence justly to be given to those from whom we draw our information on Roman moral conditions. But we may observe that there is no reason to think that the changes which took place during the centuries under examination introduced into the religion prevalent in Rome any new ideas tending to give stronger sanctions to the virtue of veracity.

Indeed in this, as in some other respects, there was a curious persistence among the Romans, through all the changes of their national existence, of certain characteristics. There was at all times an essentially practical spirit in their relations with the various divinities to which at one time or another they gave their allegiance.

---

the State and its authorities and *ius divinum*, which is conceived, not indeed as constraining the deity, but as calling upon him (*invocare*) to perform his part, in formulae which he cannot well neglect, simply because it would be unreasonable to do so, contrary to his nature as a deity of the Roman State and its *ager*." *Cf.* pp. 200, 202. To rely not upon "the god's good-will" but upon "man's devices" in the shape of formulae which by reason of the god's nature he cannot well neglect, comes very close to the constraint of magic.

> Prayer and vow were the means to win temporal blessings. The gods were expected, in return for worship, to be of use to the devotee. It is evident from the inscriptions that this conception of religion was as prevalent in the age of the Antonines, or of the oriental princes, as it was under the Republic.[1]

This considerable degree of stability in those qualities of character which we are considering renders it unnecessary for us to examine the extent to which a religion sometimes lags behind its votaries in periods of rapid change. We shall find no great difference between the various ages of Rome in an approval of disingenuousness and a resort to those pious frauds which our piety regards as unbecoming in man and unpleasing to God. But whatever criticisms the modern scientific spirit may level at the easy toleration of such practices by the devout, Roman sentiment seemed rarely to be shocked by the intimate association of what in our eyes are mental and moral incongruities.

For the special purpose of our inquiries, it is not important what may have been the real facts as to the origin of Roman theology, or what the early Romans may have thought on the subject; nor indeed are we concerned with the ideas which may have been held on it in later times, except in those classes from whom the surviving literary material on Roman affairs comes, and in those ages when the works were written. We have practically nothing earlier than the last two centuries of the Republic; and during these years and those of the early Empire, the authors upon whom we rely were nearly all either members of the governing and aristocratic classes, or were their associates or dependents who shared

[1] Dill, *Roman Society from Nero to Marcus Aurelius*, pp. 543-4.

or affected to share the ideas and prejudices of their actual or prospective patrons.[1] The conditions of book publishing made this almost a necessity. The great, silent multitude was no doubt a most important element in the state from other points of view, but not from this particular one, save that the simple-minded credulity of the many was the material on which the disingenuous ideas of the few were imposed.

Before closing these observations, prefatory to later discussion, one further remark may be made. To rely on conclusions based on the testimony of historical writers for the purpose of discrediting the trustworthiness of these writers themselves may seem to wear the aspect of sawing off the branch on which we sit, or to fall into the famous dilemma of the old logicians regarding the assertion by a Cretan that all Cretans were liars. In reality, however, this proceeding is legitimate: in the first place the evidence is in some cases directed to the establishment of a writer's own opinions, or his self-contradictions in which one of his assertions must be false; in the second place, no writer is mendacious in every statement, and many assertions of even a generally untrustworthy writer may be justly credited if we can identify them; in the third place, many statements, while valueless regarding the matters of the past with which they purport to deal, are good evidence of the thought of the writer's contemporaries. And in general either any particular statement is true, and hence properly enters into the reasoning process to establish the writer's general lack of probity, or it is false, in which case it is direct evidence of the general conclusion, instead of indirect. In the present study we are not seeking to substantiate any particular state of facts regarding any particular element

[1] Plautus may be an exception.

of Roman life—which would necessitate a special scrutiny of each alleged fact—but simply to make clear the existence of general defects in our material and the nature of these defects as a basis for sound canons of interpretation.

CHAPTER IX

RELIGIOUS SCEPTICISM

STUDENTS have often to deplore the scantiness of direct, explicit evidence available for a just knowledge of Roman religion. When we limit ourselves, however, to the members of the social class from which our authorities on Roman affairs during Republican times are derived, we find abundant evidence that their faith must have been something curiously unlike our conception of the meaning of faith. They seem not to have been supported by any distinct belief in the origin and, at times, even the existence of their divinities. This lack of foundation, as most moderns would probably regard it, for any religious sentiments at all, and the consequent unreality of their professions, demand attention.

When Roman affairs first come clearly into the light of history there are already indications of widespread religious incredulity. As early as 249 B.C., we are informed, the consul Claudius ordered the sacred chickens to be cast into the sea because they failed to give the desired indications; and a similar contempt for the auspices was manifested by his colleague.[1] We cannot feel sure of the truth of these anecdotes, for both consuls had unfortunate experiences in the war—Claudius suffering

---

[1] Cic., *de Div.*, II, 33; Val. Max. I, 4, 3; Livy, *Epit.*, XIX. Even earlier than this (293 B.C.) it appears that the consul Papirius was willing to tolerate a false report of the auspices, and even make a jocular vow to Jupiter. Livy, X, 40, 42.

impeachment—and such circumstances easily give rise
to stories. Polybius in his narrative of the battle and the
subsequent prosecution of Claudius does not mention a
charge of impiety as entering into the case.[1]   In like
manner Flaminius, who lost the battle of Lake Trasimene, was charged with neglecting omens and auspices;
but this story also may well be deemed uncertain since
Flaminius was not popular with the class that wrote
history.[2]   Such stories, however, have a certain evidential
value inasmuch as the author of a damaging tale usually
seeks to invent what his contemporaries at least may think
probable.

That the religious attitude of the commanders in question was such as to furnish occasion for anecdote indicating their impiety is not at all improbable, for early Roman
literature abundantly attests the scepticism prevalent
among the intellectual and ruling class. The popular plays
of Plautus were produced for many years under official
sanction; yet they abound in passages in which the gods
are irreverently treated as engaged in low intrigue.[3]   It
may indeed be argued that these plays were mere trans-
lations from the Greek; but they were adapted for the
Roman stage; the gods appear under Latin names, and
neither the magistrates nor the people would have tolerated
the plays had they been very offensive to Roman piety.

Ennius, the "father of Latin poetry," acquainted with

[1] Polybius I, 52. No great importance can be attached to
Polybius's silence, for he is contemptuous of such matters.

[2] Compare Livy, XXI, 63; XXII, 1, 3, 9; Plutarch, *Marcell.*,
4-5. Fabius Maximus, dictator after the battle of Lake Trasimene, seems to have been duly respectful to religion; *cf.* Plut.,
Fab., 4-5. But Claudius Marcellus, five times consul between 222
and 208 B.C., as well as augur, despised the auspices and avoided
seeing omens. *Cf.* Cic., *de Div.*, II, 36.

[3] See, *e.g., Amphitruo, Prol., et passim.*

plebeians and nobles alike, was more earnest in his scepticism than Plautus, and had no hesitation in manifesting
openly his contempt for religion and his incredulity as to
the gods, although he treated them reverently in patriotic
poems. He had dabbled in various philosophies but
always with a sceptical spirit in matters of religion.
Cicero says that his extreme Epicurean sentiments deny-
ing divine Providence and flouting religious practices were
applauded by all the Romans.[1] As a Pythagorean he
declared the gods to be only natural forces regarded as
persons for practical purposes, only physical allegories.[2]
But it was to the teachings of Euhemerus that he gave
special allegiance; following them he asserted that the
gods, including even Jupiter, were only prominent men
who had received worship after their death.[3]

That "archetype of an old Roman" as Teuffel calls Cato,
busy with incessant litigation, censure of the *Zeitgeist,*
and the reform of women, interested in magic, the medici-
nal virtues of cabbage, and whatever other ideas he conceived to be venerable, wondered that one haruspex could
refrain from smiling when he met another; and even
inserted in his *Origines* doubts regarding the importance

[1] Ennius, *Telamo;* Cic., *de Div.*, II, 50. *Cf.* G. Boissier, *Religion
romaine*, vol. I, pp. 42-43; G. Colin, *Rome et la Grèce* (Paris,
1905), p. 345ff.

[2] Ennius, *Epicharmus.*

[3] Cic., *de Nat. Deorum*, I, 42. The Euhemeristic doctrine of the
human origin and often all-too-human character of the divine
recipients of worship seems to have been widely held among the
Romans, and we find it applied by various writers to many
Roman deities. For numerous cases, see Marquardt, *Le culte chez
les Romains* (trans. by M. Brissaud, Paris, 1889, = *Manuel des
antiquités romaines*, vol. XII), I, pp. 72-73. It is worthy of note
that Ennius was brought to Rome by Cato and later became
closely attached to the Scipio family.

of the Pontifical Annals, and the character of one of the divinized recipients of Roman worship.[1]

The remarkable group of men, often referred to as the Scipionic circle, is worth our attention because they illustrate not indeed the old Roman character but the new type coming into prominence during this century, which represents a fusion of ancestral vigor and the broader cultivation taken over from Greek civilization.

Both in the eminence of its members and in the public service it rendered, the Scipio family was the most prominent of the great Roman houses during the period under discussion. Scipio Africanus the younger, by birth the son of Aemilius Paullus, conqueror of Macedonia, had been adopted by the eldest son of Scipio Africanus the elder, who triumphed over Hannibal. A daughter of the elder Scipio by his wife Aemilia, sister to the younger Scipio's own father, was the famous Cornelia, mother of the two Gracchi, with whom began the civil conflicts of the last age of the Republic. Their sister Sempronia was the wife of the younger Scipio Africanus about whom gathered the so-called Scipionic circle. The importance of this family is indicated by the fact that during the century ending with the inauspicious year of the tribunate of Tiberius Gracchus (133 B.C.) a Scipio had been consul no fewer than thirteen times, while three of the name had been censors and a like number supreme pontiffs. If we include Scipio's brother and the families of his own father by blood, Aemilius Paullus, and of his wife's father, Sempronius Gracchus, we must add nine more consuls and two censors; in all twenty-two consuls and five

---

[1] See Cic., *de Div.*, II, 24; Aulus Gellius, II, 28. Cato's speech about women in Livy, XXXIV, 2-4, doubtless expresses accurately his real attitude. Colin, *op. cit.*, pp. 356ff, 591ff, cites numerous instances of Cato's inconsistencies.

censors.[1] Even more remarkable than the large number of
magistracies held is the fact that of the twenty-seven wars
waged by Rome during the century, in a third of them the
victorious general was a Scipio; while if we add the two
closely allied families mentioned above, in fourteen of
them it was a Scipio, an Aemilius Paullus or a Gracchus
who led the successful army. In the eight wars of importance during this period, the surprising fact appears
that in five of the eight a Scipio was the triumphing
general, and in a sixth a holder of the illustrious name
shared in the final victory as consul and general.[2]

This prominence in political and military affairs was
carried over into the humanities. Around the younger
Scipio Africanus were assembled many of the most
highly cultivated men of the times.[3] The philosophical
director of the group was the Stoic Panætius, one of the

[1] A Scipio was consul in the years 222, 221, 218, 205, 194, 191,
190, 176, 162, 155, 147, 138, 134; censor, 199, 159, 142. An
Aemilius Paullus was consul in 219, 216, 182, 168; censor, 164: a
Gracchus consul in 215, 213, 177, 163; censor, 169. Scipio's
brother, Fabius Maximus, was consul in 145.

[2] These eight are the wars with the Gauls ending in 222 B.C.
(Claudius Marcellus and Cornelius Scipio Calvus); in Spain,
206 (Scipio Africanus Major); with Hannibal, 202 (the same);
with Philip of Macedon, 197 (Flamininus); with Antiochus, 188
(Scipio Asiaticus); with Perseus of Macedon, 168 (Aemilius
Paullus); with Carthage, 146 (Scipio Africanus Minor); in
Spain, Numantia, 133 (the same). The other wars ended by a
Scipio are: the war with the Istri, 221 (Scipio Asina); with the
Gauls, 191 (Scipio Nasica); in Dalmatia, 155 (Scipio Nasica
Corculum). The estimate of the total number of wars at twenty-
seven is not absolute, as it is impossible to decide satisfactorily
into how many separate wars the long continued struggles in
Spain and Liguria should properly be divided.

[3] Colin, *op. cit.*, pp. 555ff, 560ff, gives an interesting sketch of the
group.

few men of his school who showed a rather chilly scepticism towards the popular religion although he was quite willing to tolerate it.[1] Ennius, attached to the family, was an avowed sceptic. Terence, another member, was cool towards the gods; while Lucilius regarded all the miraculous as grotesque, and charged Numa with the invention of religious terrorism.[2] Perhaps the most illustrious associate was Polybius, whose long residence at Rome almost entitles him to be classed as a Roman. He seems to have accepted the doctrines of Euhemerus,[3] and on religious matters expresses his views with ample freedom. With stories of marvels he has no patience, save when they are used to preserve reverence for religion among the common people, and he reduces the occasions when a sensible man may follow the opinion of the multitude regarding Providence to those cases which are otherwise inexplicable. He praises highly the piety of the Romans, and it appears that he includes under the term the skill with which leading men used the terrors and scenic effects of religion as a check upon the desires of the vulgar. To this piety he attributes, in an early passage, the pecuniary honesty of the Romans; longer experience seems to have made him less confident of the success of religious pragmatism.[4]

---

[1] Cic., de Div., I, 3; II, 42; Acad. Prior., II, 33. Hecaton, a pupil of Panætius, dedicated to Tubero, one of the circle, a book in which conformity to established institutions was urged. Cicero (de Off., II, 14) shows that Panætius approved occasional mendacity, and (Tusc. Disp., I, 32) argued against immortality.

[2] Lucilius, Frag. Sat., I, XV; Terence, Phormio, line 704ff, Eunuchus, 584ff.   [3] Polybius, XXXIV, 2.

[4] Polybius, VI, 56; X, 9; XVI, 12; XVIII, 35; XXXII, 11; XXXVII, 9. His long argument against the advisability of sacrilegious acts in war seems to be based entirely on secular grounds (V, 9-12).

In endeavoring to ascertain the religious opinions of the Scipios, we are fortunate in having Polybius as an authority, since he not only had abundant opportunities for knowing the facts but also felt so warm a friendship and gratitude towards his patron as to give us confidence that he would not traduce the members of the family, and would represent, if not their real opinions, at least what they or their descendants wished to have known as such.[1] Polybius begins by assuring us that the elder Scipio was not dependent on divine assistance in his great labors for Rome, but inasmuch as he saw that most men could not be made to fulfil their duties without the use of religious hopes, he instilled into the minds of the crowd the idea that he was acting under the direct guidance of the gods. Then, somewhat inconsistently, follows the narrative of Scipio's brilliant exploit when, as a boy, he saved his father's life in battle through sheer pluck and vigor—a deed which was sufficient without religious trickery to ensure courageous action by the soldiers. When Scipio decided, after canvassing the situation, to become a candidate for office, he secured his pious mother's consent—his father being absent in war—by inventing for her benefit a story of repeated dreams. So, in the words of the eulogist:

[1] We may safely assume that all but the very last of his book was finished before Scipio's death, and undoubtedly seen by him. Cf. Bury, *Ancient Greek Historians*, p. 193. Polybius (X, 3) speaks of gaining his information about the elder Scipio Africanus from his intimate associates, especially from his bosom friend Laelius. It is an interesting fact that the son of this Laelius was the closest friend of the younger Scipio. For the intimacy of Polybius with Scipio, see Polybius, XXXII, 9ff. In general, he is one of our most trustworthy sources. Compare Bury, *op. cit.*, pp. 193ff, 215, 220. See, too, Polybius, I, 14; XVI, 14; XXXII, 8.

by a dexterous use of the occasion, both with the people and with his mother, he obtained his purpose, and moreover got the reputation of acting under divine inspiration.

But, so Polybius assures us, we must not, like foolish people, be misled by this stupid notion and fail to give Scipio full credit for his remarkable but unmiraculous diligence and sagacity.[1]   Later, in Spain, he made careful investigations regarding a plan of campaign, and after devising some brilliant strategy concealed his schemes for a time from all save his friend Laelius.   But at the right moment he announced impressively to the army that Neptune had suggested the plan to him and had promised to render valuable aid in the hour of battle.   In Polybius's words :

the skilful mixture in this speech of accurate calculation with promises of gold crowns, and a reference to Divine Providence, created a great impression and enthusiasm in the minds of the young soldiers.

The narrator has to complain, however, that some historians insist on attributing the success to the gods, although indubitable evidence including a letter of Scipio himself proved the contrary.[2]

The value of these statements lies not primarily in the information which they give us of the elder Scipio.   Some doubt may always legitimately exist as to how far histori-

---

[1] Polybius, X, 2-5.   The translation quoted is by E. S. Shuckburgh, London, 1889.

[2] Polybius, X, 7-11.   Polybius's praise of Scipio's continence (X, 18, 19) is not echoed by the contemporary Naevius.   *Cf.* Aulus Gellius, VII, 8; Val. Max., VI, 9, 2.   Scipio seems at all times highly pleased with himself.   Polybius, XXIII, 14; Livy, XXXVIII, 51.

cal anecdotes have grown directly and without alteration out of the acts of the characters to whom they relate, although in this case there seems to be no reason to doubt their general accuracy.[1] But their special importance is the light which they throw upon the conceptions prevailing in the circle. Even if altogether false, they would not on that account be less significant.[2] Clearly, it was not offensive to the *pietas* of the younger Scipio that his grandfather, the glory of his house, should be represented as a crafty schemer.

The part of Polybius's work dealing with the career of his patron, Scipio Africanus Minor, is extant in an incomplete state. There is no detailed statement of Scipio's religious ideas; but the account of the beginning of their close friendship contains indications that Polybius attributed to the young man a character and sentiments very much like those of the elder Scipio.[3] There is in each case the picture of a bright, precocious, ambitious youth, keenly concerned with attaining prominence and not

[1] Later writers follow the tradition set by Polybius. See Livy, XXVI, 19, 41, 45, 49, 50; Appian, *Bellum Hisp.*, 19, 23, 26; *Bellum Pun.*, 6, 21. Valerius Maximus appropriately mentions Scipio under the chapter heading *de Simulata Religione*, I, 2, 2. Appian (*Bell. Hisp.*, 23) says that after his great successes in Spain he began to think he was divinely inspired, or at any rate proclaimed it publicly with more confidence. Aulus Gellius (VI, 1), and Cassius Dio (XVI, 57, Boissevain, I, p. 240) add new touches to satisfy later tastes and represent Scipio as the son of Jupiter who appeared to his mother in the guise of a serpent.

[2] Compare Lecky, *History of European Morals* (ed. cit.), vol. II, p. 131.

[3] *Cf.* Polybius, X, 2-9, 18-19, and XXXII, 9-16. *Cf.* XXIX, 18. The young man appears to have been quite different from his own father, the very good, conscientious, and cautious Aemilius Paullus. See Livy, XLV, 27-28, 39; Plut., *Aem. Paul.*, 3, 6, 7, 17, 39, as well as Polybius, XXIX-XXXII, 6 *passim*.

averse to somewhat showy manifestations of benevolence. These and other similarities arouse a suspicion that possibly Polybius made some effort to bring the two sketches into harmony so that by this resemblance of the youth, adopted into the illustrious family, to the distinguished man who was now his grandfather, it might indubitably appear that the Scipio by adoption was a Scipio indeed. Most noticeable is the statement in each case urging the reader not to attribute the man's remarkable exploits to Fortune (Tyche) or to any other cause than his own skill and prudence.[1] Evidently in both cases some observers had insisted on making the gods responsible for so much prosperity; and in the Scipionic circle it was regarded as unseemly for allegations of the receipt of help from the gods to be taken seriously after the occasion for the making of such claims had passed. An admission of deception was deemed less objectionable than a reputation for inability to dispense with divine assistance in performing exploits.

In the century preceding the establishment of the Empire under Augustus the material bearing on the question under discussion is too abundant to justify more than a cursory examination. A few cases may be noted where circumstances, one would think, would have imposed a respectful attitude towards religion.

Q. Mucius Scaevola, a learned and respected man, held the office of consul in 95 B.C. and later that of Pontifex Maximus, but he nevertheless felt free to say that there were three sorts of teachings concerning the gods: that invented by the poets, which was unseemly; that taught by the philosophers, which it would be undesirable for the people to know; and that laid down by the political leaders, which was inconsistent with the first and second, but useful

[1] Compare Polybius, X, 2, 5; XXXII, 16.

to the commonwealth and hence not to be disturbed. Therefore the pontiff thought that it was expedient that communities be deceived in matters of religion, and that the citizen should profess belief in many things which as an individual he considered to be false.[1]

A similar division of the subject seems to have been adopted by Cotta, consul in 75 B.C. and a priest, whom Cicero represents as distinguishing between his opinions as priest and citizen and the opinions which he held as philosopher. In the former capacity, if we can take Cicero as giving us a fair picture of him, he professed to believe in the whole of the Roman religion regardless of arguments and without proofs; in the rôle of philosopher he proceeds to deliver a smashing confutation of arguments made in its support.[2]

The long and active life of Varro covered nearly the last century of the Republic. The variety of his attainments, his wide acquaintance, and the universal respect felt for his high and virtuous character make him an excellent guide to interpret for us the thought of his times. His talents as displayed in public and military life were respectable but were overshadowed by the eminence accorded him for his vast erudition in nearly every field of ancient learning. Not only were his studies widely extended, but we are able to conclude from his extant writings that he had a vigorous mind.[3] To Varro

[1] *Expedire igitur existimat falli in religione civitates.* Augustine, *Civ. Dei*, IV, 27. Macrobius (*Sat.*, I, 16, 11) cites Scaevola as laying down most conveniently broad rules as to what may properly be done on holy days.

[2] Cic., *de Nat. Deor.*, I, 22-23. III, 2ff. In chapter 38 he recognizes the poet's fables as yet a third form. *Cf.* Boissier, *op. cit.*, vol. I, pp. 47ff, 52-53.

[3] See the citations collected by Teuffel, *s.v.* Varro. *Cf.* Cic., *Acad. Post.*, I, 3; Augustine, *Civ. Dei*, VI, 2-3.

it seemed that the Roman religion was in danger of perishing from sheer neglect and indifference, and he set himself with zeal to the task of supporting it.[1] It would doubtless have shocked him had he known that a later writer was to call him "everywhere the foe of religion."[2] Like the pontiff, Scaevola distinguished three sorts of religion, those of poets, of philosophers, and of statesmen. The first he stigmatized as based on mendacious and immoral fables; the second as full of conflicting theories; while the third, resting largely on myth, was an invention of men in different communities and was consequently local and confused. As a Roman he professed accord with the Roman cult, although his personal views seem to have inclined towards a kind of Stoic theology.[3] On one point, however, he was perfectly clear and in accord with the sentiments of most of his contemporaries. This is that in religious matters "there are many true things which it is not desirable that the people should know, but rather concerning which it is expedient that they have even false opinions."[4] Deceit in religion seemed to

[1] Augustine, *Civ. Dei,* IV, 22; VI, 12. As in the case of Scaevola, one feels some hesitation about judging of a man's religious opinions from what purport to be quotations of his writings in the books of a bitter opponent; but in this matter it seems probable that Varro's views are transcribed with general correctness since they agree in so many ways with what we learn from safer sources as to the religious ideas of his contemporaries, and since Augustine seems disposed to quote fairly enough from others in cases where we can check him.

[2] Servius, *Schol. in Aeneid.,* XI, 787: *ubique expugnator religionis.*

[3] Tertullian, *ad Nat.,* II, 1-2; Augustine, *Civ. Dei,* IV, 31-32; VI, 3-10; VII, 6, 9, 17, 23, 28.

[4] Augustine, *Civ. Dei,* IV, 31: *multa esse vera, quae non modo vulgo scire non sit utile, sed etiam, tametsi falsa sunt, aliter existimare populum expediat.*

him, as to Scaevola, useful when the end justified the means.[1]

If in the case of Varro and others we have been compelled to gather their opinions from unfriendly sources, in the case of Cicero we are on sure ground. The great number of his extant writings afford abundant material from which to determine his ideas. Furthermore, his character with all its defects, and indeed because of its defects, assists the historian. Lacking a commanding will; possessing a sensitive and susceptible temperament; keenly alive to the esteem and flattery of others; having a quick mind and facile tongue, coupled with poor judgment, which made indiscreet self-revelation easy and indeed inevitable, Cicero did not impose himself on his age and *milieu*, but rather was so deeply affected by them as to reflect them from many angles. A versatile interest in all things, a lack of originality and of strong principles, a nervous instability, a power of ready expression, a thin skin and a nimble wit form no doubt a poor equipment for a statesman, but are excellent possessions in a historical source.[2]

At first glance, Cicero's statements about religious matters seem to be in irreconcilable contradiction, and so indeed in one sense they are; but we get a clue to these inconsistencies when we observe that the quality of his assertions depends not upon what he himself thought about the subject; but upon the prepossessions of the persons whom he was addressing. He nowhere discriminates the three theologies as neatly as does Scaevola or

---

[1] Augustine, *Civ. Dei*, IV, 27; cf. III, 4: *sed utile esse civitatibus dicit, ut se viri fortes, etiamsi falsum sit, diis genitos esse credant.*

[2] Compare A. Bouché-Leclercq, *Leçons d'histoire romaine* (Paris, 1909), p. 61ff.

Varro, but better than that, he illustrates the three different attitudes of a Roman towards religion by his position and environment at the moment. In his orations and political treatises he speaks as a citizen devoted to the civic cult; in his philosophical treatises he is the student with mind attuned to the liberalizing Greek systems; in his letters, where, if he were sincerely religious, one would surely look for his inmost thoughts, he is the private man, beset with cares, and the subject of religion is absent from his attention altogether.[1]

No one could display a more becoming devotion to religion than Cicero generally does in his orations and political treatises. The conclusion of his *Verrines* is almost a catalogue of the gods, to so many of them does he appeal for aid in establishing justice, promoting truth, protecting Rome, and enhancing the orator's reputation for good faith.[2] The speeches against Catiline also abound in edifying sentiments of trust and confidence in Jupiter and the other gods. Who can deny, he asks, that Rome is governed by the immortal gods? They have sent aid, omens, and portents, and he calls upon the citizens to flock to their altars with prayers and thanksgivings. Yet gratitude to the gods should not exclude due appreciation of the great merits of the consul. He even hopes that "all the gods who preside over this city will give thanks to me in proportion to my deserts." [3] And after his re-

[1] Boissier, *op. cit.*, vol. I, p. 54ff. For tripartite division of religion see also Plutarch, *Amatorius*, 18. Eusebius (*Praeparatio Evangelica*, IV, 1) comments on this classification from the Christian point of view. *Cf.* Marquardt, *op. cit.*, p. 72ff.

[2] Cic., *in Verr.*, V, 72. This oration was never delivered but we may suppose that the conclusion is as if for delivery.

[3] *Cat.*, III, 8: *quamquam haec omnia, Quirites, ita sunt a me administrata, ut deorum immortalium nutu atque consilio et gesta et provisa esse videantur. Ibid.*, IV, 2: *nam primum debeo*

turn from exile he declares that it was divine Providence
which restored him to the Republic.[1]

As for himself, Cicero declares, he is not one of those
who delight to devote themselves to studies which alienate
the mind from religion, for who can lift his eyes to the
heavens and doubt that there are gods or fail to see that
it is they who have made Rome great: for it is piety and
faith in the divine rule over all things in which the
Romans surpass all other peoples. Such was the faith
handed down by their wise ancestors, and he is blind
who would deny it.[2] Cicero's profession of faith includes
a belief in omens and prodigies, augurs and haruspices,
auspices and sacrifices, the Sibylline Books, the games
and ceremonies, and exact ritual.[3] A law which imposed
some check on the practice of announcing the intention of
taking the auspices or the observation of bad omens for
the purpose of interfering with the business of the comitia
is denounced by him as destroying the republican constitution.[4] He was prepared to assert positively that the gods
are concerned with morality and decorum, and sometimes
afflict the wicked with madness, so that by their rash acts
they are brought to destruction.[5] Cicero's zeal in asserting
his orthodoxy, however, cools when his auditor is not
likely to be affected by it, and in the speeches he makes

---

*sperare, omnes deos, qui huic urbi praesident, pro eo mihi, ac
mereor, relaturos esse gratiam.* See also I, 13; II, 13; III, 9,
10, 12; IV, 1, 2, 9-11. In other speeches also he seems to turn
from the benevolence of the gods towards Rome to his own
beneficence. *Cf. pro Sulla,* 31; *pro Muraena,* 1; *pro Rabirio,* 1-2.

[1] *De Domo,* 55-56. *Cf. pro Sestio,* 69.
[2] *De Har. Resp.,* 9: *pro Milone,* 30-31.
[3] *De Domo,* 54; *de Har. Resp.,* 5, 10-15, 17, 25; *in Vatin.,* 8;
pro Milo., 30-31.
[4] *Pro Sest.,* 15, 26.
[5] *De Domo,* 41; *de Har. Resp.,* 16-18; *pro Milo.,* 31-33.

before Cæsar, who though Pontifex Maximus indulged
in no profession of faith in the conventional beliefs of the
people, there is no attempt, save in some common form
passages, to bring in the gods.[1]

In Cicero's treatise on the ideal state—a vision of Rome
as conceived by an Optimate—orthodox sentiments prevail. The immortal gods are the rulers of the universe
and supply men with souls and virtue, but the conception
of virtue is metaphysical rather than religious. The
punishment of sin seems to be confined to the reproaches
of one's conscience and the posthumous social reprobation
of the sinner.[2] A frugal piety, not involving much expense, is recommended. The state priests should superin-
tend all suitable religious cults, and private worship of
new or strange gods should be inadmissible.[3] The importance of the augurs is asserted and illustrated by
examples of their power to intervene effectively in political matters. In response to a direct question as to
whether divination is or is not a fraud, Cicero, himself an
augur, declares his sincere belief that a true art of divination is not impossible and has existed, but that there is no
doubt of its disappearance, owing to old age and neglect;
when it existed it was sometimes a political convenience
and often gave wise counsels; or, as he remarks elsewhere,
it furnished a plausible method for adjourning mischievous
comitial assemblies, adding smugly: "for it has often hap-

---

[1] *Pro Marcello*, 2-3, *passim; cf. pro Ligario; pro Rege Deiot.*
One may note also the freer use of the religious apparatus in the
Philippics addressed to the people than those addressed to the
Senate.

[2] *De Legibus*, I, 7, 8, 10-12, 18-19; II, 7-10, 17. In the case of
Clodius, however, the gods had shown greater activity in punishing sin. See *pro Milo.*, 31.

[3] *De Leg.*, II, 10-12.

pened that the immortal gods have suppressed by means
of auspices the unjust impetuosity of the people." [1]

This matter of divination was a very important part of
the official cult, and Cicero represents the pontiff Cotta as
declaring that the whole religion of the Roman people
consisted of sacrifices and auspices, to which have since
been added prediction from portents and prodigies explained by the Sibylline Books, or the haruspices. [2]   In
a treatise written near the end of his life, Cicero exposes
the various methods of divination to a brilliant and
mordant critique and repudiates them all.   He shows in
the first place that divination in general is an impossible
art. [3]   Then he passes on to haruspication which, he says,
"I believe the interest of the state and of common religion
requires to be upheld ;" but he finds no difficulty in proving
it to be utterly ridiculous, whether it be in the form of
inspection of entrails, or the interpretation of portents,
prodigies, or thunderbolts.   He denies flatly stories of the
miraculous. [4]   Divination by auspication, omens, or presages
fares no better, though he is an augur and is willing to
see those who flout the auspices fall into misfortune, since
they ought to be obedient to the established religion. [5]
The resort to drawing lots is mere luck, complicated by
trickery, [6] while astrology is insanity. [7]   The rejection of
oracles and prophecies by the Sibylline Books, and of
reading dreams closes the catalogue of superstitions, [8] and

[1] *Ibid.*, III, 12.   *Cf.* II, 12-13; *de Prov. Cons.,* 19.
[2] *De Nat. Deor.*, III, 2.   A. Bouché-Leclercq (*Histoire de la
divination dans l'antiquité*, vol. IV, p. 177) speaks of the augural
law as a "half of the Roman religion."
[3] *De Div.*, II, 3-11.   [4] *Id.*, II, 12-32.
[5] *Id.*, II, 33-40.   Cicero's reference to divination in one of his
letters (*ad Fam.*, VI, 6) seems to relate really to predictions
based on a careful consideration of the situation.
[6] *Id.*, II, 41.   [7] *Id.*, II, 42-47.   [8] Id., II, 48-57, 58-71.

the treatise ends with a clean-cut abandonment of divination as a "superstition which has extended itself through all nations and has depressed the intelligence of almost all men and filled their minds with imbecility." [1]

To arrive at a satisfactory estimate of just how much theistic belief was held by Cicero is an impossibility for us, as it probably would have been for Cicero himself. But since the purpose of our present inquiry is to determine the extent of his conscious insincerity, or subconscious inconsistency, it is not important to determine exactly what his religious opinions really were, or indeed if he had any at all; it is enough for us to establish the existence of such a state of disharmony in his ideas, or confusion in his thought, as to make clear his deficiencies in that accuracy and honesty which may properly affect our credence of his statements of fact.

The incongruities which appear in the cases cited are but samples of those which pervade all his writings. In his great treatise, *On the Nature of the Gods,* he attributes to Cotta, one of the interlocutors, the most destructive arguments against the gods and amplifies these arguments with such warmth and evident enjoyment as to justify us in taking them as expressions of his own opinion. [2] There as elsewhere in his writings, the popular, traditional religious beliefs are dismissed with a contumely which contrasts strikingly with his toleration of them in

[1] *Id.,* II, 72.

[2] At the beginning of the treatise (I, 3; *cf. Acad. Prior.,* II, 20) Cicero ranks himself with the Academics, and it is in the character of one of this philosophic school that Cotta carried on his criticism. It seems probable that Cicero was at least as sceptical as Cotta is represented to have been. This may be gathered from scattered indications: *e.g.,* his contempt for the pious credulity of the Stoics (*de Div.,* II, 41, 70-72) and of philosophers who prefer any absurdity rather than to behave with common sense

other places; but he ends his crushing critique of religious faith by exonerating himself from responsibility with a dry statement of his acquiescence in the arguments which he has just been triumphantly destroying.[1] Whatever Cicero may think about the various elements of Roman religion, however, he is clear that "it is the part of a wise man to uphold the religious institutions of our ancestors by the maintenance of their rites and ceremonies." [2] All the apparatus and pretenses of divination are, according to him, pitifully absurd, but they are to be upheld in the interest of religion and the state. Indeed, it was for the purpose of political manipulation that they were invented by the pious early Roman, and it is outrageous to object to this deceit.[3] Intellectual honesty is a pinnacle difficult for Cicero to scale, and impossible for him to occupy long at a time. It is characteristic of him that he should commend those who prefer to go wrong with Plato than right with other guides.[4]

But we have a better source of information about Cicero than his harangues to the crowd, or his essays for dabblers

---

(57-58); his sound views regarding discretion in the use of evidence (11); his atheistic ideas of the punishment of sinners (*de Leg.*, II, 17, 43-44); his distrust of authority as proof (*de Nat. Deor.*, I, 5), and insistence on reason (3); his praise of a frank admission that one does not know, where such is the fact (30; *de Off.*, I, 6). But the real nature of his beliefs, if he had any, need not detain us here.

[1] E.g., *de Nat. Deor.*, I, 2, 22; II, 2, 28 and III, *passim.* Cf. *Tusc. Disp.*, I, 5; Augustine (quoting Cicero), *Civ. Dei*, IV, 30; XXII, 6.

[2] *De Div.*, II, 72. The pragmatic argument for religion occurs frequently, *e.g.*, *de Leg.*, II, 7, 11; *de Nat. Deor.*, I, 2.

[3] *De Div.*, II, 12, 18, 33, 35, 38ff; *de Nat. Deor.*, I, 42; *pro Sest.*, 15, 26; *in Vat.*, 7; *de Prov. Cons.*, 19.

[4] *Tusc. Disp.*, I, 17.

in philosophy. The great collection of his correspondence with most of the leading men of the times gives us a real insight into his and their unpremeditated ideas such as is furnished by no other historical source of the period.[1] An examination of the letters will indicate that what bore the name of religion in the cultivated society of Rome at the end of the Republic was nothing which we can recognize by that name. There were philosophical speculations which formed a kind of intellectual gymnastic rivaling poetry as a form of entertainment; there were superstitions which furnished a large part of the subject matter of poetry, superstitions which interested the educated and frightened the ignorant, but which had hardly more relation to religion in our sense of the word than the myths of Jack the Giantkiller or Little Red Riding Hood. They assumed more importance than these diverting tales, however, by reason of their power over the vulgar and by their supposed explanation of many rites and ceremonies whose real character might be compared to a New Orleans Carnival or a London Lord Mayor's Show but whose performance was carried out with the meticulous deference to ancient forms observable in the coronation of a king of a long established monarchy. That there was anything more in religion than these elements, the letters of Cicero and his friends give us no indication.

In his old age Cicero had to endure two bitter griefs— the downfall of the Republic and the death of his beloved daughter Tullia in the flower of her young womanhood. As to the depth and sincerity of his devotion to both, no one can entertain a reasonable doubt. Furthermore, many

[1] *Cf.* Boissier, *Cicero and His Friends* (Eng. trans., New York, 1898), p. 1; E. Allain, *Pline le jeune et ses héritiers*, vol. II (Paris, 1902), pp. 364-382.

of Cicero's friends were dead or in exile as a result of the civil war, and he and Terentia, the wife of his youth, had become estranged, and there had been a divorce. The folly of his second marriage with his young ward had become apparent. In the shipwreck of everything dear to him, with the world turned to dust and ashes, the present full of sorrow, the future menacing and almost hopeless, he pours out his inmost thoughts in daily letters to his staunch, tried, and faithful friend Atticus, with whom there seems never to have been a shadow of reserve or doubt.[1] Here then we might expect to find expressions of his really profound sentiments on the fundamental aspects of human life; but in all the letters to Atticus and others, in the messages of condolence from friends and in his replies to them, we can find nothing to indicate the possession by Cicero of any vital belief.

In a philosophical treatise written about this time he sets forth a doctrine, based largely on Plato, of the immortality of the soul; but it can hardly be said that he gives very strong indications of being convinced by his own arguments.[2] When we read his letters of these months we find him distinctly and without qualification expressing the opinion that death is the end of all things, that if he ceases to live he will cease to have any sensation; and he refers sadly to that long long time when he will not exist.[3]

[1] The fact that the opinions of Atticus inclined towards Epicureanism would be no obstacle to Cicero's writing him on any topic that occurred to him, for their correspondence reveals unrestrained intimacy and freedom. The letters to Atticus during this period comprise most of those in Book XII from 12, and a number in Book XIII.

[2] *Tusc. Disp.*, I, 9, 10, 17, 21, 32, 34, 40.

[3] *Ad Fam.*, VI, 21: *cum omnium rerum mors sit extremum. Id.*, VI, 3: *si non ero, sensu omnino carbeo. Ad Att.*, XII, 18:

The gods seem far removed from his thoughts in the letters of the period. He evinces no desire to enter into relation with them, or to find comfort and support in their cult.[1] But if he found nothing in the existing religion to which he was drawn, he played for a time with an idea that brings to light a curious phase of his religious conceptions. The *De Natura Deorum* contains a passage purporting to be spoken by a Stoic, but possibly suggested to Cicero by his own thoughts during these months of mourning. The Stoic interlocutor, in speaking of superstition as the creator of fictitious and imaginary deities says:

> they who prayed and sacrificed for days that their children might survive them (*ut sibi sui liberi superstites essent*) were called superstitious (*superstitiosi*), which word was later given a more extended signification. . . . Thus are the words superstitious and religious understood, the one being a term of reproach (*vitii nomen*), the other of commendation.[2]

In the depth of his bereavement Cicero formed a project, based on suggestions in the books he was reading, to erect something in the nature of a shrine to his beloved

---

longumque illud tempus cum non ero. Cf. *ad Fam.,* V. 21, written a little earlier. In the letters from friends there is nothing save a faint phrase: *quod si qui etiam inferis sensus est, ad Fam.,* IV, 5. *Cf. id.,* V, 13, 14, 15; VI, 2, 21; IV, 6; V, 16. A letter written in October, 46, fully confirms the conclusion regarding his disbelief in divination. *Cf. ad Fam.,* VI, 6; Boissier, *op. cit.,* vol. I, pp. 58, 59.

[1] The same indifference occurs during the other period of great distress in Cicero's life—the months of exile. *Cf. ad Fam.,* XIV, 1-4. At all times his references to the gods are the casual conventional expressions with no more theological meaning than the analogous phrases in current use.

[2] *De Nat. Deor.,* II, 28.

daughter. His idea seems to have been to found a Tullia cult of his own. He wrote to Atticus that he wished to avoid having her memorial structure resemble a tomb, but desired it to be a fane, a shrine, in order to come as near as possible to an apotheosis. Many thoughts occur to him in favor of this, he remarks in another letter.[1] But before long the *vis medicatrix naturae* and the turmoil of the political situation seem to have banished the idea from his mind.

These letters, then, which clearly give us our best information as to Cicero's real ideas on religion, indicate that he believed in it hardly at all. They show, too, that the religion to which he publicly professed so much devotion really appeared to him to be little more than a valuable engine of political chicanery, valuable and even indispensable to the satisfactory working of existing political institutions. He accepted its use as legitimate even when it worked against his side. For instance, he stigmatized the Sibylline oracle regarding the restoration of the king of Egypt as a mere bit of trickery supported not by religious scruple but by malevolence, and declared that it was generally recognized as such. But he met trick by trick. If his opponents attempted certain moves in the popular assembly, he and his supporters were prepared to stop them by producing bad omens. On one occasion he suggested a way of evading the literal terms and clear intent of the oracle by a scheme which, he thought, would meet with general approval, but on condition that there should be no failures in the military operations.[2]

---

[1] *Ad Att.*, XII, 36: *fanum fieri volo . . . sepulcri similitudinem effugere non tam propter poenam legis studeo, quam ut maxime adsequar* ἀποθέωσιν. Cf. *id.*, 18, 19, 35, 37, and *passim* through the letters to Atticus written from March to June of this year.

[2] *Ad Fam.*, I, 1, 2, 4, 5b, 7.

Throughout the letters we find references to tricks calculated to prevent the orderly conduct of government by playing upon the timid conservatism and sodden superstition of the crowd,[1] until we may well wonder how the Republic could have lasted so long as it did. Cicero was of course annoyed when these tricks were worked to his disadvantage; but what especially exasperated him was the refusal of his opponents to be bound by religious jugglery, or the attempt to impose legal limitation on their use in party politics. This was not playing the game according to the rules and was destructive of the constitution.[2] Of the existence of any sentiments against the legitimacy of skilful resort to fraud for accomplishing political aims, we find no trace in the writings of Cicero or in other literary sources of the times; on the contrary, as will appear in the next chapter, its use had been legalized in many respects as part of the *ius divinum,* and had become a recognized method of attaining desired ends with divine approval and human toleration.

Such religious conceptions as we have been examining will seem less extraordinary if we observe that the divine character, according to Roman ideas, was not composed of those superlative qualities which we are accustomed to bestow upon it or recognize as naturally inherent therein. The gods of Rome had not got far enough away from their source to have lost their resemblance to it; they retained many of the characteristics of the *populus Romanus.* They had the same lack of distinct individuality as the Romans of the earlier days, the same mediocre intelligence and very moderate morality, the same careful regard for exactness of form and indif-

[1] *Ad Att.,* IV, 3, 9, 16; *ad Q. Frat.,* II, 3, 4, *et passim.*
[2] *Pro Sest.,* 15, 26; *in Vat.,* 9; *Red. in Sen.,* 5 and notes p. 159.

ference to content.[1]   Their conception of virtue was
strictly legal in character: they were what is known in our
times as "law-honest."   What is of special interest is that
both gods and men seemed to regard the false, if told
in due and proper form, as in some way equivalent to the
true.   They would not have deemed novel the doctrine
which has been enthusiastically declared of late years as
a new discovery of the pragmatists: "truth is that which
works well."

We accordingly find that the Romans treated their gods
in much the same fashion as they treated one another, although the great powers of the immortals naturally induced mortals to proceed with caution.   The various
narratives we have of the relations of early Romans with
their gods are hardly scientific data, but are not on that
account without considerable value as indicating what
later generations conceived them to have been.   It is in
this way that writings wholly false as regards the matters
with which they purport to deal, are often more valuable,
if they are properly used, than those which are partly
true: the subjective elements, whether in the writer or his
sources, are less distorted by the intrusion of elements,
often beyond identification, of objective fact.

The easy-going irreverence of the Romans towards
those gods whose existence they assumed is worth noticing
as bearing upon the lack of religious scrupulosity, in all
but matters of form, which we have been considering, and
as indicating the training in mental confusion and disingenuousness which resulted from the disharmony between
the various classes of half-beliefs which they at once held
and discredited; while no doubt nearly all the stories

[1] Compare Wissowa, *Religion u. Kultus* (*zweite Aufl.*), p. 23ff;
C. W. L. Launspach, *State and Family in Early Rome* (London,
1908), pp. 78-80.

about the gods are foreign importations into Roman religious thought, still they were well enough established by
the period from which our literary material comes to
enable us to treat them as representing an aspect of ideas
then current.

Livy speaks reverently of the divinized Romulus as "a
god and son of a god," but follows with the suggestion
that perhaps Rhea, his virgin mother, implicated Mars in
the scandal to ennoble her lapse from a Vestal's vows.[1]
Other writers do not refrain from guesses at his human
paternity, and Ovid narrates with gusto certain details of
Mars' connection with the affair.[2]   When Livy describes
Romulus's ascension to heaven, he adds that some suspected assassination as the true cause for his disappearance
from earth; and after the theophany, resting on the unsupported testimony of Proculus Iulius, the historian
marvels that so much credence was given to the narrator
of the miracle.[3]   The divinity of Romulus seems to have
been less strongly believed than professed.

Numa was the pious and virtuous king whom the Romans revered, ostensibly, as the inspired founder of many
of their institutions; but his relations with the divine
powers, as handed down to memory, could hardly have
inspired serious belief or reverence for truth in thought-
ful men.   Seeing that his subjects ill endured the unaccustomed tranquillity of his reign, the pacific king deemed
it desirable to implant in them a fear of the gods.[4]   To
this end, so we are told, he resorted to the fiction of a
miracle and feigned to have nightly interviews with the
nymph Egeria.   At her suggestion he drew Jupiter down

[1] Livy, I, 4.
[2] *Fasti*, III, 9ff; II, 492ff; Plut., *Rom.*, 3, 4, 27, 28; *Numa*, 2.
Cicero seems rather ironical, *de Rep.*, II, 10.
[3] Livy, I, 16.   [4] Livy, I, 19.

from heaven by means of a magical spell taught him by Picus and Faunus, two coadjutors whose aid he obtained by intoxicating them and then keeping them strongly bound until they revealed the constraining incantation. This done, the king of the gods appeared, majestically angry, to Numa who stood firm and demanded knowledge of the approved expiations to avert the portents of lightning.

Jupiter begins, "cut off a head." To which Numa, deftly turning aside the suggestion of human sacrifice, hastily adds, "of an onion." The god to correct this mitigation, rejoins, "of a man," but Numa cleverly affixes "the hair." Jupiter, still intent on his savage formula, demands "a life;" to which the crafty king appends, "of a fish." At this continued display of nimble wit, Jupiter is so pleased that his sternness passes; he laughs and, lest he be again out-juggled, lets the recipe stand with Numa's qualifying addenda. Accordingly, the portent of thunder and lightning was thereafter charmed away by the peculiar mixture of onions, hair, and pilchards. Indeed, according to some, Jupiter continued so well pleased with the king's ingenuity at repartee that upon further reflection he sent from heaven a shield of celestial workmanship. No doubt those who told this story proved it by pointing to the shield.[1]

The Christian controversialists delighted in extracting from pagan books stories like that of Numa and Jupiter in the mistaken idea that they represented the beliefs of their adversaries, and with the design of giving their co-

---

[1] Livy, I, 19; Ovid, *Fasti*, II, 285ff; Plut., *Numa*, 15; Valerius Antias, quoted by Arnobius, *adv. Gent.*, V, 1; Dion. Hal., II, 60. That the story is probably a late invention does not affect its value as evidence, not of course of early beliefs, but of the attitude of men of the first century B.C. towards the gods.

religionists a pleasing thrill from such disclosures of
heathen irreverence. But probably few of the educated
Romans gave them the least credit, although they continued telling them for various reasons. Indeed, it is
probable that the Christian writers had more belief in the
myths about the old gods, whom most of them regarded
as existing dæmons, than did most of their nominal worshippers. Plutarch is on solid ground when in closing his
narrative of Numa's interviews, he says: "these ridiculous
legends show the way the people had become accustomed
to regard the gods." [1]

Roman confidence in the easy-going good nature of the
gods might well be fortified by the remarkable tolerance
with which the deities view freedom of language or boldness of conduct towards themselves. M. Boissier suggests that perhaps the political liberty of the Romans had
given them a sense of their own importance in the presence
of the gods and hence they dared even jest with them.[2]
If so, the effect of political liberty was similar to that
which Kipling observed when he sketched the typical citizen of a modern Republic in the words:

> "Enslaved, illogical, elate,
>   He greets th' embarrassed Gods, nor fears
> To shake the iron hand of Fate
>   Or match with Destiny for beers." [3]

Something of the sort might have been said of the Romans in view of Numa's tricking Picus and Faunus into
inebriety, or of Jupiter's apparent embarrassment, carried
off with a laugh, when the king had worsted him in re-

[1] *Numa*, 15. *Cf.* Lucilius, *Sat.*, XV; Livy I, 19-21; Dion. Hal.,
disapproves of those who flout these stories, II, 60-61.
[2] Boissier, *op. cit.*, vol. I, pp. 26-27.
[3] *An American.*

partee, or of a consul's careless assurance in offering
Jupiter a cup of wine and honey.[1] It may be doubted
whether the modern republican who, for literary purposes
at least, excited Kipling's aversion, could quite match the
unbecoming familiarity of the priest of Hercules who is
said to have played dice with his divinity for the stakes of
a bountiful feast and a fair woman. The priest lost and
duly produced the stakes in the temple. The winner expressed so much satisfaction with the manner in which
both parts of the wager were paid, albeit one part of it
was a somewhat damaged article, that he found a wealthy
and elderly husband for Acca Larentia, and as a result a
handsome legacy was later left to the Roman people.
Through this benefaction the Roman pantheon was en-
riched by a new divinity with an annual festival.[2]

[1] Livy, X, 42.
[2] Macrobius, *Sat.*, I, X, 12ff; Plutarch, *Rom.*, 5; *id., Rom.
Quaest.*, 35; Aulus Gellius, VI, 7.

CHAPTER X

RELIGIOUS PRACTICES

THE examination, in the preceding chapter, of the opinions held, or reported to have been held, by representative members of the classes which produced most of our historical sources, furnishes evidence of the existence of a noticeable spirit of confusion and disingenuousness in the domain of Roman religious thought. It is obvious, as has been remarked, that such defects in one phase of the intellectual life, would suggest the need for caution in accepting statements from such a source on any other subject where a motive for misstatement or an opportunity for inaccuracy might reasonably be presumed to exist. But the amount of material which affords explicit declaration of religious belief is after all comparatively meagre, until we reach the prodigally exuberant subjective material of the later religious development. It is therefore necessary to try another method of approach: that is, to endeavor to ascertain the prevalent beliefs and feelings of the classes in question through an examination of their overt acts.

This indirect mode of proof by inferring a man's beliefs from his conduct is more satisfactory than to rely on his direct statements. Words may be marrowless things, somewhat like paper money with no redemption fund be-

hind, and they not only frequently mislead the hearer but
also often dupe the speaker himself. From their use we
frequently get the delusion that we believe, when in
reality we merely believe that we believe; for we do not
ourselves know our beliefs until we have seen how we act
when an occasion arises.[1] Thought and feeling exist as
parts of one complex process whose end is action: they
are but prefatory and accessory to it, and when the ap-
propriate act does not follow, this failure, if not otherwise explained, casts grave doubts on the existence, or
at any rate on the strength and distinctness of the supposed antecedent states.[2] Action being nothing but the
belief objectified, what we call acts inspired by it are not
so much its effects as constituent parts of it, furnishing us
a concrete definition and visible criterion of its value,
reality, and sincerity—the fruit by which the tree is
judged. When an idea is attended by acts congruous
thereto, then and then only can we be said to believe in
it. Indeed, the belief often seems to be subsequent to the
acts and to be built up by them.[3]

We are then encouraged to hope that an examination
of the conduct of the Roman governing and literary classes
in matters involving probity, truthfulness, and good faith,
in connection with the proposition that the gods were made

[1] Cf. E. Tassy, Journal de psychologie normale et pathologique,
1907, p. 195. H. Spencer, Principles of Biology, vol. I, section
112.

[2] See A. Fouillée, Tempérament et caractère (Paris, 1895),
p. 186; W. James, Principles of Psychology, vol. II, pp. 314, 522ff;
J. M. Baldwin, Social and Ethical Interpretations in Mental
Development (New York, 1897), pp. 91-96; J. H. Leuba, Monist,
vol. XI (1901), p. 212.

[3] Compare James, op. cit., p. 311; Baldwin, op. cit., pp. 92, 97:
"What we do is always a function of what we think;" "what
we shall think is a function of what we have done."

in the image of their worshippers and that religious ideas expressed the general states of mind of those who held them, will enable us to understand the workings of their minds.

. The student of the religious history of mankind will find an abundance of highly irrational and contradictory ideas and practices forming a part of various faiths, but in most cases these occur in communities of primitive culture; or, as in the case of the Greeks, they are so intermingled with poetry and drama as to form a part of the æsthetic heritage of the people. Again, they may be held as part of a mystical system which is professedly out of relation to rationality; often they are based on what are believed to be definite, divine revelations, and sometimes they are only nominally accepted and their unreal character is shown by the fact that they are not acted upon. But the case of the Romans, at least of the last two centuries of the Republic, was not that of barbarians, nor mystics, nor persons impassioned over the beautiful; nor did they claim a definite revelation as a basis for most of their vagaries; nor were their irrationalities merely played with as phantoms of faith. On the contrary, they were distinctly, regularly, and unhesitatingly practiced in every-day life. Whether or not they should be regarded as properly explicable by the hypothesis of conscious fraud utilizing for secular profit the sedulously stimulated credulity of the masses is not really important; since whatever their foundation and essential nature, they indicate such a degree of mental confusion, or moral obliquity, or both, as to impair our confidence in the power or the inclination of the Romans to speak and act with habitual straightforwardness. This will appear more clearly from a glance at the official systems of divination,—that part of their religion which more than any other preserved some life and was regularly practiced in the later days of the Republic.

Nearly every important act of Roman public life had to be prefaced by a demand for some manifestation of divine approval regarding the intended proceeding. In taking the auspices the Romans did not ask to have the future disclosed to them, nor to be vouchsafed some miraculous assistance; they did not deny the uniformity of natural law, but requested the gods to intimate whether or not their suppliants had by unaided reason formulated an objectionable plan, whether or not the gods felt at the moment of inquiry inclined to oppose the project. If the auspices were unfavorable the Romans generally postponed action until either they or the gods changed their minds.[1]

The right to inquire directly as to the divine attitude was vested in the magistrates and not in the priests; but the augurs, a kind of religious jurisconsults, were at the service of the civil or military official to tender him advice at his request as to the *modus operandi* of the inquiry and as to the meaning of the signs. The divine replies to the magistrates were indicated in forms that might need interpretation, for they were such things as the flight or the feeding of birds, the motions and sounds of quadrupeds, or the more imposing manifestations of thunder and lightning. The gods, however, might intimate their objections by making signs on their own initiative, and these omens might be observed and brought to the attention of the magistrate by any one—a magistrate, an augur, or even a private citizen.

Besides these methods of divination, there was the art of the haruspices, an Etruscan method of extracting valu-

[1] Compare Cicero, *de Div.*, II, 33; A Bouché-Leclereq, *Histoire de la divination*, vol. IV, p. 176; A. H. J. Greenidge, *Roman Public Life* (London, 1901), p. 36; Wissowa, *op. cit.*, p. 523ff.

able information from an inspection of the entrails of slaughtered animals, or other portents and prodigies. In times of unusual calamity, especially earthquake and pestilence, the fears of the people were allayed by expiatory rites suggested to the officials in charge by a consultation of the carefully concealed Sibylline Books, from which some vague sentence, properly construed, was supposed to ensure the requisite panacea.

The argument in favor of divination was that the gods exist and are essentially benevolent and philanthropic; that they cannot be ignorant of events, since these take place by their direction, that knowledge of the future is serviceable to mankind and the gods are able to give men needful information and the power to understand their intimations; and finally that the experience of all nations proves its existence.[1] But if the laws for ascertaining and understanding these intimations had been the expression of a sincere faith on the part of honest men, it seems hardly possible for them to have accepted the probability that conflicting and contradictory messages would at one and the same time come from the celestial to the human sphere unless confusion were prevented by human arrangements depriving Omniscience of more than one conduit for its sacred suggestions. Yet we find it to be a fact that when a higher magistrate had set a day for an assembly, he forbade all inferiors to receive messages from the gods, or even to watch the sky for any purpose on that day, lest some unfavorable omen be seen by them. Sometimes the Senate, when it felt an interest in the adoption of some measure, ventured to forbid all magistrates to receive and announce unfavorable omens.[2] The principles of the law

[1] Cic., de Div., I, 5, 6, 38ff.
[2] See G. W. Botsford, The Roman Assemblies (New York, 1909), p. 114; Bouché-Leclercq, op. cit., vol. IV, p. 218ff.

regarding divination recognized that in the course of the same observation there would sometimes be several opposing presages, and the prescribed ritual contained rules for solving this divine confusion and unholy awkwardness. The simplest one was that the person taking the auspices might determine the precise moment for recognizing the communication, excluding all preceding and following contradictions.[1]

But there were other troublesome changes of mind by these capricious divinities as they were represented in augural science and law. After favorable auspices had been obtained, it was still necessary to guard against sudden withdrawal of divine approval. At any moment some warning omen might be sent which compelled a suspension of business, or, in Cicero's language, the immortal gods sometimes furnished a plausible method for adjourning useless and mischievous assemblies. An attack of epilepsy, a clap of thunder, a drop of rain, might manifest the desire of the gods, or at any rate of the presiding magistrate, that the assembly adjourn. The wishes of the gods seemed in their changes to synchronize remarkably with those of the consul who presided over the meeting.[2]

Indeed, so far were the Romans from believing that these warnings really came from the gods, so perfectly well was it understood by all but the ignorant crowd that

[1] Bouché-Leclercq, *id.*, pp. 201-202, with numerous citations.

[2] *Ibid.*, pp. 251-252. In the determination of the future by the inspection of entrails, the magistrate need not be cast down by the divine disapproval of a project which he had at heart. Aemilius Paullus, "very devout and learned in sacrifices" was not discouraged in failing to find satisfactory indications in twenty oxen. At the twenty-first the god concurred in the consul's opinion. *Cf.* Plutarch, *Aem. Paul.*, 17; Livy, XLI, 14-15; Bouché-Leclercq, *op. cit.*, vol. IV, pp. 71-72.

the magistrate was the fabricator of the omen, that when one announced his intention of watching the sky on a certain day, this mere declaration made it contrary to divine law for any public business to be brought before the popular assemblies. The consul Bibulus was strictly within the letter of the law when he sought to stop all legislation during the year by announcing that he proposed to remain at home and continually to watch the sky; but this was carrying things to an absurdity, and Cæsar was too determined a man to tolerate so much orthodoxy, and was strong enough with the people to overcome their timidity.[1]

Equally persuasive, perhaps, in showing the unreality of their professions of religious faith is the illuminating fact that invented reports of presages, false statements as to events which never happened at all, or took place in a way absolutely contrary to that stated, had the same efficacy as presages really observed and truthfully reported; and this by the mere fact of their announcement—"a word is a bird." [2] The voice of the augur, even mendaciously declaring the existence of the divine message, appears to have taken the place of any other sign.[3] This belief in

[1] Suet., *Jul.*, 20; Cic., *de Domo*, 15; *de Har. Resp.*, 23; *Prov. Cons.*, 19; *ad Att.*, II, 16; Cass. Dio, XXXVIII, 4. *Cf.* Botsford, *op. cit.*, p. 115; Bouché-Leclercq, *op. cit.*, vol. IV, p. 257ff; Greenidge, *op. cit.*, pp. 172-173. On assuming office, the new consul first took the auspices. These were always favorable: lightning was always announced as appearing on the left. *Cf.* Greenidge, *op. cit.*, p. 196. There was a curious doctrine in this legal fiction that the same presage, obtained by one magistrate (*impetrativa*) and favorable to the work he had in hand, might as a warning omen (*oblativa*) be unfavorable to another magistrate. *Cf.* Botsford, *op. cit.*, p. 112.

[2] Aristophanes, *Aves*, 720.

[3] Bouché-Leclercq, *op. cit.*, vol. IV, pp. 138, 174, 202, 208, 210.

the intrinsic efficacy of words, even words which were in flat contradiction to the event which they purported to describe, is so delirious a confusion of the true and the false as to seem the product of minds fundamentally and hopelessly destitute of any feeling for veracity; yet it appears to have been the regular practice of the Romans from early times, and was very appropriately called *mentiri* or *ementiri auspicia*.[1]

Livy tells of a case in 293 B.C. when the chickens, from whose manner of feeding the divine will was ascertained, had in fact refused food but the keeper reported them as eating greedily (*tripudium solistimum*). This favorable presage was reported to the consul Papirius who announced that the auspices were excellent and the gods favorable and gave the signal for battle. His nephew, whom Livy piously commends as born "before men had learned to scorn the gods," heard that the report about the birds was false and hastened to inform his uncle; but owing to the latter's "firmness of mind" which did not suffer him to be diverted by any dispute about the auspices, the youth was told that the report was enough to make the auspices favorable, and that its falsity was simply a matter between the gods and the keeper. When the unfortunate *pullarius* was killed in battle among the first, the consul declared the event was quite as it should be. In the end, the Romans prevailed; the battle was won. Thus, says Livy, did the gods conduct the auspices to a favorable issue, being pleased by the consul's promise to offer Jupiter, if all went well, a cup of wine and honey before drinking any himself.[2] Two hundred and fifty years later the same convenient practice continued. "Do you suppose," asks Cicero, the augur, "that those who take

[1] *Cf.* Livy, X, 40; Cic., *de Div.*, I, 16.
[2] Livy, X, 40.

the auspices look for presages themselves? They give orders to the *pullarius;* he makes the report." [1]

Sometimes even the services of a subordinate were not required, or perhaps the urgency of the need for "suppressing the unjust impetuosity of the mob" did not allow time for summoning assistance, and the presiding magistrate had to recognize the divine change of mind. Pompey the Great was once holding a meeting for the election of praetors. He thought that sufficient bribe-money had been distributed and was carefully watching the polling to see the voters "stayed bought." But there was a strong popular movement to elect Cato, whom the consuls greatly detested; the first tribe had already voted for him when Pompey suddenly heard a clap of thunder, quite inaudible to the others present, and dissolved the assembly.

Thereafter [says Plutarch], by employing excessive bribery and driving the best people from the Campus they (Pompey and Crassus) brought it about by violence that Vatinius should be elected praetor instead of Cato.[2]

In view of the liberal rules of divination by which a magistrate could pick and choose among the presages seen and even use false reports with as much efficacy as if the report were true, it is not always easy to draw the line between legitimate selection of the divine message and

[1] Cic., *de Div.*, II, 35. Compare I, 16 for the curious argument as to the effect of the announcement of presages made to Crassus on his departure for the fatal Parthian campaign. Ateius, who had dealt out the imprecations, seems to have been punished for the injury he had done Rome by his false statements. *Cf.* Plut., *Crassus*, 16; Cass. Dio, XXXIX, 39.

[2] Plut., *Cato Minor*, 42; *Pomp.*, 52. *Cf.* Cic., *de Div.*, II, 24; Plut., *Pomp.*, 75. Professor Oman seems to be unduly impressed by Pompey's honesty; compare *Seven Roman Statesmen* (London, 1902), p. 236.

what might fairly be considered inadmissible fraud; but it would seem that Pompey's thunder must have been near the line. Yet we may observe that there was rarely any open complaint of the unreality of the signs alleged to have happened. As all the leading men participated in these convenient practices we may suppose that a kind of political etiquette forbade such an attitude as would impair the reverence of the crowd for the mysterious ways in which the gods made known their will to men. Occasionally, of course, exasperation broke the bonds of etiquette and charges of deceit were publicly hurled. Even in the fourth century B.C. we get indications that the customary solemn swindles were sometimes hotly resented.[1]

In the desperate conflict which Cicero waged against Antony after Cæsar's death, he did indeed propose to make in the Senate the charge that Antony falsified the auspices, though this oration was in fact never delivered. His intended argument however is curious; he declares that Antony, who was both consul and augur, had months before declared his intention, in his capacity as augur, to prevent or to annul by means of auspices a certain proposed election. But, says Cicero, he could have done this more easily as consul, for in his latter capacity he had the right to observe the heavens, while augurs may only make announcements; and no one but he who determines to observe the heavens—and has the right as a magistrate so to do, we may understand—can foresee what defect there will be in the auspices.[2] We need not delay over the other defects in Antony's conduct or Cicero's argument. What is of interest for our present inquiry is that Cicero's posi-

---

[1] See Livy, VIII, 23.

[2] Cic., *Phil.*, II, 32-33, 45: *quisquamne divinare potest quid viti in auspiciis futurum sit, nisi qui de caelo servare constituit. Cf.* Bouché-Leclercq, *op. cit.*, vol. IV, p. 259, note 2.

tion in the passage cited seemed to be based upon the doctrine that a consul knows, or may know, in advance, what presages his observation of the heavens is going to disclose. In other words, the results of this observation depend not upon signs sent by the gods, but upon a pre-existing determination in the magistrate who takes the auspices. Briefly, the whole proceeding is a fraud and known to be such.

This fact seems rather startling but it is quite in line with the theory upon which another class of practices concerning omens was based. It was held that an omen had no value or efficacy independent of the will of him who observed it, for it was the acceptance and interpretation or application by the observer that in fact created the omen. Pliny the Elder correctly summarizes this doctrine in saying that

> the efficacy of presages is in our own hands and they operate according to the way in which they are received. At all events, it is a principle of augural law that neither evil omens nor presages of any kind have any effect upon those who, when entering upon an undertaking, declare that they will pay no attention to them: there is no more striking instance of the divine complaisance.[1]

After the external event had been accepted and applied by human will and intelligence to some work in hand, then indeed it became a real omen, but what gave it life was the human element. Roman history is full of cases of ingenious or far-fetched and childish applications of chance words or trivial actions to some matter utterly foreign to them, or of magistrates going in closed litters

[1] Pliny, *N. H.*, XXVIII, 17; Servius, *ad Aeneid.*, XII, 259; V, 530.

to avoid seeing anything of a sort which they might be
expected to interpret as a warning.[1] With a startling
lapse from pure rationality, Cicero, who had just
before flatly denied divination, criticised this judicious
blindness as an attempt to avoid the admonitions of
Jupiter.[2]

The doctrine as to the control exercised by the recipient
of the omen may be thought to proceed on the theory that
the sign was a sort of wager offered by the gods which
could be declined, or whose conditions could be modified,
so that the gods were bound by the response. Some such
idea seems to have been in Plutarch's mind.[3] But probably
it was merely a form of the widespread belief in the magical effect of formulæ, of the spoken word—that *logos*
which so haunted and confused ancient thought.[4] At
all events, the controlling element, the word, was of human rather than divine origin.

With all these strictly legal methods of managing the
expression of the divine will, it was not often that anything really illegal needed to be done by the skilful statesman. The chickens might be kept on very short rations
to affect their mode of feeding so that favorable auspices
could be forced, and there seems to have been no legal

[1] Compare *e.g*, Livy, I, 7; V, 55; IX, 14; XXIX, 27; Virgil,
Aeneid, V, 530; XII, 260; Cic., *de Div.*, I, 46; II, 36, 40.

[2] Cic., *de Div.*, II, 36. *Cf. id.*, 40. In 35 he asks: *quis negat
augurum disciplinam esse? divinationem nego.* At the end of
the chapter he asserts that the augural law is maintained for
political purposes. *Existimoque ius augurum, etsi divinationis
opinione principio constitutum sit, tamen postea rei publicae causa
conservatum ac retentum.*

[3] *Numa*, 14, 15.

[4] Pliny, *N. H.*, XXVIII, 10ff, has preserved some interesting
material on the subject. In general, see the excellent treatment
by Bouché-Leclercq, *op. cit.*, vol. IV, pp. 135-144.

objection to this.[1]   Sometimes a popular leader was troublesome and accused the Senate of juggling him into a false position.[2]   Once indeed they made a slip by reason of their error in thinking that Antony, the presiding magistrate at a comitial assembly, would coöperate with them; but his views had changed and hence he refused to accept the statement that the celestial signs were unfavorable, and went on with the meeting.[3]   But the elasticity of the religious law, and the "divine complaisance" rendered recourse to strictly illegal action unnecessary and uncommon.

While the Romans, as has been said, laid great emphasis on an exact and literal performance of engagements, where there was nothing else to be done but pay, they were not averse to convenient modifications.   Now gods have rarely been inclined to waive their established rights, but those of Rome were represented as being easily managed in this as in most other respects.   When there was a shortage of milk-white bulls, it was decided that Jupiter would not see any difference if red bulls colored white with chalk were offered instead, and if a solemnity must be celebrated at some particular place, the gods were thought not to notice anything wrong if an altogether different place were chosen, but called by the correct name.[4]   Such instances of substitution afford another illustration of the controlling power of the word over the fact.   This general principle runs through much of Roman cult, and the doctrine is said by a late writer to be that in matters of religion the counterfeit is to be accepted as real: *in sacris simulata pro veris accipi,* whence it follows that where beasts for

---

[1] Cic., *de Div.,* I, 15; II, 34, 35.

[2] *E.g.,* Flaminius, Livy, XXI, 63; XXII, 1, 3, 9; Plut., *Marcellus,* 4-5.

[3] Appian, *B. C.,* III, 1, 7.   [4] Serv., *ad Aen.,* IX, 52.

sacrifice are difficult to find, they may be made of bread
or wax and offered in place of the actual animals.[1]

This principle of the substitution of the false in place
of the true, and their equivalence, whose comprehensive
sway in Roman life and letters has been engaging our
attention, was not confined in the religious field to things
alone but extended also to persons, when the operation
would relieve one of the directing classes from destruction.
By the rite of *devotio* a Roman general, before seeking
death in the thick of the fight, presented to the appro-
priate deities the enemy together with himself as a sacrifice, in consideration of which the gods were to help the
Romans and destroy their adversaries. This impressive
ceremonial is said to have been performed more than
once in the earlier days.[2] But when it was better understood that the gods were equally well pleased with a sub-
stitute, we find it held lawful for the general "to devote
not himself personally, but whatever citizen he might
select out of a regular Roman legion."[3] With the growing comprehension of the possibilities of extension of the
principle underlying vicarious offerings, together with
an increase in power of the common people, who probably
were not altogether pleased with this form of human
sacrifice, we find that at the siege of Carthage the general
devotes to the infernal gods on behalf of Rome, not himself
nor one of his soldiers, but simply the hostile forces, together with their country, as substitutes: *eosque vicarios
pro me . . . pro populo Romano, exercitibus, legioni-*

[1] Serv., *ad Aen.*, II, 116: *sciendum in sacris simulata pro veris
accipi: unde cum de animalibus quae difficile inveniuntur est
sacrificandum, de pane vel cera fiunt et pro veris accipiuntur.*

[2] Livy, VIII, 9-10; X, 28-29; VII, 6; Cic., *de Nat. Deor.*,
II, 3; III, 6; Fowler, *Religious Experience of the Roman People*,
pp. 206-209; Wissowa, *op. cit.*, p. 384.

[3] Livy, VIII, 10; Cic., *de Nat. Deor.*, II, 10.

busque nostris do devoveo.[1]   By this convenient method
the Romans got rid of the enemy and the gods took them
over as offerings in behalf of Rome.   This seems highly
ingenious, convenient, and inexpensive—"a new way to
pay old debts."   As an afterthought, a suggestion is made
in guarded terms of three black sheep in addition to the
enemy.   Frugality to the gods was highly esteemed at
Rome, and Cicero, for instance, approves the cultivation of
piety—but not expensive piety.[2]

   The implication of the doctrines we have been considering and the general ease of manipulation of the gods by
very transparent tricks, suggest to us that the character
embodied and typified in these divinities had certain intellectual peculiarities which we regret to see held in honor
by those who form our historical authorities; for whether
or not it be a sound principle that "in religion the counterfeit is to be accepted as the real," we cannot be satisfied
with it in historical studies.   Furthermore, to the intellectual defects of these Roman deities there were joined
equally loose moral qualities.   Passing by the sending of
misleading presages, it appears in the ceremony of *evoca-
tio* that the Romans regarded these divine beings as amenable to bribes and not beyond being tempted to betray
every obligation to those who trusted them, where such
treachery seemed to promote their own convenience or
prosperity.   So convinced were the Romans of this being
their character, that now and then from early times, when
a city was besieged, the attacking general made a formal
offer to the tutelary gods of the enemy that if they would
betray their people, desert them, and take up their residence at Rome, the Romans would build them temples,
establish games in their honor and otherwise procure them

[1] Macrobius, *Sat.*, III, 9, 10, referring to the siege of Carthage.
[2] Cic., *de Leg.*, II, 10, 18.

personal satisfactions. We read in Livy of the Roman success in luring away the protecting divinity of Veii, and of the temple built at Rome in payment of the bribe.[1] Macrobius preserves the formula used at the siege of Carthage in which the tutelary deity is requested to desert that city, to inspire its people with terror, and to come to Rome where temples and games were promised. And a passage of Virgil is quoted to show his acquaintance with this divine characteristic.[2]

But it may be thought that only foreign gods were deemed capable of this violation of the duty of limitless devotion to the Fatherland, the virtue perhaps most highly esteemed in ancient ethics. Not so: the Roman gods themselves were considered liable to commit such treason. Hence with childish cunning the Romans kept both the sacred name of the city and the name of its special tutelary deity profoundly secret, lest any enemies might by due proceedings induce this divine protector to abandon the city.[3] Even if such were not the original reason for this concealment, it is significant that the later Romans found nothing improbable in such an explanation. It is evident in any case that they attributed no very high degree of probity to the gods made in their own image.

To attend to the cult or interpret the communications of the deities whose characters betrayed grave deficiencies obviously required no high degree of intelligence or morality. A priest need not possess any particular belief

[1] Livy, V, 21-23.

[2] Macrobius, *Sat.*, III, 9, 10-12; Virgil, *Aeneid*, II, 326; Bouché-Leclercq, *Les Pontifes de l'ancienne Rome*, pp. 163-165; Wissowa, *op. cit.*, p. 385.

[3] Pliny, *N. H.*, III, 65; XXVIII, 18; Plut., *Rom. Quaest.*, LXI; Serv., *ad Aen.*, II, 351. A revelation of the name of Rome by Valerius Soranus was punished, Solinus says (1, 5), by death. Plutarch offers an improbable alternative explanation of this secrecy.

regarding the divinities at whose worship he presided, or whose messages he declared; **nor** was he required to display in his character or conduct any of that gravity or probity which has ordinarily been deemed becoming in the sacerdotal office. Religious services might be the offering of sacrifice, a matter purely of ritual, or feasts, games, or festivals.[1] In none of these need there have been, nor was there, any more concern about the pontiff's theology or morals than there is now about an undertaker's views on the immortality of the soul.

So we read of an idle and debauched youth made *Flamen Dialis,* apparently with a view to his reform, inasmuch as one of the taboos on this *flamen* forbade him to pass a night out of his own house.[2] Because of this or some other reason, the office is said to have had an excellent effect on the incumbent's conduct. This moralizing influence was not however always easily applied. L. Cornelius Dolabella, selected for the office of *rex sacrorum* in 180 B.C., was unwilling to accept ordination at the cost of resigning a secular office held by him, and with a skilful use of the means put at his disposal by religion, he succeeded in obtaining an unfavorable omen from heaven at the critical moment.[3] Mere youths were sometimes chosen priests,[4] and neither his Epicurean scepticism nor his irregular private life was a bar to the elevation of the young Julius Cæsar to the position of Pontifex Maximus;[5] nor did Cicero's flat denial of divination seem incompatible with his office of augur, or official interpreter of the divine science whose very existence he denied.[6]

Actual conviction and banishment for crime might cost

---

[1] Macrobius, *Sat.,* I, 16, 4.
[2] Livy, XXVII, 8; Val. Max., VI, 9, 3.
[3] Livy, XL, 42.   [4] Livy, *ibid.*
[5] *Cf.* Ferrero, *Greatness and Decline of Rome,* vol. I, p. 257.
[6] *De Div.,* II, 35.

a pontiff his office, but not so an augur, however great his
offence. In this case orders were indelible.[1] The permanence of tenure of members of this college was not,
indeed, accompanied by an unquestioned repute. Even
back in the ages of Faith, we read of angry but unavailing protests by the tribunes and cogent arguments to the
effect that the augurs had falsified the divine presages.[2]
And at the end of the Republic, the augurs seem to have
commanded no great respect.[3] Cicero, while denouncing a
lack of deference in Vatinius, admits that the augurs had
become ignorant, incompetent, and corrupt.[4] A striking
incident which indicates the reputation if not the character
of the augurs is narrated by Cicero with no intimation
that the view taken of augural venality was, in his opinion,
unfounded. Two candidates for the consulate in the
year 54 B.C. deposited with the existing consuls forty
sestertia (about $1750) apiece, to be forfeited if they
failed to produce three augurs to depose that they had
been present at the passing of a *lex curiata* of interest to
the consuls—which had in fact not been passed at all—
as well as two senators of consular rank to depose that
they had helped to draft a certain decree—though there
had not been a meeting of the Senate on the subject.[5]
Evidently in the opinion of those who staked their money
on it, augural mendacity was not limited to strictly official
work. We can hardly be surprised at the attempt to extend the principle *simulata pro veris* to political affairs,
since most cogent analogical arguments could have been
made to this end.

It becomes evident from the foregoing that scrupulous

[1] Plut., *Rom. Quaest.*, XCIX.
[2] Livy, VIII, 23. *Cf.* X 40.   [3] Cic., *In Vat.*, 6-9.
[4] Cic., *de Nat. Deor.*, II, 3; *de Leg.*, II, 13; *de Div.*, II, 33, 35.
[5] Cic., *ad Att.*, IV, 17.

care displayed in striving for exactness and precision in the performance of religious ceremonial among the Romans was never paralleled by any similar attempt at accuracy of words in relation to the facts with which they purported to deal. While no doubt the Roman religion lent support to the keeping of formal oaths made in technical legal forms, yet the preoccupation with form to the neglect of spirit, put out of the reach of religious sanctions any violation of that general fidelity and integrity which we consider so valuable a possession in a historical source. Trickery or mendacity, if not in violation of a special definite pact, was judged by its success in accomplishing desired ends, or producing pleasant states of feeling. Polybius, when outlining the Roman defence to the charge of deceit practised on Carthage to effect its destruction in the third Punic War, defines treachery as covering only something done in violation of an oath or a written agreement.[1] Such conceptions need have caused no embarrassment to any writer, and indeed must have tended to regularize any degree of pragmatic liberality which he found it desirable to use. The constant public indulgence in religious mendacity, known to be such by the statesmen who used it and by their fellows who heard it, could hardly have failed to disaccustom men's minds to any invariable relation of word and fact.

In place of mental rigor in this regard, we get a certain tendency to indistinctness and confusion of thought, a complacent acceptance of inconsistencies without the speaker or writer seeming to be aware of them. There seems to have been little desire to analyze and understand precisely the thought connoted by a word. It is impossible, for example, to say whether the divinized abstractions, *Salus, Concordia, Pietas, Spes* and the like, were thought

[1] Polybius, XXXVII, 1.

to be independent entities, or merely concepts expressed in a picturesque way; and it seems probable that the Romans themselves never thought the matter out distinctly.[1] Thinking for them would be concerned with imagining rather than analysis and definition; it took the form frequently of a sort of reverie, a play-activity with personified concepts and Platonic Ideas in an intellectual twilight where words were things and things were words and both were persons, and the false and the true were aspects of each other. But speculative thought was not attractive to the Romans, and their mental activities generally found more congenial scope in producing that especial variety of truth which is "true because it works well." Mystic phantasmagoria did not lead them to ecstasies but assumed a kind of pseudo-rational order, giving birth to the convenient lie. The current superstitions were in general gross and material, and no great subtlety was necessary to construct fictions congenial to the docile crowd. In the later days of the Republic the more refined theosophies of the Orient exerted a powerful influence and promoted a state of mental incoherence, which by nullifying useful thought was finally to disgust mankind with the operations of the intellect, and to keep alive a taste for the marvellous that was henceforth stimulated by the new cults.

The states of mind indicated by the study of Roman religion would have been grave enough phenomena had they been quite out of touch with daily life and reserved for exercise on holy days. But they were matters involved in every-day action and so became a part of the general

---

[1] Cf. H. L. Axtell, *The Deification of Abstract Ideas in Roman Literature and Inscriptions* (Chicago, 1907), pp. 62ff, 88, 98; Fowler, *Roman Festivals of the Period of the Republic* (London, 1899), p. 190; *Religious Experience*, p. 285; Wissowa, *op. cit.*, p. 327ff.

mental constitution of man, affecting its whole character. The official system of divination was no idle theory since any neglect of its many and complicated rules involved the absolute nullification of the action taken. Dictators, consuls, and other magistrates were forced to abdicate for irregularity of the auspices at their election; laws were annulled by a *senatus consultum* based on a decree of the college of augurs, even though years had elapsed.[1] Indeed, it is not too much to say that the reckless application of the laws relating to divination was one of the main factors in producing the anarchy of the later Republic.[2]

During the last two centuries of the Republic, it seems reasonably certain that Roman religion continually declined, except when now and then public disaster caused a temporary recrudescence. Cults decayed and temples fell into ruins, until restored by Augustus. Some places of religious worship were quietly occupied as private property; many of the gods were forgotten, till the antiquarian enthusiasm of Varro rescued them from oblivion. Many of the minor priesthoods and priestly colleges seem to have disappeared, and even in the case of the greater sacerdotal offices it was not always easy to find incumbents. For seventy-five years there was no *Flamen Dialis*.[3] There was a general relaxation of the ancient rules of

[1] Bouché-Leclercq, *Histoire de la divination*, vol. IV, p. 249ff. Cicero's attack on the acts of Clodius as tribune was based on defects in the auspices three years before. Cic., *de Domo,* 15; *Har. Resp.*, 23; Botsford, *Roman Assemblies*, p. 106ff.

[2] Bouché-Leclercq, *op. cit.*, vol. IV, pp. 256-260; Cass. Dio, XXXVIII, 4-6, 13; XL, 45, 47.

[3] The details are sufficiently given with citations in Marquardt, *Le culte chez les Romains*, vol. I (French ed. by M. Brissaud, Paris, 1889), pp. 8off, 267; II, 17; G. Colin, *Rome et la Grèce de 200 à 146 avant Jesus-Christ* (Paris, 1905), p. 331ff; Wissowa, *op. cit.*, p. 71.

religious conduct;[1] even thunder did not always suspend
comitial business,[2] and it is impossible that Julius Cæsar
could have been chosen *Pontifex Maximus* had the general
pristine religious belief prevailed, or that Cicero could
have ventured to question the apparatus of divination.

Notwithstanding the growth of scepticism, such was
the indifference to consistency of thought and action that
Roman leaders and statesmen, in the name of a religion
which did not command their belief and whose validity
they were willing to flout, still permitted the government
to be paralysed and acts of injustice to be perpetrated.
It is rare indeed that we hear of such a case as that of
Sulpicius Gallus who on the occasion of an eclipse when
the Roman army was engaged in the campaign against
Perseus of Macedon, dispelled superstitious fear by explaining fully to the soldiers the real nature of the phenomenon and its harmless character. The action of the
consul Aemilius Paullus was much more after Roman
custom. Although he understood eclipses he preferred
to indulge in the regular religious hocus-pocus and offered
the moon a sacrifice of eleven calves, following this at
daybreak by twenty-one oxen to Hercules.[3] Sometimes
indeed the susperstitions of the people became fatiguing to
the magistrates, as in 193 B.C., when recurrent reports of
earthquakes required certain religious ceremonials. In
this case the wearied consuls finally forbade the report
of any more of these divine portents on days when religious rites had been ordered.[4]

[1] Macrobius, *Sat.*, I, 16, 35; Cic., *de Nat. Deor.*, II, 3; *de Div.*,
II, 36, 41, 57; Colin, *op. cit.*, p. 332.

[2] Appian, *B. C.*, I, 4, 30.

[3] Livy, XLIV, 37; Plutarch, *Aem. Paul.*, 17; Val. Max., VIII,
11, 1; Pliny, *N. H.*, II, 53.

[4] Livy, XXXIV, 55.

Such triumphs of the spirit of common sense were however infrequent. More often we have the disagreeable spectacle of statesmen lowering themselves to the level of the ignorant and imposing, or seeking to impose, serious penalties on what they must have been convinced were ridiculous pretexts. Thus we read of the prosecution of Aemilius Scaurus by Domitius Ahenobarbus before the people on a charge of negligence in performing certain religious ceremonies at Lavinium. Scaurus had sufficient influence to secure an acquittal, but the vote in the tribes was very close.[1]

When Cicero was banished, his vivacious enemy Clodius improved the opportunity to tear down the exile's house and consecrate to religion the ground on which it had stood. We can hardly suppose that any of the pontiffs to whom the question of the irrevocability of the consecration was later referred can have taken it seriously; but Cicero was compelled to go through a solemn farce as if his auditors really believed that in some way the immortal gods were concerned. He had to set up old religious irregularities in the adoption of Clodius into a plebeian family in order to rescue his own property from this consecration. Cicero indeed betrayed a not unreasonable exasperation at the trick, but apparently recognized it as permissible, if regularly done. It was of high antiquity and seemed to have become a recognized part of political warfare.[2] The same extraordinary proceeding stripped Metellus Macedonicus of his property during his censorship.[3]

[1] Cic., pro Scaur., 1, 2; Asconius, in Scaur. (Clark), p. 19.

[2] Cic., de Domo, 47ff, 123; Mommsen, Le droit pénal romain (French trans. by J. Duquesne, Paris, 1907 = Manuel des antiquités romaines, vol. 17), vol. I, p. 55, note 2.

[3] Cic., de Domo, loc. cit.

Clodius himself had fallen foul of the gods at an earlier period of his career; for his indecorous intrusion into the house of Cæsar, the Pontifex Maximus, during the solemnities of *Bona Dea* was regarded as sacrilege. Cæsar, however, showed no inclination to use the religious law for the satisfaction of private grievances, and gave the situation what he regarded as its proper solution by divorcing his wife. But it took some judicious bribery before the jury accepted the *alibi* set up by Clodius.

The Romans, like nearly all strong peoples, had some idea of justice and were comparatively free from wanton cruelty, although they could be stern enough when severity seemed advisable. Their penalties for infractions of law were on the whole during the later Republic singularly mild.[1] It seems also clear, as we have seen, that their governing class was to a great extent free from any strong faith in their religious institutions except as these were a useful means for political ends. Yet so far were they from having developed a high standard of honesty that even in the last century of the Republic they reverted on slight pretexts and with full deliberation to the stupid and brutal injustices of savages.

In 114 B.C. a Roman army in Thrace had met with severe losses and the daughter of a Roman knight returning from Rome to Apulia had been killed by lightning while on horseback. There was some public uneasiness and imaginative minds saw in the death of the equestrian maiden a hint of misconduct of knights and Vestal Virgins. Scandals were whispered and the Pontifex Maximus held an inquest, acquitted two of the Vestals, and found a third guilty, but probably of nothing more than some indecorum, since a conviction of unchaste con-

[1] *Cf.* Mommsen, *op. cit.*, vol. III, p. 280ff; II, pp. 273, 284, 389ff.

duct would have brought upon her the penalty of burial alive. The next year there was a serious military defeat of a Roman army by the Cimbri and suspicions revived regarding the Vestals. By an irregular proceeding, a new trial was had, an orgy of accusation and denunciation followed, and the three Vestals, as well as a number of their alleged paramours, were condemned. Whether the regular penalty was inflicted is unfortunately left uncertain by our authorities; but the religious feelings of the people were ministered to by a solemn ceremony purporting to come from the Sibylline Books, whereby four human beings, one Gallic couple and another Greek, were buried alive in the Forum Boarium.[1] This matter must have received the coöperation of the governing classes, since the Sibylline Books could be examined only by order of the Senate, and the pontifical college which declared or invented these precious revelations was composed of men of rank, most of whom, we are justified in assuming, had slight faith, if any, in their supernatural origin.[2]

It would be idle to pass moral judgments on the strange things which men have done under the influence of religious sentiment, or to observe with Lucretius: *tantum*

---

[1] Livy, *Epit.*, LXIII; Plut., *Rom. Quaest.*, LXXXIII; Macrobius, *Sat.*, I, 10, 5; Val. Max., III, 7, 9; Pliny, *N. H.*, XXVIII, 12; Ihne, *op. cit.*, vol. V, p. 124ff. The burying alive of Vestals and of a Greek and a Gallic couple seems to have been used at an earlier time (216 B.C.) to calm Roman religious sensibilities. *Cf.* Livy, XXII, 57; Wissowa, *op. cit.*, pp. 60, 421.

[2] It is said that the Senate forbade human sacrifices in 97 B.C., but the practice does not seem to have ceased entirely; there is some evidence that it was known at least until Hadrian's time. *Cf.* Pliny, *N. H.*, XXVIII, 12, 13; XXX, 12; Tertullian, *Apol.*, 9; Eusebius, *Praep. Evang.*, IV, 16. *Cf.* Boissier, *op. cit.*, vol. II, pp. 386-7; Fowler, *Religious Experience*, pp. 33, 117, 320.

religio potuit suadere malorum.[1] "Can anything," asks Cicero, forgetting his fellow countrymen in speaking of the barbarous Gauls, "can anything appear holy or religious to those men who, if ever they are so much influenced by fear as to think it necessary to propitiate the gods, defile their altars and temples with human victims, so that they cannot pay proper honor to religion itself without first violating it with crime?"[2] No people come before the bar of history with clean hands in such matters and the Romans went astray less than most of them. But such acts have generally proceeded from strong and genuine, however misguided, beliefs. In the case of the governing class among the Romans, however, their religious faith seems to have been little more than a conviction that religion was chiefly an excellent means of gaining secular ends. There was in it little or none of the emotional element, common to most religions, but much of deliberate calculation. We may fairly question, therefore, whether intelligent men, who pretended to be actuated by a belief in things at which they really scoffed, and who were willing to engage in ritualistic murders coming down from primitive times of terror so that the spectacle might promote the mental tranquillity of the crowd, possessed scruples sufficient to hold them to strict probity in their literary composition.

[1] Lucret., I, 101.
[2] Cic., *pro. Fonteio*, 14.

CHAPTER XI

THE AUGUSTAN REVIVAL OF RELIGION

RELIGION among the Romans had, as we have seen, taken on a threefold aspect, and reflective men like Cotta, Scævola, and Varro distinguished the religions of poets, of philosophers, and of statesmen, and found marked differences and even contradictions between them.[1] The first was referred to as consisting of poetical inventions, mendacious, unmoral, and often unseemly, but generally accepted by the vulgar. The second was marked by contradictions and was closely akin to atheism. It represented in most cases the real attitude of the cultivated classes, but was regarded by them as entirely unsuited to the common people and to all women. To the last form they all gave nominal adhesion in public, and used it as a convenient political instrument. Their high appreciation of its utility in this direction was all that kept them from deriding it. The form and amount of belief among the great mass of the people need not be examined, inasmuch as our present concern is limited to a consideration of the character and practices of those from whom our historical material comes; and these were either members of the cultivated and ruling classes or persons who were associated with them and had adopted their point of view.

It must not be supposed, however, that the foregoing

[1] *Cf.* above, p. 150ff.

résumé of the three religious types represents, in its brevity and distinctness, the matter just as it appeared to Roman minds, for it makes explicit and positive what to them was more or less implicit and confused. They did not draw so sharp a line of demarcation as scientific standards compel modern scholars to do, between the true and the false; they did not clearly distinguish in many cases between what they really believed and what they believed that they believed; they sometimes pretended to believe so as to induce others to entertain belief. An examination of such a state of mind regarding religion, however important a study in itself, would not form a proper part of the present inquiry were it not for the fact that it serves to indicate a general habit of mind whose defects impair the validity of testimony in historical fields. It seems fair to conclude that men who, for political purposes, would indulge habitually in the practices described in the foregoing chapter, could not have possessed a probity of character sufficient to inspire our confidence in their statements of fact in cases where self-interest might lead them to distort the truth. Many of our most important historical authorities, however, come from a period considerably later than the one examined, and justice to them requires us to follow the progress of Roman religious thought to later times.

The threefold nature of Roman religion as analyzed by Varro and others was not an accidental or arbitrary matter, but flowed naturally from the characteristics of human nature. The ideal man, who becomes an object of thought only when one falls into a Platonizing mood, would doubtless exhibit a perfect balance and harmony between the affective, volitional, and intellectual aspects of his being; but in real men these elements are not thus poised. The ordinary man, with his undeveloped mind and his generally feeble or chaotic will, naturally manifests a relative excess on the affective side, and in matters of religion, is dominated by sentiment rather than by consistent thought or steady will. The pleasing or terrifying myths of the poets impress him more than do the theological speculations of the learned, or the ethics of the self-controlled. The three sorts of religion, that of the poets, of the philosophers, and of the statesmen, are simply the three kinds which correspond to the three kinds of men distinguished by the relative prominence of sentiment, thought, or will. Objectively, they are characterized by the relative importance assigned to worship, belief, and acts.

When, as in the case of Roman society at the end of the Republic, these different manifestations are more or less clearly perceived, confusion in religious life ensues. For as no man is devoid of a considerable amount of sentiment, thought, and will, however much one of these may predominate, so none can hold rigidly to any one of the three forms of religiosity to the exclusion of the others. In a more primitive stage of development, there is not enough perspicacity to see the contradictions or to analyze the sources of confusion; in more highly developed minds the feelings are under discipline and order can be restored, to speak figuratively, by the joint action of reason and will. While the Romans at this period had, of course, emerged from their more primitive state they had not, save for the rarest exceptions, attained any remarkable height of pure intellect. Their chief concern, accordingly, henceforth became a search not for truth but for peace and tranquillity of mind.

The advent of Augustus to power marked a new era in the religious as well as in the political life of Rome. Whether or not he was a great man is a problem that will probably continue to divide historians: what is important is that a certain deflection was given to the course of human events during the years when he presided over the Roman state which was so great and so far reaching that even to-day its effects are by no means exhausted. However true it may be that others did most of the things for which he gained the credit and reaped the reward, they were nevertheless done, as was freely admitted by his coadjutors, "under his auspices," to use a favorite Roman phrase. His name may therefore be conveniently used to signify the general course of events in those years which are, by common consent, called "the Augustan age."

This is not to say that his personality stands in no closer relation to the period than does that of Queen Victoria, let us say, to the age which bears her name. We cannot regard as a mere figurehead a man who, whatever his defects of character and intellect, manifested in such an extraordinary degree that good luck which the Romans elevated to a virtue. That a boy not yet nineteen, suddenly plunged into a maelstrom of plots, intrigues, and bloody violence, should have deceived, manipulated, and ultimately crushed so many skilful opponents; that he should in a few years have emerged as the presiding genius of a state prospering under a felicitous and memorable peace; that without military skill or civic experience he should have mounted swiftly to an unrivalled and giddy eminence of wealth, power, and dignity of even divine worship, and yet have remained cool, canny, and indeed rather commonplace; more than all, that he should have held the respect, loyalty, and affection of· those closest to him—the able woman who was his wife for fifty years, the great generals and statesmen like Agrippa and Tiberius who fought his battles for him—such things as these argue the presence in him of remarkable qualities, however indistinctly they may appear in our historical sources.

It is given as a reason for his success that the prestige enjoyed by Julius Cæsar, his maternal granduncle, descended upon him. This was, no doubt, a very important factor at the beginning of his career, but even the loose notions of heredity prevalent among the Romans could hardly have attributed to a grandnephew, even though fortified by adoption, the descent of the genius of his grandmother's brother; and indeed the prestige of the great Julius was not so great among the Romans outside of his army as to have supplied the entire necessary capital for such a career as that of the younger man. It is evident that he himself counted for something.

Of the men who fill a great place in history, certainly many and probably all, so some have thought, owe their prominence not to the fact that they have led their people into fields where these would otherwise not have wandered, or have furnished them with new ideas or ideals, to which otherwise they would not have attained; rather, the great men have most amply expressed the incoherent thoughts and tendencies of those whom they appear to have led or inspired. They have merely gone a little beyond the advancing crowd and occupied some point in the line of march from which they have beckoned and called to the advancing throng. Yet so lacking in discernment and discrimination are the many that he who anticipates them seems to guide them; he who formulates their desires or feelings in words, acts, or institutions, seems to have originated the ideas of which they now for the first time begin to grow conscious. Sometimes, indeed, unless the leader be cautious, they do not recognize the contents of their own minds when put explicitly before them, and, panic-stricken at the apparent novelty, they trample down their spokesman, not dreaming at the time that he but interpreted their minds. And then they lament the martyr.

This theory of "the great men in history" is not easily applied in some cases. It is difficult to make it fit the cases of Cæsar, for instance, or Sulla, each of whom has received the distinction of being called the real founder of the imperial system. But in the case of Augustus there is much to commend it to our acceptance. Without any trace of that original, creative power to which we give the name "genius," he expressed singularly well the salient characteristics of the great body of contemporaneous Roman thought.

The world was tired of disorder, conflict, and slaughter.[1] The strain of the long civil wars had made it somewhat neuropathic, and it craved peace and the protection of a fixed *milieu* where things would go along quietly and easily, without the need for concentrated attention and important decisions and without the spectre of strife and bloodshed constantly looming up. For half a century there had been no real Republic but merely a succession of personal rulers. The Roman conception of the nature of political power expressed in their word *imperium* made every high magistrate a temporary despot; and they had now come to be familiar with proconsuls and special magistrates holding other offices for years, so that it did not startle them to see Augustus exercising in the interests of peace and good order a power apparently the same, only somewhat more extended in time and scope, provided the word "king" was not whispered and the fiction of the existence of a free Republic was maintained.

Still possessed, as ever, of a mediocre intelligence that

[1] The situation is excellently summarized by J. B. Mayor *et al.*, *Virgil's Messianic Eclogue* (London, 1907), p. 33ff.

was easily satisfied with words and forms, the Romans lacked the acuteness to penetrate beyond them to the realities for which they stood. The proconsular *imperium,* the tribunicial power, the designation of *princeps* and *imperator* were venerable and respectable names of Republican things, and their union was not alarming. Julius Cæsar had been a genius, and his keen incisive mind, the reach and grasp of his intellect, alarmed the dull and timid; but Augustus seemed nearer their level and within their comprehension.

Besides being frightened by the social and political turmoil of the civil wars, men were terrified by the disarray of their minds. It had, of course, become impossible for any one who knew how things were managed to preserve any faith in the childish charlatanry of the official or semi-official schemes of divination; but even in the most intelligent classes, while scepticism was rampant it had hardly touched the underlying strata of superstition. Rational criticism had done only negative and superficial work. The timid were appalled at the lack of positive beliefs to protect them against the delusive suggestion of ignorance and superstition, while those of stronger fibre were losing their confidence in reason as a guide to life. The effort of clear thinking seemed poorly repaid by the arid nullity of its results, and men craved a mental life which at least would be easier and less perplexing to tired brains and more productive of positive results. It was much simpler to indulge in rites and formulæ than in serious thought.[1]

To quell this disorder without and within, nothing seemed to promise so well as an attempt to return to the supposedly calm, contented, and virtuous days of their

[1] For the intellectual background of the age, see Boissier. *Religion romaine*, vol. I, p. 205ff.

ancestors. The picture of that golden age was almost entirely imaginary, but this defect did not enter into the calculation, nor did the impossibility of the attempt strike their confused minds. What they wanted was to produce in a great heterogeneous urban community which had become predatory, imperialistic, and capitalistic the imaginary civic and domestic virtues of a small homogeneous people mainly agricultural; and they thought to accomplish this by reëstablishing, of set purpose, the magical rites and ceremonials whereby that small rural state had expressed its ignorance of the unknown.[1]

It is doubtless true, as Pascal pointed out, that a persistence in acts of simulated devotion may produce a belief in the reality of the objects of the cult.

C'est en faisant tout comme s'ils croyaient, en prenant de l'eau bénite, en faisant dire des messes, etc. Naturellement même cela vous fera croire et vous abêtira.[2]

With a similar acquiescence in this method of obtaining figs from thistles, Professor James laid down, not as a mere scientific fact but as

a practical observation . . . so well known in moral and religious education that I need say no more [that] we need only in cold blood act as if the thing in question were real, and keep acting as if it were real, and it will infallibly end by growing into such a connection with our life, that it will become real. . . . Those, to whom "God" and "Duty" are now mere names, can make them much more than that, if they make a little sacrifice to them every day.[3]

[1] See above, p. 132ff.
[2] *Pensées*, X, I, (Havet, p. 262—*Les grands écrivains*, vol. II, pp. 153, 154, no. 233).
[3] *Principles of Psychology*, vol. II, pp. 321, 322. *Cf.* p. 463.

But the trouble with the project of reviving early Roman virtues by reëstablishing old religious ceremonies was that the practice of the latter could do no more than to produce a belief in the mere reality of the divine objects of the cult; these vague deities or numina, however, belonged to an age prior to any general connection between religion and ethics, and were not associated with distinct moral ideas. To establish a belief in their existence and power, which was all that could be expected, would merely suggest a resort to some magical method of securing their assistance in forwarding the worhipper's desires, instead of encouraging an inhibition of unbecoming desires. Many of the gods were of considerable moral laxity, and the believer needed only to pick out a complaisant divinity in order to receive aid towards some unmoral end. Where the crudity of this theological outlook shocked more delicate minds, there was a refuge in the oriental cults with their ecstatic states of mystical delirium.

But neither Augustus nor his contemporaries did more than to repair and rebuild temples, fill the vacant priesthoods and sacred colleges, and restore so much of the venerable religious ceremonial as the zeal of antiquaries could discover and the enthusiasm of subsidized devotees could arrange. So all the old disingenuousness took a fresh start and the attempt was again made to use a religion which commanded little belief among the intelligent and had never produced general morality among the people, for the purpose of improving human conduct. Religious activity became respectable and in some cases profitable. People set to work performing archaic ceremonies, making professions of ancient piety, or approving these practices, so as to produce the old Roman virtues— in someone else. Such apparent success in moralizing the community as followed the reanimation of cults is sufficiently accounted for by the distaste for violence produced by the excesses of the last half century, by the peace and order imposed, and by the better administration of justice resulting from the increased efficiency of government.

In the last century of the Republic the religion of Rome, as has been remarked, seemed moribund.[1] The temples were falling into ruin; most of the priesthoods were filled with difficulty; for a full seventy-five years (87-11 B.C.) there was a vacancy in the office of Flamen Dialis,[2] and for forty-one years there was no lustration of the people.[3] But one branch of religion had remained alive: divination survived in great and troublesome activity to the confusion of orderly government. Cicero declared it an indispensable part of the Republican constitution,[4] and membership in the college of augurs was still a prize to the most prominent statesmen.

Great as was the enthusiasm of Augustus for religious institutions, it was not undiscriminating. He was said to have been credulous in regard to dreams, signs, omens, prodigies, and the lore of stars.[5] Yet some doubt arises as to the sincerity of his credulity when we observe that the part of the national faith which dealt with these subjects, apparently so congenial to his alleged temper of mind, was precisely the part which he showed no interest in promoting or honoring. With the beginning of the Empire, there was a sudden cessation of talk about auspices and the opinion of the gods on mundane affairs. Augustus himself became an augur but the opinion he had regarding the seriousness of the office and the gravity

[1] *Cf.* Wissowa, *Religion und Kultus*, p. 70ff.
[2] Cass. Dio, LIV, 36; Tac., *Annals* III, 58; Suet., *Aug.*, 31.
[3] *Monumentum Ancyranum*, c. 8.
[4] *Cf. de Leg.*, II, 12; *de Div.*, II, 33; *de Nat. Deor.*, II, 3.
[5] Suet., *Aug.*, 90-96; Appian, *B. C.*, IV, 110.

and learning necessary to entitle one to interpret the divine communications to mankind may be seen from the fact that he raised to the same office his grandsons, Gaius and Lucius Cæsar, while still in their teens.[1] Claudius, his grandnephew and step-grandson, he considered too hopelessly incompetent and too nearly imbecile to be safely invested with any public office save that of augur. As Champagny neatly observes, "Auguste ne l'aimait pas, il n'en fit jamais qu'un augure; il le trouvait trop imbecile pour faire autre chose que deviner l'avenir." [2] By carefully revising the official Sibylline Books, by committing to the flames two thousand unofficial books on divination,[3] and by restricting the activities of the haruspices,[4] he destroyed absolutely the religious chicanery which had been utilized as a weapon of political opposition so abundantly and regularly during the later Republic.[5]

The results of his repressive measures touching divination were, in their way, as important as the more showy revivals and restorations which have usually engaged the attention of historians. By means of the latter, Augustus

[1] Cf. Bouché-Leclercq, Les Pontifes de l'ancienne Rome (Paris, 1871), p. 345.

[2] F. de Champagny, Les Césars (2nd ed., Paris, 1853), I, p. 331. Cf. Suet., Claud., 4. For Claudius's attempt to revive haruspication, see Bouché-Leclercq, op. cit., pp. 355, 356; Tac., Ann., XI, 24; Furneaux, Annals of Tacitus, Appendix to book XI.

[3] Cf. Bouché-Leclercq, op. cit., p. 348ff; Suet., Aug., 31.

[4] Cass. Dio, LX, 25; Cf. LII, 36; Bouché-Leclercq, Divination, vol. IV, pp. 112, 326.

[5] Mr. Fowler's meaning is not clear when he says (Religious Experience of the Roman People, p. 430) that "Augustus troubled himself little about the later political developments of religion, which we have lately been examining,—about pontifices, augurs, and Sibylline books." These so-called "later political developments" seem to be quite as old as the parts of the religion he especially patronized.

succeeded, to some extent, in stimulating the sentiments of religious awe and fear of the unknown. In the words of Mr. Fowler: "he knew that it was far more important to touch a spring in the feeling of the people, than to occupy himself, like Sulla, in mending old machinery or inventing new." [1] That is to say, he preferred to excite primitive emotions rather than to promote distinct thoughts. The former, properly played upon by elaborate ceremonial, produce more tractable subjects than do the latter. But in limiting the opportunities to oppose his designs by making use of the time-worn pretexts of religion, he lessened the chances of the dangerous development of rivals.

In one respect at least Roman religion under Augustus entered upon a phase which was peculiar to the Empire. This was the worship of the emperors. Arising ultimately, no doubt, from a complexus of associations involving the doctrine of the *genius* and the cult of the *di manes,* and certain Hellenistic cult-elements, it first took significant form when the Senate, deferring to popular sentiment, passed the decree (42 B.C.) whereby Julius Cæsar was enrolled among the gods of the state as *Divus Julius.* [2] The young Octavianus, as the adopted

---

[1] W. W. Fowler, *op. cit.,* p. 431. The same writer (p. 428) speaks of the "cool tactical attempt of Augustus to revive the outward forms of the old religion." For the Augustan revival see also Boissier, *Religion romaine,* vol. I, p. 69ff; J. B. Carter, *The Religion of Numa* (London, 1906), p. 146ff; *Religious Life of Ancient Rome* (Boston, 1911), p. 63ff; Wissowa, *Religion u. Kultus,* p. 73ff; V. Gardthausen, *Augustus und seine Zeit* (Leipzig, 1891), vol. I, 2, p. 865ff; II, 2, p. 507ff; Mommsen, *Res Gestae Divi Augusti* (2nd ed., Berlin, 1883), p. 78ff.

[2] C. I. L., IX, 2628: *Genio Deivi Iuli parentis patriae, quem senatus populusque Romanus in deorum numerum rettulit. Cf.* Wissowa, *op. cit.,* p. 343.

son of the deified Julius, was of course *Divi filius,* and
after the battle of Actium (31 B.C.) divine honors were
paid him throughout the provinces and even in a number
of Italian towns.[1] The City of Rome was the only place
where the new divinity, to whom the semi-sacred name
of *Augustus* was later granted, was not openly and even
ostentatiously worshipped. The caution of Augustus
warned him of the danger of awakening such animosities
as had proved fatal to Julius, and he took steps to limit
in the provinces the right or privilege of worshipping him
to those who were not of Roman birth.[2] By 7 B.C.,
however, he ventured to associate his genius with the
lares compitales and thus afforded an opportunity to the
common people to gratify themselves by participating
in his cult. [3]

There can be no reasonable doubt that the feeling
throughout the provinces and among most of the people
in Italy was strong and sincere. It was not based on
servility nor indulged in as a mere matter of etiquette.[4]
Man makes for himself a religion out of any idea that
fills his soul, says Fustel de Coulanges; [5] and a feeling of
gratitude and veneration grew up for the ruler who gave
to the world peace, prosperity, and good government.
The line between human and divine was never clearly

---

[1] *Cf.* Beurlier, *Essai sur le culte rendu aux empereurs romains*
(Paris, 1890), pp. 13ff; 17ff. (For critical discussions of Emperor-
worship see E. Meyer, *Alexander der Grosse und die Absolute
Monarchie* in *Kleine Schriften,* Halle, 1910; E. Kornemann,
Zur Geschichte der Antiken Herrscherkulte in *Klio,* vol. I, 1902,
pp. 51-146; Wissowa, *op. cit.,* p. 78ff.—*Editor.*)

[2] *Cf.* Beurlier, *op. cit.,* p. 17.

[3] *Cf.* Beurlier, *op. cit.,* p. 16.

[4] *Cf.* Fustel de Coulanges, *Histoire des institutions politiques
de l'ancienne France* (Paris, 1875), p. 86ff.

[5] *Ibid.,* p. 96.

distinguished in ancient times; the gods were simply more than men, not different, and the rendering of service to mankind was regarded as indicating the possession of something of the divine. There were many legends of men becoming gods, and indeed in the Orient, where the worship of the emperors was strongest, kings and Roman proconsuls had long been objects of worship.[1] It was indeed no great step from recognizing the sanctity of a tribune and the majesty of a consul, to attributing to the monarch, who in effect was both at once, the character of *divus,* especially as it involved merely outward acts of respect and no professions of belief. Indeed it had long been a custom in the pagan world to testify to one's high esteem and respect for a great man by using these appellations of divinity which seem to us so preposterously extravagant. Some philosophers adored Plato in this way; Silius Italicus established a cult to Virgil; even Lucretius called Epicurus a god.[2] So it is not surprising that as the Empire came to seem a part of the cosmic order the feeling of submissive loyalty towards the emperors grew stronger with time; so natural, so just did it seem to most men that they had great difficulty in understanding how any save the disloyal could withhold this manifestation of good-will. Whatever defects there were in the Roman imperial constitution, it had at any rate the prime merit of a government: it possessed the hearty approval of the great mass of those who lived under it.

Evidence regarding the religious sincerity of the great mass of the little people throughout the Empire is, however, not directly applicable to our present purpose, since

[1] *Cf.* Beurlier, *op. cit.,* p. 23ff; 323: Boissier, *Religion romaine,* vol. I, pp. 155-157, 169ff; Guignebert, *Tertullien,* pp. 26, 27.

[2] Pliny, *Epist.,* III, 7, 8; Lucretius, V, 8.

it was not they who produced our literary historical material. When we read Ovid's words: "it is expedient that there be gods, and as it is expedient, let us believe them to exist," and when we notice with what irreverence he treats them, setting forth the ancient stories of mythology in such a spirit and with such details as to make a kind of *Decameron* of his *Fasti* and *Metamorphoses,* the Augustan revival of the Roman religion seems to have been blighted by the incurably sceptical atmosphere of the intellectual class before the mortar in the new temple constructions could have been fairly dry.[1]

As to Augustus himself, it is difficult to see any indication that he had changed since the days when he had craftily deluded Cicero with honeyed words, calling him "father," writing him daily to beg his advice and guidance, and endeavoring to persuade him that the assassins of Cæsar would find a friend in the young heir. That he genuinely believed that it was well for the people to be deceived and that by this means they could be made better Romans may indeed be at once conceded; but this unconstrained view of truth, this readiness to make misstatements where they would apparently "work well" is, of course, not what we are looking for. Yet it is difficult to credit him with moral principles or mental clarity more to the historian's taste when we consider his patently pragmatic attitude towards divination, and his entire readiness to be a god to the provincials who wanted him to be one, but not to the Senate or the other Romans who would be offended thereby. If his attempt to infuse life into the old Roman religion was not entirely successful, it may have been because, as Seneca said, the prime re-

[1] Ovid, *Ars Amat.,* I, 637: *expedit esse deos, et ut expedit, esse putemus. Cf.* Boissier, *Religion romaine,* vol. I, pp. 202-204.

quisite for the worship of gods is to believe in their existence.[1]

Tiberius, after one act of acquiescence, flatly repudiated any divine qualities, and if the speech on the subject attributed to him by Tacitus represents his real attitude, which it probably does, he showed himself to be honest and clear-headed beyond most men of his times.[2] Gaius seems to have taken his godship with much irony and as affording an outlet for his generally sardonic humor,[3] while Claudius followed the example of Tiberius in repelling worship.[4] Vespasian's sturdy common sense was evidently not taken in by the prospect of apotheosis.[5] Yet none of these sceptics seems to have felt any compunction about recognizing the divinity of his predecessors and promoting their worship in Rome.[6] Nero, the musically minded paranoiac, is credited with a lucid witticism on the subject of mushrooms as a food for gods in reference to the supposed cause for Claudius's transfer to the celestial abode of divinities.[7] It can hardly be

[1] *Epist.*, XCV, 50. For a full discussion of the religious policy of Augustus, see Boissier, *op. cit.*, vol. I, pp. 47, 67ff, 109ff.

[2] Tac., *Ann.*, IV, 37, 38. *Cf.* Suet., *Tib.*, 26, 27; Cass. Dio, LVIII, 8.

[3] *Cf.* below. p. 382; Cass. Dio, LIX, 11.

[4] Cass. Dio, LX, 5.

[5] Suet., *Vesp.*, 23.

[6] Tiberius appears to have engaged personally in the cult of the divinized Augustus (*Ann.*, IV, 52) but seems to have prevented prosecutions for alleged irreverence to the new god (I, 73; II, 50). The town of Cyzicus lost its liberty (IV, 36): *incuria caerimoniarum divi Augusti, additis violentiae criminibus adversum cives Romanos.* Boissier (*op. cit.*, vol. I, p. 173) alludes only to the lack of religious zeal as the cause: the assaults on Roman citizens may have been the real reason.

[7] Cass. Dio, LX, 35, *Cf.* Juvenal, *Sat.*, VI, 622; Seneca, *Apokol.*, 5, 7.

believed that Seneca would have ventured to transgress
grossly the beliefs and standards of taste of his friend
and patroness Agrippina and of his pupil Nero; but if
the *Apokolokyntosis* be his—and it probably is—the divinization of Claudius must have been regarded in the
imperial circle as an *objet de risée*.

The senators seem to have felt no doubt as to the
rightfulness and propriety of elevating one of the imperial
family to the rank of *Divus* and authorizing the worship
of such a person even while living, and objected to decreeing an apotheosis only when they felt an especial degree
of ill-will towards the one proposed, and the matter was
not very urgently pressed upon them.[1] The assertion of
this power seems to have called forth no objection, and
whatever criticism there was, related, so far as we can
determine, only to the merits of the particular case.[2]
Even Seneca, however much he may jeer at the case of
Divus Claudius, does not question the general power and
the effectiveness of its exercise;[3] and Lucan, although
referring gloomily after his quarrel with Nero, to the
divinities resulting from the civil wars, had at an earlier
time expressed enthusiasm over the prospect of Nero's
becoming *divus*.[4] Tacitus represents a senator as attributing divine rank to emperors as a matter of course, and
when, somewhat later, Tiberius flatly repudiates the honor,
the historian finds the emperor blameworthy.[5] Nero is

[1] *Cf.* Cass. Dio, LIX, 3; LXX, 1; Spartianus, *Had.*, 27;
Eutropius, VIII, 7.

[2] Manilius (IV, 931) seems rather pleased with the idea that
men can now create gods, and Valerius Maximus (*Praef.*) ranks
their creations rather higher than the traditional deities. *Cf.*
Beurlier, *op. cit.*, p. 55ff.

[3] *Cf. de Clem.*, I, 10.

[4] I, 33ff; VII, 456.

[5] *Ann.*, III, 36; IV, 37-38.

represented as being advised to murder his mother and then arrange for her apotheosis.[1] It was not necessary that the proposed divinity should have been the sovereign, the mundane Jupiter; with equal ease the Senate could divinize Drusilla, the sister of Gaius, Poppæa, the wife, and Claudia, the infant daughter of Nero, and even Matidia, the mother-in-law of Hadrian.[2]

A still more surprising practice obtained in later times. In the third century we find Christians accepting positions as priests of the divinized pagan emperors without any very serious objections from the Church, provided they did not personally take part in offering sacrifices or in giving games;[3] and after the Empire became Christian, it appears that emperors—all Christian save Julian—continued for two centuries to receive from the Senate at the instance of the reigning monarch the distinction of apotheosis.[4] It would seem, therefore, that the general confusion of thought characteristic of earlier times had never disappeared.

The more attentively the cult of the emperors is examined, the more difficult it becomes to discover in the general character of the governing class among the Romans clarity of intellect and honesty of purpose. That the cult was useful is beyond question, but its utility is not here in question. The question is the intellectual honesty of the circles that were responsible for much of the material from which the later world has formed its notion of Rome. In this connection it is significant that the interpreters of the thought of the times anticipate the official apotheosis of Augustus and begin to declare him a present deity on a par, or nearly so, with the Olym-

[1] *Id.*, XIV, 3.
[2] *Cf.* Beurlier, *op. cit.*, pp. 56, 75, 76; 325ff.
[3] *Id.*, pp. 278-281.   [4] *Id.*, pp. 283ff, 329-331.

pian gods.[1] And the *façons de parler* of the Augustans continue in use.

In whatever direction the age may have been making moral progress, it was not towards the virtues which are of especial interest to us; and the ambitious moral and religious reforms of Augustus, whatever else they may have accomplished, failed to stir the springs of honesty and fair dealing. One source of trouble lay in the fact that the emperor did not himself set a good example. It could hardly have failed to be apparent to the men who were in close contact with political affairs that the whole imperial system was based on a number of pretenses. The political constitution was a mass of make-believes, not ancient fictions venerable through age and deceiving nobody, but new creations which were consciously planned to mislead, to convey the impression that the government was not a military despotism but that the Republic had been restored—a falsehood which Augustus set forth in his famous *Res Gestæ,* together with the equally glaring misstatement that thereafter he held no more power than those who were his colleagues in any magistracy.[2]

His religious reforms were based on an artificial revival of the externals of a moribund system of primitive superstition which had been for generations discredited among the relatively more intelligent classes, but had continued to be utilized by them unblushingly for the purposes of political advantage. This religious resuscitation included archaic elements, such as the *Sodales Titienses,* which had

[1] *Cf. e.g.,* Horace, *Odes,* I, 12.

[2] *Cf.* Mommsen, *Res Gestæ,* p. 144 (c.34). The statement that he twice defeated the Republicans in battle (c.2) is another example of clear perversion of historical fact. *Cf.* Tac., *Ann.,* I, 4; III, 56.

been practically forgotten, while others, like the *Fratres Arvales* were revamped into schemes of personal glorification. The presiding genius, the emperor, appeared as a hypostatic union of a spurious savior-god and a counterfeit Republican magistrate: the former for provincials whose credulity, gratitude, and remoteness rendered them innocuous, and the latter for Romans whose prejudices and proximity imposed caution on their ruler lest they penetrate the disguise.

Not the least of Augustus's measures for promoting the new patriotism was his patronage of literature. Under his direction Virgil, Horace, and Propertius glorified the faith and virtues of Republican Rome, and hailed Augustus as a god, to the end that the new Rome, the *Roma Æterna* of Tibullus,[1] might stand forth splendid in all men's eyes. Their devotion to the idea of Rome is beyond question; as for their real belief in the resuscitated religion which Augustus doubtless conceived as an instrument of the new patriotism—*credat Iudæus Apella.*

[1] II, 5, 23.

CHAPTER XII

PHILOSOPHIC HERETICS

WHEN a people is in the process of emerging from a state of ignorance, two distinct attitudes may be adopted by the relatively intelligent leaders toward their fellow countrymen. One is a firm belief in the saving power of truth as a moral and political instrument: *magna est veritas et prævalebit*. The other, amply illustrated by the Roman governing classes, is a common form of political expediency based on distrust: distrust of the people by their rulers, lest knowledge breed indocility, and distrust of the rulers by themselves, lest their authority wan without resort to fraud.

As has been indicated in the foregoing pages, the general and indeed almost universal attitude of the leading Romans toward the common people was that of encouraging among them old credulities and promoting a belief in convenient new superstitions. But now and then out of the welter of fraud and mendacity which characterized Roman life, there emerged men who were disinclined to accept the current doctrine that the moral improvement of the many or the political interests of the few were subserved by continual deceit. Mention has already been made of the case of Caius Sulpicius Gallus who shortly before the battle of Pydna, when the camp had been strongly fortified . . . and the soldiers had been called to assembly, announced—in order that no one might regard the matter as a portent—that there would be an eclipse of the moon on the following night, from the second to the fourth hour. Because this happened, he said, at stated seasons in the course of natural events, it could be both known and foretold. As they felt no surprise that the moon sometimes shone with full orb and at others in its wane, with slender horns, because both the rising and the setting of the sun and moon are regular; so they ought not to interpret as an evil omen the fact that it was obscured when covered by the earth's shadow. . . . When the eclipse took place at the hour foretold the wisdom of Gallus seemed to the Romans almost divine. The portent struck the Macedonians as an evil one, foreboding the fall of their kingdom and the destruction of their race.

The consul, however, though he well understood the matter, did not omit the usual superstitious practice.[1]

Cicero, in narrating this incident, puts it after instead of before the eclipse and significantly represents Tubero, the Stoic, upon hearing it, as expressing surprise that Gallus ventured to say such things before ignorant men.[2] Evidently they were not often explained to the common people. Nearly two centuries later, so it appears, legionary soldiers were thrown into a panic of superstitious terror by the same phenomenon of an eclipse;[3] and yet during all this time correct knowledge on this subject was the common possession of educated persons, however little

---

[1] Livy, XLIV, 37, 40; Plut., Æm. Paul., 17.
[2] Cic., de Rep., I, 15: Ain tandem? inquit Tubero; docere hoc poterat ille homines paene agrestes: et apud imperitos audebat haec dicere?
[3] Tac., Ann., I, 28.

it spread beyond them.[1]   The emperor Claudius, understanding that an eclipse of the sun was to take place on
his birthday, and fearing that the portent might cause
alarm and disturbance, gave notice beforehand not only
that there would be an eclipse and when and for how
long, but also the reasons why it must necessarily take
place; but before long the old superstitions again held
full sway.[2]

One of the few Romans who dispensed with the usual
tricks in his dealings with the people was perhaps the
greatest of them all, Julius Cæsar.[3]   He was willing to
flout the whole machinery of magical and religious lore
as well as misleading and bombastic rhetoric, both in civil
and military affairs; and certainly his neglect of these
time-honored expedients did not prevent him from receiving unequalled loyalty and devotion from those men
whom he treated candidly and justly.   After reading the
shifty mystifications and disingenuous artifices practised
on their followers by Roman statesmen and generals like
Scipio and Sulla, it is not a little refreshing to turn to
Cæsar's bold and open nullification of the conventional
chicanery attempted by his colleague Bibulus, or to the
straightforward and spirited reprimand which he addressed to his panic-stricken and half-mutinous soldiers
early in his Gallic wars.[4]   Suetonius says that when in
Africa his men were alarmed by reports of the enemy's
strength, he did not deny the truth but chaffed them by

[1] Cic., de Div., II, 6; Lucret., V, 751; cf. Pliny, N. H., II, 28ff;
53f; 56f; Sen., Quæst. Nat., I, 12.

[2] Cass. Dio, LX, 26; Cf. Juvenal, VI, 442; Martial, XII, 57.

[3] Mommsen's unrestrained eulogy of Cæsar has been followed
by a natural reaction; but in the opinion of the writer, Mommsen's
judgment is nearer the truth than Ferrero's chilly estimate.

[4] Cæsar, B. G., I, 40; cf. id., VII, 52-53; B. C., I, 7; III, 73,
85, 90

humorous exaggerations of the hostile forces, and told them that now they must make no further inquiries or guesses on the subject, or he would send them away.[1] Even when they had met with a serious defeat in Epirus which greatly embarrassed him, he pointed out to them, as the means of redressing their ill-fortune, a reliance not on favors to be extracted from divinities, but on their own hard work and courage.[2] Such things as prodigies, prophecies, and holy days never deterred nor retarded him in the prosecution of any enterprise.[3] Order and obedience he obtained by telling his men the truth frankly and by maintaining a discipline marked by strictness and even severity, but so obviously just that the soldiers themselves coöperated in its enforcement.[4] Throughout his life he was abstemious, courageous, incessantly laborious, and amazingly energetic.[5] To clients he showed the greatest zeal and fidelity; to friends he was kind, considerate and devoted, never forgetting an obligation,[6] while to his enemies among the Romans, even to faithless friends, he manifested a complete absence of rancor and even a generous clemency so incredible as to bewilder its recipients. It is the possession of these rare qualities of moral dignity and honesty, quite as much as his consummate military genius, that has made the world recognize in Cæsar one of the few supremely great men of history.

The philosophic formulation of this fearless attitude towards gods and men, the attitude of the true followers of Epicurus, may be found in the immortal poem of

---

[1] Suet., *Jul.*, 66.   [2] *Cæsar*, *B. C.*, III, 73.

[3] Suet., *Jul.*, 59, 54, 65, 77, 86; Appian, *B. C.*, II, 152-153; Cic., *de Div.*, II, 24.

[4] *Cæsar*, *B. C.*, III, 74; Suet., *Jul.* 65, 69, 70.

[5] Suet., *Jul.*, 53, 57.   [6] *Id.*, 71, 72.

[7] *Cf.* p. 288. See also Cæsar, *B. C.*, I, 39; Cic., *ad Att.*, IX, 13; *ad Fam.*, VI, 6(8); *ad Att.*, VIII, 13.

Cæsar's contemporary, Lucretius. If religion is to be defined by the modern phrase, "morality touched with emotion," then it may be said that Lucretius was one of the most religious men who ever lived.[1] He looked out upon a confused world full of terror-inspiring fictions of divine caprice and tyranny. It is his burning indignation against this terrorism, and his fervent aspiration to bring peace to men by showing them the calm law and order of the cosmos, that give to Lucretius his inspiration and eloquence. He was determined to drive out dread of natural phenomena and of the cruel anthropomorphic gods, leaving the world free to scientific investigation.[2]

> For even as children, are flurried and dread all things in the thick darkness, thus we in the daylight fear at times things not a whit more to be dreaded than what children shudder at in the dark and fancy sure to be. This terror therefore and darkness of mind must be dispelled not by the rays of the sun and glittering shafts of day, but by the aspect and law of nature.[3]

The wise teachings of Epicurus show men how to gain this end.

> When human life to view lay foully prostrate upon earth crushed down under the weight of religion, who shewed her head from the quarters of heaven with hideous aspect lowering upon mortals, a man of Greece ventured first to lift up his mortal eyes to her face and first to withstand her to her face. Him neither story of gods nor thunderbolts nor heaven with threatening roar could quell.[4]

[1] *Cf.* Sellar, *Roman Poets of the Republic* (3rd ed., London, 1889), p. 360.

[2] See C. Martha, *Le Poème de Lucrèce, passim;* G. Boissier, *Religion romaine,* vol. I, p. 277ff.

[3] Lucret., VI, 34-40 (Munro's trans.).

[4] *Id.,* I, 64-70 (Munro's trans.).

To minds debased with religion, Epicurus brings relief and strikes off their shackles. Be ye free, he proclaims, for there are no gods nor ghosts who will trouble you; such thoughts are but dreams, and after death is endless sleep. No man is consigned to Erebus, nor to black Tartarus: the region of Acheron is nowhere to be found, nor the torments across the Styx. Did men but realize that death sets a fixed limit to their woes, they would be able to defy the myths and menaces of poets. To live as a fool is the only hell, and true piety is naught but viewing all things with a serene mind.[1]

Peace of mind is the *summum bonum,* and to assist men in gaining it Lucretius gives a résumé of the scientific knowledge of the ancient world. Natural phenomena, he never wearies of explaining, are not the work of erratic dæmons or divinities. Instead, the world is an orderly cosmos governed by fixed and immutable laws. Many of the details of his scientific doctrines are wrong, but he firmly grasped—and this is the essential thing—the controlling principle of all true science, the universality of causation and the invariability of its forms of manifestation. There are no secrets and no mysteries in his philosophy, no dialectic subtleties; nor does he make a philosophic attack on theism. He attacks not the gods, but only the base superstitions about them, and the evil that false beliefs do to mankind. The keynote throughout is contained in the famous phrase: *tantum religio potuit suadere malorum.*

The spirit of kindliness towards men, and the desire to benefit them, rising in Lucretius to splendid heights of moral enthusiasm, were characteristics of Epicureanism from its foundation and made it always essentially humane

[1] Lucret., I, 71ff; II, 55ff; 610-623; III, 1ff 25, 54, 88ff, 944ff; IV, 34-45; V, 1ff, 62ff, 1161ff.

as well as humanistic. Unlike some philosophic systems, it never lost itself in the clouds; nor was it ever indifferent or contemptuous toward mankind. More than any other school of philosophy it retained an indelible and fervently affectionate devotion to the person of its founder. It developed neither heresies nor schisms, and preserved always the quality of warm-heartedness which distinguishes it from the chill and inhuman aridity of Stoicism.[1] Epicurus himself laid the greatest emphasis on friendship, not merely in abstract doctrines but in actual conduct.[2]

With this ideal continually before them, the Epicureans were relatively free from a tendency to become egoistic; they seem, so far as we can judge, to have kept in touch with their fellow men, not losing interest in them, nor desiring to turn from them to a life of abstract speculation, mystical revery, or concern for their own souls. An example of this characteristic, interesting in its naïveté, is furnished by the fragments of an inscription found among the ruins of Oinoanda, a town in Asia Minor.

A citizen of this little place, Diogenes by name, erected a colonnade in which he caused to be placed an inscription three courses high, and extending longitudinally over twenty metres.[3] Addressing it to his kinsmen, household, and friends, he states that he is ill with an affection of the heart and his life is very uncertain, but that he has shaken off all fears and nearly all pains; he would gladly live but if not—then comes a break. Being now near the

[1] *Cf.* C. Martha, *op. cit.,* pp. 344-347 and citations.

[2] See Diogenes Laertius, X, 5, 6, 10ff; Zeller, *Stoics, Epicureans and Sceptics* (Eng. trans., London, 1891), p. 491ff.

[3] See H. Usener, *Rhein. Mus.,* vol. 47 (1892), pp. 414-456; R. Heberdey and E. Kalinka, *Bull. Corr. Hellénique,* vol. 21 (1897), pp. 346-443; J. William *Diogenis Œnoandensis Fragmenta,* Leipzig, 1907; R. T. Glover, *Conflict of Religions in Early Roman Empire* (3rd ed., 1909), pp. 217-220.

sunset of life, and grieving over the way men waste their lives, he thinks it the part of a good man to help others as much as he can, to help those who are to live after us, for they, too, are ours, even though not yet born, to help even strangers. Most men are poisoned with false opinions as if by a pestilence; for them he sets up this colonnade and public inscription which, he hopes, will bring them joy and happiness more than would a theatre, or public baths; for it contains the medicine of salvation—a knowledge of the nature of the universe.

The body of the inscription consists of what is practically a treatise on Epicurean philosophy. He begins by controverting some different philosophic opinions, not, so he says, in any spirit of ill-will against these other teachers but that truth may be safeguarded. Then he proceeds to argue against the idea of divine intervention in human affairs and to deny the fabulous tales of terrors and tortures beyond the grave. By helping his fellow-citizens to know that all are entitled to peace of mind, he feels that he can do more for his city than by any political activities.

Whatever may be thought of the philosophy which seemed to him who erected this unique inscription, so valuable a human possession, there can be no question as to his sincere good-heartedness; and were the defects and errors of his medicine of salvation far greater than they are, the inscription would still indicate a sounder character than is to be found in the hypochondriacal egotisms of which the times furnish so many epigraphical and literary remains.[1]

For a life of unassuming, unsentimental, intelligent and unswerving benevolence and beneficence to his fellow-

[1] *Cf.* S. Dill, *Roman Society from Nero to M. Aurelius*, p. 459ff.

men, few characters in history have a fairer reputation than the Epicurean Pomponius Atticus, the contemporary of Cæsar and Cicero. The sketch of him by his friend Cornelius Nepos might well seem too favorable for truth, were it not so indubitably confirmed by the revelation of his character contained in Cicero's letters. He was a brilliant student as a youth, and kept up his literary studies. His father left him property and he inherited a large fortune from his crusty uncle with whom he alone could keep on good terms. By prudent investments and various business activities, including book-publishing, his opulence increased. In the Marius-Sulla civil wars, he assisted the younger Marius, a proscribed public enemy, yet he gained the affection of Sulla, who commended his good feeling in declining to engage against his friends in the civil conflicts. He helped impoverished Athens by loans without interest and donations of corn, yet refused, so long as he lived there, the honor of a public statue.

Though he kept out of active participation in the civil strifes, he was no recluse, and friends sought his valuable assistance in their political campaigns. Cæsar admired him and paid him marked favors, though he was an intimate friend of Pompey and had given financial relief to many of his friends in that party. After the assassination of Cæsar, he refused to contribute to a fund for the assassins, though Brutus and he were very intimate; but when the situation changed and Brutus's prospects were black, Atticus helped him without waiting for solicitation, and after Philippi, helped his family. When Antony's star seemed to have set, before the formation of the triumvirate, Atticus relieved the necessities of his friends and of his termagant wife; and yet all this time he was Cicero's most intimate friend. It seems to have been his custom to show an increased devotion to his friends' interests just when their affairs were at their worst. At the time of the proscription he was treated most courteously by the triumvirs, and was able to save some friends. In his old age, both Antony and Octavianus delighted in his society and wrote him regularly during their absences from Rome. He married when he was over fifty, and proved an excellent husband and affectionate father. Agrippa preferred to be his son-in-law rather than to seek an alliance with one of the great families, for Atticus remained a simple knight. Octavianus brought about the betrothal of his stepson Tiberius to Agrippa's daughter in her infancy, and later she became the wife from whom this grave prince was compelled to part for reasons of state, but whom he continued to love.

His style of living was refined and elegant, after the old manner, but was singularly free from ostentation, extravagance, frivolity, and laxity of morals; nor did he indulge in a more expensive mode of life when, by his uncle's death, he came into the possession of a large fortune. After seventy-seven years of general good health, he fell ill of a disease that was incurable and increasingly painful, and after a fair attempt at medical treatment, and consultation with his friends, he abstained from food; and after a few days of comparative relief he died and was buried, as he had wished, without pomp, but attended by all Rome.[1]

[1] G. Boissier (*Cicero and his Friends,* Eng. trans., N. Y., 1898) seems unsympathetic towards Atticus. His criticisms seem to arise from the abstention from public life charged against Atticus. Yet Atticus did not abstain from public life but only from seeking public office. *Cf.* p. 151ff. The statements purporting to be based on *ad Att.,* VIII, 2, 15; X, 16 and XIV, 10, are inaccurate, and in the matter of the attitude taken by Atticus as to Cicero's joining Pompey are not in accord with the résumé given by Cic., *ad Att.,* IX, 10.

His writings have all perished, and we may the more regret their loss, since to no other Roman, so far as we know, was there paid such a tribute regarding the matter of special interest to our inquiry. Nepos said of him: "he would neither utter a falsehood nor could he endure it." [1] This characteristic of accuracy and truthfulness in the historical writings of Atticus was sufficiently remarked by Cicero, and it is a quality that is rarely even mentioned in reference to an ancient writer.[2] But it would be necessary to think that Nepos permitted his friendship to lead him too far, were the last clause of the sentence quoted above to be interpreted, as is usually done, as referring to falsehood in others. For if Atticus had not tolerated deceit in others he would have had to diminish his circle of friends very materially. Cicero, his intimate friend, seems to have had no hesitation in sending to Atticus for his perusal copies of distinctly mendacious letters which the orator had sent to Antony, Dolabella and others; or in telling him of the use of a falsehood in a controversy with an ungrateful freedman. Indeed, if we may rely upon subsequent references in Cicero's letters Atticus did not indulge in that intolerance of his friend's duplicity which the passage in Nepos might lead one to expect.[3] It also appears pretty distinctly that Marcus Brutus had disingenuously misled Atticus regarding a rather shady financial matter without, so far as we can discover, impairing the good relations between them.[4] It is quite out of the question to suppose that the sage old man ever sought to impose on others very strict moral rules in this respect when we consider the large circle of

---

[1] *Mendacium neque dicebat neque pati poterat, Att.*, 15.
[2] Cic., *Brutus*, 3, 11.
[3] Cic., *ad Att.*, XIV, 13, 13b, 17; X, 10.
[4] Cic., *ad Att.*, V, 21; VI, 1, 2, 3.

friends he had and kept, and the abundance of mendacity in which some of them indulged. All that can fairly be inferred from his career is that he confined his attention to his own morals. Cicero, it will be observed, represents him as smilingly tolerating in the historical compositions of others a laxity which he personally disdained to use.[1]

When we have available no writings of an author whose veracity is to be determined, we cannot but feel that this lack of direct material is inadequately supplied by the statements of admiring friends, especially when their general truthfulness is not established, but in the case of Cæsar we have extant writings, his commentaries on the Gallic and on the Civil Wars. In view of the fact that these books were published as political documents to gain public favor in a time of confusion and revolution; that the former related to events of wars in wild countries withdrawn almost entirely from the eyes of the Romans and known only by Cæsar's soldiers, who, with the exception of a few officers, were thoroughly devoted to him; that the indubitable success obtained in the war rendered not improbable the insertion of favorable details; that the purpose of these books would be fulfilled if they could gain credence and exalt the reputation of the writer for a short time, however completely they might be disproved later; that Cæsar was a skilled orator and that the Roman people were enamored of rhetorical embellishment in all sorts of literary composition, and tolerant of wide departures from strict accuracy, it might be supposed that the author would embellish, garble, and invent episodes with a view to winning the commendation of readers and the support of statesmen who should hail him as the sole hope of the tottering Republic.

[1] Cic., *Brutus*, 11.

However natural such a supposition might be, it is not confirmed by the actual narrative. Instead of meretricious embellishment, we find a style dry, precise, almost bald. "Simple, correct and graceful, divested of all the ornaments of language, of all drapery, as it were," is Cicero's characterization.[1] There is no hint in the Gallic War of Cæsar's political views, no reference at all, in fact, to political questions. Even when Cato and others in the Senate had attempted to disavow and censure Cæsar's conduct in detaining the envoys of two German tribes, falling upon their camp, and massacring the entire body, Cæsar's narrative betrays no hint of the criticisms at Rome. He does no. disguise the act, nor defend it; his account merely implies that his conduct was advantageous to Roman interests.[2]

A detailed review of Cæsar's statements in these Commentaries for the purpose of judging of his veracity is a task fortunately rendered unnecessary after Mr. Holmes's able and exhaustive study of the Gallic War.[3] His conclusion accords fully with the opinion of the Duc d' Aumale that Cæsar was "le plus sincère de ceux qui ont écrit leur propre histoire."

In view of the fact that the philosophy of the Epicureans has been commonly regarded as a cloak for voluptuousness and that the stronghold of morality lay in other systems of thought, chiefly Stoicism,[4] it may be

[1] Cic., Brutus, 75; Asinius Pollio thinks they were not drawn up with due care and regard for truth (Suet., Jul., 56), but Pollio had a reputation for being hypercritical. Cf. Quintilian, I, 5, 56; VIII, 1, 3; XII, 1, 22; Suet., de Gram., 10.

[2] Cæsar, B. G., IV, 4-15; Plut., Cæs., 22. Cf. T. Rice Holmes, Cæsar's Conquest of Gaul (London, 1911), p. 99.

[3] Op. cit., pp. 211-256.

[4] Cf. Mommsen, History of Rome (Eng. trans., N. Y., 1895), vol. IV, p. 201ff; Merivale, History of the Romans under the

of interest to take a limited period of Roman history where our material is relatively abundant in an endeavor to gain definite information about the general character of the Epicureans of the time. Such a period can hardly be any other than that covered by the correspondence of Cicero.

As we have had several occasions to observe, Cicero's principles regarding veracity accommodated themselves automatically to the exigencies of the situation, but he seems always to have been ready to gird at the Epicurean philosophy and to insist on its deleterious effects. We are therefore entitled to regard his statements which are at variance with this prepossession as worthy of credence. In the nine hundred letters of the correspondence of Cicero and his friends, there are many expressions on his part of judgments regarding the moral character of most of the important men of the times. These judgments vary with the political situation and the person to whom he is writing—whether to the man himself or to some confidential friend like Atticus. To this "dearest and most delightful" of friends, he seems always to have written with perfect frankness and with absolute confidence in his friend's patience,[1] discretion, and readiness to assist, when occasion demanded, with advice, money, or action. Indeed, so great a degree of trust in Atticus do these letters display, and so amply was it justified in every case, that the eulogy which Nepos wrote seems not far removed from the truth. It is somewhat surprising, therefore, that Cicero should have felt disposed to speak in terms of

---

Empire (N. Y., 1896, 4th London ed.), vol. II, pp. 352, 401; Lecky, *History of European Morals*, vol. I, p. 175ff; Tucker, *Life in the Roman World of Nero and St. Paul*, pp. 408-409.

[1] See, *e.g., ad Att.*, XII, 22.

reprobation regarding the moral effect of his friend's philosophic principles.[1]

There were not a few of Cicero's contemporaries of whose moral character he had, whether rightly or wrongly, a distinctly poor opinion, but with the exception of Piso, of whom more hereafter, none of these blackguards—we cannot approach the richness of Cicero's vocabulary of vituperation—was charged with Epicureanism. He does not hint that the shockingly infamous conduct ascribed to Verres, Catiline, Vatinius, Gabinius, Dolabella, Antony or most of all human beings—Clodius and his sister Clodia, was the natural result of their adoption of this depraved philosophy. Not even the lesser knaves are tainted with it. On the contrary, with the exception noted, the persons whom he mentions as addicted to it are guilty of nothing but the inconsistency, as he frequently notes, of not being what their creed ought to make them. In fact, Cicero's Epicurean friends, although he is not so impressed by their marvellous virtue as he is by that of the more pretentious Stoics, seem to have been the best people he knew.

Preëminent in the Ciceronian circle was Julius Cæsar. Cicero was never really fond of Cæsar, whose political course nearly always met his disapproval, and whose assassination he hailed with rapturous but short-lived delight. He was prepared to see oppressive measures perpetrated by this destroyer of the old Republic; and he waited gloomily for the tyranny to begin.[2] But little by

---

[1] Zeller, *Stoics, Epicureans and Sceptics*, p. 415 n. infers that Atticus was not an Epicurean from the language of *ad Fam.*, XIII, 1: *non quo sit ex istis; est enim omni liberali doctrina politissimus.* The context seems rather to indicate that Cicero meant that Atticus did not neglect the liberal studies which, according to Cicero, were insufficiently appreciated and cultivated by the stricter Epicureans. *Cf. de Fin.*, I, 7; *de Nat. Deor.*, I, 26.

[2] *Ad. Att.*, IX, 2a, 18; VII, 22.

little he was forced to marvel at Cæsar's "sobriety, fairness, and wisdom," his "kind and clement disposition." And gradually the letters give us a picture of the great dictator which is attractive and the more striking in that it is so reluctantly drawn.[1] It was, perhaps, a solace to Cicero to turn from this tyranny of facts and, retiring to one of his villas, to produce a philosophic treatise containing powerful assertions—we can hardly call them demonstrations—that it is not possible for an Epicurean to be brave, temperate or just, nor to possess even kindness, liberality, or friendship.[2] It is only in these treatises on ethics, with their convictions based not on experience but upon disappointed ambition and a reading of Greek philosophers, that Cæsar appears as an oppressor whom it would be an honorable exploit to slay.[3]

In the little circle which Cæsar gathered about him there were several Epicureans whose characters seem to satisfy Cicero. Of the two consuls in the year of Cæsar's death, Pansa is mentioned as a man whose character is good and is approved by good people, and whose word can be trusted.[4] He was on terms of friendly intimacy with Cicero, visiting him shortly after the assassination. The break in Cicero's agreeable references to him comes when Pansa seems unlikely to show sufficient vigor for the restoration of the Republic; then the fear is expressed that he and his colleague Hirtius are sunk in wine and sleep. The events of the next few months showed this

[1] *Ad Fam.*, VI, 6; cf. IV, 13; VI, 10, 13, 14; XIII, 19, 29, 35, 36; *ad Att.*, XI, 6, 7; Sallust, *Cat.*, 54.

[2] *De Off.*, I, 2; III, 3. That Cæsar was an Epicurean is sufficiently indicated by his attitude towards divination and man's posthumous state. *Cf.* Sallust, *Cat.*, 51, doubtless largely apocryphal but confirmed in this respect by Cicero, *Cat.*, IV, 4.

[3] *Cf. ad Att.*, IX, 7, 9, 11a; *de Off.*, III, 21.

[4] *Ad Fam.*, XV, 17; VI, 12; VII, 12; XV, 19.

fear to be groundless, and Pansa's sentiments and political conduct having proved satisfactory, his character recovers in Cicero's eyes its customary excellence.[1] The philosophic opinions of Hirtius are not mentioned; like Pansa, he met his death in the successful campaign which the two consuls made against Antony (April 27, 43 B.C. at Mutina).[2] He was on the same friendly terms with Cicero as was his colleague, and we read that together with Pansa and Balbus, another intimate associate of Cæsar, he was Cicero's guest at his villa on the bay of Naples a few weeks after the death of Cæsar. In May he is again a guest at the same place.[3] These men, who were of Cæsar's inmost circle and among whom Epicureanism was the reigning philosophy, seem to have followed their leader in manifesting towards Cicero a courtesy and consideration [4] which contrast pleasantly with the attitude of Brutus; and Cicero's frequent comments on them to Atticus would not suggest that they were men of bad character. It might be urged that Cicero concealed his real opinions from considerations of personal safety, but this seems improbable in view of the fact that he felt free enough to express severe judgments on Antony, who had also treated him with courtesy.

Another of Cicero's friends was Trebatius Testa, who

[1] *Ad Att.*, XVI, 1; cf. *ad Fam.*, XVI, 27; XI, 5; XII, 22, 25; *ad Att.*, XVI, 9.

[2] *Ad Fam.*, IX, 16, 20; XI, 9; *ad Att.*, XII, 34, 44; XIII, 37; XV, 1; *de Fato*, 1; *ad Brut.*, I, 3a.

[3] *Ad Att.*, XIV, 11; XV, 1. For Balbus see *ad Q. Frat.*, III, 1; Oppius, another of Cæsar's intimates, is commended for honesty and conscientiousness, *ad Fam.*, XI, 29; *ad Att.*, XVI, 2; *ad Q. Frat.*, III, 1.

[4] *Ad Fam.*, IX, 16; VI, 6, 12; VII, 24; *ad Att.*, XIII, 49, 50. Cicero's own brother was playing him false before Cæsar (47 B.C.) but unavailingly, *ad Att.*, XI, 8-16.

embraced Epicureanism while serving at Cæsar's head-quarters during the Gallic Wars. Cicero speaks of him as modest and industrious, and the change of philosophic faith seems to have been followed by an increase of energy, in which he had previously been somewhat deficient. His relations with Cicero continued to be cordial and intimate. A note written by Cicero in 44 B.C. indicates that he had tarried late at the table one evening over the wine. The guest was Cicero himself and the pastime was a discussion of abstruse legal problems; the next day Cicero sent a note saying that although he arrived home late and full of wine, he managed to hunt out in his law books some passages confuting his host's side of the controversy. On the whole he inclined to think that Trebatius was right in his opinion of the law, although wrong in declaring that it was not a disputed point.[1]

Cassius, who later became a prime mover in the tyrannicide plot, was also one who had embraced Epicureanism while serving under Cæsar. He retained enough of his earlier Stoicism to be vain and vindictive, but was sufficiently enlightened by his new philosophy to argue with Brutus against the reality of dæmons and especially of that particularly menacing one who is said to have announced to the latter his intention of appearing again at Philippi.[2] Cassius was far from being an admirable character, although he had some ability and even a little humor, and was free from the coarser vices which Cicero liked to declare the natural results of the Epicurean doctrines. On the whole, he compares favorably with his fellow-conspirators of loftier pretensions. In one of his letters he checks Cicero's idle misrepresentations of his philosophy, pointing out that it teaches the impos-

[1] *Ad Fam.*, VII, 6-22. [2] Plut., *Brut.*, 37, 38, 48.

sibility of living pleasantly without living justly and decently; that active happiness as well as its passive form of tranquillity, is obtained by virtue, equity, and rectitude, and that those whom Cicero calls "pleasure-lovers" are lovers of the good and just, cherishing and practising what is right.[1]

Other friends of Cicero, whom neither their support of Cæsar nor their Epicurean principles prevented Cicero from recognizing as men of high personal character, are Fadius Gallus[2] and Papirius Pætus.[3] Both manifested that amiability, helpfulness, and faithful friendship which seem to have been almost universal characteristics of members of their school of thought.[4]

A few adherents of this philosophy were not in the party of Cæsar, and among these may be mentioned Lucius Manlius Torquatus, whom Cicero makes the Epicurean representative in his *De Finibus* and refers to elsewhere with the greatest approbation.[5] Aulus Torquatus, a man of the same high character, was, we may infer, of the same sect, from the Epicurean tone of the consolations which Cicero addressed to him in exile.[6] Saufeius, the intimate friend of Atticus, seems also to have been of good repute.[7]

Cicero has occasion to mention various persons who had the double moral taint, according to his prejudices, of

---

[1] Cic., *ad Fam.*, XV, 16, 18, 19.

[2] *Ad Fam.*, II, 14; VII, 23-26; IX, 25; XV, 14; *ad Att.*, VIII, 12.

[3] *Ad Fam.*, IX, 16-26; *ad Att.*, I, 20; XIV, 16. *Cf. ad Fam.*, IX, 24 (43 B.C.).

[4] Matius Calvena may have been an Epicurean, although there is no direct evidence as to his philosophical affiliations. *Cf. ad Fam.*, VI, 12; VII, 15; XI, 27-28; *ad Att.*, IX, 11, 15; XIV, 1.

[5] *De Fin.*, I, 5ff; *Brut.*, 76; *ad Att.*, XIII, 5, 19, 32.

[6] *Ad Fam.*, VI, 1-4 (especially 3); *ad Att.*, V, 1; *de Fin.*, II, 22.

[7] *Ad Att.*, IV, 6; II, 8; VI, 1; VII, 1; XV, 4; *cf.* Nepos, *Att.*, 12.

being Greeks as well as professional teachers of Epicureanism. Such were Phædrus,[1] Patro,[2] Philodemus,[3] Syro,[4] and Xeno,[5] yet in every case save one the references to them are commendatory and even laudatory in character. In the case of Philodemus the statement in Cicero's philosophic treatise is favorable, but in the course of a political tirade against Piso, he involves Philodemus, as Piso's teacher, in his general invective.[6]

Besides these there are complimentary references to his eminent Epicurean friend Velleius,[7] and a colorless mention of the lately deceased Catius and the earlier Amafinius.[8] In speaking of the action of the Senate in refusing a *supplicatio* to Albucius—an event which took place about the time Cicero was born—he exculpates Albucius from any moral defect save indiscretion and thoughtlessness. He was condemned for irregularities in his provincial administration and retired to Athens, where he took up the study of philosophy and became an Epicurean.[9] Hence his misdeeds antedated his speculative errors.

---

[1] *Ad Fam.*, XIII, 1; *ad Att.*, XVI, 7; *de Fin.*, I, 5; V, 1; *Phil.*, V, 5; *de Nat. Deor.*, I, 33.

[2] *Ad Fam.*, XIII, 1; *ad Att.*, V, 11; VII, 2; *ad Q. Frat.*, I, 2, 4.

[3] *De Fin.*, II, 35; *in Pis.*, 28-29; author of the philosophical works discovered in Herculaneum; Zeller, *op. cit.*, p. 413.

[4] *Ad Fam.*, VI, 11; *de Fin.*, II, 35.

[5] *Ad Att.*, V, 10, 11; VII, 1; XVI, 3; *de Nat. Deor.*, I, 21. There seem to have been two of this name; *cf.* Zeller, *op. cit.*, p. 412, n. 3.

[6] *In Pis.*, 29.

[7] *De Nat. Deor.*, I, 6, 21; *de Orat.*, III, 21, 78.

[8] *Ad Fam.*, XV, 16; *cf.*; 19; *Acad. Post.*, I, 2; *Tusc. Disp.*, IV, 3, Memmius, to whom Lucretius dedicated his poem, was not an Epicurean, if we may judge from the language of *ad Fam.*, XIII, 1. For Asclepiades see Zeller, *op cit.*, p. 415.

[9] *De Prov. Cons.*, 7; *in Pis.*, 38; *de Fin.*, I, 3; *Brutus*, 35; *Tusc. Disp.*, V, 37.

Three men are mentioned by Cicero in his philosophical writings as having lived lives of refined luxury but without excesses or indulgence in vice. These are Thorius Balbus,[1] Sergius Orata,[2] and Postumius,[3] who are possibly put forward by Cicero as Epicureans, although not explicitly so. The extent of their offending seems limited to the invention of such things as heated baths and artificial oyster beds, an interest in fish ponds, or undue attention to their *cuisines*. It is, however, a proceeding of doubtful propriety to class men as Epicureans merely because Cicero's description of them approaches his theoretical Epicurean type, especially when the characteristics of the theoretical type are seen to be inconsistent with the real Epicureans whom he describes.

The foregoing, with one addition, are all the Epicureans mentioned as such by Cicero, nor do other historical authorities indicate any important additions which should be made,[4] save of course the great name of Lucretius, unless we include Cornelius Gallus; Horace, Varus, and Virgil, to whom no great reproach can be justly attached, belong to the next generation.

We have omitted, however, the name of L. Calpurnius Piso Cæsonius, the father of Cæsar's wife Calpurnia, who was an object of Cicero's heated denunciation as a

---

[1] *De Fin.*, II, 20.

[2] Cicero quoted by Augustine, *de Vit. Beata,* 26; *cf. de Fin.*, II, 22; *de Off.*, III, 16; *de Orat.*, I, 39; Varro, *de Re Rust.*, III, 3; Pliny, *N. H.*, IX, 171.

[3] *De Fin.*, II, 22.

[4] Plutarch (*Brut.*, 12) refers briefly to a certain Statilius as an Epicurean approached by Brutus but refusing to join in the plot. Possibly he is the Statilius of Plutarch's *Cato Minor* (66, 73). Suetonius (*de Grammaticis,* 8) mentions Pompilius Andronicus, a Syrian, who neglected his grammatical teaching for his Epicurean studies, and who, though writing much, remained poor.

complete rogue. The charges made against this pupil of Philodemus are of special interest as an example of much of the historical material commonly relied upon to establish the moral character of prominent Romans. A glance at the political situation will serve to show the utter baselessness of most of Cicero's charges.

Had Cicero understood himself and the situation, he might have become the public orator of the first triumvirate. When he opposed the powerful coalition, his greatness as the savior of Rome and *pater patriae* fell like a house of cards. In 58 B.C., while the consuls Piso and Gabinius stood aloof, they allowed the vivacious Clodius to harry the bewildered Cicero and drive him into an exile that was appalling to his vanity. His opportunity for revenge on the two consuls came in the middle of 56 B.C., when a scheme was proposed in the Senate by the oligarchy to assign provinces to the consuls to be elected later that year. The real purpose of the measure was to deprive Cæsar of Cisalpine or Transalpine Gaul, or both,[1] under the pretext of making places for the new consuls. Piso and Gabinius were now governors respectively of Macedonia and Syria, and were they to be recalled, the necessary two provincial governorships would be vacant for the new consuls without disturbing Cæsar. Here was a great opening for Cicero; in the first place he could render service to those whom he must satisfy, and in the second place he could gratify his own longing to punish some of the enemies who had laughed at his distress.

With these motives operating, and with the free hand given him by the absence of Cæsar in Gaul and Pompey in

---

[1] In 56 B.C., the triumvirs renewed their understanding, which involved the extension of Cæsar's proconsulate for five years and the election of Pompey and Crassus as consuls for the year 55.

Sardinia or Africa, Cicero proceeded to indulge his great talent for vituperation, whose unreality he had explained in a speech, delivered shortly before this one.[1] He begins his speech (*de Provinciis Consularibus*) by declaring that he is entitled to have a strong detestation of Piso and Gabinius, but he will reserve it for the day of vengeance. He will also pass over the notorious wickedness they displayed in getting their assignments to these provinces, not least of which was their unsympathetic treatment of the orator. There have been, he declares, many incursions of barbarians into Macedonia whereby it has been greatly harassed, and the entire Roman army there has perished from war, capture, famine, and disease. The allies have been oppressed by the governor; Byzantium has been plundered and would have been stripped by Piso of all its numerous statues had not Caius Vergilius, the legate, intervened.[2]

Then, as Cicero warms to his work, there is found to be not a statue nor an ornament left in a temple or sacred place in all Greece. He omits Piso's murders and acts of lust as well as reference to highborn maidens who cast themselves into wells that by a voluntary death they might escape dishonor.

> I do not omit these things [he says] because they are not most atrocious, but because I am speaking now without having any witnesses to produce. . . . Let his dark acts of lust remain hidden, those acts which he used to conceal by effrontery and arrogance, not by modesty and temperance.[3]

The orator then proceeds to deal with Gabinius in somewhat the same way; complains of him for having sent

[1] *Pro Caelio*, 3; *aliud est dicere, aliud accusare*, etc.; *cf.* 13.
[2] It is strange that a legate could interfere with a proconsul.
[3] *De Prov. Cons.*, 1-4.

letters to the Senate narrating victories, and of Piso for not having done so; and then passes on to a laudation of Cæsar, explaining how it is that the speaker is now supporting the triumvirate.

Piso came back to Rome the next year; complained in the Senate of Cicero's scurrility; defended his provincial administration, and worst of all, chaffed Cicero about his writing sorry and self-laudatory verse. We are also told by Cicero that his exile was referred to by Piso in a slighting and insulting manner, but that the senators crushed the insolent frenzy of this abject monster not merely by murmurs but by a loud outcry.[1] It would seem extraordinary, one might suppose, that the Senate should display so much zeal for one whom most of them probably regarded as a clever upstart.

The first part of Cicero's *Oration against Piso* survives only in fragments, but enough remains to show us that it consisted of general abuse of Piso's maternal ancestors. Scattered through the speech are heated assertions that all despise and hate him—senators, knights, people, soldiers, all Italy and the provinces—and believe him guilty of enormous crimes.[2] He is ignorant, coarse, and beastly, and has spent his life in drunkenness and debauchery in the lowest and vilest resorts. He is an Epicurus, brought forth from his stye, and the orator proposes in the future to raise the question of his thefts, sacrilege, and murders.[3] Numerous charges are interjected in the form of questions, or in such phrases as: "what shall I say of" so and so, or "I pass over," this and that.[4] Piso dared not send reports to the Senate, or at any rate if he did, they were not read to that body.[5] He lost his army, or at least

[1] *In Piso.*, 14.
[2] *Ib.*, 12-14, 20, 27, 40-41.
[3] *Ib.*, 1, 6, 8, 10, 18, 27, 36.
[4] *Ib.*, 16, 36-37.
[5] *Ib.*, 16-19, 40.

brought none of it to Rome, and even disbanded some of it. He failed to demand a triumph; he says that he never had any desire for a triumph. What wickedness is this! What business had he not to desire a triumph! "O, thou gloom! thou filth! thou muck!" [1] Such is the language, mitigated in deference to modern taste, of this lengthy oration, apparently irrelevant to any question before the house.

It is to be noticed that the remarkable intervention of the legate to control the governor, set forth in the earlier sketch of the *de Provinciis Consularibus,* does not figure in the oration against Piso; so, too, the penchant for collecting Byzantine statuary. The loss of the army is now confused with a mere discharge of the soldiers; [2] nor do we hear any details about the highborn maidens who flung themselves into wells. Cicero admitted he had no evidence for these charges in the earlier speech, and the careful, detailed examination of Piso's iniquities, which he claims to have made, seems to have failed to substantiate these counts of the earlier indictment. [3]

Only once does Cicero give us any indication of the character of the evidence on which he is relying, and it is instructive to see what it is. After some particularly tart assertions of the low vulgarity of his private life, the orator pauses. "But someone will say, 'whence did the knowledge of these things come to you?'" Well, a Greek philosopher (Philodemus) had endeavored to instruct Piso, but no sooner had he made the statement that pleasure was the *summum bonum* than Piso refused to hear further explanation and proceeded to put this lesson into practice. The Greek was impressed by the austere countenance which had deceived even the wise Romans,

[1] *Ib.,* 20-26.   [2] *Ib.,* 20.
[3] *Ib.,* 34, 38.

and let himself be turned into an obscene poet. He was compelled to put into most polished verse the various debaucheries of the wicked pupil; and in these poems, so Cicero says, any one who wished could see as in a mirror the life of Piso.[1]

Even the Romans with all their liberality in the matter of evidence seem to have paid no attention whatever to this vituperation. At the next election of censors, although the adherents of Cæsar were in a minority, and although Piso was said not to have cared for the position, he was elected to this high office,[2] and was later referred to as among the most illustrious Romans.[3] What is even more to the point is that the conduct of Cicero himself was not that of a man who took the charges seriously. After almost continuous threats of what is going to happen to Piso, he ends with the lame statement that all he wishes to do is to frighten Piso, to tear his reputation to pieces; he has no intention of prosecuting him.[4] It may be urged that this was because of fear of Cæsar; but were this consideration a reason to refrain from prosecuting, it might have suggested a less savage and insolent vituperation. But we have another expression of Cicero in a letter to Atticus, when the civil war had begun and Piso's political conduct was satisfactory to Cicero, an expression which seems unduly gentle to apply to one whose lifelong character was

[1] *Ib.*, 29: *rogatus, invitatus, coactus ita multa ad istum de ipso quoque scripsit, ut omnes libidines, omnia stupra, omnia cenarum conviviorumque genera, adulteria denique eius delicatissimis versibus expresserit, in quibus, si qui velit, possit istius tamquam in speculo vitam intueri.* A number of Philodemus's amatory epigrams have been preserved in the *Anthologia Graeca.*

[2] Cass. Dio, XL, 63.

[3] Appian, *B. C.*, III, viii, 50.

[4] *In Pis.*, 18-20, 41. For Cicero's later attitude toward Gabinius see *pro Rabirio Postumo*, 8.

believed to be that of an obscene monster. It is: "Indeed, I love Piso." [1]

Now the query suggests itself, was this speech ever delivered; was it anything more than a fanciful rhetorical exercise, expressing in whirling words Cicero's wounded vanity of the moment? Some of his wildest harangues were closet declamations and intended only for private circulation, or perhaps merely to relieve his feelings. There is a story in Cassius Dio that Cicero about this time composed a violent invective against Cæsar and Cassius, but fearing trouble if it became public, he sealed it up and left it to be opened only after his death. [2] Some of his best known orations were never used in public, at least in their present form. [3] As to the one under consideration, it seems to be purely declamatory; it is not a speech urging some course of action upon the Senate. Furthermore, there is no indication in the correspondence or other writings of Cicero or his friends or any other person that such a speech was ever delivered. After the time when it is supposed to have been made, [4] Cicero was frequently interchanging letters with his brother Quintus and with his friend Trebatius Testa, both of whom were with Cæsar in Gaul, and there was some correspondence with Cæsar himself, but no hint appears that Cicero was inquiring or was desirous of knowing how the powerful triumvir took this vile assault upon his wife's father. There are several letters to Atticus, but no reference is made to it,

[1] *Ad Att.*, VII, 13: *amo etiam Pisonem. Cf. ad Fam.*, XIV, 14, where Cicero commends Piso to his wife and daughter. In *ad Fam.*, IV, 4; XII, 2, Cicero seems to have been working harmoniously with him. Brutus, it appears, praised him highly. *Ad Att.*, XVI, 7.

[2] Cass. Dio, XXXIX, 10. *Cf. ad Att.*, II, 6; XIV, 17.

[3] See *e.g.*, *in Verrem act. sec; pro Milone, Philippica*, II.

[4] In the summer of 55 B.C.

nor is it mentioned in a very long explanation of his
political acts covering this year which he wrote to Lentulus
Spinther.[1]

On the contrary, there is a letter from Cicero to his
brother Quintus in Gaul, in which this passage occurs:

> The next thing is about the speech of Calventius Marius
> (this name is probably a pseudonym for Piso[2]). I am
> surprised at what you write—that you are of the opinion
> that I should make an answer to it; particularly as no
> one is likely to read it, unless I do write an answer,
> while every schoolboy learns mine against him as if it
> were a school exercise.[3]

This letter was written about the end of September, 54
B.C., a year after the supposed oration against Piso. It
seems clear from it that the orations then in existence
were: one from Cicero against Piso, which schoolboys use
as an exercise, and one from Piso against Cicero, which
would not be read unless Cicero advertised it by answering
it. When Quintus suggested making this reply, Cicero
was surprised that his brother overlooked the fact that
this would bring Piso's speech to public attention. Inasmuch as there had not yet been a reply to Piso, it is
evident that the speech referred to in Cicero's letter was

[1] *Ad Fam.*, I, 9 (54 B.C.). *Cf.* I, 7.

[2] Calventius was the name of Piso's grandfather which Cicero
applied to him in contempt for his Gallic ancestry (*in Pis.*, 6, 23;
Asconius, Clark, p. 5). Marius may refer to an idea of Cicero
that he left Rome to escape a contest with Piso as Metellus had
done in the hopeless contest with Marius (*in Pis.*, 9). No one
by the name Calventius Marius is known.

[3] *Ad Q. Frat.*, III, 1, 4; *alterum est de Calventi Mari oratione
quod scribis. Miror tibi placere me ad eam rescribere, praesertim
cum illam nemo lecturus sit si ego nihil rescripsero, mam in illum
pueri omnes tamquam dictata perdiscant.*

De Provinciis Consularibus delivered in the year 56; that Piso's speech was the one delivered on his return from Macedonia in 55, containing the allusion to Cicero's poetry; and that Cicero had not delivered the speech now known as the *Oration against Piso* up to September of the year 54. Yet the oration purports to have been spoken before the return of Gabinius to Rome, which was September 27 of the year 54.[1] Indeed, we can fix the purported date more closely, for the reference [2] to the near approach of the most elaborate and magnificent games "in the memory of man, such as not only have never been but can never occur in the future" can hardly mean anything else than the games exhibited by Pompey in the year 55, when, as consul, he dedicated the great theatre which he was presenting to the people.

The foregoing argument has been based on the strong probability that the cryptic name "Calventius Marius" [3] in the letter to Quintus Cicero refers to Piso. If the assumption is correct the conclusion seems inevitable that the oration against Piso was not in existence for more than a year after the date of its supposed delivery (55 B.C.). But the same conclusion arises independently of that letter.

It was perfectly natural that in June, 56 B.C., when Cicero had just been roughly awakened from his dream of heading the optimates in their opposition to Pompey and Cæsar,[4] when both Pompey and Cæsar were far away and he had been left to choose his own means of carrying out their orders to oppose the attempt to cut short Cæsar's

---

[1] *In Pis.*, 21-22; *ad Q. Frat.*, III, 1, 4. He did not appear in the Senate for ten days, *ad Q. Frat.*, III, 2.

[2] *In Pis.*, 27.

[3] Cf. *in Pis.*, frag. 11; Asconius, Clark, p. 5.

[4] *Ad Fam.*, I, 7-9.

proconsular imperium in the Gallic provinces, and when the best course might well seem to be to urge the recall of Piso and Gabinius in order that the necessary vacancies might be created without disturbing Cæsar, Cicero might have felt free to solace his animosity by indulging in verbal extravagance against Piso. He could say with apparent good faith that this course was necessary and that he had not been told to refrain from doing so.[1]

But the situation was very different the next year. Pompey was in Rome and had given Cicero his views on political matters.[2] There was no occasion whatever, from the point of view of Pompey or Cæsar, for Cicero to indulge in vituperation of this sort. Indeed there was a special reason why Pompey would not wish any animosity stirred against Gabinius, and that was this: the dethroned king of Egypt had promised an immense bribe, ten thousand talents, if some Roman force would restore to him his throne. Pompey had desired the task, but his senatorial enemies had produced a Sibylline prophecy against it and had balked him. Gabinius, Pompey's confidential supporter, was in Syria with an army—although the Senate had cut short his governorship—and to him Ptolemy went with his bribe and to him Pompey sent a message to accept it—joint account, we may suspect. News was just beginning to reach Italy that this barefaced scheme was in course of execution. Pompey and Crassus were consuls this year, and one or the other would be presiding over the Senate. Pompey and Cicero were meeting one another and discussing the situation in April on the shores of the bay of Naples just as the first vague rumors from Egypt were arriving. Pompey was returning to Rome in a few days, and it appears from Cicero's

[1] *Ad Q. Frat.*, II, 6 (56 B.C.); *Ad Fam.*, I, 9.
[2] *Ad Att.*, IV, 1, 9; *ad Q. Frat.*, II, 7.

letter that the great games were to be held shortly there-after.[1]

If, then, the oration against Piso was really delivered at its supposed date, it must have been just after these interviews and before the games; that is to say, about the month of May or of June. But in view of the situation, it does not seem reasonable to suppose that Cicero would venture in the very face of Pompey to deliver, apropos of nothing, a very lengthy tirade against Piso in the course of which he would go out of his way to denounce in the bitterest terms the infamous character of Gabinius and his shameless conduct in hiring out a Roman army for a bribe, in violation of "the prohibition of the immortal gods, the answers of the priests, the authority of the Senate, and the commands of the Roman people." [2]   If Cicero had thus recklessly exhibited his independence, his *volte-face* in engaging to defend Gabinius a little later for accepting the bribe,[3] would have seemed not a little remarkable.

It seems probable, therefore, that the oration against Piso was nothing more than a rhetorical exercise written by Cicero after September in the year 54, when his brother's suggestion on further consideration commended itself to him, and when he thought he might safely get up a neat bit of invective for private circulation in the

---

[1] *Cf. ad Att.*, IV, 9, 10; *cf.* IV, 1; *ad Q. Frat.*, 11, 7.

[2] *In Pis.*, 21; *cf.* 12.

[3] Cicero writes of his strong position with Pompey and Cæsar, *ad Q. Frat.*, II, 14 (54 B.C.); he offers to do anything for Crassus, *ad Fam.*, V, 8 (54 B.C.); he acknowledges his subservience to Pompey, *ad Q. Frat.*, III, 4 (54 B.C.); he accepts a position of legate under Pompey, *ad Att.*, IV, 19 (54 B.C.); he defends Gabinius, Cass. Dio, XXXIX, 55, 63, *pro Rabirio Postumo*, 12, which he had formerly said would be infamous, *ad Q. Frat.*, III, 4-6, 9 (54 B.C.); *cf. ad Fam.*, I, 9; VII, 5.

guise of a speech delivered more than a year before.[1]
Now this conclusion is supported by a bit of nearly contemporaneous evidence. When Asconius Pedianus, about
a century later, came to write his comments on Cicero's
orations, he had no difficulty from internal evidence—
the reference to Pompey's games and the like—in assign-
ing this one to the year 55 B.C. He was, however, surprised to find that Fenestella placed it among the works
of Cicero of the year 54. Fenestella lived half a century
before Asconius and was reputed to be a careful writer,
but Asconius, not suspecting the real character of the
oration, attempted to show that the later date was inconsistent with its contents.[2] It did not occur to him that
the great orator was writing something which was intended not for public delivery but for the relief of his
irritation and for the delectation of discreet connoisseurs
in vituperation. The value of the supposed speech, from
which modern historians have extracted data on the moral
degradation of Roman Epicureans,[3] lies solely in the
discredit which it casts upon the charges in the speech on
the Consular Provinces and on Cicero's veracity.

This long digression on the subject of the general trustworthiness of Cicero's oration against Piso has led us
almost out of sight of the individual Epicureans whom we

[1] Mommsen (*op. cit.*, vol. V, p. 135) refers to this production
as "an equally envenomed and insipid pamphlet." Fowler (*Social
Life at Rome*, p. 123) remarks: "we cannot believe a tithe of what
he says about this man, Calpurnius Piso, consul in 58." [Sihler
(*Cicero of Arpinum*, New Haven, 1914, p. 245), delivers a Del-
phic utterance: "thus this speech, record and document of 55
B.C. remains also a curious monument of that blending of prudence and passion so characteristic of Cicero."—*Editor.*]
[2] Fenestella (born about 50 B.C., died about 21 A.D.) is called
diligentissimus scriptor by Lactantius, *Div. Inst.*, I, 6, 14.
[3] *Cf.* Fowler, *Social Life at Rome*, p. 123.

were investigating, yet it may not be without profit in giving us an example of the sort of material upon which has been built the conventional idea of the Roman Epicureans. We have examined what Cicero had to say about all the men who professed this philosophy and who were known to him well enough to be mentioned by name. He was prejudiced against their philosophic faith and unconsciously drew a caricature of himself when he represented his imaginary Piso as incapable of carrying on any thinking after he had heard the word "pleasure."[1] By a process of deduction based upon his notions of the underlying principles of human nature he constructed a typical Epicurean. He recognized that this was not the picture which the authoritative members of that school themselves drew; that Epicurus denied that any man "who does not live honorably can live agreeably." "As if I cared to know what he said," Cicero remarks with philosophic scorn, "or what he denied. What I inquire is what it is consistent for a man to say who puts pleasure as the *summum bonum*. . . . I am not asking what he said but what he can possibly say consistent with his own system."[2] The Epicurean doctrines as actually laid down are entirely satisfactory to him,[3] but he insists that they are illogical and that his deduced Epicurean is the subject of his rhetorical moralizing.[4] He professes himself bewildered when he hears Epicureans speak of duty, dignity, good faith, honor, dying for one's country, and the like; for he cannot see how they can consistently have such moral ideas. And when he sees them continually faithful in their friendship and consistently moral in their conduct, he declares that they refute their doctrines by their lives.[5]

[1] *In Pis.*, 28.
[2] *De Fin.*, II, 22, 26.
[3] Cf. *in Pis.*, 18; *Tusc. Disp.*, III, 20; *de Fin.*, II, *passim*.
[4] *De Fin.*, II, 25, 31.
[5] *De Fin.*, II, 23, 25, 28.

It is a favorite joke of his in writing to his Epicurean friends to insist that they ought to be vicious.[1] Such a source affords excellent material for judging the members of this school of thought, since the writer is looking for bad qualities in them to satisfy the exigencies of his *a priori* theories while every item of favorable testimony has the value of an admission against a prepossession. Against most of the Epicureans he also had other prejudices. The Greeks he expected to be dishonest and base because they were Greeks. He felt a strong bias against those who did not idealize, as he could not refrain from doing, the old Republican constitution with its immemorial features of religious trickery and reverence for respectable ineptitude. Like most men who are clever but shallow,[2] he was secretly afraid of real intelligence. Notwithstanding the more than generous consideration which he always received from Cæsar, it is probable that he really disliked him, and was more drawn to the dull Pompey.[3]

Yet Cicero was not fundamentally a dishonest man; he lied only when his personal interests seemed to require it, or when he was angry. Though he detested the politics and the philosophy of the group who with Julius Cæsar were laboring at the gigantic task of making the Roman government better adapted to carry the burden of Empire

---

[1] *Ad Fam.*, XV, 16, 18, 19.

[2] *Cf.* Mommsen, *History of Rome*, V, p. 504f.

[3] Cicero's deficiency in the presence of genius is well illustrated by his commonplace remark about the poem of Lucretius: *Lucreti poemata, ut scribis, ita sunt, multis luminibus ingeni, multae tamen artis. Ad Q. Frat.*, II, 9. We seem to hear some one saying, "Yes, indeed, you're right about Shelley, he gets in some good touches—very neatly done. When I see you, I've got Young's *Night-Thoughts* for you; I am curious to see whether you're up to it."

which had come to rest upon it, and though he felt convinced that they ought to be idle debauchees, he lets us see they were not.[1] Of the nineteen, or possibly twenty-four, whom we can identify in Cicero's writings as Epicureans, there are but two, Catius and Amafinius, who are mere names to us.

The life of Albucius seems to have been un-Roman rather than unmoral.[2] Piso, so far as we can see him through the clouds of Cicero's scurrility, was not far below the average of his class. Philodemus, who suffers with Piso, is even *optimus vir* and *doctissimus homo* in another connection.[3] The other Epicureans have distinctly better characters than the average man of the times, so far as we can judge that average from Cicero's correspondence. None of them is dissipated, idle, or self-centered, and most of them are credited with characteristics of marked kindliness. Furthermore we hear of no other Epicureans in Cicero or elsewhere of a different sort, none who correspond to that ideal type which Cicero kept insisting half-humorously they must be. More than once, in treatises written towards the end of his life, Cicero expressed his conclusions regarding the personal characters of the Epicureans. He declares that while he opposes that philosophy, yet among its votaries he recognizes "so many friends, such good men, so affectionate to one another," [4] and again he refers to them as "the best men, for no men

[1] *De Oratore*, III, 17, charges the Epicurean philosophy with calling men from the rostra, the courts, and the Senate to recline softly in gardens. When Cicero wrote this work (47 B.C.) he was himself in philosophic retreat, while nearly all his Epicurean friends were hard at work with war and government.

[2] *De Fin.*, I, 3; *Tusc. Disp.*, V, 37.

[3] *De Fin.*, II, 35.

[4] *Acad. Pr.*, II, 36: *sustinuero Epicureos, tot meos familiares, tam bonos, tam inter se amantes viros.*

are less evilly disposed than they." [1] Even in the vituperation of Piso he exculpates them, in a moment of fairness, from responsibility for that moral shipwreck—"would that you had listened to them as they deserve to be listened to; never would you have plunged into so many wickednesses." [2]

Cicero is far and away our most ample historical source on the morals of his contemporaries, and it would seem not beyond the powers of modern writers to discriminate between what he says about the real, living Epicureans, most of whom he liked and admired, and what he describes as the nature of his imaginary Epicurean deduced from what he thinks ought to be the conduct of a believer in this philosophy, and held by him in moral reprobation. Yet it seems as if the latter character had to a large extent been put in the place of the former. One eminent scholar remarks that Epicureanism became popular only in the last century B.C., "and then in its most repulsive form," but surprises us in his next sentence with the observation: "it was indeed destined to inspire the noblest mind among all Roman thinkers (Lucretius) with some of the greatest poetry ever written." [3] Other scholars are positive that the ordinary Epicurean tended not only to become lazy, but to become vicious; [4] or that under the influence of this philosophy at the end of the Republic "the cultivated patrician, enervated by vice and luxury . . . . accepted frankly a lawless universe

---

[1] *Tusc. Disp.*, III, 21: *Epicurei, viri optimi (nam nullum genus est minus malitiosum)*.

[2] *In Pis.*, 18: *quos utinam ita audires, ut erant audiendi; numquam te in tot flagitia ingurgitasses*.

[3] Fowler, *Religious Experience of the Roman People*, pp. 358-360.

[4] Tucker, *Life in the Roman World*, p. 409.

and a life of pleasure or power, to be ended by death." [1] Mr. Lecky thought that Epicureanism proved to be "little more than a principle of disintegration or an apology for vice." [2] Dean Merivale, after praising the public and private virtues of several of Cæsar's associates classed by him as Epicureans, slips into describing a character whom we can recognize as Cicero's imaginary Epicurean.

> The dogmas of Epicurus, while they indulged political indifference and made time-serving respectable, were also easily distorted to cloak vice and voluptuousness: to disclaim the inference which so many of their professors drew from them in favor of licentiousness both of action and principle was the faint and hypocritical endeavour of a few sanctimonious pretenders. [3]

The only case of something like a use of Epicurean doctrines to cloak a vicious life is in the fancy sketch of Piso, already examined; and "sanctimonious pretenders" is a unique phrase as applied to Epicureans.

In all these writers on Roman morals there is evident the same strange disparity between the abstract Epicurean who is uniformly condemned, and the individual Epicurean who is singled out for praise. So Professor Sellar paints the philosophy as a lazy form of hedonism, depressing spirit and energy, and then, like Mommsen,[4] instead of supporting his generalization, proceeds to sketch sympathetically the poet Lucretius, an individual Epicurean,

---

[1] Dill, *Roman Society from Nero to M. Aurelius,* pp. 499-500. Mr. Fowler's objection is not that Epicureanism was lawless but that it was too full of law—too mechanical to admit of belief in a personal Providence. *Op. cit.,* p. 360.

[2] *European Morals* (ed. cit.), vol. I, pp. 175-176 and note.

[3] Merivale, *History of Romans under the Empire,* vol. II, p. 352.

[4] Mommsen, *op. cit.,* vol. IV, p. 201.

who possessed qualities of mind and heart that militate against the generalization. With that fine sketch of Rome's lofty poet, whose vision rose *extra flammantia moenia mundi,* no lover of literature would venture to disagree; what is strange is that here, as elsewhere, the tradition of the stye should have acquired so dominant a prestige in the face of contradictory particulars.

The sources of the general disapprobation of the Epicureans were many and complex. One of them, it must be admitted, was their attitude toward established religions.[1] To Romans like Cicero, Scævola, Cotta, or Varro who, like jugglers tossing balls, showed their dexterity by keeping three religions in the air, the philosophy of the Epicureans must have seemed an element of danger and disintegration in the state. Criticism of popular beliefs, it is true, was common enough in the ancient world from Xenophanes on, and on purely theoretical grounds Epicureanism could not have been unwelcome. But the Romans were not metaphysicians, and philosophy was interpreted in terms of conduct. The Epicurean opposition to all forms of religious superstition was dangerous, they thought, because it undermined confidence in divination as a political instrument; but more dangerous still was the doctrine that pleasure was the chief end of life, a doctrine that was especially unwelcome to the Stoics and Eclectics, who easily misinterpreted it as coarse hedonism. Furthermore, in Rome, where politics and religion were inextricably intermingled, the Epicurean doctrine of neglect of public affairs, except where special circumstances made participation advisable, stood out in marked contrast to the teachings of the Stoics. Stoicism, as Zeller has well said,[2] found its political expression in the stubborn

[1] *Cf.* W. Wallace, *Epicureanism* (London, 1880), p. 245ff.

[2] *Stoics, Epicureans and Sceptics,* p. 492.

spirit of Republican Rome; and Republican Rome remained an ideal enthusiastically championed by many who could not, or would not, see that the Republic had proved inadequate long before it had ceased to function.

CHAPTER XIII

IT is not difficult for the student to see how impossible it was to resuscitate the Roman Republic after the death of Cæsar and to build it up into a satisfactory organization for governing the ancient world. This venerable polity had come to have for the work it was called upon to do almost every possible fault. It had in fact been moribund half a century and a series of oligarchies, ochlocracies, and anarchies had been masquerading under its name, to the confusion and distress of the world. Possibly the great Julius, had he lived another decade, might have been able to devise a better political constitution than that which was gradually developed under his heir and successor in supreme power; but this is mere surmise. It is, however, not too much to say that on the whole, in view of all the conditions, including that vastly important one of the existing prejudices of men, the Augustan constitution was probably as good a form of government as the Romans of that era could have constructed. Its long life, the peace and order prevailing under it, and the absence of any serious attempt to discard or even alter it, are strong tributes to its merits.

Yet there was, and long remained, a deep and persistent opposition to the rule of the emperors—the opposition of the old Roman aristocracy, small indeed in numbers and not very formidable in character and intelligence, but still possessing an indelible prestige, profound discontent, and abundant means. All these made it continually dangerous unless it was closely watched.[1] This opposition is even more important for us in our present study than it was for the Cæsars in their attempt to govern the world, because by reason of the educational system and of the social prominence of this order, it perpetuated its class ideas among the wealthy families of the Empire; and because this class, on account of the special conditions of literary production then obtaining, controlled to a great extent the literary sources from which our historical information is derived. Only in the principate of Augustus was an attempt made to establish an imperial literary bureau which, under the patronage of Mæcenas, was no small factor in transmitting to posterity a relatively favorable opinion of the emperor's public and private career.[2]

To this class the Cæsars were no more than enthroned demagogues; they were "tyrants" in the ancient sense of that word, irrespective of how well they ruled or how indispensable they were to the well-being of Rome and even of the nobility itself. That the emperors were for a century sprung from the highest aristocracy was only an aggravation of the wrong felt by those other families of

[1] See G. Boissier, *L'Opposition sous les Césars* (3rd ed., Paris, 1892). Dill, *Roman Society from Nero* (pp. 38-39), says justly: "Thus the Senate remained an imaginative symbol of the glory of Roman power, down to the last years of the Western Empire, . . . a body which was surrounded by the aureole of antiquity, which had such splendid traditions of conquest and administration." A valuable monograph is that of C. O. Reure, *de Scriptorum ac Litteratorum Hominum cum Romanis Imperatoribus Inimicitiis*, Paris, 1891.

[2] Virgil, Horace and Propertius might almost be said to have been "retained" by Mæcenas for Augustus.

equal pride, who were once their associates in ruling the world and were now their subordinates.[1]

> The old noblesse were the natural enemies of the new régime, which had raised the Julii and Claudii so far above the rest of their order; they resented their diminished importance, and while afraid openly to oppose Caesar, they no less disliked obeying him. . . . Even the rule of Augustus himself was not borne always with acquiescence; under his successors there was a standing quarrel.[2]

A glance at the historical situation in its bearing upon the interests of the small but important aristocratic class will bring out clearly the full significance of the position in which they found themselves, and will explain the attitude they adopted. The one danger that had always menaced them was the rise of a demagogue, who would organize the supreme but incoherent strength of the mass of the people and thereby deprive the ruling class of its hegemony. In the eyes of the nobles he would be a "tyrant." The rhetorical denunciations of tyrants—of those who deprived a dominating caste of its privileges—had been eagerly accepted by the educated Romans from Greek declamation, and had flourished mightily in Rome. It was no mere imaginary peril which barbed the arrows of aristocratic invective, for there had arisen from time to time in Roman history demagogues dangerous to their order. But in one way or another they had been disposed of, and had passed like a summer storm before

[1] Dill, *op. cit.*, pp. 185-186, comments on the strong feeling of caste obligation among the Roman aristocracy.

[2] Pelham, *Outlines of Roman History*, 1905, p. 492. See also the same writer's *Essays on Roman History* (Oxford, 1911), p. 33ff; Merivale, *History of the Romans Under the Empire*, vol. V, pp. 59-60.

which the nobles had needed only temporarily to bow their heads.

But now a far more menacing condition had arisen. After the discipline of the long and deadly war with Hannibal, the Roman state had become irresistible; all other political organizations in the Mediterranean world had crumbled at its touch. A vast Empire had come into existence, but because of the increased complexity of the problems of government, or the decreased competence of the Roman administration, or both, Rome and its dependent world had come near to anarchy. The words "demagogue" and "tyrant" had lost their power to frighten most thinking men, who saw that even more important than the form of government was its ability to maintain order and secure justice. For these boons men had come to be willing to accept the yoke of one competent ruler rather than perish from the incompetence of many.

Then a terrible disaster befell the old order of things. That supreme military genius, Julius Cæsar, belonged by birth to the ranks of the high nobility, but he turned away from most of his social peers, or was repudiated by them, and appeared as leader of the popular party. His daring scepticism gave him courage to break through the conventions of political strife, and although he was Pontifex Maximus he flouted the whole machinery of religious checks,[1] carrying the populace enthusiastically with him. His opponents had not sufficient skill to break him, and they unwisely fell into a weak position by disregarding the sanctity of a tribune. When resort to arms was tried, he overwhelmed and crushed them.

Some of the more enthusiastic republicans assassinated him, justly enough according to the traditional opinions regarding tyrannicide, but the ensuing years of bloodshed

[1] See above, p. 218.

wrought havoc among the conservatives and disposed the world more than ever to accept a permanent "tyranny" as the price of peace. Men were forced to look facts in the face, to take glimpses of the reality that lay behind words, and most of them were ready to sacrifice the form for the substance, provided the loss were decorously veiled. Many of the surviving aristocracy, however, found it difficult to detach themselves from ancient principles and prejudices, and to submit to the rule of one of their order. A few of them frankly accepted the new order; more accomplished a superficial conformity to the government which had prizes to bestow. Those who acquiesced with more or less grace could not fail to observe that their property was safer than in the days of the turbulent, sovereign crowd. It was evident that in some ways one "tyrant," who had no motive to resort to further proscriptions and confiscations, was less perturbing than a swarm of petty and predatory demagogues.[1] Yet neither rational considerations nor a sense of benefits received prevailed with the irreconcilables. They had lost some of their old privileges, and such boons as they received at the prince's hands were less than their indelible rights and did not constrain them to loyalty, "since it was by a wrong that Cæsar had come to be in a position to bestow these benefits. A man," so argues Seneca with aristocratic feeling, "has not saved your life who does not kill you, nor has he given a benefit, but gives you quarter."[2]

The prospects of public life for such as had revived from the stupefying calamities of the civil wars were restricted in many ways, and their political activities were

---

[1] Compare Tacitus, *Ann.*, I, 2; *id.*, 4.

[2] Sen., *de Ben.*, II, 20. His argument as to whether Brutus owed an obligation to Cæsar is significant. Suet. (*Jul.*, 76) gives the complaints of the opposition.

forced into channels which have a direct bearing on the
general subject under discussion. It was evident to the
dullest that open rebellion was hopeless unless a military
mutiny could be effected. In and near Rome the emperor
had nine or ten thousand highly trained and privileged
Prætorian guards, as well as about three thousand soldiers
in the urban cohorts; and with the loyalty of this force it
was dangerous to tamper. In the background were twenty-
five legions entirely under imperial control and in general
loyal to their commander-in-chief. From him alone all
the soldiers received their pay and other gratifications;
to him alone were they bound by their military oath.[1]

Nor was any help to be found in the Comitia, which had
been in Republican times the supreme legislative and electoral organ of the commonwealth and still retained a
theoretical importance. The emperor was independent in
matters of finance, the levy and use of armed forces.
Even if the opposition could gain control of a majority
of the votes, nothing of importance could be effected by
legal means, since the emperor could block everything by
virtue of his tribunicial veto and could, to an extent not
easy to define, exercise direct legislative power by edict,
decree, or rescript.[2] A shadowy participation in the elec-

---

[1] Attempts to curry favor with the soldiers by grants of privileges by the Senate were sharply resented on the part of the
emperor. Tacitus (Ann., VI, 3) reports Tiberius as saying in
regard to a proposition of this sort: "What business had he
(the senator) with the soldiers, whose duty bound them to
receive their orders and rewards from the emperor alone." The
indiscreet proposer, Junius Gallio, was expelled from the Senate
and banished from Italy. Cf. Suet., Claud., 25.

[2] Compare Mommsen, Droit public romain (Manuel des
antiquités romaines, French edition, 1896), V, pp. 152ff, 157, 166,
185-197, 284ff; VI, 1, p. 395; Greenidge, Roman Public Life
(London, 1901), pp. 339ff, 346, 371, 378.

tion of magistrates still remained to the Comitia, but practically they were named or at least approved by the emperor, and at any time he could coerce or suspend them. Furthermore, much of the public business was now carried on by the imperial officials directly appointed by him.[1]

The Senate afforded no better field for opposition to the emperor than did the Comitia. Its numbers were practically chosen by him and he could in fact dismiss them by dropping their names at the revision of the senatorial list. If they showed any disposition to adopt measures not to his liking, his tribunicial veto was available,[2] and in one way or another his control over them was absolute.[3] Doubtless some senators who were far from satisfied with the situation felt, as did Favorinus in the time of Hadrian, that it was absurd to argue with the master of thirty legions.[4]

So deep was the discredit into which the old republican government had sunk that only on the occasion of the death of Gaius was the question of reviving the Republic suggested in the Senate, and apparently it was never seriously considered outside that chamber. Furthermore, although the Empire came to an end with the death of each prince and had to be recreated *de novo* by the passing of new laws granting powers to the new sovereign, we have no hint in our authorities that it was ever even pro-

---

[1] See Mommsen, *op. cit.*, V, pp. 193ff, 204ff, 215ff; VI, 1, 397-398; Greenidge, *op. cit.*, pp. 346-349, 371.

[2] See Mommsen, *op. cit.*, V, pp. 155, 173, 179, 222, 232ff, 395, 451, 467; Greenidge, *op. cit.*, pp. 346-347, 374.

[3] It was out of the question for the ordinary tribunes to veto an imperial measure. Compare Tac., *Ann.*, XVI, 26; I, 77; VI, 47; *Hist.*, IV, 9.

[4] Spartianus, *Had.*, 15.

posed to insert in these constituent acts any checks upon the powers and prerogatives of the monarch. The tendency was indeed the other way, and new functions were added to his office from time to time, for his government alone seemed efficient.

Yet there was opposition of a subtle sort whose purpose and efficacy have not been sufficiently recognized by the conventional accounts of the Empire. According to the traditional view, the almost limitless absolutism gave rise speedily, through craven fear, to an equally limitless political servility which gradually deepened into appalling debasement and abjection. So Dean Merivale, commenting on the banishment of Ovid, draws a vivid picture of the irresistible absolutism of the imperial power.

> When the emperor wished to rid himself of a disagreeable citizen, he directed him to remove from Rome to some distant spot indicated to him; and such was the authority of his mere word, that without defence, without trial, without sentence, without the use or even threat of force, the culprit at once obeyed, and plunged silently into oblivion. . . . Our awe is enhanced on hearing that a citizen condemned to banishment on the frontiers of the empire should simply receive an order to repair there, and be left to find his way, perhaps even unattended, without fear of his lingering on his route, or diverging from it.[1]

Instances of servility are not far to seek. Some of them, if we may believe the reports of them, cannot have

---

[1] *History of the Romans Under the Empire*, vol. IV, pp. 258-260. The source of our information is Ovid himself. From Tacitus (*Ann.*, III, 24, the case of Silanus) it would appear that Tiberius recognized the right of any one who had left Rome by reason of an imperial intimation of this sort to return whenever he wished.

failed to give a certain æsthetic satisfaction to at least one of the persons concerned. Early in the principate of Augustus, for instance, it occurred to Sextus Pacuvius, a tribune, to devote himself to the emperor after the Spanish fashion, and to force those he met on the streets to do the same. By this vow the maker bound himself to share the destiny of the other and to commit suicide at his death. Dio tells us that he made every one offer a sacrifice on this occasion, and again, before an assembly of the people, he announced he had made Augustus his joint heir with his own son which in view of the paucity of the testator's estate was a benevolence rather than a benefaction. But it was not an idle flourish, for it might serve to extract some substantial recognition from the nominal beneficiary. Our informant says that the expedient succeeded, but Macrobius declares that when the hopeful Pacuvius mentioned to the emperor the existence of a rumor that an imperial gift had been made in return, the canny prince said: "don't believe it." [1]

On a somewhat similar occasion, when a sycophant had under oath vowed his life if Gaius should recover from an illness, this emperor with more wit than humor is said to have compelled a literal fulfillment of the vow lest an oath be broken.[2] Vitellius, father of the emperor of that name, is reported to have saved himself from Gaius's suspicions by openly paying him divine honors. Once the prince declared that he had been intimate with Selene, the Moon goddess, and asked Vitellius if he saw her. And the crafty courtier, lest he make the wrong answer, lowered his eyes as if dazzled and said: "only to you

[1] Cass. Dio (LIII, 20) reads also *Apudius;* Macrobius (Sat. II, 4, 4), *Pacuvius Taurus. Cf.* Cæsar, *B. G.*, III, 22; Val. Max., II, 6, 11.

[2] Cass. Dio, LIX, 8; Suet., *Calig.*, 14, 27.

gods, O master, is it permitted to see one another." This
discretion, we are told, procured for him the boon of
intimate imperial friendship.[1]

A striking exhibition of servility was the acclamation
with which the senators are said to have greeted Nero
on his return from Greece. This chant seems too imbecile to have been wholly invented and its resemblance to
later absurdities suggests its authenticity. It runs: "Hail,
Olympian victor! Hail, Pythian victor! Hail, Augustus,
Augustus! To Nero the Hercules, to Nero the Apollo!
thou art the one complete champion, the only one of all
time, Augustus, Augustus, O sacred voice! Blessed are
they who hear thee!"[2]

In some cases such language may of course be taken
as the eager bidding for favors on the part of would-be
parasites, like Martial; in others, Paterculus, for instance,[3]
the overwrought phrases probably resulted from the
attempt in a rhetorical age to express genuine regard. At
times the servility was due to the anxiety of a very
timid man as in the case of Seneca's fawning on the
powerful freedman Polybius in order to obtain recall
from exile;[4] much of it doubtless arose from *façons de
parler* characteristic of the age, which it would be misleading to press too literally.[5] One need not go very far
back in modern times to find conventional modes of ad-

[1] Cass. Dio, LIX, 27; Suet., *Vitell.*, 2.

[2] Cass. Dio, LXIII, 20. *Cf.* Suet., *Nero,* 25. For acclamations
under Claudius see Cass. Dio, LX, 5; on the death of Commodus,
see Lampridius, *Com.*, 18 and Dio (who was present), LXXIV, 2.
Cf. idem, LXXII, 20.

[3] II, 129-131.

[4] See above, p. 83, for Seneca's pathological timidity. *Cf.* Ovid's
Tristia and *Epistles.*

[5] For the prevalence of certain habitual modes of adulatory expression, see Tac., *Ann.,* V, 6.

dress which would be considered bad form to-day.[1] But
even when ample allowance is made for the foregoing
conditions, many cases still remain of what appears to be
gross adulation on the part of the senatorial body towards
the emperor, which are imperfectly explained and still
need interpretation.

The most obvious, and perhaps generally accepted, explanation is that the tyranny of the early Empire was so
relentless as to crush men of dignity and self-respect,
and leave only those who could save themselves by continual fawning. But the theory when fully examined does
not seem to fit the facts satisfactorily.

In the first place the relative number of years covered
by the so-called tyranny is not enough to account for a
servility which manifested itself as early as Julius Cæsar,
who pardoned his enemies and paid no attention to personal abuse,[2] and which continued under every emperor.
It is, on the whole, doubtful whether any absolute
monarchy in history has shown a succession of more
efficient princes than the rulers of the Roman Empire from
Augustus to Marcus Aurelius. Government was ably
administered during the entire reigns of Augustus, Vespasian, Titus, Nerva, and his successors to the death of
Marcus, and half of those of Tiberius, Claudius, and
Domitian, as well as the earlier years of Nero—in all

[1] Compare Disraeli, *Curiosities of Literature* (London, 1858),
vol. I, p. 340, for a dedication addressed to Cardinal Richelieu.
"Who has seen your face without being seized by those softened
terrors which made the prophets shudder when God showed the
beams of his glory! But as He whom they dared not to approach
in the burning bush, and in the noise of thunders, appeared to
them sometimes in the freshness of the Zephyrs, so the softness
of your august countenance dissipates at the same time, and
changes into dew, the small vapours which cover its majesty."

[2] *Cf.* Suet., *Jul.*, 73-75; Paterculus, II, 56-57.

about one hundred and seventy-three years out of two hundred and nine. This computation leaves thirty-six years of "tyranny," which could hardly be much extended by the most pessimistic scholar. If we scrutinize the evidence more closely, however, and even assuming the general correctness of the facts narrated by our authorities as distinguished from their invective, it is difficult to see how the period during which abject servility could have seemed beneficial to the average senator can be extended beyond the last three or four years of Gaius, Nero, and Domitian—in all some ten or twelve years scattered over a period of sixty.

It is a remarkable tribute to the power of dramatic, if inaccurate, narrative of personal incidents, that the details of the controversy between emperors and Senate during these years have, in every succeeding age, driven from the minds of most men the other historical elements of that era, and left as the history of the early Empire little but a series of pictures of despotic cruelty and shameless lust.

If twelve, or even thirty-six, out of the first hundred and twenty-five tyrannical years could produce such depths of servility, surely it would seem that the ensuing three generations of liberal rule might have left some trace of increased self-respect; but we find the Senate indulging freely in sycophancy at the end of the period. The bitter conflict between Domitian and the senators, the most painful of all similar periods for them, seems to have passed without lessening the tendency to servile speech on the part of the nobles who then held high office and who later became emperors, officials, or men of letters.[1]

---

[1] *E. g.*, Nerva, Trajan, Tacitus, and Pliny the Younger. Men of humbler rank, like Juvenal, Epictetus, Plutarch, and Dio Chrysostom, retained their independence.

During the first ten years of Nero's reign, apart from cases of provincial misgovernment and apart from condemnations of members of the imperial family, not a single death sentence was rendered and only two sentences of banishment for charges of treason or libel of the emperor were pronounced. Two other accusations of treason, the only ones of the sort, ended in acquittals and banishment of the accusers.

> The Senatorial nobility had not suffered at Nero's hands, and were not likely to suffer at Nero's hands, any injustice or oppression or peril of their life.[1]

There was certainly no reason why senators should feel the need of indulging in servility under Augustus to save themselves from peril. During his long reign the nobles were not harried or exposed to any severity. On the contrary, this prince endeavored to conciliate them and induce them to accept high office and join him in the labors of government. To this end he accorded full liberty of speech and showed benevolence to individual senators; even under exasperating provocations he smiled at their rudeness and tolerated everything but dangerous conspiracies.[2] Timagenes made scurrilous jests on

---

[1] B. W. Henderson, *The Life and Principate of Nero* (London, 1903), p. 265. In Tacitus, *Ann.*, XIV, 48, Thrasea is represented as praising Nero and saying that the Senate's deliberations are free from constraint (62 A.D.).

[2] Compare Sen., *de Clem.*, I, 9-10, 15; *de Ben.*, II, 25, 27; III, 27; Cass. Dio, LV, 3, 12, 22; LIV, 15, 27; LIII, 32, 21; Macrobius, *Sat.*, II, 4; Suet., *Aug.*, 51, 54-56; W. T. Arnold, *Studies of Roman Imperialism* (Manchester, 1906), pp. 170ff, 13ff. A limit to this tolerance was set in the case of writings vituperating persons of distinction, but this measure, far from injuring the senators, was designed for their protection. *Cf.* Tac., *Ann.*, I, 72; IV, 21; Cass. Dio, LVI, 27.

Augustus, Livia, and the imperial family, and continued to do so after a warning. The emperor finally forbade him the palace, but he

> passed the later years of his life as the guest of Asinius Pollio, and was the favorite of the whole city; the closing of Cæsar's door did not close any other door to him. . . . He was at enmity with Cæsar, but yet no one feared to be his friend.[1]

Nor can we discover in the acts of Tiberius any reason for a resort to adulation for the purpose of ensuring personal safety. Indeed, all the authorities make it clear that he abhorred flattery, rebuked adulation, was disgusted with manifestations of servility, and declined to accept honors offered him, deprecating in many cases even merely complimentary phrases.[2] To the Senate he displayed marked courtesy and deference, encouraging it to participate actively in government and tolerating a freedom of debate that sometimes bordered on insolence.[3] Where he disapproved of its action, his rebuke was phrased with civility, sometimes, indeed with irony, but rarely with sternness.[4]

Men might think and speak their thoughts;

> he was unmoved by abuse, scandalous gossip, and lampoons directed against himself and his relatives,

[1] Sen., *de Ira*, III, 23; *cf.* Plut., *de Adulatore Amico*, 27.

[2] See Tac., *Ann.*, II, 87; III, 18, 59, 65; IV, 38; Suet., *Tib.*, 26, 27; Cass. Dio, LVII, 8-10; LVIII, 12.

[3] See Tac., *Ann.*, IV, 6, 15; III, 35, 53-54, 60, 69; VI, 27; I, 15, 74; Suet., *Tib.*, 24, 28-32; *idem, M. Pomp. Marcell.* (Roth, p. 266); Cass. Dio, LVII, 7, 17; LVIII, 19.

[4] Compare Tac., *Ann.*, III, 51; IV, 30; VI, 2, 3; Cass. Dio, LVIII, 17-18; Suet., *Tib.*, 28.

and often declared that in a free state the tongue and the mind ought to be free.[1]

An examination of the cases given by Tacitus of those who calumniated the emperor will show how little the nobles had to fear from speaking their minds with freedom and even with license. Notwithstanding the lurid generalizations of Tacitus, we find on scrutinizing the facts of the prosecutions reported by him, that of the thirteen cases under Tiberius in which there was a question of written or spoken words, in three the case proceeded on other charges;[2] in one the Senate precipitately condemned the man without the emperor's knowledge, and was rebuked by him for the act;[3] in one, the accused committed suicide before trial;[4] one case involved merely the transfer of the libeler from one place of exile to another;[5] in one, the accused was already in prison under a capital sentence and seems to have called further attention to himself by writing scurrilous poems;[6] one man was forbidden the prince's table;[7] another was exiled for a very grave libel;[8] and in four instances the prosecu-

[1] Suet., *Tib.*, 28, 29. *Cf.* Tac., *Ann.*, II, 34, 50; IV, 31, 42; VI, 5-7, 38; Cass. Dio, LVII, 23; LVIII, 25. Even ridicule of his person was ignored. *Idem*, LVIII, 19.

[2] Silanus (*Ann.*, III, 66), Sabinus (IV, 68-70), and Scaurus (VI, 29).

[3] Priscus (*Ann.*, III, 49-51); *cf.* Cass. Dio, LVII, 20.

[4] Cremutius Cordus (*Ann.*, IV, 34-35). The statement of this case by Tacitus may not be correct. Seneca, who was intimately acquainted with Cordus, gives an entirely different narrative and imputes no blame to Tiberius. *Cf. Cons. ad Marc.*, 1, 2, 15, 22, and Cass. Dio, LVII, 24.

[5] Cassius Severus (*Ann.*, IV, 21).

[6] Sextius Paconianus (*Ann.*, VI, 3, 39).

[7] Sextus Vistilius (*Ann.*, VI, 9).

[8] Votienus Montanus (*Ann.*, IV, 42); banished to the Balearic Islands, according to Jerome, *Chron. Euseb.*, 782 = 29 A.D.

tion under this perplexing "tyrant" failed through his intervention or, as in one case, through his acquiescence.[1] During the seventeen years of Tiberius's reign up to the discovery of Sejanus's conspiracy, not a single senator was sentenced to death; and of the five suicides of accused persons none can be regarded as due to tyrannical oppression.[2]

Perhaps the most objectionable form of servility during this reign was that of delation; but clearly this was not a means of ensuring one's personal safety. The fate of thirty-one delators is known, and a comparison of their lot with that of the twenty-nine persons accused by them is instructive.

Fate of persons accused by delators	Fate of the delators themselves
12....Acquitted, pardoned, or proceedings squashed..................	2
	(escaped any penalty)
3....Condemned: executed	7
7....Condemned: lesser penalties................	19
6....Committed suicide pending trial.............	2
1....Died before judgment	1
Total 29	Total 31

[1] Marcellus (*Ann.*, I, 74), Appuleia Varilla (*Ann.*, II, 50), Cominius (*Ann.*, IV, 31), and Cotta Messalinus (*Ann.*, VI, 5-7).

[2] Tacitus (*Ann.*, II, 27-32) suggests the innocence of Libo Drusus, saying however that Tiberius declared he would have pardoned him. The only contemporary evidence seems to prove his guilt clearly (Paterculus, II, 130; Seneca, *Epist.*, LXX; Suetonius, *Tib.*, 25, agrees). Cn. Calpurnius Piso was clearly guilty of military insubordination (Tac., *Ann.*, III, 14) but was hounded into a probably premature despair, not by the prince but by the prince's enemies. C. Silanus is conceded by Tacitus (*Ann.*, III, 67) to have been guilty of extortion and rapacity as a governor. Plautius Silvanus had murdered his wife (*Ann.*, IV, 22). For Cremutius Cordus see above, p. 269.

Ten of the condemnations of delators were for failure to substantiate their charges; the others were on other charges at later times, six or seven of them in later reigns.

A notable career was that of Manius Lepidus, a noble whom Augustus had declared a proper person to be emperor. Neither this invidious designation, nor his undertaking the defence of Piso, charged with treason, nor that of his sister, accused *inter alia* of magical inquiries regarding members of the imperial house, nor his activities in limiting the rewards of delators and antagonizing the proposals of sycophants—none of these things prevented him from enjoying uninterruptedly the esteem and favor of Tiberius, gaining high office and great influence with the prince and dying at a ripe age, near the end of the reign, renowned for his dignity, wisdom, and conduct.[1] A similar career was that of Gnæus Lentulus. When some one accused him of plotting against Tiberius, the emperor brushed the charge aside, declaring, "I am indeed no longer worthy to live, if Lentulus, too, hates me."[2]

Under Gaius, and in the latter part of the principates of Nero and Domitian, we read of some instances of prosecution for written or spoken words consisting in most cases of reflections on the reigning emperor, but we are also told of the very general freedom of speech which prevailed.[3] The writings of Seneca abound in anti-imperialistic sentiments and there is no indication of an attempt to suppress free political comment and even savage criticism. Indeed, the general liberty accorded to every one has probably been equalled only in recent times.[4] The "tyranny of the Cæsars," even when viewed

---

[1] Tac., *Ann.*, I, 13; III, 11, 22, 35, 49-51; IV, 20, 56; VI, 5, 27.

[2] Cass. Dio, LVII, 24; Tac., *Ann.*, I, 27; III, 68; IV, 29, 44.

[3] *Cf.* Suet., *Cal.*, 16; *Claud.*, 15; *Nero*, 39; *Vesp.*, 13, 15.

[4] See Merivale, *op. cit.*, vol. VI, p. 178ff.

under the lurid light of Tacitus, pales into insignificance
when compared to the powers exercised by popes and
kings in certain epochs of mediæval and modern history.
Instead of one emperor, the very vastness of whose juris-
diction ensured general toleration, there were in every part
of Europe jealous and ruthless despots whose savage
suppression of opposition fills many a page of European
history.[1]

It is, then, a question whether the servility and adulation of the Senate were prompted by fear of personal
safety. The prestige of the Senate, attested not only by
the deference paid it by most of the emperors but also
by the animosity towards it on the part of Gaius, Nero,
and Domitian during at least part of their reigns, militates
against the theory that it was merely a cringing body of
time-servers.   Although the Senate possessed little corporate power under the Empire,

> Senators governed the Emperor's provinces, com-
> manded his legions, levied his recruits, watched the
> frontiers, and looked after the highroads and the food
> supply.   They did all those things in the Emperor's
> name, and as his delegates; but no man who had once
> been admitted to the Senate-house ever forgot that he
> was a Senator, and the solid powers which the Senate
> did not wield directly, it wielded to a certain extent
> indirectly through its individual members.[2]

Later, of course, a civil service grew up, recruited mainly
from the equestrian order,[3] but when an early emperor
wanted generals, governors, and high officials he was
practically compelled to seek them in the Senate.   Hence
it was that Augustus "made it his business to win over

[1] See L. W. Vernon-Harcourt, *His Grace the Steward and Trial
of Peers* (London, 1907); *Spectator*, Aug. 10, 1907, p. 198.

[2] Arnold, *Roman Imperialism*, pp. 63-64.

[3] *Cf.* Arnold, *op. cit.*, p. 70ff.

the representatives of the great Roman families, and was never happier than when he could induce a Piso to take a consulship." [1]

Tiberius, as we have seen, paid marked deference to the Senate; [2] Claudius bespoke its friendship; [3] Verginius Rufus and the legions recognized it as entitled to dispose of the Empire, [4] and Otho declared it to be the *caput imperii*. [5] Augustus and most of his successors sat personally in free interchange of opinion with the senators, to coöperate in the determination of public measures. [6] The emperors from Nerva to Marcus Aurelius [7] deferred to the Senate in every way, and thereby reaped their reward in a literary tradition so eulogistic as almost entirely to obscure the causes for the striking decline in the strength of the Empire during that period. This puzzle is almost equal to that afforded by the phenomenon of the maintenance of the Empire in full vigor during the preceding century, characterized in great part, if we are to credit most of our literary sources, by imbecile misgovernment and depressing tyranny.

It may seem strange that with all the emperor's powers, he was not able to bring the Senate into closer relations with him by seeing to it that the choice of new senators

---

[1] *Op. cit.*, p. 170; *cf.* Pelham, *Essays on Roman History*, p. 125n. 1: "In the consular *fasti* from 27 B.C. to 14 A.D. comparatively few new names of families appear."

[2] See above, p. 268.   [3] Josephus, *B. J.*, II, 11, 2.

[4] Cass. Dio, LXIII, 25; Plut., *Galba*, 6; Tac., *Hist.*, I, 12, 55.

[5] Tac., *Hist.*, I, 84.

[6] Compare Suet., *Tib.*, 30; Tac., *Ann.*, IV, 6; Cass. Dio, LVII, 7; LXVI, 10; Capitolinus, *M. Ant.*, 10, 11; Mommsen, *Droit public romain*, vol. VII, p. 496.

[7] The Senate was not altogether satisfied with Hadrian although he seems to have done much to conciliate it. *Cf. Spartianus, Had.*, 7-8.

fell upon persons who were in full harmony with him. But nearly omnipotent as he was in most respects, he was constrained by general opinion and the necessity of strengthening his government to have at least the nominal participation in it of those whose names were recognized as giving, by their participation, the emperor his right to rule. Hence he was forced to treat senatorial rank as practically hereditary, and to give the broad purple stripe to the scions of great houses. Even the emperors of the first two centuries most hostile to the Senate did not venture to raise to that body those freedmen who administered most of the routine work of government.[1] But independently of this need for recognizing hereditary claims, the persistence of the *esprit de corps* of the Senate was, no doubt, an important factor. The effect of the traditions of an ancient body like the Senate upon the young men, who entered it in small numbers yearly and continued in it all their lives, would be to impose upon them the senatorial point of view. It has been observed in the case of the British House of Lords that it is difficult to maintain a fair minority of Liberal peers. The Senate could not be made imperialistic, and the emperors dared not destroy it. The difficulty was met by the emperors becoming senatorial after 96 A.D.

A glance at the membership of the Senate in the early Empire is instructive. Thanks to the labors of Professor Willems, we have more or less complete information regarding three hundred and ninety persons who were certainly or probably members of the Senate in the year 65 A.D.[2] Nearly ninety were of families which had

[1] Compare Fustel de Coulanges, *Histoire des institutions politiques*, p. 242; Pelham, *op. cit.*, p. 126ff.

[2] *Le Sénat romain en l'an 65 après Jésus-Christ, publié d'après les notes de P. Willems par J. Willems, Le Musée Belge,*

attained senatorial or equestrian rank in Republican times; more than thirty belonged to the ancient aristocracy. Even the meagre information which has come down to us shows that eleven were of high military rank; five were philosophers; and three or more were jurisconsults, while nineteen others were prominent in letters or eloquence. The active part taken by senators in the administration of the Empire is shown by the fact that no fewer than one hundred and forty-seven of them had governed provinces. The total number of such offices held by them aggregated two hundred and three, of which ninety-two were in senatorial provinces, and one hundred and eleven in those directly administered by the Emperor. In this Senate sat six men who attained the imperial throne, as well as the ancestors of all the other emperors for the ensuing century and more, save perhaps those of Hadrian.[1] It was esteemed no derogation of his position for an emperor to regard himself as one of this body, *primus inter pares*.[2]

It is, then, difficult to regard the various hypotheses which have been referred to in the preceding pages as affording an adequate explanation of this phenomenon of apparently servile adulation towards the emperor. To understand its real nature and thus perceive its effect upon historical sources, it is necessary to know just what it

---

vol. IV (1900), pp. 236-277; V (1901), pp. 82-126; VI (1902), pp. 100-151. (See Bruno Steck, *Senatores Romani qui fuerint inde a Vespasiano usque ad Traiani exitum* in *Klio, Zehntes Beiheft,* 1912.—Editor.)

[1] But Hadrian's grandfather must have been a senator about this time; *cf.* Spartianus, *Had.,* 1.

[2] Martial, writing in eulogistic phrases, calls Hadrian a senator.
> *Non est hic dominus sed imperator,*
> *Sed iustissimus omnium senator.*

X, 72; *cf.* Pliny, *Pan.*

was that the members of the Senate desired from the holder of the imperial position, and how they set to work to secure it. As has been indicated, the weakness of the Senate in the later Republic was that, being the assembly of the rich, it was exposed to the predatory action of the discontented poor; and for defence against this danger it did not have in its corporate capacity that direct control of armed force which is the *ultima ratio* of all governments. The consuls had no regular, armed force available for quelling popular disturbances in the city, and were hampered by the right of every citizen to appeal to the people against any criminal sentence. Hence that "short way with the demagogues," so much desired by the opulent classes, was intolerably obstructed.

For the rise of this troublesome sort of politician, there was every facility. In the sovereign assembly of the tribes, there was no clear preëminence of property owners; and from this body could easily come forth popular leaders invested with the power and sanctity of tribunes to suggest to the crowd schemes of legislation thoroughly offensive to most of the senators and sometimes dangerous to prominent individuals. Then, too, a demagogue sometimes reached the consular seat, for the lack of means of preserving public order in the city made it possible for even the centuriate assembly to be packed and wrested from the control of the conservatives. Sometimes these popular leaders were themselves members of the threatened order, who placed their personal interests, or what they considered the welfare of the people, above the obligations of class loyalty.

In most cases, of course, it was possible for the senators to block disagreeable reforms by clever use of legal or religious chicanery. But the people were losing, little by little, their respect for legal technicalities and the warnings of the gods : it was not always easy for a noble augur to stop a bold demagogue who had the people behind him. The first consulate of Julius Cæsar was highly disconcerting to large numbers of prominent citizens, for he flouted the venerated checks upon popular sovereignty with complete disregard of his colleague's confident inspection of the heavens for reactionary omens. Most radical movements, however troublesome for a time, had not lasted long; but there was aways the danger, so frequently illustrated in Greek history with which the nobles were becoming acquainted, of the demagogue turning into a tyrant and, by steady coöperation with the popular assembly, recasting the constitution in such a way as to deprive the aristocracy of its immemorial privileges.

In the earlier days of Rome, the controlling class could meet dangerous movements of the people by the expedient of securing, or threatening to secure, the appointment of a dictator, whose irresponsible and unlimited power over the lives of citizens without any appeal to the people would serve to check undesirable reformers. The dictatorship, however, had become obsolete since the second Punic war and while not expressly abolished until after the death of Julius Cæsar, it had for all practical purposes ceased to exist.[1]

The Senate's need of absolute power to crush aspiring demagogues with predatory projects grew stronger with the increasing danger during the last century of the Republic. Any group of men needs a delegate to undertake its defence when the occasion for the use of force arises, for it is of the essence of military power that, to be

---

[1] The so-called dictatorships of Sulla and Cæsar were established by special laws, not by old constitutional usage : they were consecrations of existing absolute power *de facto*. *Cf.* Mommsen, *Droit public romain*, vol. III, p. 194; IV, p. 427.

effective, it must be wielded by one hand and directed by
one mind. So there was evolved, by a process which we
cannot trace, and defended by arguments of very doubtful constitutionality, the theory that the Senate could by
its decree call upon one or more magistrates possessing
the imperium "to see to it that the Republic suffer no
harm." [1] By this *senatus consultum ultimum,* it was held,
the magistrate was vested with what were in effect
dictatorial powers, and had the right to put to death
without appeal any one who was troubling the state. The
measure was first put into operation against the Gracchan
party and continued in use at intervals down to the
contest between the senatorial government and the friends
of the deceased Julius Cæsar in 43 B.C. [2]

It was, then, a political construction of this sort which
the Senate desired:—the grant to one of its members
possessing "sound" political views, of unlimited powers to
safeguard his creators against turbulence and depredation
by the crowd or the soldiery under the lead of demagogues. Such they nearly had in Pompey, but Pompey
lacked force. This ideal of a glorified but manageable
Pompey obsessed them for ages, and the emperors were
judged by their approximation to the ideal. The Senate
seems to have made some attempts to persuade Claudius
of the beauty of their theory, urging upon him that the
promiscuous use which had been made of the title "Father
of his Country" made it less suitable to characterize his
unusual merits than the title "Father of the Senate;" but

[1] At times warning was given of an intention to resort to this
senatus consultum ultimum by a preliminary one, *contra rem pub-
licam factum videri. Cf.* Willems, *Droit public romain* (6th ed.,
Louvain, 1888), p. 212.

[2] Compare Greenidge, *Roman Public Life,* p. 281; Mommsen,
op. cit., vol. VII, p. 470ff; Willems, *op. cit.,* p. 212.

Claudius, whose wit has been underestimated, modestly checked the Senate from doing him this honor.[1] The *quinquennium Neronis* promised well, and Nero was for a time correspondingly praised; but disappointment followed.

The difficulty which the Senate experienced with the Julio-Claudian Cæsars was that the Empire had been founded on a diametrically opposite principle. Julius Cæsar came to power as the representative of the classes below the nobility, and while he did not live to work out a clear constitutional theory of his autocracy, his successor, Augustus, based his position upon the tribunicial power; and the emperors became in theory as well as in fact the representatives of the people rather than of the aristocracy. The title *princeps* which they bore was, in all probability, not an abbreviation of *princeps senatus* but of *princeps civitatis*.

This was not, of course, in harmony with the Senate's notion of a proper constitution, and it was some time before the emperors were in sufficiently close association with the Senate to adopt its doctrine unconsciously. Augustus was a revolutionary ruler before he was a senator, and his imperial position continued to dominate his conception. Tiberius was a senator for many years, but these were mostly spent away from Rome, and his disposition unfitted him for becoming a very enthusiastic member of that body. Executive administration and military command were more to his taste. Nor was he enamored of the characters of many of the senators. Gaius, Claudius, and Nero became monarchs without much senatorial experience. But with the first two

[1] See Tac., *Ann.*, XI, 25. At a considerably later time when the feud was ended, the emperors did not hesitate to take this title.

Flavians conditions changed somewhat and after Domitian, who may be classed with the last three Julio-Claudian Cæsars as to senatorial experience, the emperors for nearly a century were distinctly senatorial in sentiment, except, perhaps, in the case of Hadrian who passed but little time at Rome.

After the senators took account of their position under the early Cæsars, another constitutional theory took firm root in their minds and formed an important part in their picture of the ideal emperor. We cannot trace this claim very distinctly to its origin, but before long it seemed to them to be a sound doctrine of public law, or at least of decent administration, that a senator should be tried on a criminal charge only by his peers. If we may suppose that Tacitus gives us a correct idea of senatorial sentiment in the time of Tiberius, there seems to have been an inclination then to deprecate the condemnation of a senator in any tribunal for any offense against the emperor or the provincials.[1] It was, however, not until the reign of Titus that imperial recognition was given to this senatorial theory of exemption from the ordinary criminal law. He did not indeed accede to it formally, but he extended clemency and pronounced no capital sentence against members of that body during his short principate.[2] Domitian refused to permit it to be made a rule of law or custom, but henceforth the emperors generally began their reign with an express pledge not to pass a capital sentence on any senator.[3] Under Septimius Severus the rule of con-

[1] See Tac., *Ann.*, II, 37-38; III, 22-23, 48, 66-67; IV, 18-20, 31; VI, 29.

[2] Cass. Dio, LXVII, 2; Suet., *Tit.*, 9.

[3] For Nerva, *cf.* Cass. Dio, LXVIII, 2; Trajan, LXVIII, 5; Eutropius, VIII, 4; Hadrian, Spartianus, *Had.*, 7; Cass. Dio, LXIX, 2; LXX, 1; for Antoninus Pius and M. Aurelius, Capitolinus, *Ant.*, 7, 8, 13; *M. Ant.*, 10, 25.

fining the right of capital condemnations of senators to their own tribunal was established in law.[1]

This doctrine forms the negative aspect of the senatorial theory of a satisfactory principate, the positive aspect of which is supplied by the conception of the emperor as a delegate or at least a protector of the Senate; and the two constitute the touchstone by which emperors are judged in most of our authorities. Attempts to assassinate those who were satisfactory in respect to their substantial conformity to these principles were deprecated by general aristocratic sentiment,[2] and are usually treated sympathetically in our sources. Yet, so well established a habit of public life had it become for every one who disliked the acts of an emperor to seek his life, that we find conspiracies against all of them, even those who are said to have been universally beloved.

The form taken by the long continued hostility of the senatorial party to those emperors whose actions did not correspond to that party's theory of the principate was, therefore, almost inevitable. Open warfare, as has been observed, was out of the question unless the irresistible strength at the disposal of the emperor could first be weakened by undermining the loyalty of the army. He could of course be assassinated, but if this took place while he still enjoyed the confidence of the legions, there was little profit to be gained from the deed; indeed the

[1] Cass. Dio, LXXIV, 2; Spartianus, *Sev.*, 7. The speech, favoring this idea with an extension to the whole family, attributed by Dio to Mæcenas (LII, 31), doubtless represents the senatorial views in the time of Alex. Severus. *Cf.* Mommsen, *op. cit.*, vol. V, p. 249ff; Greenidge, *op. cit.*, pp. 386-387.

[2] For cases in which senatorial conspirators against Trajan or Hadrian were promptly condemned by the Senate during the emperor's absence and without his knowledge, *cf.* Eutropius, VIII, 4; Spartianus, *Had.*, 7.

later state of the opposition was likely to be worse than
the former.

In preparing for the destruction of an emperor unsatisfactory to the Senate, an open show of force would
defeat its own ends; concealment and mendacity were,
therefore, clearly suggested by the situation.   In the
old Republican days, when a magistrate had shown himself refractory to the *patres conscripti,* it had generally
been possible to paralyze his administration by that resort to religious chicanery which formed one of the most
common elements of political warfare; but this convenient expedient had been rendered less amply available in
the new order of things.[1]   The state of mind, however,
which used and approved it had not disappeared but had
only changed its methods.   A more distinctly secular
guile, more directly and precisely adapted to its objects,
was speedily put into operation and flourished mightily.
It was far indeed from being unknown in earlier Rome,
and the history of mankind of other ages and places has
not been without it; but never, perhaps, has it been more
skilfully organized and persistently carried on than was
the case in the long conflict between the Roman Senate
and the emperors; and, it may be added, rarely has it
more successfully falsified history.   This political weapon
on which the nobles placed so much reliance appears in
three forms of disingenuousness, all of which have been
damaging to the trustworthiness of the historical authorities of the period.   These three forms, not always neatly
distinct, are (1) deceptive adulation; (2) scandalmongering, and (3) narratives, historical in form but primarily
artistic in character with moral, polemical, apologetic or
other purpose, masquerading as veracious history.   The
third form, except where it overlaps the other two, will

[1] *Cf.* above, p. 178ff.

be examined later in more detail.[1] At present the use of the first and second forms will be noted.

The occasion and, speaking unmorally, the justification of these artifices will readily appear if we consider what it was desired to accomplish. In the first place, it was helpful, as a preliminary to putting a conspiracy against the prince into operation, to lull him into a feeling of security and thereby induce him to relax apprehensions regarding attacks on his person or power. Were he suspicious that those who had access to him intended his death, or that his legions were being tampered with, his abundant powers would enable him to protect himself. Hence those who cherished designs against him went as far as possible in giving indications of unlimited esteem and reverence. If successfully done, this would avert suspicion until the time to strike had come.

The more abject manifestations of abasement had a second motive no less important. Nothing has a more deleterious effect on character than an environment of flattery, adulation, and sycophancy. Such an atmosphere undermines good sense and a just estimate of realities, and depraves any but the strongest character. Rarely in history has there appeared a young man, or indeed men of any age, who could long endure it unharmed. It is the surest means of ruining a man, of driving him from indiscretion to folly; and the phrase *"la folie des Césars"* exists as a reminder of the results in Roman times.[2]

The second form of disingenuous conduct practiced by the opponents of the emperors was of a less subtle and more direct kind, and consisted of mendacious stories originating in Rome but generally intended for provincial

[1] *Cf.* below, p. 360ff.
[2] See P. Jacoby, *Études sur la sélection chez l'homme* (Paris, 1904), p. 8ff.

consumption. This is a form of political opposition not unknown in modern times. When the emperor was not vigilant, when he did not remember as did Tiberius that "he held a wolf by the ears," [1] his opponents found it easy to spread tales which would cause discontent or disgust among the soldiers who, although they were slow in discovering it, were from the beginning the real sovereigns of Rome.

It is significant that writers nearer to the period under examination were themselves struck by the existence of this disturbing element in their material.

> After the battle of Actium [writes Tacitus], truth (in historical writings) was violated in many ways; first from lack of knowledge of the State, as though it were foreign to them, and presently from an extravagant propensity towards flattery or from hatred towards their rulers: hence no concern was manifested for posterity by either foes or flatterers. But a writer's partiality is easily rejected, while spleen and calumny are received with greedy ears; since the base crime of servility is associated with flattery, whereas a deceptive parade of independence accompanies malice. [2]

Cassius Dio refers in much the same way to the greater publicity of political matters under the Republic, and the consequent greater chance of determining the truth about them. But from the time of the establishment of the Empire under Augustus he says the affairs of government were less well known, and even if a matter were made public this publication inspired little confidence since its accuracy could not be verified, and it was suspected that everything said and done was according to

[1] Suet., *Tib.*, 25.
[2] Tac., *Hist.*, I, 1; *cf. Ann.*, I, 1; III, 19; Cass. Dio, LIII, 19; Boissier, *L'Opposition sous les Césars*, p. 76ff.

the wishes of the prince or his officials. Hence many things were reported that never happened, and many that did occur never became known, and hardly anything was published as it really took place. Wherefore, so this writer frankly informs us, he proposes to set forth the version of events commonly current, whether it be true or not.[1]

The peculiarities in the treatment of the emperors mentioned above were abundantly manifested as early as the days of the first Cæsars; the facts from which these generalizations have been drawn will receive detailed examination in the following chapter.

[1] Cass. Dio, LIII, 19; *cf.* LIV, 15; LXI, 8 and 11. See also Josephus, *Ant. Jud.*, XX, 8, 3; Tertullian, *Apol.*, 34, 35, 36; *ad Nat.*, I, 10, 17.

CHAPTER XIV

THE SENATE AND THE CÆSARS: JULIUS, AUGUSTUS, TIBERIUS

In passing from the old Republic of Rome to the Monarchy—or to the Dyarchy, as some would say, which for two centuries or more partly veiled the essentially monarchical character of the new régime—there appear great changes in the outward aspect of Roman life; but however much a people's circumstances may be suddenly altered, its character does not rapidly change. Yet there may be marked differences in the modes of manifestation of this character which demand the student's scrutiny, in order that he may not lose sight of the persistence of fundamental traits.

Thus in the matter of the use of fraud and mendacity in Roman public life, the new form of government made certain ancient methods no longer available, but the spirit of disingenuousness found fresh fields in which to display itself. One of the most important of these was in the relations between the emperors and the Senate, concerning which some general statements were made in the preceding chapter.

Our words "fraud and mendacity" connote so much moral reprehension that a digression may be permitted to disavow the impression probably conveyed by the use of these words. It is not suggested that a cause supported by such means is thereby discredited. In the first place, questions of desert are, or should be, foreign to the historical student. He is engaged in ascertaining facts, not in appraising values, and the only moral defect with which he is concerned is that form of fraud which obscures or perverts the facts. Roman emperors may or may not have been pernicious despots, but the fact that their opponents used falsehood in the conflict is evidence of nothing except that the Senate was the weaker party and that historical material emanating from it needs scrutiny.

Furthermore, in dealing with this subject it would be a psychological error to think that the making of false statements necessarily means conscious and deliberate lying. Human actions are rarely based on careful reasoning. The conduct which we are considering probably went on with no more distinct planning than there was in the earlier religious chicanery previously examined. It simply seemed the natural and obvious thing to do, as it does to-day, in regard to the object of one's dislike or hatred. A man does not often pause and say to himself: "Now I am going to invent a falsehood about my enemy." He merely finds it easy to believe, and pleasant to report, derogatory statements about the foe; nor does he often distinctly observe that he is selecting and arranging his materials to fit his conception of the object of his animosity. Tacitus tells us that any tale against Tiberius and Sejanus, however fabulous and monstrous it might be, found ready credence by those who hated them.[1] Cassius Dio says that what was thought harmonious to the characters attributed to Nero and Agrippina was declared to have actually taken place, and again he expresses his uncertainty as to whether a certain base act

[1] Tac., *Ann.*, IV, 11.

attributed to them actually occurred or was merely invented to fit their supposed characters.[1]

It would possess more formal correctness were the evidence regarding the nature and use of adulation and scandalmongering in the early Empire to be classified under the heads indicated in the preceding chapter: namely, (1) That adulation was intended to discredit the emperor or to lull him into a feeling of security; (2) that it sometimes had one or more of these effects; (3) that conspiracies against the emperor were nearly always preceded by an outburst of flattery; (4) that the emperors often recognized its character and purpose; (5) that many false stories about the emperors were invented and have entered into our historical sources. But the evidence is only imperfectly divisible into these categories, and the attempt involves so much repetition that the facts can be reviewed more satisfactorily by proceeding chronologically.

That the excessive adulation of the ruler, which was so prominent in imperial times did not arise out of tragic experiences of despotic harshness, appears from the fact that it burst full-fledged into existence with the victory of Cæsar.[2] He had shown clemency towards his opponents even on the field of Pharsalus, and this readiness to forgive his enemies characterized all periods of his life.[3] Yet to call this aspect of Cæsar's character by the name of forgiveness of enemies is misleading in that the phrase connotes those irritating qualities of moral ostentation, with the preliminary requirement of abasement and

[1] Cass. Dio, LXI, 8 and 11.   [2] Dictator, 49-44 B.C.
[3] Suet., *Jul.*, 73-75; Plut., *Cæs.*, 46, 48, 54, 57; *id.*, *Brut.*, 6; *Cato Min.*, 72; Vell. Pat., II, 52, 55, 56; Appian, *B. C.*, II, chap. XI, 81; XVI, 106; Sen., *de Ira*, II, 23. No harm came to those who voted against decrees made to honor him, Cass. Dio, XLIV, 8; XLIII, 15ff; 20, 50. *Cf.* Cic., *ad Fam.*, VI, 6; *ad Att.*, IX, 16; Reure, *op. cit.*, p. 67ff.

humiliation on the part of the person to be forgiven, which have so frequently accompanied the exercise of this virtue in modern times as to form part of our idea of the words. Cæsar did not forgive in this sense; he rather seemed to forget, or at least ignore, past hostility and to restore, as it were, his enemies to the place in his regard which had been theirs. His relations to Cicero, for instance, furnish a striking example of kindness without condescension.

The Senate, however, began immediately and continued incessantly to vote him extravagant honors: among others they declared him sacred and inviolable, and bound themselves by oath to defend his person.[1] Much of this adulation he deprecated, and many honors he declined, saying that those granted him needed to be lessened rather than enlarged.[2] He was a man who in matters of importance saw through appearances to realities, and there seems no adequate reason to doubt his good faith in rejecting a royal title, which would obviously have weakened rather than strengthened his position.

That the motives for the excesses of adulation were not disingenuous appears explicitly in the authorities. Plutarch says that after the first distinctions were granted,

> some persons, by adding still further honors and vying with one another in this regard, made Cæsar odious and an object of dislike even to those who were of the most moderate temper, by reason of the extravagant and unusual character of what was decreed;

[1] Plut., *Cæs.*, 57, 60; Suet., *Jul.*, 76ff, 84; Appian, *B. C.*, II, chap. XVI, 106-107; Cass. Dio, XLII, 19-20; XLIII, 14-15, 44-45; XLIV, 3-6.

[2] Suet., *Jul.*, 79; Vell. Pat., II, 68; Appian, *B.C.*, II, chap. XVI, 107-111; Cass. Dio, XLIII, 15, 46; XLIV, 3. Dio partly contradicts himself at *ibid.*, 7. Cf. 9-11.

and it is supposed that

> his enemies who hated Cæsar conferred these measures
> no less than those who were his flatterers, in order that
> they might have as many and as great pretexts as pos-
> sible for attacking him.[1]

Cassius Dio declares that

> various men kept proposing sundry greater marks of
> distinction, all in excess, some out of extreme flattery
> towards him, and some out of sarcastic ridicule. . . .
> Others, and the majority, followed this course because
> they wished to make him envied and disliked as quickly
> as possible, that he might the sooner perish. Of course
> precisely that happened. . . .   In order to embitter
> even his best friends against him, they did their best
> to traduce the man, and finally called him King. . . .
> They secretly adorned with a diadem his statue which
> stood on the rostra.[2]

The dishonesty of these proceedings is plainly indicated
in our authorities, most of whom declare that the conspiracy against him was due to envy and malice, and that
the alleged patriotic zeal was a mere pretense.[3]   The
senators who had lavished extravagant honors upon him,
publicly spread injurious reports that he was glad to
obtain them, and had behaved himself in a haughty
fashion, although to have thrust all the honors aside
would have seemed to them contemptuous. The duplicity

---

[1] Plut., *Cæs.*, 57; *cf.* 60.

[2] Cass. Dio, XLIV, 7, 9; *cf.* Appian, *B. C.*, II, chap. XVI, 108.
Suetonius collects some of the general scandals about Cæsar,
Jul., 49-65, 77.   The verses of Catullus (29, 54, 57, 93) are
striking examples of abuse.

[3] *Cf.* in addition to the foregoing references Sen., *de Ira*, III,
30; Appian, *B. C.*, II, chap. XVI, 112; Cass. Dio, XLIV, 1;
Plut., *Cæs.*, 60; Vell. Pat., II, 56.

of the Senate was brought out at his funeral when Antony had the herald read its decrees pressing upon him all distinctions, human and divine.[1] Cæsar himself saw clearly that its acts did not all spring out of good-will, and that a faction was conspiring to make him odious by artfully accusing him of aiming at royalty.[2] He appears to have been disgusted at the carping criticism to which he was subjected, but disdainfully passed over, with nothing more than an intimation of his knowledge of them, or a warning to those concerned, all the plots and treasonable meetings, as well as the virulently scandalous lampoons and libels so lavishly circulated against him.[3]

That his enemies by their flattery succeeded in rendering Cæsar conceited and thus impairing his natural sanity is asserted by some writers but it is not probable. No well established acts on his part give any indication of it. Cassius Dio, indeed, in one passage attributes Cæsar's acceptance of the excessive honors voted him to his disinclination to seem contemptuous were he to decline them, though to take them rendered his position unsafe; and then he goes on to declare that by these excessive honors his mind was sent soaring, that he became vain, that he was delighted with them and accepted nearly all of them, including those voted in ridicule.[4] But Plutarch seems to be nearer the truth in speaking of him as stimulated to great ideas and projects for the future by the tre-

[1] Cass. Dio, XLIV, 3; Suet., *Jul.*, 84. *Cf.* Cass. Dio, XLIII, 47, for anonymous pamphlets in circulation.

[2] *Cf.* Appian, *B. C.*, II, chap. XVI, 108; Vell. Pat., II, 68; Cass. Dio, XLIII, 15.

[3] See Suet., *Jul.*, 73, 75; Plut., *Cæs.*, 60. *Cf.* Appian, *B. C.*, II, chap. XVI, 110; Cass. Dio, XLIII, 20, where, in one instance, Cæsar was moved to deny a vile charge, and was ridiculed for his pains. *Cf.* Suet., *Jul.*, 49.

[4] Cass. Dio, XLIV, 3, 6-8.

mendous deeds he had already performed.[1]   Brutus in a letter, the authenticity of which is under suspicion, blamed the weakness of the Romans towards tyrants as having incited in Cæsar the audacious desire for sovereignty;[2] but this is putting the cart before the horse. Brutus was constitutionally incapable of understanding a great man or a complicated political situation.[3]

There was, however, another effect, which may be attributed, with better evidence, to the protestations of loyalty and esteem so lavishly made to Cæsar.   His enemies possibly succeeded thereby in making him believe that his life was safe in their hands.   Cæsar neglected to safeguard himself.   It need not surprise us if he underestimated the malice of his opponents, nor if his high intelligence found it difficult to imagine that others would commit the terrible mistake of killing him.   As a result of the grant to him of the sacrosanctity of a tribune with all the penalties entailed for any one who should commit a breach of it, and of a body-guard of senators and knights bound by oath, he is said to have believed

> that he would never be plotted against by men who had voted him such honors, nor by any one else whom they could prevent and in consequence of this belief he even dispensed in the future with his body-guard.   For nominally he accepted the privilege of being watched

[1] *Cæs.*, 58; cf. Cass. Dio, XLIII, 41.

[2] Cic., *ad Brut.*, I, 16: *et Caesarem in cupiditatem regni impulit,* Cf. Plut., *Brut.*, 22.   In another of these doubtful letters Brutus says (to Atticus) that Cicero is slavish and cringing. *Ad Brut.,* I, 17.

[3] The episode of Brutus's loan at 48% to the town of Salamis in Cyprus, his refusal to accept 12%, and his starving some of the town council to coerce them casts considerable light on his character. *Cf.* Cic., *ad Att.,* V, 21; VI, 1, 2, 3.

over by the senators and knights, and therefore dismissed his former guard.[1]

It would no doubt have been difficult for him to believe that, for instance, a man like Cicero, whom he had treated with the greatest generosity as well as courtesy and consideration,[2] who had written him the most friendly letters and had made addresses to him full of eloquent, and apparently heartfelt, commendation, declaring that the safety of all depended on his safety; that he, the speaker, and all others exhorted and entreated him to take every care of himself; saying, "we promise you not only to exert our vigilance and our wariness to assist in this case, but also to oppose our bodies as shields against every danger which can threaten you"[3]—it would indeed have been difficult to believe that this man was hoping for his benefactor's death, and that when the murder took place, he would fall into an ecstasy of delight and declare the joy with which he feasted his eyes upon the just execution of a tyrant; that he could not praise Brutus and Cassius enough, and that on them, he urged, should be bestowed all care and protection.[4]   It is not

[1] Cass. Dio, XLIV, 5-7; Suet. (Jul., 84, 86), speaks of his reliance on these senatorial decrees and oaths and consequent dismissal of his Spanish guards who had theretofore attended him with drawn swords.   Plutarch (Cæs., 57) says that he even declined a body-guard of his personal friends.   Cf. Appian, B. C., II, chap. XVI, 109.   Cicero (ad Fam., IV, 4, 46 B.C.) speaks of the devotion displayed by the Senate to Cæsar.

[2] Cf. e.g., Cic., ad Att., XI, 6; ad Fam., IV, 13.

[3] Cic., pro Marcello, 10 et passim. Cf. pro Ligar., passim; and pro Deiot., ad Att., XIII, 50; ad Fam., IV, 4. This letter written at the time of the speech for Marcellus (46 B.C.), shows the mendacious character of Cicero's expressions quoted in the text. Cf. ad Att., XII, 45; Phil., II, 11-13.

[4] Ad Att., XIV, 14; ad Fam., VI, 15; IX, 14; ad Att., XIV, 6. 13.

surprising that the triumvirs failed to follow Cæsar's example of sparing his enemies, and that Cicero and many others came to experience what has been called in a rather metaphysical phrase, "the self-vindicating power of great moral laws."

There is, then, nothing improbable in the idea that the flattery and adulation heaped upon him may have led Cæsar to underestimate the dangerous malevolence which lay beneath. It was so clear to him that "the commonwealth was more interested in his safety than was he himself" [1] that he may have been deceived into an unintentional carelessness regarding his personal safety.

But there is another hypothesis which receives equal support from authority and is better grounded in our general knowledge of the minds of great men. To the average man, important only by his numbers, clinging desperately to his own existence, there is something incredible in the idea that a man whose life is full, rich, and felicitous should fail to be concerned about spinning it out to the last possible moment, and that he should consider a meticulous absorption in the means of accomplishing its prolongation too high a price to pay. It may be that men like Cæsar feel that they have struck all the keyboard of human experience, while the others feel that they have not yet begun to live; or it may be that the former cherish so highly the sentiment of personal dignity as to deem it compromised by petty diligence in securing their personal safety, or that they are too much occupied in their relations with the larger objective things to be willing to spend their time in watching for manifestations of human folly and malice. At any rate, however it comes about, a man of the calibre of Cæsar seems generally to feel, as Paterculus and others say that he felt, that he would

[1] Suet., *Jul.*, 86.

rather die than be constantly dreading death; or as Shakespeare renders it: "Cowards die many times before their deaths; the valiant never taste of death but once." [1]

But this digression as to how Cæsar was misled by the machinations of his enemies is really not germane to the question of the extent of disingenuous adulation and scandalmongering of which he was the object. It is sufficient to know that these elements in Roman political life show themselves in full operation in the lifetime of the first and most merciful Cæsar, and hence that they were not the results of oppression or tyranny.

The history of the years of confusion (44-31 B.C.) shows likewise how little dependence the phenomena under discussion had upon the so-called tyranny of the Cæsars; how it was a recognized expedient of Roman public life to defame in order to destroy an opponent; to wheedle and flatter, in order to deceive or deprave, and then betray. Each of these forms of guile finds interesting illustrations in the orgy of mendacity that followed its successful use against Cæsar. The remarkable civic virtues of Brutus and Cassius did not prevent them from putting out false declarations in order to increase the odium against Antony; [2] nor did the absurdity of their attempts prevent Cicero and Antony from endeavoring to deceive each other as to their mutual sentiments. The dissatisfaction felt by Cicero regarding the glorious tyrannicides was probably the reflection that the job had not been completed by not having killed Antony as well. [3]

[1] *Cf.* Suet., *Jul.*, 86; Vell. Pat., II, 57; Plut., *Cæs.*, 57, 60; Appian, *B. C.*, II, chap. XVI, 109. Suetonius reports that some of Cæsar's friends thought that failing health contributed to his indifference.

[2] *Cf.* Vell. Pat., II, 62.

[3] *Cf.* Cic., *ad Att.*, XIV, 21, 22; *ad Fam.*, XII, 4; X, 28; *ad Brut.*, I, 15.

No two men could be more antipathetic than these, and Cicero repeatedly expressed the lowest opinion of the other's character,[1] and the desire that things might go badly for him.[2]   The sentiments of Antony towards Cicero, we may fairly infer, were much the same.   Yet about six weeks after the death of Cæsar, we find Antony writing in a complimentary and deferential way to Cicero, and the latter replying with fulsome words about his love for Antony, and declaring that no one is dearer to him, that he has never felt any bitterness to him, that he will always zealously and unhesitatingly do whatever may conform to Antony's wishes or to his advantage.   The next day Cicero writes Atticus commenting on Antony's unprincipled and iniquitous character, and enclosed a copy of the affectionate letters exchanged—perhaps as model exercises in mendacity.[3]   But for the time, so Cicero said to Tiro, he wished to be in amicable relations with Antony, and a similar desire seemed just then to animate Antony, whose brother Lucius wrote Cicero courteously assuring him that he need have no anxieties.[4]   A little later, however, the situation had changed, and Antony again appears as the beast.   It is worth noting

[1] See ad Att., XIV, 12; ad Fam., X, 28; XII, 2; ad Brut., II, 5.

[2] Ad Att., XV, 3.

[3] Cf. Cic., ad Att., XIV, 13, 13a, 13b. Among Cicero's expressions to Antony are, e.g.: nam cum te semper amavi primum tuo studio, post etiam beneficio provocatus, tum his temporibus res publica te mihi ita commendavit ut cariorem habeam neminem. In writing to Atticus, however, he says: quam dissolute, quam turpiter quamque ita perniciose ut non numquam Caesar desiderandus esse videatur facile existimabis.

[4] See Cic., ad Fam., XVI, 23; ad Att., XV, 12. Cicero's opinions about Lucius are expressed in Phil., III, 12; V, 7; XII, 8ff. Cf. ad Brut., II, 5.

that Cicero says without any indication of surprise that Antony is charging him with being the instigator of Cæsar's assassination for no other reason than to incite the veterans against him.[1]   The use of mendacity to discredit an opponent was a recognized trick.   Opportunism was the guiding principle of public life, as Cicero wrote to a friend about this time,[2] and there was the inevitable accompaniment of false reports and forged documents.[3] That material of this sort passed into the received history of the period is only too probable.

Cicero and others met their match at this sort of statesmanship of deception in Octavianus, who arrived in Italy, not yet nineteen, to take the position of heir of his granduncle Julius.   One of the first things he did was to obtain the active support of the veteran politician Cicero, who wrote Atticus that Octavianus treated him with extreme deference and friendliness and is entirely devoted to him.[4] He called Cicero "father," wrote him every day urging him to take hold and save the Republic, though he was perhaps not wholly successful in endeavoring to persuade Cicero that the tyrannicides would find a friend in Cæsar's heir.[5]   He exhibited, in Cicero's opinion, "a remarkable

[1] Cic., *ad Fam.*, XII, 2.
[2] *Fecimus id quidem temporibus cedentes, quae valent in re publica plurimum, ad Fam.*, XII, 1.
[3] Cf. Cic., *ad Att.*, XVI, 14; *ad Brut.*, II, 5.
[4] Cf. Cic., *ad Att.*, XIV, 11, 12.
[5] See Plut., *Cic.*, 45; Cic., *ad Att.*, XVI, 9, 11, 15.   The wise Atticus suggested caution, *ib.*, XVI, 15.   Octavianus seems also, with about equal good faith, to have called Antony "father," Appian, *B. C.*, III, chap. II, 15.   It was charged that he was concerned in a plot to assassinate Antony, a charge which Cicero believed and approved, *ad Fam.*, XII, 23.   Our authorities are in conflict on this matter.   Seneca (*de Clem.*, I, 9) and Suetonius (*Aug.*, 10) credit the report.   Plutarch (*Ant.*, 16) is non-committal, while Appian (*B. C.*, III, chap. VI, 39) denies it.

natural inclination towards virtue," behaving most excellently and following the old statesman's advice.[1] Cicero actively supported him in the Senate and was instrumental in procuring for him various grants of honors, distinctions, and privileges.[2]

But this does not mean that Cicero's course was taken in good faith, nor that he was not ready to turn on his protégé whenever it seemed desirable.[3] Antony declared that Cicero had boasted of his success in cajoling and deceiving Octavianus by compliments and honors.[4] Testimony about Cicero from that source is, of course, open to suspicion, but the charge is confirmed by Cicero's epigram that "the young man is to be lauded, honored and"— here follows a word which bears the double meaning of "exalted" or "strung up." The *mot* reached Octavianus's ears and may have been in his mind when, a few months later, the list of the proscribed bore Cicero's name among the first.[5]

For reasons other than his possession of eminent military talents Augustus (31 B.C. to 14 A.D.[6]) emerged from the long period of confusion and civil war ending

[1] *Ad Brut.*, I, 3, 10, 15; II, 5; *ad Fam.*, X, 28.
[2] *Cf. Phil.*, V, 17-18; XIV, 9; Vell. Pat., II, 62; Appian, *B. C.*, III, chap. VIII, 51; Cic., *ad Brut.*, I, 15; *ad Fam.*, XI, 14.
[3] *Cf.* Cic., *ad Att.*, XVI, 15.
[4] *Cf. Phil.*, XIII, 19.
[5] The epigram (*laudandum adulescentem, ornandum, tollendum*) attributed to Cicero, appears in a letter from Brutus (*ad Fam.*, XI, 20) as reported to him by a person who had lately talked with Octavianus. Cicero's reply (*id.*, 21) seems to bear the interpretation that he admitted the authorship. This is also affirmed by Velleius Paterculus, II, 62. Suetonius (*Aug.*, 12) mentions the remark but does not give the authorship. It sounds very much like one of Cicero's *jeux d'esprit*.
[6] The title Augustus was not given to Octavianus until 27 B.C.

in the battle of Actium, the undoubted master of the Roman world; and for the remainder of his life he continued to be, under a thin disguise, its sovereign ruler.

Our information regarding his principate is extremely defective in both quantity and quality, and yet it is probably safe to say that the Senate opposition to him was less keen and active than it had been to Julius, and was again to become in the following reigns. It must have taken many years for the aristocracy to catch its breath and get on its feet after the stunning blows it had received during the civil wars; and the memory of the results flowing to it from its participation in the killing of Julius Cæsar, or its approval of the deed, must have tended to depress its enthusiasm for revolutionary adventures.

Then, too, several things tended to mitigate its antipathy to Augustus. Neither his father, mother, nor stepfather had incurred the ill-will of those who opposed Cæsar, and the latter two had endeavored to dissuade the young man from accepting the stormful inheritance of his granduncle.[1] There was no career of demagogic opposition to the Senate on the part of the young Octavianus to be overlooked, and he had done them the great service of disposing of Antony, whom many of them feared and detested, and on whom they were quite willing to saddle most of the blame of the proscriptions. When Augustus got well established he showed himself most liberal in pardoning and reinstating all the nobles who had survived.

The Octavian family had not long been great and its genealogical tree did not invite a scrutiny. Possibly for

---

[1] Compare Plut., *Cic.*, 44; Suet., *Aug.*, 8; Vell. Pat., II, 60; Appian, *B. C.*, III, chap. II, 10; Cic., *ad Att.*, XIV, 12. Philippus, the stepfather, had remained neutral in the civil war, and was on good terms with both Cæsar and Cicero. *Cf.* Cæsar, *B. C.*, I, 6.

this reason its present head, though raised to a giddy height by his adoption into the Julian family with the tremendous inheritance of a claim to the power acquired by Julius Cæsar, yet remained somewhat impressed by the greatness of the ancient stocks among whom he now found himself. Only one born in a great line, as were Julius and Tiberius, could without effort despise the degenerate bearers of glittering names. One of more humble origin would more quickly recognize it to be his duty, as did Augustus, to make a clearance from the Senate of those new men whose presence was offensive to such as had nothing but ancient lineage to their credit.

It was a pleasure in which Augustus indulged himself as often as possible, to induce the nobility to lend the aid of their prestige to his experiment in government; and his new magistracy lacked one element most objectionable to an oligarchic caste, for it had not come to him by inheritance, however much his position as the heir of Julius may have given him the opportunity to obtain it. Not being hereditary, it was in theory open to any ambitious candidate at his death. Although in the earlier part of his reign he had seemed to indicate Agrippa as his successor, this must have appeared to the nobles as a mere amiable eccentricity on his part. However, when in the later years he clearly designated Tiberius as his choice, the element of heredity became obvious, and this was probably one of the things which contributed to cause his popularity with the senators to wane.

Another factor of very considerable importance in strengthening his position with the aristocracy must be taken into account, the influence of Livia. Early in his career he had become deeply attached to a woman who possessed the remarkable combination of great personal beauty, indubitable virtue, a kind and benevolent disposition, excellent judgment, tact and discretion, a strong intelligence, and a courageous heart; and who was withal a member by birth and family connection of the most ancient nobility.[1] Such a woman was Livia, who enjoyed for over half a century, unimpaired and unquestioned to the last, her husband's devotion.[2] Her services to her husband were real, and his career was, it is almost certain, greatly forwarded by the establishment of a fair understanding and some mutual confidence between him and those elements which had bitterly opposed Cæsar and were with equal bitterness to oppose the later Julio-Claudian emperors.

Then, finally, there were two factors which made things go smoothly with Augustus, but which we may be inclined to underestimate. They counted as virtues however in Roman times:—Augustus enjoyed great personal pulchritude and remarkable good fortune.

The effect of all these factors was, as we have said, to make the perennial feud between the Senate and the emperor less sullen and rancorous than at most other times in the first century of the Empire. The conspiracies against him do not seem to have had much bitterness or vindictiveness, nor do they appear to have commanded a wide support or approval. The opposition in general hardly went beyond the invention and propagation of base stories about his private conduct—conventional scandal-mongering, indulged in as a pastime, or to express a patriotic antipathy to what men called "tyranny." It was apparently not difficult to keep them within these limits and to counteract their influence by the activities of the im-

[1] See Tac., *Ann.*, V, 1; IV, 71; Vell. Pat., II, 75, 79, 130; Suet., *Aug.*, 62, 99; *Claud.*, 4; Cass. Dio, LVIII, 2; LV, 18ff; Sen., *Cons. ad Marc.*, 3ff; *de Clem.*, I, 9.

[2] Cass. Dio, LVIII, 2, explains the secret of her influence.

perial subsidized literary bureau managed by Mæcenas.[1]
Augustus in his earlier career had been familiar enough
with plotting to be able to judge when it was becoming
dangerous, and it was not often necessary to execute a conspirator.[2] Tacitus, with the best will in the world to make
out a case for what he calls a "bloodstained peace," mentions but three names of persons executed, but very
characteristically puts them in the plural to conceal their
paucity.[3]

Still there were a few conspiracies. We know of seven
in which nobles were engaged—members of such families
as the Æmilian, Cornelian, and Plautian—some of whom
had accepted favors from him and passed for his friends; [4]
but none of these plots seems to have commanded the support or approval of any large proportion of the Senate.

From the beginning of his career, however, there was
an abundance of scandalous charges against him, many
of them most odious in character. Suetonius spends no
small part of his sketch of the emperor in preserving for
us an anthology of what we may hope were the most obscene of these stories.[5] The extravagance and absurdity
of many of them make it probable that they could have had
no particular effect in compromising his position; they
were perhaps not even seriously designed to that end, but

[1] If Martial (XI, 20) may be trusted, Augustus seems to have
given his opponents as lively abuse as he received.

[2] His pardon of conspirators is often mentioned; e.g., Sen.,
de Clem., I, 9-11; Cass. Dio, LVI, 40; Suet., Aug., 51.

[3] Ann., I, 10.

[4] See Suet., Aug., 19, 66; Sen., de Clem., I, 9; Pliny, N. H.,
VII, 147; Cass. Dio, LIV, 3, 15; Vell. Pat., II, 88, 91. Dio
(LIV, 15) gives some intelligent reflections on the subject of
reports of plots against monarchs.

[5] Aug., 55-56, 68ff; Cf. Pliny, N. H., VII, chap. 45 (46); Tac.,
Ann., I, 10.

represented merely ebullitions of peevish scurrility and blatant indecency. Their value consists not in what they tell of Augustus but in the evidence they give of what Suetonius thought would appeal to the public taste of his times, and in the indication afforded by them of credulity on the part of some moderns in accepting them as serious historical material. Augustus himself proceeded wisely in ignoring or smiling at such feeble attacks.[1]

To the fairly cordial relations existing between Augustus and the Senate may be attributed not only the unofficial character of the plots against him and the general triviality of the scandalmongering of which he was the object, but also the absence of senatorial orgies of laudation and the pressing upon him of insidious honorific extravagances. There seems to have been no concerted effort to make him ridiculous or detested, as appeared so distinctly in the case of Julius Cæsar. Probably warned by his grand uncle, he was careful to discourage any approach to sycophancy and to decline excessive distinctions; and in the general good feeling which prevailed, there does not seem to have been any serious attempt to embarrass him in the matter.[2] The world was anxious to pay him divine honors, and he sanctioned this in the provinces where it was done in connection with the worship of Rome; but in Rome itself, not at all.[3]

---

[1] Cf. Sen., de Clem., I, 11; de Ira, III, 23; Suet., Aug., 51, 55, 56; Tac., Ann., IV, 34. Cassius Severus was punished as a general libeler of various men and women of distinction. Tac., Ann., I, 72. Cf. Cass. Dio, LVI, 27. Direct incitements to revolution were of course treated as criminal: Cass. Dio, LV, 27.

[2] See Suet., Aug., 52-54, 57, 58; Cass. Dio, LV, 12; LVI, 17, 25. We rarely hear of such a case as that mentioned in Dio, LIV, 3, where hostility was excited by honors paid to Augustus.

[3] Cf. Suet., Aug., 52; Tac., Ann., IV, 37. The political aspect of emperor worship is of course a factor in this distinction.

If our information about the details of the events happening during this reign were less meagre, we might be able to discover some significance in the possibly suggestive fact that just prior to each of the conspiracies against him in which nobles were engaged, there were grants to him of additional powers or distinctions. In the present state of our authorities, however, importance cannot be attributed to this synchronism, and it would be hardly worth mentioning save that in certain other reigns these premonitory laudations seem to have some relation to the subsequent attacks; wherefore the suspicion—but nothing more—arises that we may be here in the presence of similar phenomena. At any rate it appears abundantly in our sources that whatever manifestations of servility or sycophancy there may have been during this reign, they were not imposed or suggested by any danger attaching to a more reserved attitude.[1]

While it seems probable that Augustus and the Senate got on together without serious friction, and that he had no very bitter enemies in that body, the same cannot be said of his successor. The existence, extent, manifestations, and results of the hostility felt towards Tiberius (14-37 A.D.) form the subject of a more detailed study later in this book,[2] and will be passed over here; it is enough to deal at this point only with the adulation of which he was the recipient. We may anticipate conclusions hereafter reached to the extent of saying that from various causes there existed no small amount of enmity towards him.

At the same time, however, there was tendered him much adulation, and we need to consider to what extent it

[1] Cf. Cass. Dio, LV, 4; Suet., *Aug.*, 51ff.
[2] See below, p. 319ff; (cf. L. Lévy, *Quomodo Tiberius . . . Erga Senatum se Gesserit* [Paris, 1901].—*Editor*).

was unreal and factitious, and how far it was used, not as a shield of protection against a suspicious tyrant, but rather as a subtle weapon against an undesired prince. Far from Tiberius's desiring or being gratified by sycophancy or the heaping of honors upon him, all authorities agree that he at all times and in positive terms detested and refused them for himself and so far as possible for those under his control. He declined to accept various honorific distinctions which were pressed upon him; the title of *Pater Patriae* [1] and the prænomen of *Imperator* [2] were refused, and the name or title of *Augustus* he used only in diplomatic correspondence.[3] He would not allow his name to be given to a month nor accept a civic crown, nor an elaborate birthday festival,[4] nor an ovation,[5] nor proposals to renew ceremonially the oath of allegiance and obedience to his acts.[6] He was easy of access, deferential to the Senate and consuls, tolerated opposition and refused to consider himself slighted or insulted.[7] He sharply rebuked a citizen who addressed him as *dominus,* rejecting the appellation as contumelious; and adulatory references to his occupation as "sacred," or to acts as done "by his authority," he insisted should be changed to the words "laborious" or "persuasion." [8] From one attempting to kneel to him, he started away in disgust; even ordinary compliments offended him; [9] and an embassy of congratulation he refused to receive.[10] Sycophantic prosecutions

---

[1] See Tac., *Ann.,* I, 72; II, 87; Suet., *Tib.,* 26; Cass. Dio, LVII, 8.

[2] *Cf.* Suet., *Tib.,* 26.   [3] See Suet., *Tib.,* 26; Cass. Dio, LVII, 8.

[4] See references in preceding note.   [5] *Cf.* Tac., *Ann.,* III, 47.

[6] *Cf.* Tac., *Ann.,* I, 8, 72; Suet. *Tib.,* 26, 67; Cass. Dio, LVIII, 17; LVII, 8.

[7] *Cf.* Cass. Dio, LVII, 9, 11, 15, 17; Suet., *Tib.,* 31.

[8] *Cf.* Suet., *Tib.,* 27; Cass. Dio, LVII, 8.   [9] Suet., *ibid.*

[10] See Cass. Dio, LVIII, 13.

for offences against his dignity he was sedulous to quash;[1] and he rebuked the Senate for its undue haste in putting to death a man charged with this offence without giving the prince time to intervene with his tribunicial veto, requiring for the future a lapse of ten days before the execution of a sentence.[2]

After once so far yielding to the precedent set by Augustus as to permit a temple to be erected to himself and the Senate in the provinces of Asia, he thereafter persistently forbade anything like worship of himself, or the ascription to him of divine honors, or the erection of his statues without his permission, which he granted only where it was clear that there was no intention of instituting a religious cult. He was but a man, he said, trying to perform worthily the duties of a man with that tranquil spirit which he prayed the gods to grant him to the end; in place of temples and images he hoped for approval and kindly recollection in the hearts of the citizens and subjects of Rome. This attitude seemed to his enemies to be mean-spirited, *degeneris animi*.[3]

Tiberius understood the danger involved, in the acceptance by the emperor of new powers whose exercise was bound to provoke odium, and several times frankly explained it to the Senate,[4] while as to honors and distinctions, he had early in his reign, in declining some that were offered him, told the Senate emphatically that every increase of their number increased the perils of his position.[5] He had deprecated, and often forbidden, the extravagant

[1] *E.g.*, Tac., *Ann.*, I, 73; II, 50; III, 70; VI, 5; Suet., *Tib.*, 27.
[2] *Cf.* Tac., *Ann.*, III, 51.
[3] Tac., *Ann.*, IV, 37-38; Suet., *Tib.*, 26; Cass. Dio, LVII, 8-9; LVIII, 8.
[4] *Cf.* Tac., *Ann.*, II, 36; III, 54, 69.
[5] Tac., *Ann.*, I, 72: *quantoque plus adeptus foret, tanto se magis in lubrico dictitans.*

distinctions offered to his aged mother, who, with the enfeeblement of advancing years, had shown some disposition to regard not only herself but her friends as exalted above the law.[1]

The granting of excessive and unmerited honors to the young men and children of his family he positively forbade, sometimes with heat, as damaging to them. When he asked the Senate to grant the tribunicial powers to his son Drusus, he explained that the young man was now in his thirty-fifth year, had been tried in battle and government for eight years, had quelled mutinies, concluded wars, and filled the high offices of state, so that he was fairly entitled to the promotion.[2]

It would seem from the foregoing, and there is no conflicting evidence in our authorities, that Tiberius had done everything possible to make it clear that he did not desire and would not receive flattery and adulation, or the granting of honorific distinctions.[3] Yet notwithstanding his consistent attitude the Senate continued to make fulsome proposals for fresh titles and flatteries, offering prayers and sacrifice to his image and taking oaths in the name of his *Fortuna*.[4] It appeared to be of no avail that Tiberius made a direct command that the offensive nonsense cease, that no more resolutions of this character be passed, and finally, that no more such business be even brought before the Senate.[5] In a little while he was besought to accept an armed body-guard of twenty senators.

[1] *Cf.* Tac., *Ann.*, I, 14; II, 34; III, 64; IV, 21; Suet., *Tib.*, 50; Cass. Dio, LVII, 12; LVIII, 2.

[2] See Tac., *Ann.*, III, 56, 57, 59; IV, 17; Suet., *Tib.*, 54. The Senate was displeased that Drusus sent a letter of thanks instead of coming to Rome to thank them in person.

[3] *Cf.* Tac., *Ann.*, III, 65; IV, 6; Suet., *Tib.*, 26.

[4] *Cf.* Tac., *Ann.*, III, 65; Cass. Dio, LVIII, 2, 4, 8, 12.

[5] See Cass. Dio, LVII, 8; LVIII, 8, 12.

Remembering, perhaps, the fate of Julius Cæsar, he is said to have grown very suspicious of the Senate, and to have devoted special attention to assuring himself of the loyalty of the Prætorian Guard. His suspicions were naturally increased by the fact that just at this time it was proposed in the Senate to grant to the veterans of the Prætorian Guard the privilege of occupying equestrian seats at the Circus. This Tiberius regarded as an attempt to stir up sedition, and the proposer was expelled from the Senate and from Italy, and later given to the custody of the magistrates. We may note in this connection that Tacitus ascribes to him a different sentiment regarding the proposal for a guard—a sentiment more like that of Julius Cæsar—representing him as saying that life was not so great a thing to him as to make him care to preserve it by such precautions.[1] But "the senators were devising and decreeing new honors for the emperor, each according to his wont," when finally his end came, and whether or not he would have declined them all, was never known.[2]

This uncontrollable persistency and even effrontery in fawning and cajolery may well excite our suspicions, as it did those of Tiberius, and suggest that there may be something more than mere coincidence in the immediate anteriority of special outbursts of adulation, or the declarations of loyalty in the Senate, to the discovery of plots by senators against the emperor. In the endeavor to reach a true understanding of the nature of these incessant manifestations, incidents which taken individually amount to little may in cumulation have some probative value. It may be of some significance, then, that each special period of adulation or protestation of fidelity is followed, either

[1] Cf. Cass. Dio, LVIII, 17-18; Tac., Ann., VI, 2-3.
[2] Tac., Ann., VI, 45.

later in the same year or in the following year, by what
was claimed to be the uncovering of a disloyal project or
conspiracy. Thus flattery in the years 15, 16, 22-23, 27,
28-30, 32, 33, is followed by plots in 16, 24, 28, 30,
32, 34.[1]

But the evidence recapitulated, while raising a doubt as
to the motives for the eulogy poured out upon Tiberius
in and out of season, is lacking in direct proof of the
motive. It seems hardly probable that those indulging
in sycophancy seriously expected to turn the emperor's
head, and they ought to have realized finally that he was
too clear-sighted to be lulled into a careless neglect of due
precautions against them; yet the offer of a senatorial
body-guard which came as late as the year 32 seems to
indicate some such idea. But, as we have seen, Tiberius
was more cynical than Julius Cæsar, and its effect was just
the reverse.

If we are left largely to conjecture as to the motives for
the distinctions pressed upon the emperor, we are permitted a clearer sight in the case of Sejanus, who for a
long time was almost a colleague in the imperial power,

---

[1] 15 A.D., flattery and loyalty (Tac., I, 72); 16 A.D., plot
(Tac., II, 27-31; Vell. Pat., II, 130; Suet., *Tib.*, 25); 16 A.D.,
sycophancy (Tac., II, 32, 35, 36); revolutionary attempt (Tac.,
II, 39-40; Cass. Dio, LVII, 16; Suet., *Tib.*, 25); 22-23, adulation
and loyalty (Tac., III, 47, 57, 65, 70; IV, 8, 12); 24, projects
(Tac., IV, 17-21; Vell. Pat., II, 130); 27, adulation (Tac., IV,
64); 28, plot (Tac., IV, 68-70; Cass. Dio, LVIII, 1); 28-30,
sycophancy (Tac., IV, 71, 74; Cass. Dio, LVIII, 2, 4, 6, 8);
29-31, conspiracies (Cass. Dio, LVIII, 3-16; Suet., *Tib.*, 54;
Josephus, *Ant. J.*, XVIII, 6, 6; Tac., V, 8; Suet., *Vitell.*, 2);
32, protestations of loyalty (Tac., VI, 2; Cass. Dio, LVIII, 17-
18; 32-33, plots (Tac., VI, 3, 4, 7, 9, 10, 14); 33, adulation
(Tac., VI, 25; Dio, LVIII, 22); plots (Tac., VI, 29-30; Dio,
LVIII, 24; Tac., VI, 38, 39).

and attracted even more dislike from the nobles than did Tiberius himself.[1]   In his case we can more easily trace the working of this mode of opposition.

It has been sagely observed with reference to Sejanus, that a man of his type is avid of adulation, craves distinction, and resents the withholding of it, while a person of more profound self-esteem is indifferent to the applause of others.[2]   Sejanus certainly seems to have accepted with complaisance all that the Senate could offer him, and the Senate was not niggardly in the bestowal of statues, festivals, honorific embassies, and ostentatious sycophancy.[3]   Tiberius, who seems to have long been genuinely fond of him—from whom indeed he received devoted and unwearying service for years—,is said to have warned him that the nobles bore him abundant ill-will, and that their fawning upon him was hypocritical.[4]   But with infatuated folly Sejanus drank in all the flattery and increased in arrogance at the sight of undisguised servility.[5]

Finally the senators, disregarding Tiberius's express directions, offered prayers and sacrifices to the emperor whom they could not well omit—and to his coadjutor; swore by their Fortunes, and finally by the Fortune of Sejanus alone.   Tiberius, on learning of these excesses, renewed his prohibition against the paying of divine honors to mortals, as well as the granting of honorary distinctions.   But it was too late; the head of Sejanus had become completely turned, as had undoubtedly been

[1] Cf. Tac., *Ann.*, IV, 1ff., 40; V, 4; Cass. Dio, LVIII, 2, 4, 6; LVII, 19; Seneca, *Cons. ad Marc.*, 1, 22; Juvenal, X, 90ff.

[2] See Cass. Dio, LVIII, 5.

[3] See Tac., *Ann.*, III, 72; IV, 74; Cass. Dio, LVIII, 2, 4, 5, 7; Suet., *Tib.*, 65.

[4] Cf. Tac., *Ann.*, IV, 40.

[5] Cf. Cass. Dio, LVIII, 2, 4, 6, 8.

intended from the first.[1] Confident of support from the
Prætorian Guards, he formed a conspiracy, so we are told,
to place himself on the imperial throne, and induced some
senators to join, or to appear to join, his project.[2] We
may fairly imagine that most of that body sat back with
a good deal of interest, now that their scheme to tempt
Sejanus into ruin was succeeding, and waited to see
just how the astute—indubitably astute—emperor would
handle the situation; for in that period of Rome there was
no reason to believe that the legions would tolerate a
Sejanus as their emperor: the Julian prestige was still
too strong. Some no doubt prepared to fish in troubled
waters; probably many more hoped that both protago-
nists would be destroyed. It is not probable that Tiberius
was long in ignorance of what Sejanus was doing: the
conspirator had too many enemies for that. The emperor
is said to have had his suspicions awakened for some time
before the end, though it may well be, as Josephus says,
that Antonia, his friend and sister-in-law, was the first
to send him definite proof.[3] A less resolute mind than
that of the aged emperor—he was well over seventy—
might easily have been appalled by the situation. He had
just ceased to tolerate and had declared open war on the
factions which, centering around the redoubtable Agrippina, had for years kept up a nagging attack upon him.

[1] See Cass. Dio, LVIII, 12. Some said that Asinius Gallus
paid especial court to Sejanus to discredit him with Tiberius.
Cf. Dio, LVIII, 3.

[2] *Cf.* Cass. Dio, LVIII, 4; Josephus, *Ant. J.*, XVIII, 6, 6.

[3] *Ant. J.*, XVIII, 6, 6. Suetonius (*Cal.*, 12) puts the date of
these suspicions at the time of Gaius's marriage, which took place,
according to Tacitus, (*Ann.*, VI, 20) two years after the death
of Sejanus. This might also be inferred from Gaius's age as
Suetonius gives it (*Cal.*, 59). Exact chronology was a weak
point with the ancients.

Sejanus had apparently full control of the only large armed force in Italy, the Prætorian Guard, and had long been the active administrator of the Empire and the right-hand man of Tiberius, and apparently his loyal and devoted friend. The latter had no one on whom he could rely; the young men of his family were dead, or were children, or worthless. The senators were slippery and untrustworthy, or disloyal and secretly hostile; many were still pushing Sejanus on; and the legions were far away.[1] So the old man, lacking the control of force sufficient to enable him to fight openly, adopted with superior skill the expedients which his enemies had always used against him when he was powerful—the traditional expedients of Roman public life. He resorted to artifice and finesse, to deceit and mendacity. He tricked and misled Sejanus until the time came to strike, and then he struck him down.[2]

The episode is worth examining as showing what a powerful weapon mendacity could be when skilfully used. In the first place, so we are told, Tiberius wished to get Sejanus away from Capri, the more easily to conceal from him what was being prepared. Sejanus thought—mistakenly as the issue showed—that his arrangements were perfect for getting word of the least step that the emperor took. So Tiberius, under pretext of doing him great honor, assumed the consulate with Sejanus as colleague, and further deceived him by holding out to him the prospects of marriage with Livilla, the daughter of German-

---

[1] Tiberius is said to have been seriously concerned regarding the conspiracy and to have arranged for taking refuge with the legions if the rebellion began successfully. Suet., *Tib.*, 65; Cass. Dio, LVIII, 4, 13.

[2] *Vix tandem et astu magis ac dolo quam principali auctoritate subvertit*, Suet., *Tib.*, 65; *cf.* Cass. Dio, LVIII, 4.

icus and widow of Drusus, and of a grant of the tribunicial power, which would amount to a definite association in the imperial office. In the meanwhile, he termed him "sharer in my cares" and "my Sejanus," and sent him on to Rome to exercise the consulate, parting from him with most affectionate farewells and assurances that he would soon follow. To Rome Sejanus went and there he was kept by frequent letters from the emperor announcing his impending arrival.[1]

It was necessary that Tiberius gain an accurate knowledge of the real intentions of Sejanus and the true disposition and probable action of the leading Romans, and obviously it would be futile to ask this information directly from men so permeated with the spirit of mendacity. Furthermore, it is actions rather than words that give the true index to a person's real opinions and intentions, and Tiberius was probably sufficiently expert in empiric psychology to know this.[2] So he set about gaining this knowledge in a method most ingenious and most skilfully carried out. He kept continually sending despatches to Rome containing contradictory news: in one he spoke of himself as moribund, in another as in good health and about to start for Rome; in one highly praising Sejanus, in another sharply criticizing him; now extending favors to one friend of the minister, and now abasing another; on one day granting honorary offices to Sejanus and his son, and on another to Gaius.

All this time he himself was obtaining minute information as to what went on in Rome. So while Sejanus was kept always in a fluttering suspense, deferring any irrevocable step from day to day as it seemed possible that to-morrow would bring his hope to safe fruition, the first

[1] *Cf.* Cass. Dio, LVIII, 4-7.
[2] *Cf.* above, p. 39.

of May came. Tiberius vacated the consulship, Sejanus
necessarily doing the same—he afterwards regretted he
had not taken action during his period of office—yet
nothing had been done save to give Tiberius time to find
out how matters stood and what might safely be undertaken.[1] The effect of the emperor's policy was first to
perplex and confuse the senators, and thus gradually to
lead them to extreme circumspection from doubt as to
Sejanus's prospects. Probably the psychological moment
for Sejanus to launch his project had gone while he was
being cajoled into uncertainty and delay—a revolution
cannot be long kept on tiptoe without the enthusiasm
cooling—and people were relieved when a strong hint
came from Tiberius that Gaius was to be the coming
emperor. This lead must have met with the hearty
approval of the faction devoted to Agrippina and her
children, and have ranged them actively against Sejanus
from whom they had nothing to expect, while Tiberius
they knew could not at the most have many years to live.
Many sycophants began to drop away from Sejanus, and
the usual indications that public opinion expected a mis-
hap to a man or a cause were not wanting—omens were
reported; most ominous of all, the strain began to show
in Sejanus's temper.[2]

Matters had not ripened sufficiently in July for a
decisive blow to be struck on the part of the emperor,
and Trio, a friend of Sejanus, had been put in place of
one of the consuls of May. We may suspect that this
was done to keep Sejanus from feeling that things were
going badly for him. But by October everything was
arranged, and Memmius Regulus, whom Tiberius deemed
courageous and trustworthy, succeeded the other consul.
On the night between the 17th and 18th of this month,

[1] See Cass. Dio, LVIII, 6-7.   [2] See Cass. Dio, LVIII, 5-9.

Macro arrived from Capri, ostensibly on some other errand, but really to carry through the plan for the destruction of Sejanus. This he communicated to the consul Regulus, who, as it was no doubt arranged, was to preside over the Senate the coming day, and to Laco, commander of the regular police force—the *vigiles*. At dawn the senators began to assemble, and Sejanus was reassured by the information that Macro bore a letter from the emperor to the Senate directing the grant to the anxious plotter of the coveted prize, the tribunicial power, in effect his association in the Empire.

The session began with Sejanus surrounded by flatterers. When it was seen that he was safely in the chamber awaiting his supposed elevation, Macro turned to the Prætorians who had escorted Sejanus to the meeting, exhibited to them his commission, heretofore concealed, as their commander; declared that he brought with him authority to distribute a largess to them, and directed the delighted guards to return to their camp whither he would come immediately to pay it. The regular police force under Laco was quickly stationed around the Senate in place of the deluded Prætorians. Macro at once entered the Senate, delivered the imperial letter to the consuls, and without waiting followed along after the Guard, to keep them at their camp in good humor, and to prevent their knowing of Sejanus's plight or attempting a rescue or rising. Should such an event develop, Tiberius had ordered him to bring forth the young Drusus, Gaius's brother, then imprisoned in the palace, and use him as a figurehead to oppose the insurrection.[1]

The imperial letter was opened in the Senate and the reading began. It was of great length, doubtless to give Macro time for his arrangements; it rambled on in a

[1] *Cf.* Tac., *Ann.*, VI, 23; Suet., *Tib.*, 65; Cass. Dio, LVIII, 13.

desultory fashion so that Sejanus should not take alarm and rush out to gain the protection of the Prætorians. Gradually, after enough time had elapsed, the letter grew chilly in tone towards Sejanus. Sycophants slipped away from the bench where he sat, and their places were taken, probably at the consul's suggestion, by trustworthy prætors and tribunes to prevent the victim escaping and rallying his forces. Laco entered also to guard against the danger. The letter grew more severe and it ceased to be vague and rambling; two senators, friends of Sejanus, were declared worthy of punishment, and finally the end came with the thunderclap of the traitor's denunciation and the demand that he be cast into prison.

Passions broke loose; Sejanus and his friends were stunned. The consul declared carried without debate a motion for his incarceration, and in charge of Laco he was led away amid curses and blows from senators and the mob, and the sound of his statues tumbling. Later in the day, when it was made certain that Macro was successful in keeping the Prætorians entertained at their camp, the Senate resumed its session, and forthwith condemned Sejanus to death. The sentence was immediately carried out, and his corpse given over to the rabble to abuse.[1]

Then the Senate decreed a statue to Liberty, a festival, and annual games in memory of the event.

To celebrate the ruin of the man whom they had by their extravagant and unprecedented laudations led to destruction, they voted solemnities greater than are offered to the gods. So well did they understand that it was chiefly by these honorific distinctions that he had been bereft of his senses, that they explicitly forbade the further grant of excessive marks of esteem to any one.

[1] See Cass. Dio, LVIII, 10-11; Suet., *Tib.*, 65; Juvenal, X, 56ff.

Yet a little later, they began to flatter Macro and Laco, granting them sums of money and honors. "But these two did not accept the distinctions, for the recent example served to deter them." Tiberius also declined all that they decreed in his behalf, and gave notice anew that no one should propose any such thing.[1] Gaius, whose mind however eccentric it may have been was acute and penetrating, declared at a later time to the Senate: "it was you who killed Sejanus in corrupting him by the conceit with which you puffed him up, wherefore I cannot expect anything good from you."[2]

The foregoing narrative, which is all that our sources contain, may not be history; the character of our authorities forbids us to feel too much confidence in it. But if it is false, then, as has been said before, we have a direct instance of the untrustworthiness of our material, instead of being forced to reach that conclusion by indirect methods; and at least it gives us a good example of what the Romans preferred to strictly scientific history. In a negative critique like the present one, we are certainly at liberty to consider the hypothesis—adverse to our general position—that any particular narrative is substantially true.

On the assumption, then, that the foregoing episode is given with general correctness by the historians who deal with it, we have an excellent concrete example of the nature and effect of mendacious adulation as applied by the statesmen of the times. We see three motives for its use: to turn the adversary's head, to discredit him, and to lull him into a false security. The first two motives are most prominent in the flattery poured out by the Senate, the third in the proceedings taken by the emperor.

[1] *Cf.* Cass. Dio, LVIII, 12.
[2] Cass. Dio, LIX, 16; *cf.* Suet., *Cal.*, 30; Vell. Pat., II, 127-128.

But whether true or not, the narrative has a value in the light it throws upon the moral principles of the Romans belonging to the class from which our historical sources almost exclusively emanate; and in the indication it gives of the extent and amount of deceit and mendacity which were regarded as legitimate expedients for the accomplishment of a desired end. We should, however, remember that this has been and still is the practice of many who profess a much stricter attachment to the obligations of veracity than was the case with the Romans. But the severer moral reprobation which as moralists we might pass upon these others for their hypocrisy must not be permitted to blind us to the fact, important for our purposes as students of historical material, that fraud and falsehood were employed by the Romans without hesitation or apology, and were tolerated without surprise or contempt, indeed, almost without blame. Otherwise, it must be observed, this ethical laxity was characteristic of the writers on whom we are forced to rely.

CHAPTER XV

In the twelfth year of the reign of Tiberius and the sixty-seventh of his life, shortly before the retirement of the emperor to the Island of Capri, ambassadors sent by the province of Further Spain requested from the Roman Senate permission to erect a temple to Tiberius and his mother Livia. Upon this occasion, says Tacitus,[1] the emperor, always resolute in rejecting honors, spoke in opposition to the granting of the permission:

I know, conscript fathers, that some ascribe it to a lack of firmness in me, that when the cities of Asia lately preferred a similar petition I withstood them not. I will therefore now disclose both the motives of my silence at that time, and my determination for the future. Since the deified Augustus had not opposed the founding at Pergamum of a temple to himself and the city of Rome, I, with whom all his deeds and words have the force of law, followed an example already approved, the more readily because the veneration of the Senate was attached to the cult bestowed upon me. But while the admission of it in one instance may be pardoned, to permit my worship as a divinity throughout all the provinces would denote a mind swelled with vanity and pride. And the honor paid to Augustus will fade if it is cheapened by indiscriminate adulation. As for myself, conscript fathers, I call you to witness

[1] *Ann.*, IV, 37-38.

that I am but a mortal and do but discharge the duties of a man, content to fill worthily the highest place; and this I would have remembered by those who come after me. They will render enough, and more than enough, to my memory if they believe me to have been worthy of my ancestors, watchful of your interests, unmoved in perils, and fearless of enmities in defence of the public good. These are the temples I would raise in your hearts, these are the fairest images and such as will endure. For monuments of stone, if the judgment or posterity turns into hate, are despised as no better than sepulchres: Hence it is that I invoke our allies, fellow citizens and the gods themselves: the latter, that they may grant me a tranquil spirit conscious of the rights of gods and men; the former, that when I shall have departed this life, they may honor my deeds and name with their praise and their kindly remembrance.

To these noble words, as if to break their force, the historian adds this comment:

And thereafter he persisted in rejecting, even in private conversations, such worship of himself. Some ascribed this conduct to modesty; many to distrust of self, and others to a degenerate spirit. . . . All other things, they said, come readily to princes; but one object should be pursued without faltering: a favorable memory of themselves. For a contempt of renown indicates a contempt of virtue.

The comment, which Tacitus ascribes to popular report in his usual manner, with seeming approval, does not grow out of the emperor's language. To pass by the innuendo that the declaration shows self-distrust or degeneracy, there is a clear distortion of ideas in the final suggestion that Tiberius showed a contempt for his posthumous reputation and therefore disdained the virtues by which it could be procured. In fact, Tiberius expressly asks for the approval of posterity and for a real approval as distinct from empty honors. And for the present purpose, it is immaterial whether the speech as reported be authentic or not. It appears in the text as the basis of the historian's comments and they must be judged in the light of the speech he gives. If the speech be pure invention, the reader can only marvel at the motives of Tacitus in composing a speech so entirely inconsistent with his general conception of the character of Tiberius.[1]

The speech and its comment raise at once the whole question of the truthfulness of Tacitus's description of Tiberius as a savage tyrant and loathsome monster. So impressive is his method that, as Dr. Dill has well said,[2] the portraits

> burn themselves into the imaginative memory, so that the impression once seized can never be lost. Tiberius, Claudius and Nero, Messalina and Agrippina, in spite of the most mordant criticism, will live forever as they have been portrayed by the fervid imagination of Tacitus.

Until recent times, indeed, the correctness of the judgment so persuasively suggested by Tacitus was accepted almost without question. Far from receiving the tribute of approval he so desired, Tiberius's name has been received with an almost universal chorus of contempt and horror. We find him described in the principal classical biographical dictionary in English[3] as a man without

---

[1] Tacitus claims to have had under his eyes some at least of Tiberius's speeches, as well as the journals of the Senate (*Ann.*, I, 81; II, 74; VI, 47; XV, 74). The speech accredited to Claudius (*Ann.*, XI, 24) is confirmed in substance by C.I.L., XIII, 1608. *Cf.* Furneaux, *Ann.*, II, Appendix I to Bk. XI.

[2] *Roman Society from Nero to M. Aurelius*, p. 25.

[3] Smith's *Dict. of Greek and Rom. Biography and Mythology*, *s.v. Tiberius* (based on Tacitus).

sympathies and affections, "indifferent about pleasing or
giving pain to others," possessing "all the elements of
cruelty; suspicion nourished his implacable temper, and
power gave him the opportunity of gratifying his long
nourished schemes of vengeance" by frightful murders.
He is depicted as a man drunken, obscene, and debauched,
indulging his monstrous and revolting lust "in every way
that a depraved imagination could suggest;" as "the
prince of hypocrites," and the events of his reign are
declared to be little more than the exhibition of his depraved and detestable character.   Such expressions as
these may be taken as fairly representing the general
reputation which Tiberius bears among all but a few.
This minority, however, includes practically every competent modern scholar, since the penetration of Voltaire
and the quick intuition of Napoleon were supported by
the learned labors of Sievers, Freytag, Stahr and others [1]
in the middle of the last century.

It may prove worth while to examine the nature of
some of the evidence furnished by Tacitus, not so much
to establish the untrustworthiness of details in his sketch
of Tiberius—that is generally conceded in varying degree
by scholars—as to illustrate the methods of writing history practised by Rome's foremost historian.   The moral
aspect of the question is quite as interesting as the
historical.   For many who question certain generalizations
still retain profound belief in his honesty of purpose and
love of truth.   So Gaston Boissier, while recognizing in
him serious inaccuracies, yet believes that he was an
honest man who loved the truth and never wilfully
resorted to deception; that he made careful use of numerous sources; that he saw things as they were, and that

[1] For a brief bibliography see Schanz, *Geschichte d. röm. Lit.*,
section 439.

on the whole we may feel assured of his veracity and trustworthiness.[1] The late Professor Pelham cannot assent to any theory of malevolence or dishonesty in Tacitus, and attributes the severity of his judgments to his acceptance of an established tradition whose shadows he merely deepened by skilful touches.[2] In stronger terms, Dr. Rhodes declared in his Presidential Address before the American Historical Association in 1899 that

> we approach Tacitus with respect. We rise from reading his Annals, his History, and his Germany with reverence. We know that we have been in the society of a gentleman who had a high standard of morality and honor. We feel that our guide was a serious student, a solid thinker, and a man of the world; that he expressed his opinions and delivered his judgments with a remarkable freedom from prejudice. He draws us to him with sympathy. . . . The merits we ascribe to Thucydides, diligence, accuracy, love of truth and impartiality, are his. . . . Had he not possessed great strength of mind and character, [he] might have lapsed into gloomy pessimism.[3]

For our present purpose it is hardly necessary to inquire whether his departures from fact were the result of a conscious intention to deceive or of unconscious bias; we are here concerned with the degree of credit to be given to his repeated assertions of accuracy and impartiality. We may determine, in part at least, his possession of these high and indispensable qualities by inquiring whether his judgments do in fact arise from his accepting an established tradition, as Pelham asserts; and furthermore—while we cannot control most of his statements of fact—we may consider whether the facts

[1] *Tacite* (Paris, 1903), pp. 67ff, 83ff, 120, 127, 133, *etc.*

[2] *Essays on Roman History*, pp. 33-37.

[3] *Atlantic Monthly*, Feb. 1900, p. 162.

as he narrates them warrant the conclusions he draws from them. In case we find that they are unsupported by the facts even as he narrates them, we may fairly conclude that the perturbation—whatever may have been its nature —which had sufficient strength to influence his logic would also have tended *a fortiori* to influence his selection of material.

A favorite means, adopted repeatedly by Tacitus to influence the mind of his reader, is to suggest incriminating charges without explicit affirmation or denial.[1] A critical historian would have weighed the evidence. Thus we have the hint that "when Agrippa died" his children, Lucius and Gaius, were murdered by Livia, their stepmother, the mother of Tiberius.[2] As a matter of fact, Agrippa died in the year 12 B.C., Lucius Cæsar, 2 A.D., and Gaius, in 4 A.D. It would seem, if the charge were true, that in waiting fourteen years in the first case and sixteen in the second, Livia strangely neglected her opportunities during all the years the boys lived under her roof, in delaying until one was in Gaul and the other in Armenia.[3] Again, with no attempt to affirm it or deny it, Tacitus alludes to the rumor that Livia poisoned Augustus,[4] with whom she had lived in harmony for more than half a century. In like manner he reports the charge that Augustus went with Fabius Maximus as his sole companion, without Livia's knowledge, to Planasia to effect a reconciliation with Agrippa Postumus and restore him to the succession—a secret journey of over forty miles and a proposal that the historian must have known to be highly improbable.

Hints, innuendoes, and epigrammatic phrases in which strict truth is sacrificed for the sake of pungency are

[1] *Cf. Ann.*, I, 3, 5; II, 43; III, 10.   [2] *Ann.*, I, 3.
[3] *Cf. Ann.*, I, 10; IV, 71.   [4] *Ann.*, I, 5.

constantly employed in the creation of his unforgettable tableaux.[1] So the acquiescence of Tiberius in the wishes of the Senate is characterized as "arrogant moderation;" [2] the military escort which Tiberius provided for the funeral procession of Augustus suggests general servitude; [3] in the balanced rhetorical expositions of the reign of Augustus, the one laudatory and the other condemnatory, the peace of Actium is "a blood-stained peace;" "there had been the disasters of Lollius and Varus abroad; at home the executions of Varrones, Egnatii and Julli." [4] This is an impressive use of plurals for the execution of Varro Murena (22 B.C.) and of Egnatius Rufus (18 B.C.) for conspiracies, both in due course of law, and of the suicide of Jullus Antonius (2 B.C.) to escape condemnation for adultery with Julia. Again, in the guise of common report, Tiberius is represented as spending the time of his exile at Rhodes in brooding over his resentments, indulging in deception and in secret sensuality.[5] The secret thoughts of a character, in fact, form a constant element in the historian's descriptions of him. These prefatory insinuations, inserted with the skill of a trained rhetorician, actually evoke in the reader's mind the image of an astute dissembler, whose path to power had been carefully prepared by a designing mother,[6] and whose secret debauchery was notorious. There is no suggestion of his austere life, of his recognized ability as a military commander and administrator, of his devotion to the state at the sacrifice of his domestic happiness. There is no attempt to portray a man, only a monster.

---

[1] The reader should consult Edmond Courbaud's *Les Procédés d'art de Tacite dans les "Histoires"* (Paris, 1918), a scholarly work which appeared since Mr. Jerome's death.—*Editor.*

[2] *Ann.,* I, 8. [3] *Ibid.* [4] *Ann.,* I, 10.

[5] *Ann.,* I, 4. [6] *Cf. Ann.,* IV, 6-7; I, 3.

The way having thus been prepared, Tacitus proceeds to develop systematically the character of the complete tyrant. Suspicion and cruelty are of course his leading traits, and may be observed in the means he took to revenge himself upon his enemies. He had long hated Asinius Gallus, we are told,[1] because Asinius had married Vipsania, the wife whom Augustus had constrained Tiberius to divorce, and because Asinius had appeared to him to be harboring ambitions beyond his rank as a private citizen. He was next offended by a laudatory speech made by L. Arruntius—the speech is not given, although that of Asinius is—and suspected him because of his wealth, ability, and popularity. Furthermore Augustus had once mentioned him as worthy and willing to take the supreme power, naming also in less favorable terms Manius Lepidus and Asinius Gallus. After noting that some authorities gave the name of Gnæus Piso instead of Arruntius, Tacitus remarks that "all of them, except Lepidus, were soon cut off on various criminal charges trumped up by Tiberius."[2] Quintus Haterius and Mamercus Scaurus also excited his enmity because of remarks made in the Senate, which as they are reported to us seem trivial enough. Towards Scaurus his anger was implacable; Haterius, after a clumsy appeal to the emperor, obtained safety only through the intercession of Livia.

What actually happened to these victims of the wrath of Tiberius? Asinius Gallus had in 11 B.C. married Vipsania, after she had been divorced by Tiberius. Twenty-five years had now elapsed and for many years to come he continued to be one of the leading senators.

[1] *Ann.*, I, 12.

[2] *Ann.*, I, 13; *omnesque praeter Lepidum variis mox criminibus struente Tiberio circumventi sunt.*

He spoke often in the Senate, sometimes with the approval and sometimes with the disapproval of the emperor.[1] Vipsania died in 20 A.D.[2] In 30 A.D., he was ordered arrested by the Senate, on a charge not known, unfortunately the portion of the *Annals* covering this period is lost, but it appears from Cassius Dio [3] that he was then a guest of the emperor at Capri, who forthwith forbade actual arrest, told him to be of good cheer, and ordered him to remain under the nominal custody of the consuls, until the emperor should next visit Rome. Asinius had been consul in 8 B.C., and now after an interval of thirty-eight years, must have been advanced in age. In the year 33 A.D., nineteen years after the accession of Tiberius, Asinius is said to have died of starvation—here we have the narrative of Tacitus again [4] —with the characteristic suggestion that whether the act was voluntary or by compulsion was held uncertain. When he was asked whether he would permit a proper burial, the emperor, says Tacitus, did not blush to grant the request and even expressed his regret that Asinius had died before being brought to trial. So far as we can see, the only connection that Tiberius actually had with the arrest of Asinius was to suspend indefinitely the proceedings without requiring bail or imprisonment. If we bear in mind Roman criminal procedure, it is evident that the career of Asinius Gallus, when considered in detail, gives little support to the picture of Tiberius, presented early in the *Annals* [5] as moved by anger and suspicion of an old enemy.

The second of the victims of the emperor's suspicion, Lucius Arruntius, had been consul in 6 A.D., and remained prominent throughout Tiberius's reign. In 15

---

[1] *Cf. Ann.*, I, 76, 77; II, 32, 33, 35, 36; IV, 20, 30, 71.
[2] *Ann.* III, 19.   [3] LVIII, 3, 23.   [4] *Ann.*, VI, 23.   [5] I, 12.

A.D., Tiberius appointed him a member of a committee to devise a plan for keeping the Tiber within its bounds.[1] This action was preferred by Tiberius to Asinius Gallus's proposal to consult the Sibylline Books on the subject, a practical measure which the historian stigmatizes on a logic that is not apparent as evidence of the emperor's love of mystery in all things human and divine. Arruntius further was governor of Spain (*in absentia*) for ten years;[2] about 30 A.D., some prosecution was instituted against him when he was acquitted and his accusers were punished,[3] and shortly before the death of Tiberius, in 37 A.D., he was accused by Macro. Seeing that Gaius was about to succeed to the empire and that Macro would be in power, Arruntius committed suicide in disgust at the prospect.[4] On Tacitus's own showing, the case of Arruntius does not bear out the generalization made in *Annals* I, 13 (14 A.D.) that he was one of those who were "soon cut off on various charges trumped up by Tiberius."

Neither does the case of Gnæus Piso square with the rhetorical generalization. He was sent to the east by Tiberius in 17 A.D.,[5] to act as a check on Germanicus. When he was accused by Agrippa and the friends of Germanicus, he was treated by Tiberius with conspicuous fairness. When Piso lost courage in the face of charges of inciting the troops to rebellion, a charge for which he seems to have had no defense, he committed suicide (20 A.D.). The story of Piso's conspiracy against Germanicus is told with consummate skill, with constant recourse to unsupported gossip culminating in a tale heard from one

[1] *Ann.*, I, 76.   *Cf.* 79.   Cass. Dio, LVII, 14, is free from Tacitus's religious bias.

[2] *Ann.*, VI, 27; *Hist.*, II, 65.   [3] *Ann.*, VI, 7.

[4] *Ann.*, VI, 47-48.   [5] See *Ann.*, II, 43.

of Tacitus's elders of a secret document, whose contents
had never been disclosed to anyone, implicating Livia or
Tiberius in the death of Germanicus. Tiberius restrained
the Senate from vindictive proceedings against Piso's
family; cleared his son and widow from the charges
against them, and refused to permit the erection of a
statue commemorating the event.[1] In the light of Tacitus's
own narrative, nothing could be more absurd than the
statement that he, like Arruntius, "was soon cut off on
various charges trumped up by Tiberius."

Manius Lepidus, after a distinguished career, died in
33 A.D.[2] Tacitus's enumeration in I, 13 of persons
who were all (*omnes*) soon cut off simmers down to two
persons, Asinius and Arruntius, three if Piso be included,
none of whom died *soon* after 14 A.D., or on charges
preferred by Tiberius. Mamercus Scaurus, another object of the emperor's keen anger at the time of his accession, and Quintus Haterius both died at an advanced age.[3]

A more subtle method of painting Tiberius as a cruel
tyrant, and a far more damaging one, is the historian's
graphic account of the workings of the *lex maiestatis*.
Tiberius is charged [4] with reviving and craftily extending
the "deadly system." Under the Republic, so we are told,
only deeds were punished, and words were disregarded.
Augustus extended the law to apply to libelous writings.[5]
Tiberius, like Augustus, was "exasperated by the publication of anonymous verses exposing his cruelty, haughty

[1] *Cf. Ann.,* II, 43, 57, 69, 74-75, 80; III, 8-19.

[2] See *Ann.,* VI, 27. *Cf.* III, 35; IV, 20.

[3] For Scaurus *cf. Ann.,* III, 23, 31, 66; VI, 29; for Haterius,
II, 33; IV, 61.

[4] *Ann.,* I, 72ff.

[5] Under the Republic the magistrate's *coercitio* was ample to
take care of derogatory remarks. *Cf.* Mommsen, *Droit pénal
romain,* II, pp. 287-288.

temper, and dissensions with his mother." The historian continues:

> it will not be amiss to relate the crimes charged against Falanius and Rubrius, two Roman knights of moderate means, that it may be known from what beginnings and by what subtlety on the part of Tiberius, this deadly mischief crept in, then again was checked, and finally blazed out and consumed everything.[1]

Falanius was charged with having admitted a base actor into a college of priests instituted for the worship of Augustus, and with having sold a statue of Augustus along with a garden. Rubrius was charged with having sworn a false oath by the divinity of Augustus.

> When these charges were made known to Tiberius, he wrote to the consuls that divine honors had not been decreed to his father for the purpose of ruining citizens. The actor Cassius, along with others of his profession, had been accustomed to take part in the games which his mother had instituted in honor of the memory of Augustus. Nor was it sacrilegious to include his statue, like other statues of divinities, in a sale of houses and gardens. The perjury should be judged as if he had sworn falsely in the name of Jupiter: the wrongs done the gods were their own concern.[2]

It is difficult to see how any one whose sense has not been dazzled by syntax could find in this shrewd, practical wisdom a subtle extension of the *lex maiestatis*.

Tacitus next takes up the case of Granius Marcellus who was accused by Cæpio Crispinus, his quæstor in Bithynia, and Romanus Hispo, a base informer, of speaking evil of the emperor, of placing his own statue above those of the Cæsars, and of cutting off the head of Augustus from a statue and substituting that of Tiberius.

[1] *Ann.*, I, 72-73. [2] *Ann.*, I, 73.

"As the things said were true," Tacitus remarks with more irony than evidence, "they were believed also to have been said." Tiberius became enraged and declared that he would pronounce his opinion openly and on oath, which, Tacitus implies, meant forcing a conviction. Perhaps it did, but Tacitus himself adds that the emperor proposed that Marcellus be acquitted on the charge of treason, and then adds "the charge of extortion was referred to the assessors." [1] It will be observed that the count which figures most impressively in the indictment is that of lèse-majesté, on which there is acquittal. Nothing more is said about the matter of the statues, although the substitution, if true, was really a grave offence in that it implied Tiberius's divinization—which he always refused—and dishonor to Augustus, whose memory he guarded jealously. This doubtless was the cause of his wrath. And, most important of all, the charge of extortion is referred to incidentally without any previous intimation that such a charge had been lodged against Marcellus. Where several counts figure in an indictment Tacitus is sure to stress that of *maiestas* as if it were the chief factor in the case. It is the black paint in which he is always ready to dip his brush.

The next case of this sort is introduced two years later with the introductory flourish "meanwhile the *lex maiestatis* was growing to its maturity." [2] But the instance adduced fails lamentably to substantiate the generalization. Appuleia Varilla, a great-niece of Augustus, is accused of slandering the divinized Augustus as well as Tiberius and his mother, and of having committed adultery—a charge of more than usual gravity in one related to the emperor.

[1] *Ann.*, I, 74; *cf.* Suet., *Tib.*, 58.
[2] *Ann.*, II, 50.

As to the charge of treason, Cæsar asked that a distinction should be made and that she should be condemned if she had spoken blasphemously about Augustus, but that he did not wish her to be called to account for invectives against himself.

And after consultation with his mother, he told the Senate on its meeting next day that "no words spoken against her, whatever their tenor, should be considered criminal." He therefore acquitted Appuleia on the charge of *maiestas;* nothing more is said about the charge of slandering Augustus. Instead of punishing her according to the *lex Iulia,* he left the penalty for the adultery to be inflicted by her relatives after the ancient custom—removal two hundred miles from Rome. Manlius, her paramour, was interdicted from Italy and Africa.

The next case occurs four years later (21 A.D.). In the absence of Tiberius the Senate condemned and immediately executed Clutorius Priscus, a poet, who composed and read before a select circle a poem on Drusus while Drusus lay ill, in the hope of gaining a recompense if he died. The charge seems trivial enough—something like the old English law of treason in imagining the death of the prince. When the case came to the emperor's knowledge

he reproved the Senate in his usual two-edged fashion, praising them for their loyalty which led them to punish severely wrongs done to their prince, however slight, deprecating so precipitate a punishment of words; lauding Lepidus and not censuring Agrippa

(who had spoken on the case before the Senate). It was then resolved, in order that the emperor might have opportunity to prevent such miscarriage of justice in the future, that no decree of the Senate should be put into effect until ten days had elapsed.[1] And without a shred of evidence to support the statement, Tacitus concludes the chapter by remarking that Tiberius was never moved to exercise clemency by the interval.

In the prosecution of Gaius Silanus in the year 22 A.D.,[2] there is mention of outraging the divinity of Augustus and despising the majesty of Tiberius, but the case was one of manifest cruelty and extortion by a provincial governor. Why Tacitus should cite this case as one of persecution it is difficult to see: the man was clearly guilty, indeed Tacitus himself says: "there was no doubt of his being guilty of cruelty and extortion." [3] In the next year Lucius Ennius, a Roman knight, was accused of *maiestas* because he had used a statue of the emperor as ordinary silver.[4] But Tiberius forbade the prosecution.

Tacitus begins the fourth book of the *Annals* with the statement that after more than eight years of tranquillity, Tiberius gave himself up to cruelty or gave scope to the cruelty of others.[5] Sejanus now appears upon the scene, but all that Tacitus can find to report for the year is two cases of banishment of officials for oppression in their provinces and two acquittals under charges of treasonable correspondence with Tacfarinas, a public enemy with whom Rome was then at war.[6] The next year (24 A.D.) Cassius Severus, who had been banished to Crete by the Senate under Augustus for libeling prominent men and women, was found to be continuing his practices and

---

[1] *Ann.*, III, 49-51.   [2] *Ann.*, III, 66ff.
[3] *Ann.*, III, 67.   [4] *Ann.*, III, 70.
[5] This refers to the year 23 A.D., but in V, 3 (29 A.D.) he remarks: "from this time began a period of sheer and relentless tyranny."
[6] *Ann.*, IV, 13-15.

was therefore transferred to the less desirable Seriphus.[1] Gaius Cominius, who had been convicted of writing a scurrilous poem against Tiberius,[2] was pardoned by the emperor.

In his preface to the events of the year 25 A.D., Tacitus remarks that in want of the more moving themes of history he can only "record savage commands, incessant accusations, treacherous friendships, the destruction of the innocent, and trials terminating in the same event." [3] In the details, however, of the year we find one suicide, a calumniator and an adulteress exiled, a senator stricken from the rolls for failure to take the prescribed oath, one case of banishment for vilifying the emperor in which the accused "paid the penalty for his treason," and the suicide of a Spaniard accused of assassination.[4] This, in an Empire, is certainly not a record to justify the sentiment quoted above. Indeed, it is not until three years later that there was an execution for *maiestas,* the first in seven years.

The *Annals* for the years 29-31 A.D. are lost. In the year 32 we meet with the next case of prosecution for defamatory speech. Cotta Messalinus, according to Tacitus,[5] was accused on various counts including vituperation of Gaius Cæsar and Tiberius, but the emperor quashed the proceedings and requested in a letter characterized by good sense that garbled words and the freedom of convivial conversation should not be distorted into crimes. The accuser was punished; but the incident

---

[1] *Ann.,* IV, 21.　　　[2] *Ann.,* IV, 31.　　　[3] *Ann.,* IV, 33.
[4] *Ann.,* IV, 34, 36, 42; *cf.* Hieronymus, *ad Euseb., Chron.,* A.D. 29 (Schoene, vol. II, p. 149). The case of Titius Sabinus (IV, 68-70) turned on bribing the emperor's freedmen in an attempt to assassinate him.
[5] *Ann.,* VI, 5-7.

gives Tacitus occasion to burst out into a fine frenzy against the "tyrant" as little justified on moral as on historical grounds.[1] In the same year Sextus Vistilius was charged "whether rightly or wrongly" with calumniating Gaius Cæsar, and was in consequence forbidden the emperor's table, whereupon he committed suicide.[2] Sextus Paconianus, whom Tacitus seems to regard as richly deserving his fate, was condemned in 32 A.D., for complicity in the plot of Sejanus to destroy Gaius, but escaped immediate execution by offering to turn informer. We hear nothing more of him until three years later when he injudiciously called the Senate's attention to the undue delay in his case by composing in prison lampoons against the emperor. He was thereupon executed under the pending sentence.[3]

But one other case can, it appears, be found in Tacitus which falls within the alleged extension and severity of the *lex maiestatis* which he attributes to Tiberius. A joint prosecution for treason of five distinguished nobles aroused apprehension among the senators, but it appears that two of the accused were exculpated and the trial of the other three was indefinitely postponed.[4] There

[1] *Cf. Ann.*, VI, 8-9, for the case of Marcus Terentius who was acquitted of crime although he openly avowed friendship with Sejanus. His accusers were punished. Lentulus Gaetulicus (*Ann.*, VI, 30) was acquitted on charges similar to those of Terentius. Compare V, 6-7.

[2] *Ann.*, VI, 9. [3] *Ann.*, VI, 3, 39.

[4] *Ann.*, VI, 9. In the following chapter Tacitus remarks that even women were not exempt from danger; they could not be charged with designs to usurp the government, hence they were prosecuted for their tears. Vitia, the mother of Fufius Geminus, was put to death because she wept over the death of her son. Tacitus does not mention any case against the son, but it appears from Cassius Dio (LVIII, 4) that he committed suicide two

is every reason to believe that Tacitus meant to give a fairly complete record of all the cases which would illustrate the tyranny of Tiberius.[1] But when it is borne in mind that the period covered by Tacitus's narrative is twenty out of the twenty-three years reign of Tiberius, it is abundantly manifest that the data do not bear out the lurid generalizations.

Indeed when we come to analyze the details of all the criminal proceedings under Tiberius recorded by Tacitus, we find a startling discrepancy between the facts as he narrates them and the generalizations. The gloomy phrases about despotism, glut of blood, ruin of the innocent and the like,[2] upon which the historian dwells with morbid delight, are so impressive that an uncritical reader accepts the picture without question. Leaving out of the count the cases against the Greek provincials (VI, 18), Vitia, already referred to, the exaggerated massacre of prisoners charged with complicity in the plot of Sejanus, Albucilla and her lovers (VI, 47-49), and the mother of Papinius, when Tiberius was in his last illness and not responsible for the conduct of the cases, we find one hundred and five cases mentioned in the course of twenty years. These may be divided into four classes.

I. Of revolutionary attempts, insubordination, slander of the prince and the like there were fifty-eight cases, resulting in twenty-two condemnations (thirteen of them capital), twenty-six acquittals or quashing of proceed-

---

years before as a result of prosecution by Sejanus. The prosecution of Vitia, if it actually took place, is to be charged to the Senate, not to the emperor, who was not in Rome. Chapter 10 narrates also with approval the condemnation to death, on charges not known, of two former friends of the emperor.

[1] Cf. Ann., IV, 32-33, 7; VI, 7, 29, 38, 47.
[2] Cf. Ann., IV, 20, 32-33; V, 3; VI, 7, 19, 29, 38-39, 47.

ings, and ten suicides before trial. In the case of some of the suicides, the emperor declared that he would have pardoned or acquitted had the offender lived. In only a very small number of cases does Tacitus even suggest that the accused were innocent. The average of about one execution in two years seems not very bloody, and but a very small number of cases can be charged to Tiberius at all.

II. Of plunder, extortion, or illegal acts by provincial governors there were nine cases, of which seven were convicted and sentenced to exile, and two committed suicide.

III. Of false accusations there were ten cases, resulting in ten sentences of exile.

IV. Of unspecified and miscellaneous cases, of which adultery was the most frequent, there were twenty-eight cases, resulting in fifteen convictions, three of them capital. Seven committed suicide and six were acquitted. That is to say, in the cases where the tyranny of Tiberius is especially denounced, convictions ensued in about thirty-eight per cent of the cases, whereas in the other cases of the second, third, and fourth classes the percentage of convictions was sixty-eight.[1]

These represent criminal cases of enough importance to reach the Senate and the emperor. The great mass of ordinary criminal business was of course brought before the lower courts. Regarding this we have no information, but it does not appear from Tacitus or other writers to have excited complaint.

Inseparably associated with the working of the *lex maiestatis* was the activity of informers (*delatores*) who, since there was no public prosecutor, served to set in

[1] For instances of sentences mitigated, *etc.*, cf. *Ann.*, III, 24, 28, 52-56; II, 50; III, 50, 69; IV, 6-7; VI, 5, 16-17, *et passim*.

motion the machinery of the *lex maiestatis*.[1]   Their
activity is a favorite theme with Tacitus and he reiter-
ates his charges with an impressive show of moral indignation and historical research.   In 15 A.D., (I, 74)
Cæpio Crispinus, we are told, began the vocation which
became so notorious in the reign of Tiberius.   He crept
into the good graces of the cruel prince and by secret
charges imperilled the lives of the most distinguished
citizens.   Notwithstanding this statement we are told
(II, 27) that in the following year, when the next informer appears, there were first disclosed those acts
which for so many years ate into the state.   In the year
17 A.D., the case of Appuleia Varilla is cited to show
the growth of the system.[2]   And after detailed description of the next cases brought by informers against
Clutorius Priscus in 21 A.D.,[3] Gaius Silanus,[4] and
Lucius Ennius in 22 A.D.,[5] we are informed (IV, 30=
24 A.D.,) that in consequence of Tiberius's refusal to
sanction a proposal that in cases where the accused
committed suicide the rewards of the prosecutors should
be forfeited, "thus rewards enticed forth the *delatores,*
a class of men called forth to the ruin of the state, and
never sufficiently checked by punishment."[6]   In fact,
"an accuser became inviolable the more aggressive he
became."[7]   In 27 A.D., "the power of the accusers
continued daily to grow stronger and more relentless,
without alleviation."[8]   Leading citizens practiced the
basest forms of *delatio,* and neither friends nor relatives

---

[1] *Cf.* Mommsen, *Droit pénal romain,* vol. II, pp. 34ff; 195ff;
Boissier, *L'Opposition sous les Césars,* p. 161ff.

[2] *Ann.,* II, 50: *adolescebat. Cf.* above, p. 331.

[3] *Ann.,* III, 49-51.   [4] *Ann.,* III, 66-69.

[5] *Ann.,* III, 70. *Cf.* p. 333.

[6] *Ann.,* IV, 30.   [7] *Ann.,* IV, 36.   [8] *Ann.,* IV, 66.

were free from the dangers of chance conversation in public or private.[1]

Tacitus must have known that *delatio,* that is the enforcement of the criminal law by the activity of private citizens in bringing complaints, was a long established practice of the Roman state. As early as 210 B.C., we hear of accusers stimulated by rewards of money and in 186 B.C., the practice is again recorded.[2] Appian mentions other cases in 89 and 43 B.C.,[3] and Cicero thinks the institution should be encouraged.[4] Sulla's law on murder, Cœlius's agrarian law and the *senatus consultum* of 11 B.C., provided money rewards for those who instituted proceedings which the state deemed beneficial. Great rewards were paid informers against the proscribed, and the *delatores* of the assassins of Cæsar received parts of the estates of the murderers.[5] Tacitus himself in his *Dialogus de Oratoribus* mentions the practice and remarks upon the glory and the stimulus to eloquence it produced.[6] And in the *Annals* themselves he admits that Tiberius sought to alleviate the system.[7] The emperor, as we have seen, regularly intervened to prevent the extension of the law of *maiestas* to derogatory words and acts.[8]

In this matter, as in that of *maiestas,* Tacitus himself furnishes material for distrusting his generalizations on the malevolent tyranny of Tiberius. His treatment of the

[1] *Ann.,* VI, 7.   [2] *Cf.* Livy, XXVI, 27; XXXIX, 19.
[3] *Cf. B.C.,* I, 54; III, 54.
[4] *Cf. pro S. Rosc.,* 20; *Cat.,* IV, 5; *in Vat.,* 11; Sallust, *Cat.,* 30 and 50.
[5] See Cass. Dio, XLVI, 49; Appian, *B. C.,* IV, 7, 11; Mommsen, *op. cit.,* p. 199ff.
[6] *Dial.,* 40; *cf.* 34.
[7] *Cf.* III, 25, 28; see also II, 50; III, 24, 52-56; II, 33.
[8] See above, p. 330ff.; *Ann.,* III, 36.

informer, Firmius Catus, and of Libo, the accused, certainly does not justify Tacitus's introductory remark, or the suggestions of disingenuous behaviour by Tiberius.[1] In like manner, the actual record of the year 25 A.D., fails to substantiate the lurid generalization.[2] Forty-three *delatores* appear in Tacitus's account of the reign of Tiberius. The fate of twelve of them is not mentioned. Of the remaining thirty-one, ten were condemned for failure to substantiate their accusations, and sixteen fell into the pit they dug for others—five or perhaps seven of them suffering capital punishment. Two or perhaps three committed suicide to avoid condemnation. Only two, or possibly three, seem to have escaped scatheless, and of these one, Veranius, was not a regular *delator* but joined in the prosecution of Piso as a personal friend of Germanicus. The relation of the fate of the accused to that of the informers has been referred to in another connection (p. 270) and need not be repeated here. An examination of the list will show that under the bloody tyranny of Tiberius it was much safer to libel the tyrant or to be accused of high treason than to engage in bringing accusations against the tyrant's enemies; but we should not suspect this from the historian's generalizations.

[1] Compare *Ann.*, II, 27-31.   [2] See above, p. 334.

CHAPTER XVI

TACITUS ON TIBERIUS: THE CHARACTER OF TIBERIUS

It may be interesting to observe, as the next step in the study of Tacitus's conception and writing of history, to what extent he possessed the "unusual mastery of refined psychological observation" with which Teuffel credits him.[1]

In the summary with which he closes his narrative of the reign of Tiberius,[2] Tacitus gives us a brief but striking note on his character.

> His character also varied as did his fortunes. He was admirable in conduct and reputation so long as he was a private citizen or in service under Augustus; he was dark and crafty in affecting virtue so long as Germanicus and Drusus lived; he displayed, while his mother was alive, the same mixture of good and evil; while he loved or feared Sejanus his cruelty was fiendish but his vices masked, and at the last he broke out in wickedness and wantonness alike, when, unchecked by shame and fear, he revealed no character but his own.

In saying that his character and conduct were admirable until he came to the throne, Tacitus seems to have forgotten the widespread rumor which he is at pains to record

[1] *Op. cit.,* II, section 333, 13 (vierte Aufl., Leipzig, 1882).
[2] *Ann.,* VI, 51.

(I, 4) that Tiberius's life at Rhodes was spent in brooding over his resentments, indulging in deception, and in secret sensuality; he seems to have forgotten also that what he here states as rumor he records as fact in *Annals,* IV, 57. "At Rhodes, too, he was in the habit of shunning company, and concealing his sensuality." [1]   In saying that he was dark and crafty in affecting virtue while Germanicus and Drusus lived (*i.e.,* until 23 A.D.,), Tacitus seems to detract from the relatively favorable view taken in IV, 1 and 6, of the first eight years of the emperor's reign.   If the efficient conduct of public business there mentioned, the freedom of debate in the Senate, the emperor's checking of sycophancy, meritorious appointments to office, wise administration of the provinces, and high regard for the due processes of law were all a dark and crafty affectation of virtue, one can only conclude that Tacitus's psychological analysis was neither precise nor penetrating.

Throughout the entire account of Tiberius, this charge of inveterate duplicity occurs again and again.   There can be no doubt that Tacitus conceived him to be a consummate hypocrite.   Clear language, we are told, came with difficulty from his lips and "even in matters which he did not seek to disguise, his words, whether from nature or from habit, were always doubtful and obscure." [2]   He delighted in none of what he regarded as his virtues so much as in dissimulation, and he took it very ill that what he desired to keep secret should be revealed. [3]   To this charge of wilful obscurity of expression and conduct,

[1] For other instances of the same practice see *Ann.,* II, 69, 73, the guilt of Piso for the death of Germanicus; IV, 67, the vicious life at Capri, and VI, 1.

[2] *Ann.,* I, 11.   Contradicted, in part, by IV, 31.

[3] *Ibid.,* IV, 71.

Tacitus frequently returns.[1] From his first mention of
Tiberius to his final characterization this conception colors
everything the emperor does or says. Only after the
death of Sejanus does the dissembler cast off all restraint
of shame and fear; yet even in this period of six years of
comparatively straightforward wickedness, Tacitus cannot
refrain from suggesting dissimulation in some ten or
twelve instances, culminating in a deathbed duplicity in
seeming to die and then revive again.[2]

It is of course a commonplace that all scientific knowledge depends upon some postulate of uniformity; if a man
never says or does what he means and never means what
he says or does, we are obviously in the presence of chaos.
We cannot pretend to the clairvoyance of Tacitus in purporting to penetrate into the secret thoughts of a man long
dead; but we can compare his general allegations of inveterate duplicity of language with what he gives us as
quotations of the words of Tiberius. Mere assertion that
every time Tiberius pardoned an accused man or quashed
a proceeding he was really intending to extend the law
under which the proceedings were being held and to increase its severity, cannot be admitted as evidence by
modern historical research.

In this connection there is suggested the preliminary
question of the authenticity of the speeches, remarks, and
letters which appear in the *Annals* purporting to emanate
from Tiberius. Tacitus claims to have had under his
eyes some at least of the emperor's speeches [3] as well as
the journals of the Senate [4] and the *acta diurna*.[5] We
have seen above [6] that in reporting the speech of Claudius

---

[1] *Cf. Ann.*, I, 33, 46, 73; III, 16, 44, 64; IV, 31; V, 1;
VI, 50, 51.
[2] *Cf. Ann.*, VI, 50.   [3] *Ann.*, I, 81; II, 63.
[4] *Ann.*, V. 4; XV, 74.   [5] *Ann.*, III, 3.   [6] *Cf.* p. 321 n. 1.

he made very considerable alterations from the authentic text, but that these alterations do not materially affect the substance of the speech: they rather confirm it. Tacitus begins with the general statement, frequently repeated, that Tiberius's language, written and spoken, possesses certain characteristics which betray the character of its author. The examples of speeches, observations, and letters are numerous and are frequently accompanied by a repetition in some form of his original declaration. These alleged quotations were either copied by Tacitus from sources more or less authentic or they were invented by him. If he copied these statements and made alterations or omissions in them, what possible motive could he have had in omitting or changing the one special element which he repeatedly asserts they possessed and which is a very important element of his general picture of the tyrant? If he invented them, how could he have failed to stress in them the one particular characteristic which would serve to justify their introduction into the narrative at all?

We cannot be absolutely sure that the expressions credited to Tiberius are authentic transcripts of his actual words, either in part or whole. In all probability few of them are exact quotations. But that is not the point at issue. The point is that the historian presents us with the generalizations and also with the data upon which he bases them. In judging of the correctness of his generalizations we are entitled to take the data precisely as he gives them, regardless of their complete authenticity. We have the right to examine the data to learn whether they substantiate the character assigned to them by the historian, and to judge whether he has passed from data to generalization by legitimate induction. If we find that he has done correctly this inductive work, the further ques-

tion as to the accuracy of the data may properly arise.
But if it appears that incompetence, bias, or some other
cause has rendered him incapable of making sound inductions, then we are justified in distrusting not only the
generalization in question but others as well. If a writer
cannot or, for any reason, does not correctly state the
substance of the very material which he sets before his
readers—and that is what a generalization amounts to—
it is surely a fair conclusion that the same intellectual or
moral weakness which becomes apparent in this comparatively simple part of his work, extends to the more difficult matters of selecting, assembling, judging, and interpreting his material.

Coming then to the passages which purport to be quotations of the emperor's words, what do we find? They
begin with the narrative of the proceedings in the Senate
on the inauguration of the new reign,[1] in which Tiberius
is said to have dissembled his real intentions. It must
be remembered that the position occupied by Augustus
was a special and extraordinary one and not at all a regular magistracy. In fact, for many years the principate
legally came to an end with the death of each prince and
was recreated by a new *lex de imperio*. All this had no
doubt come to be largely a matter of form by the time
of Tacitus, when there had been eleven cases of the trans-
mission of imperial power; but on the first occasion in
14 A.D., the whole matter was new and it would have
been remarkable if there had not been a slight uncertainty
and momentary hesitation as to the proper course to adopt.
This hesitation would be natural in a man who was to become the new monarch, but who neither then nor later,
so Tacitus admits, showed any manifestation of a grasp-
ing disposition, whose self-respect would not permit him

[1] *Ann.*, I, 11-13.

to stand forth as demanding power, and who showed long afterwards by his words and acts that deference to the Senate which was to be expected from one of his conservative disposition.[1] A brief discussion soon made it apparent to the Senate and Tiberius that there was but one course to adopt and it was adopted definitely and distinctly.[2]

The same attempt to force an interpretation of simple facts appears in the last event of Tiberius's reign. The strength of the aged ruler was failing, says Tacitus,[3] but not yet his dissimulation. He exhibited the same vigor of mind, the same energy in his looks and discourse; he sometimes essayed, by affecting affability, to hide his decaying strength, although it was too manifest to be concealed. The physician endeavored to feel his pulse surreptitiously, whereupon the emperor remained at table longer than usual as if to do honor to a friend and guest who was departing. In one sense it was no doubt dissimulation for a proud old man, who had lived most actively his seventy-eight years in full vigor of body, to resist surrender and to meet the last great enemy standing as became an emperor; but it is a dissimulation that may well be deemed a virtue. No better evidence can be adduced of the utter and unreasoning unfairness on the part of the historian than his sneer at this as an act of cunning subterfuge and crafty mendacity. Indeed, with the exception of a very few instances, not half a dozen in all, where the emperor acted as any one might naturally act in keeping his opinions or intentions to himself, we shall not find in the seventy or more quotations any indications of ob-

[1] See *Ann.*, IV, 6, 15; III, 60.
[2] *Cf.* P. Fabia, *L'Avènement officiel de Tibère*, in *Rev. de Philol.*, vol. XXXIII (1909), pp. 28-58.
[3] *Ann.*, VI, 50.

scurity, concealment, trickiness, or disinclination to let his auditors know his purpose, nor any of that difficulty on their part in understanding him which Tacitus continually asserts. As to the charges that he never meant what he said nor what his actions implied, an unprejudiced reader will fail to discover any basis save the historian's direct intuitions which certainly appear to be at variance with the facts given in detail and with which, it would seem, they should be in harmony.

An analysis of the contents of the first six books of the *Annals* seems to disclose that they are composed of clearly separable elements. In the first place there is a great mass of statements of fact, which so far as regards visible manifestations of conduct are favorable to Tiberius as a man and ruler; but to this class of facts are in most cases attached sneers, hints, innuendoes, or assertions that the act should not be taken in its apparent and obvious significance, but that it meant sómething quite different. In the second place we find a small number of statements of actions by Tiberius quite inconsistent with the general mass, and highly reprehensible. The third category consists of broad and sweeping assertions regarding Tiberius's conduct and character which are not legitimate inductions from the facts of the first class, and which in some cases are not based on any facts at all appearing in the narrative, or are contradicted thereby. Either they arise out of facts not set forth, or else, as seems more probable, they are in the nature of deductions from some undisclosed premises—the same apparently as give rise to the sneers, hints, and innuendoes; or else the writing defies any logical analysis whatever.

The attitude taken by scholars in the presence of these disharmonies has varied. Until recent years it was the general custom to extend the doctrine of verbal inspiration to Tacitus, and to swallow all contradictions on the *credo quia impossibile* principle. Lecky refers to a certain type of mind which confronted by a manifest contradiction declares it a mystery and an occasion of faith. Now this mental attitude of sturdy credulity, while not extinct, has declined together with a belief in other miracles. Another and much less mediæval position regarding Tacitus is that taken by some eminent scholars, among whom the late Professor Pelham may be cited as giving a clear statement of it. This theory is that Tacitus merely followed an established tradition regarding Tiberius, perhaps somewhat heightening the colors of it. Says Pelham :[1]

There is, however, a prior question which has hardly received its due share of attention, at any rate in this country [England]. We may grant that Tiberius, for instance, was not so black as he is painted; but it is important to try to understand why he was painted so black. In other words, why did Tacitus—for it is he who has given the tradition its currency and authority— paint the rule of the Cæsars from 14 to 69 A.D. in such unfavourable colours? The theory that he was himself malevolently disposed towards these Cæsars has deservedly fallen out of favour.

And again :

Tacitus was, in truth, above all things an artist, aiming at painting, from the materials before him, a picture of the period with which he is concerned and of the chief actors in it. He found ready to his hand an established tradition of the characters and doings of the last four Cæsars of the Julio-Claudian line. This tradition, in the main, he accepts, and he sets himself to reproduce it as effectively as possible, throwing in skilful touches and deepening the shadows, so as to give the desired impression. He was not malevolent or dishonest,

[1] *Essays*, pp. 33-37.

but he exerted the whole force of his genius to give to his own generation and to posterity a presentation of this old régime, with its extravagant luxury, wild excesses, and terrible catastrophes, which has held the attention of men ever since. . . . For the comparatively sober, bourgeois society in which Tacitus lived, the *ancien régime* that perished with Nero had a weird fascination. . . . .

It is necessary, therefore, to go behind Tacitus to the tradition which he followed. It was a tradition bitterly hostile to the Cæsars; it emanated almost exclusively from writers who belonged to the senatorial order; and it reveals something like a standing feud between the Cæsars and the nobility of Rome.

After examining the explanation of the feud, the same writer continues:

but it had a more far-reaching effect. It gave to the contemporary literature its tone of bitter hostility, and so provided the materials for that portrait of Tiberius which, thanks to the genius of Tacitus, has fascinated posterity.

But with all possible respect for the supporters of this theory, we are compelled to say that the hypothesis of an established tradition as the source of a great part at least of Tacitus's sketch of Tiberius is absolutely unsupported by any legitimate foundation.

Have we any evidence, then, of an established tradition? Little of value for our purpose can be found in the several writers who were probably contemporary—Phædrus, Strabo, Valerius Maximus, Manilius, Ovid, Celsus, Columella, and the elder Seneca. Valerius Maximus refers with abhorrence to Sejanus's treachery to Tiberius,[1] praises the emperor and speaks warmly of his fraternal affection.[2] Strabo's references are highly

---

[1] IX, 11, 4.   [2] *Cf.* V, 5, 3; VIII, 13, 1 and *præf.*

commendatory in two passages written about 19 A.D.[1]
The freedman Phædrus, who survived to the time of
Claudius, seems, like ambitious people of low station in
all ages, to have had occasion to resent the actions of his
superiors.[2] He intimates that by obscurity one escapes
the perils that are incident to great men.[3] He seems to
have had some special grievance against Sejanus, and two
fables are probably applicable to him.[4] In his direct
references, the poet seems to admit that he merited punishment and to complain only of the way Sejanus applied
it.[5] He refers plainly to the fate that regularly overtook
those who mendaciously accused others or profited by
their misfortunes.[6] The only fable referring directly to
Tiberius comments not unfavorably on his perspicacity
in seeing through those who sought to deceive him.[7] All
that one can affirm, therefore, is that there is nothing in
the fables to suggest the "established tradition."

Manilius [8] and Ovid, who were alive in the early years
of Tiberius's reign, as well as Columella, Celsus, and the
elder Seneca contain nothing bearing on our inquiry.
The only other contemporary writer is Velleius Paterculus, whose history extends to 30 A.D., and who of
all writers extant was in the best position to know
Tiberius. His picture of Tiberius is so utterly at variance
with that of Tacitus and the literary tradition after him,
that his testimony has generally been rejected as flattery
of an emperor who, all agree, detested flattery. From
the fact that Paterculus speaks well of Sejanus and that
we know nothing of him after the year 30 A.D.,—in-

---

[1] *Cf.* VI, 4, 2; XIII, 4, 8.
[2] See III, *prol.* I, 1; I, 8; I, 30-31; II, 6.
[3] See II, 7; IV, 6, 12; *cf.* I, 15; V, 1.   [4] I, 2 and 6.
[5] Compare III, *prol.*   [6] *Cf.* I, 17; V, 4; *cf.* I, 10.
[7] *Cf.* II, 5.   [8] *Cf.* IV, 761ff.

deed he is mentioned by no ancient writer until Priscian
—it has been assumed that he perished in the slaughter
of the friends of Sejanus. It is needless to say that this
writer furnishes no material tending in any way to assist
in the establishment of such a tradition as Tacitus is
said to have utilized for his *Annals*.

The books written after Tiberius's death, say Tacitus,[1]
were written under the influence of recent detestation. In
writings published after Tiberius's death we might, therefore, expect to find the tradition in process of establishment. There are extant the works of four men—Philo,
Seneca, Pliny, and Josephus—three of whom were living
during the reign of Tiberius, while the fourth was born
in the year of the emperor's death. They represent entirely different environments and points of view; they
all wrote after his death, and we have as a guaranty of
their independence the freedom with which other emperors
are mentioned. All were in positions to be well informed
about Tiberius. In their writings Tiberius might possibly
be described under the influence of detestation but at
any rate without fear.

Philo, the Alexandrian Jew, was a philosopher and
publicist who was nearly sixty years old at Tiberius's
death and was in Rome and about Naples some two
or three years thereafter on an embassy to Gaius. Later
he wrote an account of the embassy [2] in which he denounced Gaius as a debauched madman, a drunken and
monstrous beast. Consequently we can see no reason
why he should have hesitated to give his opinion about
Tiberius. He refers frequently to Tiberius—his information must have come from some one who had lived
under the emperor—describing the excellence of his
government and the general felicity under him, the fair-

[1] *Cf. Ann.*, I, 1.   [2] *Legatio ad Caium.*

ness and impartiality of his reign, his justice and benevolence to the provinces; declaring that he bestowed the blessings of peaceful rule up to the end of his life with a rich and bounteous hand upon the whole Empire, that no one lived who was more sagacious, nor who reached a more prosperous old age. He was from his youth, Philo says,[1] of a solemn and serious disposition, caring nothing for amusements. Life at his court where Gaius lived (*i.e.*, Capri) was very simple and free from intemperance and luxury.[2] Even as a boy Tiberius was called old, as a token of respect, because of his remarkable wisdom: "He was exceedingly wise, good, and great."

Seneca, the moralist and censorious Stoic, who was about forty years old at the death of Tiberius, writes savagely of Gaius and Claudius, declaring the former to be a disgrace to the Empire and a shame to the human race.[3] To Claudius he devotes an entire book of vituperation.[4] But in referring to Tiberius he mentions the emperor's self-restraint, frugal life, and disapproval of debauchees and spendthrifts.[5] There was among the people, he says, a regular epidemic of criminal accusations on trivial charges. He seems, in this connection, to attach no special blame to the emperor.[6] Seneca seems to confine this craze to the later part of the reign when Tiberius had withdrawn to Capri, where it was less easy for him to intervene in every absurd case. The responsibility he attributes to Sejanus whom he regards not so much

[1] *Leg. ad Caium*, 26.

[2] *Ibid.*, 2, 6, 21, 26, 38; cf. *Flacc.*, 3, 12.

[3] Cf. *de Const.*, 18; *de Ira*, I, 20; II, 33; III, 18-19; *de Brev.*, 18; *ad Helv.*, 10; *ad Polyb.*, 17; *de Ben.*, II, 12, 21; IV, 31.

[4] *Apokolokyntosis*.

[5] Cf. *ad Polyb.*, 15; *Epist.*, CXXII; *de Ben.*, II, 7-8; *Epist.*, XCV (42).

[6] Cf. *Epist.*, LV; *ad Marc.*, I, 22; *de Ben.*, II, 26.

imposed upon Rome by Tiberius, as imposing himself upon
Rome and Tiberius. That he does not regard the emperor
as having indulged in some at least of the tyrannical acts
on which later writers lay so much stress, is plainly
indicated in his writings. For instance, Libo, he says,[1]
fully deserved his fate, and the divergence between
Seneca's views and the later opinions appears clearly from
his letter of friendship to Marcia on the death of her son.
She was a daughter of Cremutius Cordus whose suicide
years before is described by Tacitus as due to Tiberius's
harshness.[2] Seneca's account[3] differs from that of
Tacitus. Had Seneca believed Tiberius blameworthy regarding the death of Cordus, or thought that Marcia
believed it, it is hardly probable that he would have made
two laudatory references to him in this very letter to her
—once as an affectionate son consoling his mother for
the loss of Drusus, and again as displaying true Roman
fortitude at the loss of his own son. This would surely
have been an unthinkable lack of tact, even of common
sense.[4] It is clear that we cannot find the "established
tradition" in Seneca.

Pliny the elder, a rigid moralist of a less philosophic
but perhaps more practical sort than Seneca, was about
fourteen years old at the death of Tiberius. He was a
man of wealth, prominence, industry, and benevolence,
becoming a trusted adviser of Vespasian and Titus.
Tacitus twice (*Ann.*, I, 69; *Hist.*, III, 28) refers to him

[1] *Epist.*, LXX; Tacitus, *Ann.*, II, 27ff.
[2] *Cf. Ann.*, IV, 35.   [3] *Ad Marc.*, I, 22.
[4] In *de Ben.*, IV, 31, he draws a distinction between the normal lives of Gaius's predecessors, as compared with the bloodthirsty career of that mad monarch, who tried to change a free
state (*i.e.*, Rome under Tiberius) into an Oriental despotism.
On Tiberius further *cf. Epist.*, CVIII; *de Ben.*, V, 25; *Epist.*,
LXXXIII.

as an authority. The *Natural History* contains many severe comments on the imperial family. All the descendants of Agrippa, he says, proved curses to the earth: the two Agrippinas especially were firebrands among mankind. Evidently it was not from Pliny that Tacitus got his tenderness for the elder Agrippina and her family.[1] In his twenty-five or more references to Tiberius there is nothing to support Tacitus's picture. He speaks of his simple life;[2] in the time of Sejanus there was much mourning, but the only prosecutions mentioned are those against tavern-keepers for improperly assuming the rings which marked the equestrian order,[3] and a probably mistaken reference to Mela, accused of maladministration as provincial governor.[4] It must have grieved Augustus, so Pliny surmised, to have had no sons and to see the Empire pass to the son of a man who had fought against him in the civil wars; again, Tiberius's retirement to Rhodes was disrespectful to Augustus.[5] In his youth he was somewhat too much inclined to wine, but in his later years was austere and even severe. He was one of the saddest of men—*tristissimum hominem*—and little given to affability.[6] The most serious charge which Pliny makes against Tiberius is that people thought Piso was selected as *præfectus urbis*[7] because of his drinking.[8]

Josephus was born the year of Tiberius's death, and came to Rome in his later life as the friend of Vespasian, where he continued to live and write for many years. Like the other writers, he has no hesitation in speaking

---

[1] *Cf.* VII, 45f; XXII, 92f; XXX, 14f.
[2] *Cf.* XIX, 137; XIX, 64.   [3] *Ibid.,* VII, 129; XXXIII, 32.
[4] *Cf.* XIX, 110; Tac., *Ann.,* XVI, 17.   [5] *Cf.* VII, 149f.
[6] XXVIII, 23; XXXV, 28.   [7] *Cf. Ibid.,* XIV, 145.
[8] Seneca (*Epist.,* LXXXIII) says he proved an excellent official. Tacitus, too, (*Ann.,* VI, 10) praised him highly.

freely about preceding emperors, especially Gaius and Nero, although he warns his readers against the falsehoods current about them.[1] Josephus is distinctly critical as to Tiberius, possibly resenting his expulsion of the Jews from Rome in consequence of frauds perpetrated by a few of them. This bias, if it is a bias, makes his criticism the more valuable. He complains of Tiberius's habit of procrastination in making appointments to office, leaving provincial governors in their positions for many years. He gives the emperor's explanation, however, that a governor was less likely to abuse his office if he understood that his tenure depended on his conduct.[2] Tacitus assures us that he chose good men, kept them long in their places, and saw to it that the provinces were not oppressed.[3] According to Josephus, the emperor was dilatory in trying and punishing criminals, because of his desire to augment their punishment. This charge is contrary to the evidence afforded by Tacitus. During the supposed orgy at Capri, of which Josephus gives no hint, there existed a warm friendship and mutual esteem between the emperor and his high-minded sister-in-law Antonia, and he was much influenced by her advice.[4] He strongly disapproved of the Jew Agrippa and excluded him from his presence, because of evasion of just debts. Later, when Agrippa openly expressed his desire for the emperor's death, he was put into prison.[5] The Romans rejoiced, we are told, when Tiberius died, since he had brought many miseries on the aristocratic families and was stern and implacable in his punishments.[6] Tiberius was, as

---

[1] Cf. *Ant. J.,* XIX, 2, 1 and 5; 1, 1-2; 3, 1; XX, 8, 2-3.
[2] Cf. *Ibid.,* XVIII, 6, 5.   [3] Cf. *Ann.,* I, 80; IV, 6.
[4] Cf. *Ant. J.,* XVIII, 6, 6.
[5] Cf. *Ibid.,* XVIII, 6, 4-7; *B. J.,* II, 9, 5.
[6] Cf. *Ant. J.,* XVIII, 6, 10.

we have seen, implacable to those of high station who interfered with military discipline, robbed the provincials, made false charges of crime, and committed adultery. The only instance of Tiberius's severity that Josephus gives us is the entertaining anecdote of the enterprising young Roman lover who had wooed in vain a rich, beautiful, and modest, but simple-minded, Roman matron. She was devoted to Egyptian worship; and a bargain was made between the Roman lover and the priests of Isis whereby he dressed as the god Anubis and manifested his divine condescension to the flattered worshipper. But a few days later the lover himself informed the matron of his deception, whereupon she told her husband who complained to Tiberius. The emperor instituted an examination, banished the lover, had the temple torn down, the statue of Isis thrown into the Tiber, and the priests crucified.[1] The story may or may not be true but it is significant that Josephus makes no suggestion that there was any incongruity between the emperor's severity and his own moral character.

Among the writers who wrote after Tiberius's death, Plutarch, Quintilian, and Juvenal can be dismissed briefly. Plutarch wrote a life of the emperor, unfortunately lost. The moral and miscellaneous essays, in which the evil ways of Tiberius might have been fittingly introduced as illustrative material, give no intimation that Plutarch conceived of the emperor as Tacitus did. There are in all six references, four of which do not bear upon our inquiry. A favorable inference is suggested by a passage [2] which mentions the learned group of men who formed the emperor's companions. And it does not appear that Plutarch, with his fondness for moralizing, knew the foul charges of Tacitus when he wrote:

[1] *Cf. Ant. J.,* XVIII, 3, 4.   [2] *Cf. de Def. Orac.,* 17.

Tiberius Cæsar passed the last seven years of his life on Capri; and the sacred governing spirit that so long swayed the whole world, and was inclosed, as it were, in his breast alone, never changed its residence. The burdens indeed of the Empire which poured upon him and invaded him from every side, prevented the tranquillity of his island home from being perfect and undisturbed.[1]

Quintilian [2] mentions Tiberius only as a constant attendant at the lectures of Theodorus at Rhodes. Martial launches no obscene epigram against him; and Persius does not thunder against him as a type of vice. In Statius [3] he is contrasted favorably with Gaius. Even Juvenal, avid of scandal and master of a biting phrase, finds no tarter phrase for the emperor at Capri than *secura senectus* [4] and attributes to him on "the narrow rock" no worse companions than Chaldæan soothsayers.

For eighty years after Tiberius's death, then, we find writers making statements which give no indication of an "established tradition." It is conceivable of course that there may have been writings in existence that represented the emperor in altogether unfavorable colors; it is commonly assumed that the *Memoirs of Agrippina* were of this character.[5] But it cannot be safely said that these established a tradition, for there is nothing in the extant authors—and they are the principal ones of the time—to substantiate the hypothesis. Indeed it would appear from Tacitus himself that his sources were rebellious to his general theories, since how else can we explain the preponderance in his work of statements of public actions by Tiberius contrary in character to the historian's

[1] *De Exilio*, 9.   [2] *Inst.*, III, 1, 17.
[3] *Silv.*, III, 3, 66.   [4] *Sat.*, X, 75, 93.
[5] Tacitus refers to them, *Ann.*, IV, 53.

generalizations, statements whose force and effect he is continually weakening by innuendo.

An explanation on which more reliance can be placed, and in which there are doubtless some elements of truth, is that the picture of Tiberius has been distorted by personal, social, and political bias—either the bias of earlier writers taken over and dressed up by Tacitus, or the bias of the historian himself, or a combination of the two. But the theory of the bias of earlier writers as the source of Tacitus's characterization, is subject to the same weakness as the "established tradition" theory of which indeed it is a part. It is not, in many important particulars, borne out by any extant material. Passages can be found in Seneca, Pliny, and Josephus indicating that he was not a sympathetic character and that he was severe in the matter of punishments, but a good deal more than that is needed for the purposes of this theory.

It may also be seriously doubted whether Tacitus was influenced by feelings of strong hatred against Tiberius. Hate is a powerful mental stimulant: it takes possession of the mind, dominates it, directs it. It creates an abundance of justificatory beliefs and evidential facts, and suppresses those facts which make against it. It produces in the mind a creative, transforming, and selective activity, which can be felt in all parts of its products. It diverts the mind from all mental presentations which are inharmonious with itself. Were Tacitus dominated by a real hate of sufficient intensity, for instance, to cause him to invent the Capri scandal, it would have had a greater unifying power on his mind; it would have made him more consistent, more watchful for a non sequitur, more keen to drop out facts which made against him, or to garble them into relevancy and consistency. It would not have been possible for us, in view of his literary skill, had he been possessed by this passion, to see through the haze of his comments, innuendoes, and unsupported generalizations, and to discern behind that thin veil the lineaments of the real Tiberius. Clodius, for instance, does not appear thus in the writings of Cicero, nor Claudius in the *Apokolokyntosis*. Moreover, Tacitus attributes some of the worst tyranny to the Senate and exculpates Tiberius. How then, if we reject the trustworthiness of Tacitus's picture of Tiberius, are we to explain it?

CHAPTER XVII

TACITUS ON TIBERIUS: THE MENTAL ATTITUDE OF TACITUS

To understand how a characterization like that of Tacitus came into existence we must bear in mind the fact, so often inadequately realized, that there were certain respects in which ancient customs, ideals, characters, and ethical doctrines and practices differed from ours, and that these differences had a profound influence on their historiography. The subject would involve, if adequately treated, a consideration of the entire intellectual development of ancient times. It must suffice to call attention to the implications of certain conceptions of the nature of historical writing, discussed in previous pages, and to certain aspects of Roman life which bear upon the question.

In the first place, Roman education from the time of the later Republic was devoted almost exclusively to the study of rhetoric. To use beautiful language effectively, regardless of the nature, value, or truth of the ideas conveyed by it, became a passion which dominated men throughout their lives. As Quintilian says, the literary work of a man bears the impress of his school education.[1] The object of this training was frankly avowed to be

[1] *Cf. Inst.*, IX, 2, 81; II, 17, 26f., 39; V, 12, 22; Cic., *de Off.*, II, 14; Sen., *Epist.*, XL, XLV, XLVIII, XLIX, LII, LXXXII; Petronius, 1-4; Tac., *Dial.*, 26, 29, 31-35.

the production, not of truth, but of the imitation of truth
—of verisimilitude. The result, naturally, was seriously
to impair the feeling for veracity and sincerity. As
Merivale justly says:

> the pernicious effects of this solemn trifling seem to
> have perverted the moral sense of the Romans more
> speedily than even their literary style.

There was, it is true, some criticism of this rhetorical
education, but rather because it failed to produce really
great eloquence than because it destroyed the feeling
for truth.

Another point we must remember is that the Romans
were a very free-spoken and highly censorious people
who, from an early period, indulged habitually in scurrility, vituperation, and invective with a freedom calculated
to bring a blush to the cheek of the traditional Billings-
gate fishwife. What is especially difficult for moderns
to understand is that this kind of talk was a mere inveterate habit, "which the rhetorical education of the day
encouraged and which no one took very seriously."
Cicero clearly explains that to call a man an adulterer, a
pervert, was mere outcry and abuse, intended to provoke
the adversary by insult, and that it was regarded, if well
done, as "facetious" and "urbane." It was not in the
least a real assertion of the truth of the matters alleged.[1]
Indeed shocking scurrility, or what we should regard as
such, was often indulged in affectionately, as by soldiers
to a beloved general, possibly with an idea of averting
the malevolent Nemesis.

In some quite different fields of thought there is to be
found the same habit of using words in other than their
plain natural sense. Thus the Stoics argued that every-

[1] *Cf.* Cic., *pro Cael.*, 3, 13.

one who did not attain to the height of the *sapiens* was a *stultus,* and that the *stultus,* not being entirely good, was entirely bad—Stoicism not admitting moral *nuances*—and consequently possessed every vice *in posse* if not *in esse.* Being a potential debauchee, coward, and traitor, he might be so stigmatized.[1] The same method of justifying the ascription of every vice to those who held erroneous speculative opinions passed on to Christianity, and the Fathers agreed that pagans or heretics might properly be charged with every sin and crime, because idolatry implied them all.

The lack of any grasp of scientific principles was another characteristic of the Romans which must be kept in view. While there are some adumbrations towards it in some ancient philosophers, the ancients in general had no clear idea of the uniformity of natural phenomena. Fortune, fate, chance or the gods intervene in human affairs.[2] Partly at least from this uncertainty in their general *weltanschauung,* it resulted that they really had no science in our sense of the word, certainly no science of history. Their knowledge was often vague and inexact, although the opportunity for observation and verification lay within easy reach.[3] Without any clear idea of the nature of causation, they relied in reasoning mainly on sophistries and fallacies, on happy phrases and verbal juggling. Most striking is their apparent blindness to contradictions, either in themselves or in others. The juxtaposition of mutually exclusive propositions did not seem to shock them or even to attract their attention, and they rarely

[1] *Cf.* Sen., *de Ben.,* IV, 26-27; Quintilian, XII, 1, 23.

[2] *Cf.* Tac., *Ann.,* VI, 22; also III, 18; IV, 20; *Hist.,* I, 22.

[3] Bury (*Ancient Greek Historians,* p. 227) calls attention to Livy's neglect of inscriptions and his failure to visit Lake Trasimene.

seem even to be aware of incongruities between statements about facts and the facts themselves.

In view of all this, we are not surprised that their notions on veracity were very loose. Perfectly shameless mendacity characterized Cicero, as we have seen.[1] Quintilian, in his *Institutes of Oratory,* finds frequent occasion to treat of lying as a fine art.[2] Eusebius has a chapter in his *Præparatio Evangelica* on the "Use of Falsehood for the Benefit of Those Who Need It;" and most of the Fathers regarded it as a valuable medicine in their ethical pharmacopœia.[3] The leading Romans for centuries used religion in political warfare as a scheme with which to trick the people, and the pagan gods were represented as frequently practicing mendacity. What is less generally known is that some of the Christian Fathers did not hesitate to attribute mendacity to God and to Jesus,[4] while curiously enough certain Christian legends always represent the devil as trustworthy and veracious. Such facts are highly significant in view of the fact that men's moral ideas may be seen in the character they ascribe to their gods.

It is evident that persons whose education was mainly devoted to rhetoric and who remained all their lives vastly enamored of fine phrasing, who furthermore were frankly mendacious, even regarding a good reputation for honesty

[1] *Cf. ad Fam.,* II, 16; *de Orat.,* II, 59; *de Off.,* II, 14; *Brut.,* 11, and above, p. 56ff.

[2] *Cf.* II, 17, 26-39; IV, 2, 89-94; 123-24; XII, 1, 1-14, 34-45; *ibid.,* 7, 7.

[3] *Cf.* Jerome, *Epist.,* XLVIII, 13; LII; John Chrysostom, *de Sacerd.,* I, 6-8; Clem. Alex. *Strom.,* VII, 9.

[4] *Cf.* Ambrose, *de Fide,* V. 16-18; Jerome, *Epist.,* XLVIII, 13; Hilary, *de Trin.,* IX, 62-75; Gregory I, *Moral.,* XXXIII, 7, 9; *cf.* Harnack, *Hist. of Dogma* (Eng. trans.), vol. III, p. 307; V, p. 264.

a valuable asset on occasions when one wishes to deceive,[1] will approach the writing of history with somewhat different ideas from those which we regard as suitable. So indeed we find it. Historiography was generally regarded as a branch of rhetoric; and that mendacious inventions might properly be used therein seems to have been conceded. Cicero calls them *mendaciuncula* and cites Panætius, the gravest of Stoic philosophers, to justify his liberality of view.[2] Some, like Livy, Diodorus, and Plutarch, held history to have for its aim the enforcing of moral truths. Quintilian, after defining the aim of poetry as that of giving pleasure, to which the invention of pleasing falsehoods contributes, declares that history borders on poetry and indeed may be said to be poetry unfettered by meter.[3] And Ælius Aristides puts history somewhere between oratory and poetry.[4] In this conception of history as a branch of rhetoric, the Romans were simply following the later Greek tradition which, as Bury points out,[5] was so profoundly influenced by Isocrates.

So well was all this understood that none of the ancient historians, although they often asserted their own veracity, seem to have had much confidence in the historical writing of others. Thucydides, whose critical standards approach most nearly the modern, begins his work by pointing out the weakness of his predecessors. Similarly Polybius speaks of the inextricable maze of falsehood into which his predecessors had fallen; Sallust is sceptical

[1] *Cf.* Quintilian, XII, 1, 12.

[2] See *de Orat.,* II, 59; *de Off.,* II, 14; *Brut.,* 11; *ad Fam.,* V, 12; Sallust, *Cat.,* 14, 22.

[3] See the passage of Hegesias quoted by Bury (*Ancient Greek Historians*), p. 171.

[4] *Cf.* Quintilian, X, 1, 28-31 (*ad narrandum non ad probandum*). Ael. Arist., *Panath. disc.,* II, 513.

[5] *Op. cit.,* p. 161ff.

about many of the stories about Catiline; Josephus asserts that the histories of Nero and of those before him are full of falsehoods; Tacitus declares that after the battle of Actium true history ceased to be written, and comments most severely on the worthless character of what passes for the history of the early Empire—a judgment in which Cassius Dio fully concurs, adding that much that has been written is false and almost every incident has been distorted. Vopiscus defends a contemporary against a charge of inaccuracy by claiming that Tacitus and all the great historians have made misstatements; whereat the critic graciously yields and admits that one may with an easy conscience indulge in mendacity in company with these masters of historical composition. Lucian, the belated rationalist, deplores the inability of writers to distinguish between history and oratory, or even between history and poetry.[1] As Cotter Morrison well says:

> The old masters of history resembled . . . the old masters of painting. Both thought little of what we call "local colour," of close conformity to the scene or object delineated, provided they produced striking compositions with grand outline and rich tints which were attractive and beautiful for their own sake.[2]

When we take into consideration the foregoing elements of Roman life—the exclusively rhetorical education and the craze for it which pervaded Roman society, the generally loose ideas as to veracity and the blindness to contradictions, the lax views as to the duties and obligations of the historian, the hypothesis suggests itself that the *Annals* of Tacitus, who was a skilled orator devoted to

[1] See Josephus, *Ant. J.*, XX, 8, 3, 11; Tacitus, *Ann.*, I, 1; *Hist.*, I, 1; Cass. Dio, LIII, 19; LIV, 8, 11; Vopiscus, *Vit. Prob.*, 1; *Vit. Aur.*, 2; Lucian, *Scrip. Hist.*, 7, etc.
[2] Art., *History* in *Enc. Brit.*, 9th ed.

rhetoric from his youth, may be an example of historical writing done according to the method of the rhetorician, and that this is the true explanation of those disharmonies between fact and generalization which we have noted. Now it would contribute very greatly to establish this hypothesis if an examination of the settled rules of rhetorical composition and of Tacitus's narrative showed indications that he followed the rules carefully in detail.

By the time of Tacitus the labors of many generations of rhetoricians had reduced that art to a body of definite rules, a sort of applied psychology. Fortunately we have an elaborate treatise on this matter by Quintilian, the leading Roman educator during the years of Tacitus's youth, whose precepts and doctrines may be taken to represent the rules of rhetoric as they existed when Tacitus was acquiring his mastery of them. Whether or not Tacitus was actually a pupil of Quintilian cannot be ascertained, nor does it greatly matter.

1. The Color. Historical narration, being treated as if it were the narrative part of an oration, should, like the oration, be treated as a work of art and possess the unity which belongs by the general principles of æsthetics to an artistic creation. Its facts should be in relation to its general idea; a general "color" must infuse it and unify it, making it organic and hence artistic. This general "color" or conception of the characters should pervade the whole treatment and tint each act set forth. It is not sufficient, says Quintilian, to adopt a certain color in our statement of facts unless it preserves a consistency throughout the whole case; especially since the only mode of establishing certain points lies in vehemence and persistence in asserting them.[1] To allow the under-

[1] Cf. IV, 2, 94ff; Sen., Controv., I, 3, 9; II, 7, 4f; Boissier, Tacite, pp. 211-212.

lying ideas to be controlled and modified by the natural
color of each fact would not be art. In adopting a
general color for a person, what one does is to select
some ideal typical character, *e.g.,* the miser, the lover,
the hero, the coward, and then bring the person chosen
into harmony with the "type." It is much easier mentally
to deduce a person's qualities from a selected type than
to observe and discriminate its actual manifestations in
acts, and thence induce the general picture. And this
method is still in high favor with many men. We may
recognize modern types upon which much character-
drawing is built in the "plutocrat," the "honest farmer,"
the "rum-seller," and others. We find in ancient writers
frequent recognition of the fact that episodes are invented to fit the characters ascribed to individuals, as
Tacitus intimates was done in the case of Tiberius and
Sejanus.[1]

A type that had long been in high favor with rhetoricians was that of the "Tyrant"—the ruler whose power
was, from the standpoint of the aristocracy, illegal *ab
initio* because it deprived them of their special privileges.
The Romans took this over from the Greeks along with
the rest of their rhetoric, and with the Roman love of
invective and the aristocratic detestation of Tyrants—
for the emperors were technically tyrants in that they
deprived the nobles of their right of plundering the world
—the denunciation of tyrants flourished mightily. The
schools rang with declamations against them and tyrannicide was evidently in high favor with Quintilian.[2] *Ex
hypothesi,* there was no good tyrant;

[1] *Cf. Ann.,* IV, 11; above, p. 365, n. 1.
[2] *Cf.* XII, 1, 40; Juvenal, VII, 151; Tac., *Dial.,* 35; Reure,
de Script. ac Litt. Hom. cum Rom. Imp. Inimicitiis, pp. 23-24.
See also Plato, *Rep.,* 565ff; *Gorgias,* 468, 525.

he is a ruffian who usurps power in order that he may gratify his lusts at the expense of all justice and mercy. Feeling himself the enemy of mankind, he is perpetually in a panic of suspicion, and surrounds himself with mercenaries who carry out his behests. He plunders, confiscates, and violates the sanctity of the family and the virtue of the young.[1]

The elements composing the character of the "Tyrant" were long definitely established as cruelty, injustice, suspiciousness, craftiness, and sensuality, from which followed naturally anguish of soul. These characteristics were as well-established conventions as with us are the depravity of the Politician, and the greed of the Capitalist. Writing perhaps while the memory of the terrible years of Domitian colored his view of earlier emperors, Tacitus proceeded to apply to Tiberius the characteristics of the Tyrant denounced in the schools of rhetoric. From the major premise that all tyrants are cruel, unjust, crafty, sensual, and the minor premise that Tiberius was a tyrant, it followed that Tiberius was cruel, unjust *etc.*

2. Argumentation. To argument, in our sense of the word, rhetoric paid little attention. The method of rhetorical narration was not to argue but boldly to assert and to persist in asserting—*asseveratio et perseverantia.* History is written to tell a tale, not to prove it—*ad narrandum non ad probandum.*[2] We may note that a modern psychologist asserts that this is a sound method of persuasion.[3]

3. Appeals to passion. In place of argument great stress was laid on appeals to the feelings or passions of

---

[1] J. P. Mahaffy, *Problems of Greek History* (London, 1892), p. 81.
[2] Quint., IV, 2, 94f., 103, 108; V, 13, 15, 22; X, 1, 31.
[3] *Cf.* Le Bon, *Op. et Croy.*, p. 194.

those whom one wished to persuade. This is the greatest glory of the art, says Cicero, and Quintilian urges his pupils frequently to keep their narratives sufficiently embellished to stir the feelings of the auditors, for the chief power of the rhetorician lies in exaggeration and disparagement.[1] For this purpose one should have "purple patches" ready at hand to interject into the narrative, so as to enliven it, catch the attention, stimulate the emotions, and gain the sympathy of those whom one addresses. These prepared passages had various names depending on their length and character, and much was written about them which need not detain us.[2]

These bits of embellishment, say our guides, should artfully be made to appear artless, and here as elsewhere all bias and prepossession must be carefully concealed. To this end it may be valuable to feign an air of doubt, and it is here that a good reputation for gravity and uprightness is valuable.[3] We may note the frequency with which Tacitus protests his veracity and impartiality, and gives an appearance of scrupulous fairness by expressions of scepticism regarding some more than usually improbable story of which we have no trace elsewhere. At times he seems almost to be defending Tiberius.[4]

4. Personal attacks. When you wish to attack a person who stands well, says Cicero, it is safer at first

[1] Cf. Quint., II, 17, 26-29; IV, 2, passim; IV, 5, 5-6; VIII, 3, 89; IX, 3, 27; Cic., de Orat., III, 25-27; II, 53. Cf. de Rhet. Inv., I, 16.

[2] Cf. Quint., II, 4, 21f., VIII, 5, passim; Cic., de Rhet. Inv., II, 16; Sen., Controv., I, 1, 3, 7; II, præf. I; VII, 5; IX, 5. For examples see Ann., III, 33, 65; VI, 6, 19, 22, 39-40, 50.

[3] Quint., IV, 2, 57, 117; IX, 2, 19, 65f.; X, 3, 18; XII, 1, 11-13; Cic., de Rhet. Inv., I, 17; II, 16.

[4] Cf. Ann., I, 1, 76; IV, 11.

to conceal your intentions and subtly undermine him. After having propitiated the minds of your auditors it may be well to deny that you are going to attack, so as not openly to seem to do so, but yet go on doing it cautiously and gradually alienate their favorable disposition toward the person charged, and in some way bring him into unpopularity, hatred, or contempt. Irrelevant things may be brought in if they will arouse prejudice, and you may refer to his relatives or the circumstances of his past life. Touch lightly the points favorable to him, lay stress on the unfavorable. If it cannot be shown that he has committed any wrong or even been suspected of it, it is well to suggest that he formerly concealed his wickedness, or that he had no opportunity to manifest his evil disposition, or had some reason to refrain from evil acts.[1] This passage from the great model of Roman oratory and rhetoric might be taken to be a summary of the introduction of Tiberius to the reader of the *Annals*. Tacitus first professes his detachment and impartiality, concealing the savage arraignment which is to come. With what brilliant but misleading generalizations this is done we have seen in a preceding chapter. In preparing the scene for the entrance of Tiberius, nothing very important is said, nothing very precise is asserted, but by rhetorical innuendo, used in the manner recommended by Cicero, the reader is prejudiced against Tiberius as a brutal tyrant.

5. Dealing with hostile facts. This disingenuousness in undermining a person's character was not limited to introductory matter. The rules of rhetoric about handling facts which are incongruous with the writer's prepossession are most instructive. It should be borne in mind that

[1] *Cf.* Cic., *de Rhet. Inv.*, I, 16-17, 21, 24-25; II, 8-17. *Cf. ad Heren.*, I, 7.

these rules had been built up in relation to forensic oratory where there was an opponent present, but historiography being regarded as akin to rhetoric, was subject to the same rules. In forensic debate to pass over a known fact when it is hostile to your general contention, would amount in effect to admitting it, while to deny its existence or grossly to misstate it may be highly dangerous. Hence the student is cautioned against injudicious suppression of facts.[1] The proper procedure is to admit these troublesome elements into the narrative, but in some way to destroy their effect.[2] Of course some things are better treated by general language boldly and confidently used, sometimes with an affectation of contempt; and students are warned against too meticulous attempts to wipe out every adverse fact.[6] Where this kind of treatment will not do, there are other methods of meeting the situation. As we have seen above, Cicero suggests manipulating the emphasis, arousing prejudice by irrelevancies, and suggesting that the person in question may have reason to conceal his misdeeds. This method of denaturalizing facts was used by the great orator himself in explaining his relations with Catiline and Dolabella.[4] It is the keynote of Tacitus's attempt to explain his own incongruities and disharmonies. From the first day of Tiberius's reign, when he appeared to be modest and deferential to the senators so as to penetrate, says the historian, into their designs and warp their words and looks into crimes, though we are told of no cases of the sort; in his acquittals of the accused, against whom, it is said, he secretly raged; in his quashing of proceedings, lest his wicked

[1] *Cf.* Quint., IV, 2, 66-67, 76-78.
[2] *Ibid.*, V, 13, 7f., 37.
[3] *Ibid.*, V, 13, 22, 36-37, 51.
[4] *Cf. pro. Cael.*, 4-6; *Phil.*, XI, 1-4.

character be discovered; up to the last chapter where his reasons for never saying what he meant and rarely doing what his heart desired, are said to be his fear or consideration for his stepfather, for his son, his nephew, his mother, or Sejanus, we find Cicero's precepts amply applied. Consistency in this psychological analysis is far to seek. Sometimes, we are told, the emperor hesitated only when the matter concerned the Senate, or when he was not acting as an advocate; again, he feigned; again, his mind was naturally irresolute and perplexed; again, he was actuated by subtle policy, and finally, he liked to deceive.[1]

Other ways of lessening the effect of troublesome facts are laid down. Much can be done by cleverly handling the facts narrated, changing the order, and juggling the words. A judicious use of vituperation, pathos, wit, or ridicule may carry us over thin ice; and an epigram may often serve as the vehicle of invective. A very safe thing is to dwell on the atrocity of the act. An accuser will always insist that every bad act was the result of deliberate wickedness and cruelty, while the good acts were done for some selfish object. In the field of motives, the rhetorician has full swing. A great deal can be effected by a careful choice of words to give color and character to an act; we may call a somewhat disingenuous man a thief, or a woman who has committed an impropriety a harlot. Illustrations of this practice have already been noted in the *Annals*.[2]

6. Hints and innuendoes. Indeed great reliance of the

---

[1] Compare *Ann.*, I, 7, 46-47, 74, 80; II, 65-66; IV, 30, 71; VI, 51.

[2] See Cic., *de Rhet. Inv.*, I, 16, 21; II, 16, 36; *de Orat.*, II, 53, 59; Quint., IV, 2, 52, 76-77, 80, 83; VI, 3, *passim*; VIII, 1f.; IX, 2, 93.

rhetorician seems to have been placed on hints to awaken suspicion and to discredit that part of the evidence which makes against the rhetorician. Besides the methods suggested above, there is one highly commended by Quintilian and effectively practiced by Cicero—that of describing vividly the enemy's personal appearance, how he was inflamed with wickedness and fury, how his eyes glared, how cruelty showed itself over his whole countenance. In making these word pictures, says Quintilian, it is permitted to invent details; and he further tells us that while in earlier times these purple bits were generally put forth distinctly as imaginative, in his day they were treated as actual occurrences. With more boldness still one may give to his discourse wonderful effectiveness, says Quintilian, by displaying the thoughts of an adversary as he might declare them himself.[1] Here we find the rules laid down which so strikingly characterize the treatment of Tiberius in the *Annals*. As we have seen, the great mass of the bare facts narrated, stripped of disguises, either contradicts or fails to support Tacitus's theory. But to nearly every fact is attached a gloss, comment, or interpretation suggesting that the act, however fair it seemed, was in reality base or contemptible. All this is done with sufficient art to prevent the ordinary reader from giving the natural interpretation of the facts. These additions are not parts of the events narrated; they are either mere assertions, innuendoes, or descriptions of facial expressions—even when the emperor was in Capri—or private conversations which could hardly have been known; or inner motives, thoughts, desires and intentions which Tacitus or whoever invented them could have discovered only by direct

[1] *Cf.* IX, 2, 29f., 40, 44; VIII, 3, 70; IV, 2, 123-124; III, 8, 49f.; Cic., *in Verr.*, V, 62; *cf. pro. Milo.*, 32.

intuition.[1] They are in fact undoubtedly deductions from the historian's preëstablished "color" or general theory used according to the rules of rhetoric to break the force of the great mass of material so rebellious to the picture he set out to draw. But being set forth in biting phrases, they have been ordinarily taken to be facts out of which the generalizations were obtained by induction; and the real facts, more soberly stated, have passed out of the dazzled minds of most readers.

7. Invention of episodes. But the foregoing expedients were not the only ones suggested by the rhetoricians and practiced by Tacitus. We sometimes need—and it is quite permissible—to insert pure inventions, so says Quintilian. These must be carefully fabricated so as to seem probable, and if possible be connected with something which is true. They should not contradict one another, or what is acknowledged to be true; nor should they be liable to easy disproof. It is well to have them so far as possible free from effective contradiction, as, for instance, by basing them on one's own knowledge, or on that of a dead man. Cicero says that the truth of the matter is of no importance, provided an air of verisimilitude is obtained, and they can be done with boldness so as to catch the attention. That these were common enough in historical writings we have seen in the foregoing

---

[1] Mere assertions: *Ann.*, I, 75; III, 3, 8; *cf.* I, 6, 53; III, 16, 44; VI, 23, 25, 26. Sneers: I, 74, 80; II, 38, 52, 84; III, 12; IV, 8, 9, 38. Facial expressions: I, 74; II, 29; III, 15, 16, 44; IV, 34; VI, 9. Statements elsewhere contradicted: I, 72, 74 (*cf.* II, 27); II, 50; III, 44 (*cf.* IV, 6-7); IV, 29 (*cf.* 30); VI, 30 (*cf.* 8), 38. Private conversations: I, 6, 69; III, 15; IV, 3, 7, 17, 39; VI, 21, 26, 46. Inner thoughts, *etc.*: I, 4, 7, 11, 14, 52; II, 52; III, 64; IV, 1, 31; V, 2; VI, 13, 40, 46, *etc.* The secret thoughts of Livia, Sejanus, Haterius, Nerva, *etc.*: III, 3; IV, 3, 12; VI, 26, *etc.*

pages; and there are few cases of a writer who, like Seneca, is ready to confess that his imagination sometimes triumphed over his veracity.[1]

Tacitus certainly would make no such confession; yet we may feel reasonably sure that he did not refrain from availing himself of invented episodes. Real events have antecedents and consequences: they are interconnected by innumerable bonds of cause and effect. An assumed event is betrayed by the inevitable patch work. Real events do not happen suddenly and then vanish utterly, leaving no impression on the minds of contemporaries.

The tale of the eleven years' orgy on Capri may be classed as an episode of this sort. Passing by the fact that there is no hint of it in any writer prior to Tacitus —and indeed most of them use language which would have been impossible had such an event occurred—we find enough to condemn it in Tacitus himself. It has no relation to anything told of Tiberius's past life, save the statement of what he secretly meditated at Rhodes thirty years before. Tacitus tells us that Tiberius hated vices, *vitia oderat,* that men of loose life dreaded correction by a prince who lived with old-time severity, and that he was severe in punishing all forms of debauchery. His friends and associates were men of gravity, and in the suite who accompanied him to Capri there is no mention of other than learned and decent men.[2] No scandal is charged against him by Tacitus, or by any one else, in all his life up to his retirement to Capri at the age of sixty-seven. It would seem that in locating this purple

[1] *Cf.* Quint., IV, 2, 19, 88-94, 101, 123-124; Cic., *de Orat.,* II, 59; *de Rhet. Inv.,* I, 16, 21, 29; II, 16; Sen., *de Ben.,* I, 10; *de Tranq.,* 15; *Epist.,* XCVII.

[2] *Ann.,* I, 80; II, 50, 85; III, 52; IV, 14, 20, 42, 58; V, 3; VI, 26, 27.

story at Capri where Tiberius was living in strict retirement, and where consequently the known details of his life must have been few, Tacitus is following the precept quoted above—to make your inventions such as are least likely to be contradicted easily. The practice is followed in other cases.[1] The hypothesis of some terrible senile insanity cannot be accepted in view of the fact that such a pscyhosis would unquestionably have caused, or have been accompanied by, a physical and mental collapse in a very much shorter time than eleven years. Yet Tacitus describes him at the end of his life as still energetic in looks and speech, strong in intellect, and but a few days before his death, at the age of seventy-eight, exhibiting clearness of mind and strength of will.[2] The general charge that he abandoned public affairs and spent his time in debauchery is wholly inconsistent with the repeated references to his active oversight of governmental matters.[3] Although Tacitus gives so many details with names and places in matters of trivial importance, he leaves vague and indefinite the general accusation of the brutal seizures of high-born children. Yet any one of these acts, if true, would have furnished more harrowing details harmonious to Tacitus's purpose than any other matter he narrates.[4]

It is probable that most of the material that went to form the Capri tale was derived from the long discredited and forgotten scandals circulated in Rome by Julia and her lovers during the retirement of Tiberius at Rhodes (6 B.C. to 2 A.D.) in their endeavor to discredit him and perhaps compass his destruction. The statements of

---

[1] *Cf. Ann.*, III, 16, 44.   [2] *Cf. Ann.*, VI, 50 and 46.
[3] *Cf. Ann.*, IV, 67, 70, 71, 75; V, VI, *passim*.
[4] *Cf. Ann.*, VI, 1. In VI, 7, he asserts he will spare no horrors.

Suetonius (*Tib.*, 41) regarding the military and political events during the Capri years are flatly untrue of the period from 26-37 A.D., but are substantially correct if referred to the Rhodian retirement; and the poem quoted (59) is clearly applicable only to the earlier period.

An examination of the first few chapters of the sixth book of the *Annals* will show how "rhetorical" history can be written. The failure of the facts narrated to substantiate the glittering generalizations has been sufficiently indicated in a preceding chapter. By skilful application of the rules of rhetoric, the author produces a powerful picture of a bloody tyranny. The picture fades away when analyzed critically, but it did its work to the confusion of historical knowledge, and in popular opinion it has probably damned Tiberius beyond rescue.

It would be obviously absurd in seeking to reconstruct the mode of composition used by an ancient writer for one to pretend to any exactness of details, or to think it possible to dispense altogether with some guarded use of the imagination in establishing probabilities; but in a general way the methods by which Tacitus produced his sketch of Tiberius may be inferred from inherent indications, and briefly outlined as follows. In making these surmises we should adopt as a general canon for determining the probable order in which certain ideas were taken up by Tacitus, the principle that this order of adoption is indicated by the relative completeness of the fusion of the idea with all the facts narrated.

His "color" was not fully developed when he began. Probably he started with the conception of Tiberius as cruel; the Romans were getting soft, and serving less and less in the army; were less familiar with the old severity of Roman discipline; but much of Tiberius's life had been passed in that school. His rigorous punishment of adultery, false accusations, and oppression by the public officials seemed harsh to many noble culprits.[1] Furthermore, the cool-headed, far-sighted, self-controlled person, especially if disillusioned and somewhat dour, always seems to the impulsive and emotional to be cruel. Tiberius was unsympathetic and perhaps scornful to the decadent nobles and the pleasure-seeking crowd; hence he was deemed proud. He was probably the ablest man of his times, but the circumstances of his earlier life had developed much reserve in him; hence he seemed crafty, appallingly so to the weak minds of most of his contemporaries; and as he could see through their shallow schemes and silly flattery, he seemed suspicious.

From these attributes of pride, cruelty, craftiness, and suspicion, all characterizations of the Tyrant, Tacitus seems to have made certain generalizations, such as severity in administration of the criminal law, extension of the *crimen maiestatis,* encouragement of delation and the like. He then probably drew from his sources a generally correct transcript for his narrative, slightly garbling it and adding innuendoes to endeavor to make it harmonize more completely with his "color." Such established facts as were rebellious to the picture could be accounted for by charging the emperor with duplicity and dissimulation.

At this point we may perhaps assume that he went over his work and added the embellishments *secundum artem*—protestations of veracity, spirited assertions of imperial despotism, punishment of careless words, remorseless pursuit of personal enemies, rage against critics, and the like, accompanying them with the suitable allegations of a face distorted by evil passions, or a mind filled with wicked thoughts. Some inventions were added

[1] *E.g., Ann.,* II, 50; IV, 31.

where the narrative seemed to flag, and facts were phrased
to harmonize with the preconceived theory. But still
certain passages from the first stage seem to have been
too pleasing to his rhetorical taste to be sacrificed to the
exigencies of a scientific demand for consistency.[1] The
ancient mind was not, as we have observed, very intolerant of contradictions.

His artistic enthusiasm may be supposed to have grown
with the progress of his work, to have made him more
venturesome and audacious. At any rate it appears
probable that certain additions were made at an even later
stage of the work; they are so incongruous and so detached
from, and unsupported by, the other parts. We may not
unreasonably suppose that he felt the need of following
the rules of art and of keeping his readers' emotions stimulated. The characteristics of the typical Tyrant had not
yet been exhausted by him, and seem to have suggested
to him certain piquant developments of his color. We
may infer his artistic enthusiasm from the lurid character
of some of these additions. A strong excitement was
needed to push him to the point of attributing horrible
injustice, disgusting sensuality, and blatant anguish to
Tiberius, the law-respecting old Roman of austere life and
dignified self-control. Hence we have Tiberius's attitude
toward Cremutius Cordus,[2] the slaughter of Vitia for her
tears, the Capri orgy and the tyrant's groan of despair.
The book was then published, fortunately for the cause of
historical truth, without that final revision which was necessary to bring all its parts into harmony with the various
changes and insertions that had been made since the work

---

[1] E.g., ibid., IV, 6-7; V, 1; III, 52-55, 69. Some of the
harmonizing attempts are conspicuously feeble, e.g., I, 75, 76;
IV, 38.

[2] Cf. Sen. ad Marc., I, 3-5, 15, 22.

was first begun. The last chapter, at least in part, was added, or rewritten, and there was apparently a revision of the introductory part of the first book; but many most patent incongruities were left untouched in the body of the work. Perhaps this was due to haste; or perhaps Tacitus had become so suffused with his "color" that everything seemed to him harmoniously tinted—the failure of the critical faculty in artists in relation to their own work.

In some such way as this a great literary creation was made, which, however unreal as a piece of history,[1] has impressed itself on the imagination of the world with a strength that modern criticism has done little to weaken; and so the artistic heritage of mankind, together with its Hamlet and King Lear, its Don Quixote and Mephistopheles, contains the imposing figure of Tacitus's Tiberius.

[1] It is important to remember that Tacitus, like Livy (*praef.* 10), looks upon history as a department of ethics; he is more a moralist than a historian, and a rhetorician more than either. *Cf. Ann.,* III, 65: "It is my purpose to set forth in detail only such motions of the Senate as were of remarkable honesty or of noteworthy disgrace; for I deem it the chief function of history to rescue merit from oblivion, and to inspire base words and deeds with the fear of the reprobation of posterity." See also *Agric.,* 1. Dr. Johnson was not far wrong in saying: "Tacitus, Sir, seems to me rather to have made notes for an historical work, than to have written a history."

CHAPTER XVIII

THE HISTORICAL TRADITION ABOUT GAIUS, 37-41 A.D.

THE history of the last three emperors of the Julio-Claudian family is one of the most startling passages in the long rôle of human annals, and has at all times commanded the horrified interest of mankind. Before it, and for a long time after it, we are a world of men who, whatever conclusions we may reach as to their morals, were at least sane. But when we read the narratives of these thirty lurid years we seem to be looking into a madhouse where men writhe under the lash of the maniac Gaius, the imbecile Claudius, or the paranoiac Nero.

There is nothing inherently improbable in the notion that all three were insane, and starting from their careers as reported to us, psychiatrists have coined the terms "Cæsaritis" and "la folie des Césars." It is, however, unsafe to accept the biographical data as trustworthy clinical observation.[1] In the case of Gaius our authorities are particularly unsatisfactory. While no attempt to rehabilitate the character of Gaius can ever hope to succeed, it may not be amiss to point out some defects in the received accounts of his life. Two of the principal

[1] The carelessness of earlier psychiatrists is pointed out by Dr. Naegeli-Akerblom, *Quelques résultats de l'examen des preuves historiques employées par les auteurs traitant de l'hérédité* (Geneva, 1905).

writers on whom we most rely were Jews—Philo, who was in and around Gaius's court for some months as ambassador endeavoring to dissuade the emperor from his project of associating the imperial cult with the Jewish religion, and Josephus, who came to Rome as a friend of Vespasian and Titus about thirty years after Gaius's death.

The nature of the "worship of the Cæsars" has been discussed in another place.[1] It was almost purely political in character, and was encouraged as a concrete expression of the subject's gratitude, reverence, and loyal submission. The usefulness of this idea as a means of strengthening the dominions of Rome had strongly appealed to Augustus, and, as applied to the deified Julius and Augustus, was approved by Tiberius, although the latter, save in one instance, refused to permit any direct cult to himself. These earlier rulers had sufficiently understood the intolerant monotheism of the Jews to refrain from any attempt to urge upon them a practice which they, unlike the other peoples of the Empire, could not perform without violation of religious scruples.[2] Gaius, however, was encouraged by the Jew-baiting Alexandrians to think that the attitude of the Jews indicated disloyalty, or at least disrespect, and finally, exasperated by their opposition, planned to erect his statue in the great temple at Jerusalem. After the emperor had yielded to the urgent appeal of the Jews, and countermanded the offensive order, he attached a provision that people outside Jerusalem should not be prevented from worshipping such gods, even deified Cæsars, as they wished. But religious toleration was highly offensive to the chosen people, and they proceeded to persecute those who differed from them, whereupon Gaius is said to have reverted

[1] Compare above, p. 208.   [2] *Cf.* Philo, *Leg. ad Caium,* 37ff.

to his intention of erecting his statue in the temple. Death, however, overtook him before his intention was fulfilled.[1]

It is needless to say that this proposition, on whatever provocation it might be based, struck every pious Jew as an unutterable outrage. Neither party in the least understood the situation as it appeared to the other, and Gaius in arrogating to himself divine worship seemed to the Jews to be a blasphemer, preposterous, and insane. From that time forth, they hated him with a bitter hate, and viewed him with unspeakable horror. In Philo this was a profound and vital passion, and while the destruction of Jerusalem had given Josephus more moving grief, yet he looked back on Gaius as an impious enemy of his countrymen and their worship.[2]

These writers are perhaps the most trustworthy of our authorities in that their bias is open and avowed. Both have left us accounts of the controversy between the Jewish people and the emperor, and it is from them that we learn of his attempt to impose the imperial cult on Judæa. Yet the two accounts of this public matter with which both appear to have been thoroughly familiar, contradict each other in many important details. Philo is no doubt the better source as he was an eye witness and participant in many of the episodes of the controversy, although his detestation of Gaius was probably more intense than that of his later fellow countryman. But if we take Philo's narrative as our basis we can see departures from facts in Josephus on a matter for which, but for the preservation of Philo's book, he would be regarded as a fairly good authority.

According to Josephus, the embassy headed by Philo

[1] See Philo, *op. cit.*, 30, 42.
[2] *Cf.* Philo, *op. cit.*, 11ff; 16, 17, 20, 25, 44-46; Josephus, *Ant. Jud.*, XVIII, 8, 1ff; XIX, 1, 1.

consisted of three men who came to see Gaius regarding tumults between the Jews and pagans in Alexandria. They attempted to gain a hearing but he in a great rage refused to listen to Philo and violently bade them begone. Philo then withdrew and Gaius ordered Petronius, the governor of Syria, to lead an army to Judæa and cause his statue to be erected in the temple. The army was led thither and wintered in Ptolemais, a fact which would seem to put the date of the embassy in the autumn of the year 39.[1] Philo, however, represents the embassy as consisting of five men, as coming to Italy in midwinter, as being courteously received by the emperor at Rome on some specified date, and as being assured that he would hear them personally. Before the hearing they learned of the order for the erection of the statue, but the order was later cancelled on the petition of King Agrippa. Thereafter the embassy was heard by Gaius, and presented arguments on the loyalty of the Jews, interrupted by imperial humor to their great disgust. Finally Gaius took compassion on them and dismissed them amiably.[2]

The Jews *en masse* implored Petronius to desist from the contemplated sacrilege; this according to Josephus was early in the spring at sowing time, but Philo puts it at harvest time.[3] Moved by the difficulties of the undertaking Petronius wrote a letter to the emperor. According to Josephus [4] this letter did not arrive until the project had already been countermanded, but it filled the tyrant

[1] The Latin writers, however, seem to think that Gaius was in Gaul and Germany at this time, not returning to Rome till August of the year 40. *Cf.* below p. 391.

[2] Philo, *op. cit.*, 28, 29, 31, 42, 44-46; Josephus, *Ant. Jud.*, XVIII, 8, 1.

[3] Josephus, *op. cit.*, 3-6; Philo, *op. cit.*, 33-34.

[4] *Op. cit.*, 5-6, 8-9.

with rage, and he wrote the governor to commit suicide. But before this mandate arrived, Petronius had news of Gaius's death. It would seem that if the letter was sent to Rome in the spring of 40 the reply should have reached Judæa before Gaius's death, January, 41. Philo's account puts the sending of Petronius's letter in the summer. On receipt of it Gaius swelled with fury but concealed his rage and sent a civil reply directing Petronius to go on with the project. This, however, was later countermanded on receiving Agrippa's memorial.[1]

Josephus[2] tells us that King Agrippa, who lived in Rome, intervened in the matter by arranging a supper of unapproached splendor to entertain Gaius; that after the emperor had drunk himself into a merry state, he expressed his satisfaction with the banquet by telling his host to ask any boon he desired and it would be granted; that Agrippa asked for the abandonment of the design to set up the statue, and that Gaius, admiring Agrippa's virtue and disinterested care for the public tranquillity and for divinity itself, granted the request and so wrote to Petronius. Philo's story, however, is that Agrippa came to Rome to pay his respects to Gaius, knowing nothing of the correspondence with Petronius, but found the emperor in a state of great excitement. Agrippa, on hearing him charge the Jews with disloyalty, changed into all sorts of colors, becoming at the same time bloodshot, pale and livid, and ended by falling into a prolonged faint which continued till the evening of the following day. Then he wept and ate and wrote Gaius a well-composed letter, setting forth the practices of earlier Roman rulers as regards the Jews, and begging a reconsideration of the present plan. The emperor, on reading the letter, was very angry but controlled his rage and allowed himself to

[1] Philo, *op. cit.*, 32-34, 42.   [2] *Op. cit.*, 7-8.

be moved by the appeal to his justice and by Agrippa's noble disposition, to grant the request; and so wrote Petronius to drop the matter. However, he spoiled his boon, in effect "annulling his gift," by "mingling with it a more dreadful source of terror." For he enjoined the governor to enforce toleration in Judæa outside of Jerusalem. To this order the Jews were disobedient, and Gaius a second time commanded a colossal statue of gilded bronze to be made in Rome which he was intending to transport to Judæa when he made his trip to Egypt and the east, that "while the people were calm and free from suspicion he might quietly transport it in secret and erect it suddenly to their surprise." [1] The surreptitious transport of a colossal gilt statue from Rome to Jerusalem and its erection in the temple without attracting public notice would seem to have been beyond even Gaius's intention.

Continuing the examination of our authorities, it seems that Seneca, besides his general senatorial antipathy to Gaius, had personal grievances. We are told, in the first place, that the emperor, who had a sharp tongue and strong distaste for the prevailing fashion in letters, characterized Seneca's literary compositions as "mere prize declamations" and his style as "sand without lime." [2]

But we hear of a more serious matter. Gaius is said to have been so jealous of Seneca's eloquence that he ordered him to be executed; but the philosopher was saved, so the story has come down to us, by the friendly representations of a woman who enjoyed imperial intimacy and who pleaded that he was suffering from a mortal disease. At any rate, as appears from his letters, oratory was dropped,

[1] Philo, *op. cit.*, 35-43.
[2] *Commissiones meras* and *harenam esse sine calce*, Suet., *Cal.*, 53.

but whether or not for the reason alleged is unknown. It is barely possible that the real explanation of his strained relations with Gaius was his friendship with Gætulicus who was executed for conspiracy in 39. Seneca declares he was guilty of no disloyalty to his prince; one might therefore infer that he had been accused of it.[1]

Another cause of Seneca's unpopularity may have existed in his intimacy with Julia Livilla, the sister of the emperor. Julia and her sister, the younger Agrippina, were banished on a charge of adultery to the Ponza Islands.[2] After the death of Gaius, Claudius, the uncle of the two young women, recalled them from exile, but later in the same year (41) Julia was again banished on a new charge of impropriety, and this time Seneca was condemned by the Senate and banished to Corsica.[3] In his obsequious appeal which the exile wrote to Polybius, the powerful freedman of Claudius, he touches upon his condemnation, and says that the emperor mitigated the punishment when he was struck by misfortune and was falling.[4] This is not so strong an assertion of his innocence as we should expect. But it may be urged that in a letter obviously intended for the emperor's eye, the suppliant did not think it wise to assert the injustice of his sentence. To this it may be said that not even in the letter of consolation which he wrote in exile to his mother does Seneca give any intimation that the consciousness of innocence sustains him. We read only that

---

[1] *Quaest. Nat.*, IV, *praef.* 13-15.
[2] *Cf.* Suet., *Cal.*, 24; Cass. Dio, LIX, 3, 22, 26.
[3] See Cass. Dio, LX, 4, 8; LXI, 10; Tac., *Ann.*, XIII, 42.
[4] *Cons. ad Polyb.*, 13: *sed impulsum a fortuna et cadentem sustinuit et in praeceps euntem leniter divinae manus usus moderatione deposuit.*

if one ponders upon the fact that amorous desires have been given to man not for the sake of pleasure but to promote the propagation of the race, then all the other passions will pass harmlessly by such a one, unpolluted as he is by that secret scourge which battens on our vitals.[1]

Quite so: but any one, save perhaps a mother, would see that this falls short of claiming innocence at the time of his downfall. Seneca's intrigue with Julia seems fairly well established, and inasmuch as Julia had been in exile for some time before her second banishment, it is not improbable that his relations with her began in the reign of Gaius and aroused that emperor's hostility. Seneca was not incapable of garbling the truth when his feelings were excited, and some measure of bias undoubtedly characterizes his invective against Gaius.[2]

Other writers who furnish data for the history of Gaius's reign are Pliny the Elder, Juvenal, Plutarch, Tacitus, Suetonius, and Cassius Dio. Pliny, writing during the years of reaction against the Julio-Claudian Cæsars under the first Flavian emperors, to whom he was clearly attached, is no friend of Gaius or of his family, but has not much to say about him save to call him and Nero firebrands.[3] Juvenal speaks of the potion with which it was said that Cæsonia drove her husband mad, to the ruin of senators and knights. These love potions commanded much confidence among the Romans, but the recipes of them which we find so abundantly in Pliny

---

[1] *Cons. ad Helv.*, 13; *cf.* 1, 4, etc.

[2] *Cf.* Sen., *Cons. ad Helv.*, 10; *Cons. ad Polyb.*, 17; *de Ira*, I, 20; II, 33; III, 18, 19, 21; *de Const. Sap.*, 18; *de Ben.*, II, 12, 21; IV, 31.

[3] *Faces generis humani, N. H.*, VII, 45; *cf.* XI, 143f; XXXIII, 79; XXXV, 18; XXXVI, 111ff.

seem hardly calculated to produce anything more than
nausea.[1] Plutarch, in speaking of Gaius, uses a word
which has perplexed commentators; "Gaius, who ruled
for a brief time with distinction"—at least such is
the ordinary meaning of the word.[2] Tacitus evidently
painted Gaius in black colors as a madman, but the
books dealing specifically with that prince have not
survived.[3] Suetonius, and later Cassius Dio are, with
Philo, the most voluminous sources, but neither of them
possessed independent, critical judgment. In Suetonius's
account chapters 14, 15, 16, 17, and 18 are, favorable; the
remaining chapters (19-60) furnish most of the mad
stories with which most modern historians eke out the
meagre details of his reign.[4]

We need not go far to satisfy ourselves that the stories
are not all true, and certainly not all the truth. It should
be noted in the first place that in the matter under discussion there is shown a curious lack of knowledge of what
we might suppose to be well-known and uncontested facts.
The writers who tell us so confidently of hidden and un-
observable things, of private conversations, and even of
secret thoughts, are in conflict when it comes to such
matters as the birthplace of Gaius, and that of his only

---

[1] Cf. Juvenal, VI, 616ff; Statius (*Silv.*, III, 3, 70) indicates
that the tradition of Gaius the despot was well established by
the time of the third Flavian.

[2] Plut., *Anton.*, 87, ἐπιφανῶς ; other references *e.g.*, *Galba*, 9,
12, are unimportant.

[3] Cf. Tac., *Ann.*, VI, 20, 45, 46; XII, 6, 5, 4; XIII, 3;
XVI, 17; *Germ.*, 37; *Agr.*, 13; *Hist.*, IV, 48.

[4] Later epitomizers are: Capitolinus, *M. Ant.*, 28; *Verus*, 4;
Gord., 33; Gallicanus, *Avid. Cass.*, 8; Lampridius, *Comm.*, 10;
id. *Heliog.*, 1, 33, 34; Vopiscus, *Aurel.*, 42; Eutropius, VII,
12, 14; *Aur. Victor, de Caes.*, III. The Christian tradition
was taken directly from Philo and Josephus. *Euseb. H.E.*, II, 4-7.

child, and the details of his assassination.[1]   The circumstances of his accession to the imperial power are told in various ways.   It is not even agreed where Tiberius died, or how: whether the death was natural, as seems probable, or whether Macro or Gaius, or both, murdered him; and if so, whether the means was poison, starvation, smothering by clothes or pillows.   All are mentioned, together with various tales of the thoughts and actions of the dying emperor when he was quite alone; "so grave are the doubts which encompass the greatest affairs."[2]   We are even left in doubt as to whether the funeral was held with the utmost pomp, and whether Gaius's speech in praise of the deceased monarch was interrupted by his bursting into tears; or whether the funeral was a mean one, and the speech mostly about Augustus, Germanicus, and the orator himself.[3]   It would seem that the writers drew their material from some source other than known objective facts.

One of the best known stories is that of the extraordinary bridge of ships which Gaius is said to have constructed on the bay of Naples.   About ten years after the death of Gaius, Seneca wrote a treatise on "The Brevity of Life," dedicating it to Paulinus, who seems to have been a young man connected with the service of the food supply of Rome, and possibly his brother-in-law.   In the course of the essay Seneca begs him to retire from the dangers of active life, dangers which the philosopher, having just

[1] See Tac., *Ann.*, I, 41; Suet., *Cal.*, 8, 25; Josephus, *op. cit.*, XIX, 1, 2, and 13ff; Cass. Dio, LIX, 28, 29.

[2] See Tac., *Ann.*, III, 19; Suet., *Tib.*, 73; *Cal.*, 12, quoting Seneca and giving other versions; Josephus, *Ant. Jud.*, XVIII, 6, 8-10.   For different versions of the adoption of Gaius, cf. Tac., *Ann.*, VI, 46, and Suet., *Tib.*, 72.   Cf. Cass. Dio, LVIII, 28.

[3] Compare Suet., *Cal.* 15; Cass. Dio, LIX, 3; Suet., *Tib.*, 75, and Cass. Dio, LVIII, 27.

returned from eight years of exile, could well appreciate. In the course of the argument he strongly maintains that the occupant of such a position may incur grave peril from the failure to keep up the due supply of grain, although the default may be entirely due to the misconduct of the emperor himself. To emphasize the point he declares that at the time when Gaius perished there was but seven or eight days' supply of food in Rome, "while he was making bridges with ships and playing with the resources of the Empire." The existence of the shortage, he adds, was absolutely concealed on account of the danger which would be incurred by the officials in charge were the actual state of affairs to become known.[1]

But there are difficulties about the story even in this vague form. We may pass over the question of how Seneca could have known a dangerous secret, kept so profoundly quiet—for he was then in disgrace and out of public life, and in the first year of the next reign was exiled:—a glance at the chronology of the period will disclose others. Gaius went to the German frontier in the summer of 39 A.D. In the autumn of that year and the following winter he was in Gaul, where he suppressed a conspiracy against him and assumed his third consulate. Early the next summer he made his military expedition to the British channel, and hence could hardly have returned to Rome before the date which Suetonius gives, August in the year 40.[2] Later in the year he was at the bay of Naples. The language of Philo shows that the emperor did not come down to the bay of Naples immediately after his arrival in Rome, for the embassy had an interview with him there, and after a year's absence many things must

---

[1] Sen., *de Brev.*, 18: *dum ille pontes navibus iungit et viribus imperi ludit.*

[2] *Cal.*, 49.

have required his personal attention. Indeed, there are indications in the same authority that it was already winter when he left Rome.[1] Philo writes of his being at Naples to attend upon him, and although the Jewish ambassadors were carefully studying him, and although Philo put into his book whatever strange things he observed in the prince or heard about him to support his theory that Gaius's impiety to Jehovah made him insane, no mention is made of this bridge; Philo merely says that the emperor was sojourning around the Gulf.[2] From Naples Gaius returned to Rome before the first of the year, and was there assassinated on January 24, 41 A.D. All this accords ill with the bridge idea.

Furthermore, the corn harvest of Egypt was in March and April, that of Roman North Africa, Sicily, Sardinia, and Southern Spain in May and June, and these were the countries which supplied Rome. The season of navigation in those days was considered to extend from May to the middle of September, with a possible dangerous extension of a month at either end; but from the middle of November to the middle of March the seas "were closed."[3] Exceptionally a ship ventured on a winter trip, but this was rare.[4] Therefore had Gaius been seized with the idea of building a bridge with ships, and had he used the complete fleet for that purpose, it would have been some time—perhaps even six months—after the harvests, the corn would long since have arrived in Italy, and his

[1] Cf. Philo, op. cit., 28, 29. He speaks as if the bad news they received regarding Gaius's order reached them soon after their arrival at Puteoli, and as if it were then winter.

[2] Op. cit., 29: κατελήλύθει δὲ ἐπὶ θάλατταν καὶ διέτριβε περὶ τὸν κόλπον.

[3] Cf. Vegetius, Epit. Rei Mil., IV, 39; Josephus, op. cit., XVI, 2, 1ff; Bell. Jud., VII, 1, 3.

[4] Cf. Pliny, N.H., II, 122ff; Philo, op. cit., 29; Tac., Ann., XII, 43, speaks of supplies being brought in a very mild winter.

use of the ships could have worked no such inconvenience as Seneca suggests. Indeed the ships would not have been in Italian waters at all; they would undoubtedly have long returned to their home ports to be in readiness for the next spring's voyage. The harbor at Puteoli was but small.

The conclusion that Seneca's suggestion was a rhetorical flourish, inserted for the double purpose of converting Paulinus to a realizing sense of the dangers involved in holding public office, and of venting his anger against the "tyrant" who had broken him, is fortified by the fact that under Gaius's predecessor Tiberius, and his successor, Claudius, who are not suspected of using the corn-transports for building bridges, there were serious difficulties in keeping Rome supplied with bread. Claudius built a great harbor at the mouth of the Tiber to assist in this service. If there were any shortage in the quantity of corn on hand in Rome at Gaius's death, it may have arisen from crop failures similar to those which caused difficulties in the next reign.[1]

Pliny, however, seems not to have heard of the bridge. He described many remarkable constructions including some made by Gaius whose extravagance he duly reprehended. He dealt at length with the country about the bay, and had he known of the bridge could scarcely have resisted the temptation to mention it. Nor do we find any reference to it in the inscriptions or in the poets, although an apparently inevitable place for a mention of it occurs in the *Pharsalia*.[2]

Josephus, however, writing half a century after Gaius,

---

[1] See Suet., *Claud.*, 18-20; Cass. Dio, LX, 11; Tac., *Ann.*, XII, 43; IV, 6. Josephus, *Ant. Jud.*, XIX, 2, 5, says that Gaius began and partly completed a haven at the Straits of Messina for the protection of the grain fleet.

[2] II, 672ff.

takes up the tale. In speaking of the last months of his reign he mentions briefly the building of a bridge—nothing is said about ships—from Dicearchia (Puteoli) to Misenum, a length of thirty stadia (18750 feet), because Gaius thought it a tedious thing to be rowed across, and because he wanted to show his lordship of the sea.[1] By the time of Suetonius, another generation later, the western end of the bridge has swung around to Baiæ, about two miles and a half from the terminus according to Josephus, its length remaining nearly the same (18000 feet), although the distance across the water from Puteoli is only about eleven thousand feet. Different authorities —vague enough, as usual—are cited for the reason why the bridge was built. "Many" thought Gaius sought to rival Xerxes, who bridged the Hellespont; "others," that the rumor of the great task might frighten Germany and Britain. But Suetonius himself as a boy had heard his grandfather say that the reason given by the courtiers of the palace was that Thrasyllus the astrologer had assured Tiberius that "Gaius would no more be emperor than he would drive across the gulf of Baiæ."[2] The tales of a grandfather may be interesting but are not always true; in any case we may note that the prophecy was already disproved because Gaius was already emperor. It would have been more to the point had Gaius driven across as prince to prove that he would be emperor.

When Cassius Dio came to write about it a century later, the western terminus and the distance have again changed, while on the bridge there appear an aqueduct, rest-houses, cavalry charges, captives and spoils, and a preposterous harangue by the emperor; then an illumination of the

---

[1] *Ant. Jud.*, XIX, 1, 1.

[2] *Cf.* Suet., *Cal.*, 19, 32. None of the distances given by any of the writers is correct of the true distance across the bay.

whole bay, and a banquet with the treacherous murder of companions as a finale. From Seneca to Dio the story has lost nothing in the telling.[1]

In scrutinizing the stories of sexual irregularity with which our authorities teem, it is well to remember that the Romans, as Cicero said, regarded it as "facetious" and "urbane" to charge one with the vilest debauchery: this was often simply rhetorical abuse, "mere vituperation recklessly poured forth by an angry enemy."[2] When defamatory assertions can be controlled in any way, they often present grave contradictions. For instance, Suetonius preserved for us the anecdote that Gaius, when a daughter was born to his wife Cæsonia, was satisfied that he was the father of the infant for no better reason than that of her savage temper, which was such that she would attack with her nails the eyes and faces of the children at play with her. This seems not improbable until we consider that the age of the child, who could hardly have been over a year old at her father's death, makes her indulgence in such outbreaks appear exaggerated.[3]

Again, it is highly improbable that the emperor's poison box was so extremely lethal as to kill numbers of fish when it was thrown into the Mediterranean.[4] Nor does it command credence that when Gaius was short of money in playing dice, he was able to call for the census papers of Gaul containing the assessment rolls of the province, pick out the wealthiest citizens, order them off for execution, and, having replenished his means with a few millions, return to the game.[5] Such swiftness of action

---

[1] Cf. Cass. Dio, LIX, 17. [2] Pro. Cael., 3, 13. Cf. above p. 64.
[3] See Suet., Cal., 25; Cass. Dio, LIX, 23, 28.
[4] Cf. Suet., Cal., 49.
[5] Cf. Cass. Dio, LIX, 22. Suet., Cal., 41, gives quite a different version.

occurs only on the stage.   Suetonius seeks to arouse indignation at the tyrant's allowing noble senators to run beside his chariot for several miles: the source of the incident probably lay in the fact that Galba, then a hardy officer at the head of the Guard, accompanied the emperor's chariot for twenty miles along the Rhine frontier and distinguished himself by his bodily vigor.[1]

It is improbable that the authorities tell the whole truth of the military exploits of Gaius. If the stories are the whole truth, the Roman legions and provinces must have been in a state of cowardly impotence incredible at that period of Roman history. We are told that Gaius took a sudden resolve to visit the legions on the Rhine frontier.[2] After harsh and hasty levies, he made a very irregular march with a throng of dissipated camp-followers, and arriving at the frontier headquarters proceeded to dismiss most of the oldest centurions who had earned their discharge so as to deprive them of their pensions; as for the others, the allowances to which they would become entitled were reduced.[3] Then followed a military comedy —victories over persons arranged for capture, and branches of trees borne back for trophies. In the course of these manoeuvers he killed many of his own soldiers, cutting them down one by one or butchering them *en masse*. The general of the army, Lentulus Gætulicus, was an excellent general and much beloved by the soldiers; therefore the emperor put him to death and appointed a

---

[1] Suet., *Cal.*, 26; *Galba*, 6.

[2] B. Niese, *Römische Geschichte* (München, 1910), p. 311, note 2, cites, with disapproval, an attempt by Al. Riese to prove that the cause of the emperor's expedition was the conspiracy of Lentulus Gætulicus.—*Editor.*

[3] Suet., *Cal.*, 43ff.

strict commander who forbade the men even to applaud.[1]
Then he marched the whole army to the sea as if to
invade Britain, but on reaching the water's edge he sailed
only a little way, then sailed back, took his seat on a high
platform, gave the battle signal, and ordered the legionaries
to fill their helmets with sea shells, announcing that these
were the spoils to be exhibited in his triumph, becoming
vastly elated and feeling that he had enslaved the ocean.
A far from impressive donation was then promised the
soldiers with the grandiloquent announcement that now
they were to depart rich. In further preparation for his
triumph, he procured counterfeit prisoners whose hair he
caused to be dyed red, who were given German names, and
directed to learn the German language.[2]

He was, so we are assured by Suetonius, an arrant
coward, and in the face of his troops on the Rhine, made
a shameful exhibition of poltroonery at the first whisper of
possible danger. But other authorities, and even Suetonius
himself, make statements which ill accord with cowardice.[3]
We are told that before leaving the province he formed
the design of putting to the sword four legions, because on
the death of Augustus, over twenty-five years before when
his father commanded them and Gaius was an infant in
the camp, they had mutinied, and had endeavored to persuade their commander to revolt against Tiberius and seize
the Empire—an offence for which they had requested and
received punishment. Being with difficulty dissuaded

[1] Tac. (*Ann.*, VI, 30) speaks of him as if he may have been
rather lax in command, and Suetonius (*Galba*, 6) speaks of
the restoration of discipline by his successor, Galba. In the
latter passage there seems to be a more serious view of these
military operations than in *Cal.*, 44-46.

[2] *Cal.*, 51; Cass. Dio, LIX, 25.

[3] *Cf.* preceding note.

from the general massacre, he had obstinately persisted in the design of decimating them; but when he attempted to put this into effect, he became frightened at the prospect of resistance and made off for Rome. So far as we are told, it did not occur to the emperor that inasmuch as the term of enlistment of legionary soldiers was twenty years, none of the soldiers present in the year 14 A.D., would still remain in the legions in the year 40; nor did it strike him that the massacre of four Roman legions, a half of the army on the Rhine, would doubtless meet some resistance.[1] If the relations of Gaius with his army were as Suetonius described them, it is not altogether clear why he should inform us that when Gaius was killed, the assassins sought to tranquillize the disorderly soldiers by the false report that the emperor had committed suicide in alarm at the tidings of a defeat.[2] Gaius may have been insane; but we cannot believe that everyone else was imbecile. Unless we are prepared to doubt the veracity of Suetonius, or his sources, we must believe the Roman legionary soldiers were as mad as their emperor.

The people of Rome, too, must have exhibited touching, unresentful loyalty under great provocation, if what is told is true. We read of the emperor occasionally shutting the grain warehouses and obliging the people to starve for a while,[3] and mixing bits of iron with largesses which he flung at the people, whereby many were badly and even fatally injured.[4] He did not hesitate to invade the rights

---

[1] Compare Suet., *Cal.*, 43-51; *Galba*, 6; Cass. Dio, LIX, 21, 22, 25. All the legions which were on the Rhine in 14 A.D., were still there in 40; *cf.* E. G. Hardy, *Studies in Roman History*, (2nd ed. London, 1910), pp. 188-194.

[2] See Suet., *Cal.*, 51.

[3] Suet., *Cal.*, 26.

[4] Cass. Dio, LIX, 25.

of the many Romans who were descended from freedmen by declaring that the citizenship previously granted to freedmen and their posterity included only the first generation of descendants.[1] He forced testators to put him in their will as legatee, and then sent them poisoned cakes.[2] He levied taxes on everyone and had the decrees written in such small letters and posted in such a place as to be illegible, that he might cause the people to incur penalties by ignorance of the law; and when they clamored they were cut down by soldiers and perished in numbers.[3] The least remissness on the part of those engaged in his building operations was made a capital offence.[4] The games were mean affairs, and when the sun was hot he had the awnings removed so as to broil the spectators, forbidding exit to them.[5] Strangely enough people still flocked to the games and when they disturbed him with the noise of taking their seats, he had them driven away with clubs.[6] When there was a shortage of criminals to be fed to the beasts he ordered spectators to be thrown into the arena with their tongues cut out to prevent their vituperating him.[7] His general feeling towards the people was indicated by the phrase: "Would that the Roman people had only a single neck." [8] The idea of decapitating the person he was addressing is said to have occurred to him frequently on most inopportune occasions, as for instance when sitting next to the consuls at a banquet, or "as often as he kissed the neck of his wife or mistress." [9] To the upper classes,

---

[1] Suet., *Cal.*, 38.   [2] *Cf.* preceding note.
[3] Suet., *Cal.*, 40-41; Cass. Dio, LIX, 28; Josephus, *Ant. Jud.*, XIX, 1, 4.
[4] Suet., *Cal.*, 37.   [5] *Ibid.*, 26.   [6] *Cf. Ibid.*
[7] Cass. Dio, LIX, 10.
[8] Suet., *Cal.*, 30; Cass. Dio, LIX, 13, 30.
[9] Suet., *Cal.*, 32, 33.

even to his guests and personal friends, his conduct was
such as only a Suetonius could describe.[1]   Yet the immediate cause of his death and was comparatively venial
offence of giving an obscene watchword to a serious
minded officer of the Prætorian Guard.[2]

It is evident that to form any sort of consistent idea
of Gaius we must get away from this gossip of a hyposta-
sized monster and endeavor to reconstruct a real human
being moving in a real world.   To attain anything like
completeness is of course a vain hope, but it is not difficult to go far enough to see that there existed conditions
apt to create in the class responsible for the literary tradition, that bitter enmity towards the emperor which is
indicated by the tales handed down to us.   And the attempt
need not involve the taking of any undue liberties with the
existing authorities, scanty, confused, and improbable as
they are.   We need only to remember that psychological
miracles do not happen, and that in interpreting testimony
manifesting a strong bias special weight should be given to
those statements which are made casually and incidentally
as well as, of course, to those which make directly against
the prepossession shown.   Where insanity is alleged in
explanation of conduct bordering on diabolism, we are
entitled to inquire whether all his actions as narrated are
characteristic of any known psychopathy.   If so, it would
seem probable that the picture was drawn from real life;
but if not, the alleged insanity would appear an inaccurate
invention of details of conduct.   In that case, as in some of
the lives of the saints, we are dealing with literature that
is frankly romantic.

[1] *Cal.*, 26, 27, 30ff.   *Cf.* Cass. Dio, LIX, 15, 18, 28; Josephus,
Ant. Jud., XIX, 1, 1ff; Philo, *Leg. ad Caium,* 4, 6, 9, 17.
[2] Suet., *Cal.*, 56; Josephus, XIX, 1, 5; Cass. Dio, LIX, 29;
Sen., *de Const. Sap.*, 18.

Tacitus [1] tells us frankly that the histories of Tiberius and Gaius, of Claudius and Nero, were falsified by fear if written during their life-time; or were composed with fresh hatred after their death. Gaius was born August 31, 12 A.D., at Antium, the son of Germanicus and Agrippina, the daughter of Marcus Agrippa and Julia, only child of Augustus. Till his mother's exile in 29 A.D., he lived in her household. Agrippina, as is well known, was possessed by the firm conviction, whether well founded or not is immaterial here, that Tiberius was the inveterate enemy of her family and was responsible for all their troubles. [2] In view of the destruction of his mother and two brothers under Tiberius, and the opinions prevailing in his home and among the faction that gathered about his mother, it is not unreasonable to suppose that he shared in this belief. After his mother's exile he lived for a time with his grandmother Antonia, [3] and then from the age of nineteen to twenty-five with Tiberius on Capri. He married early but his wife did not live long, and his life was strict and simple, [4] and probably somewhat dull. His education from his youth was carefully directed; he responded readily to instruction, and was capable of delivering the oration at Livia's funeral when he was less than seventeen. [5] While under the care of Tiberius, he manifested no indications of abnormal depravity; it is agreed that he was under discipline and possessed abundant self-

[1] *Ann.*, I, 1.

[2] *Cf.* Suet., *Cal.*, 12.

[3] Suet., *Cal.*, 10, says that after his mother's exile he lived with Livia, his great-grandmother, until her death. But it seems clear that Livia died before Agrippina's exile (Tac., *Ann.*, V, 1, 3).

[4] *Cf.* Philo, *op cit.*, 2, 26.

[5] *Cf.* Suet., *Cal.*, 53, 54; Tac., *Ann.*, V, 1; Josephus, *op. cit.* XVIII, 6, 8.

control. That he must have conducted himself in a fairly
satisfactory way is indicated by Tiberius's treatment of
him and by the statements which hostile writers occasionally disclose.[1]   Tiberius was careful not to let him be
spoiled by flattery.[2]

His conduct on becoming emperor was marked by good
feeling and sound judgment.   Whatever his private grievance towards his predecessor may have been, he observed
all the proprieties of the occasion, even asking the Senate
to decree posthumous honors for Tiberius, though not
pressing the matter against the Senate's reluctance.   For
the living, as well as for the memory of the deceased
members of his family, he appears to have done everything
which warm affection could suggest.[3]   His generosity
towards his sisters and his grief when one of them died
were of course maliciously interpreted by later writers;
but neither Philo nor Seneca gives any support to the
charge, and the story in Josephus falls far short of the
later version.[4]

The tale of the murder of Tiberius by Gaius and Macro
may also be dismissed.[5]   As to the other alleged murders
or compulsory suicides in the early part of his reign,
the various stories told by the different writers are
not such as to impose conviction.   One may suspect that
Macro's suicide was due to chagrin at great expectations

[1] See Philo and Josephus, *loc. cit.*   His conduct for some time
after Tiberius's death indicates no extraordinary depravity;
cf. Tac., *Ann.*, VI, 20, 45-46, 48; Suet., *Cal.*, 10-12; Cass. Dio,
LVIII, 23, 27.

[2] Cass. Dio, LVIII, 23; Suet., *Cal.*, 10.

[3] See Suet., *Cal.*, 15, 16; Cass. Dio, LIX, 3; Sen., *de Ira*,
III, 21.

[4] *Ant. Jud.*, XIX, 2, 5.   *Cf.* Tac., (*Ann.*, XIV, 2) who seems
to be unaware of the scandal.   Suetonius knows all the details,
Cal., 24.   *Cf.* Cass. Dio, LIX, 3, 11, 22, 26.   [5] See above, p. 390.

ending in a mortifying dismissal from office. In the case of Silanus, we can but remark on the strength of the temptation to use harsh language when a bore commits suicide upon a mere suggestion. Regarding Tiberius Gemellus, under whatever circumstances the youth died, it was inevitable that murder would be charged.

It is abundantly clear that Gaius, on coming into power, received an enthusiastic welcome. The serious and gloomy old man who had never been popular had given place to a descendant of the beloved Drusus, and of Germanicus idealized and idolized by the people's imagination.[1] Everything combined to make things easy for the young man, not the least important factor being the possession of an overflowing treasury which he inherited from his predecessor's thrift. Gaius probably accepted the anti-Tiberius version of the cause of his family's ill-fortune, and was prepared to be on the best of terms with the nobles who, so long as he could remember, had sympathized with his mother and brother against the machinations of the stern Tiberius and the diabolical Sejanus. An era of good feeling began, and the long hostility between Cæsar and Senate seemed at an end.[2] He severely criticized the actions of Tiberius, and seemed to take Augustus as his model. He showed great deference to the senators; declared that he would share his power with them and do whatever would please them; called himself their son; abolished prosecutions for lèse-majesté; refused to listen to delators, and to put everyone at ease brought out what were said to be the files and records in the cases against his mother and brothers and publicly burned them.[3]

[1] Cf. Josephus, Ant. Jud., XVIII, 6, 8; Suet., Cal., 13ff.

[2] Cf. Philo, op. cit., 2-3; Josepnus, op. cit, XVIII, 7, 2; Suet., Cal., 14-18; Cass. Dio, LIX, 7.

[3] See Suet., Cal., 15, 16; Cass. Dio, LIX, 4, 6, 7.

Exactly how long this happy state continued it is not possible to say. From Philo we should conclude that it was about a year, with which Suetonius agrees, while Josephus and Dio make it about two years.[1] But at some time towards the middle of his reign the situation changed, and we observe that there was a bitter feud existing between emperor and senators. No overt action had been taken by the Senate, so far as we are informed, of a nature calculated to exasperate the prince, yet he was evidently exasperated.

There seem to have been prosecutions and condemnations of senators.[2] Seneca's troubles began about this time, but we do not hear of any particularly important conspiracy unless it be the one discovered while Gaius was in Gaul, by reason of which Gætulicus and Lepidus were executed. This, however, was after the new hostility to the Senate was in full swing. It seems not unlikely that Gaius had discovered that in the later years of the previous reign, Gætulicus, since the year 29 commander of the important army of Upper Germany, had in effect asserted his independent position, a defiance which Tiberius had thought it expedient to overlook. The assembling of an armed force by Gaius and the expedition in person to the Rhine, the destruction of Gætulicus and the substitution of the strict disciplinarian Galba, may be taken to be the energetic reply by the emperor to the governor's disobedience of Tiberius, and the reëstablishment of imperial supremacy. There is no other reason apparent for Gaius's going to the frontier and sojourning

---

[1] Philo, *op. cit.*, 24; Suet., *Cal.*, 37; Josephus, *op. cit.*, XVIII, 7, 2; Cass. Dio, LIX, 2ff, 21.

[2] Cass. Dio, LIX, 18-19, 23; Josephus, *op. cit.*, XIX, 1, 1 and 8; 2, 2; Suet., *Cal.*, 26; Sen., *de Ira*, III, 18, 19; *de Ben.*, II, 12. Philo, *op. cit.*, 14.

there so long.[1]   The absurd stories told regarding his actions were probably confused tales and misconceptions which had floated back to Rome and had been manipulated in senatorial circles.

This discord between the emperor and the Senate cannot have grown out of any failure to grant desired distinctions to the former, since, contrary to the idea sought to be conveyed by most of our authorities, it appears from them that Gaius was chary of accepting those honors which the Senate was always pressing upon him. We read of his refusals to have them decreed to him and his prohibition of adulation of himself or his relatives.[2]   In language which resembles that of Tiberius and which seems to have been quite misunderstood by Dio who reports it, he told the Senate that their honorific resolutions did not so much augment his glory as diminish his power.[3] The statement as to his assumption of a variety of titles is clearly contradicted by the inscriptions which, with the exception of *Pater Patriae,* are modest and show that he bore only those customary titles strictly incident to his position.   It was very different in the case of emperors like Commodus and Elegabalus.[4]

Furthermore, the vigor of his administration does not in the least suggest a prince whose mind was filled with thoughts of empty distinctions and whose time was occupied in receiving vain adulations.[5]   In the words of Dean Merivale,

---

[1] *Cf.* Tac., *Ann.,* VI, 30; Suet., *Cal.,* 43ff; *Claud.,* 9; *Galba,* 6. See above, p. 396.

[2] Suet., *Cal.,* 24, 49; Cass. Dio, LIX, 4, 7, 22-24.

[3] Cass. Dio, LIX, 23; *cf.* Tac., *Ann.,* I, 72.

[4] *Cf.* C.I.L., XIV, 28543, 3449.   Suet., *Cal.,* 22-24; Cass. Dio, LIX, 3, 24.

[5] For an excellent account of Gaius's activity in administration, building, *etc., cf.* H. Willrich, *Klio,* III (1903), p. 419ff.—*Editor.*

his activity was certainly remarkable; many of his plans of public improvement were as wise as they were bold; the vigilance of his government never relaxed; though well aware of the perils of his position, he was harassed by no craven timidity; we hear of no complaints under him of affairs neglected and foes encouraged; yet he yielded himself to no minister or favorite.[1]

Another respect in which our authorities give indications by their details of serious exaggerations in their generalizations is regarding the alleged bloodthirstiness of Gaius and his delight in the murder of opponents. There appears to be more harshness of language than of acts on the part of the emperor, and an expectation by the senators of their general massacre rather than much actual slaughter. Philo tells us that he was savage, raging, insatiable in revenge, and that he looked upon all attempts to advise him as insults; yet it appears from the narrative that the letter of urgent admonition from the Jewish prince Agrippa appealing to the practice of Gaius's predecessors and to his sense of justice was received by him in good spirit, admired, and allowed to effect a change in his "implacable" mind. Philo, of course, is altogether dissatisfied with his attempt to impose religious toleration on the Jews.[2] Josephus lets us understand that the bloodshed in the games was fictitious, and gives us an instance of Gaius's being so moved by the tortures endured by a freedwoman examined as a witness in a case of treason, that he dismissed the case altogether, and did what he could to make amends to the unfortunate

[1] *History of the Romans under the Empire*, V, p. 323.
[2] *Cf.* Philo, *op. cit.*, 4, 6, 8, 9, 17, 21ff., 42. *Cf.* 5; he "remembered the laws amid his lawlessness and had piety in his impious deeds, mocking the nature of truth." For Agrippa's intervention, *cf.* Josephus, *op. cit.*, XVIII, 8, 7-8.

girl. Cassius Dio also speaks of the episode.[1] This would
not seem a very remarkable case of mercy in a modern, but
we rarely find Romans betraying humane sentiments regarding such a matter.

In Seneca's case, the philosopher was no doubt terribly
frightened, but nothing happened to him,[2] and in the
apparently serious affair of Gætulicus we hear of but one
execution besides the recalcitrant governor.[3] Gaius's exasperation towards the senators must have been very great,
for after a year's absence, he is said to have returned to
Rome still breathing fire and slaughter against them. He
came very near destroying them all; but we do not learn
that any real slaughter occurred, and we are put off with
stories of lists of persons whom he was *intending* to murder, of *designs* to destroy the flower of the nobility, of
a box of poison that killed the fish in the sea, and the
projecting of deeds of unsurpassed wickedness.[4] Our
authorities are full of tales of his intentions—he *intended*
to make his horse *Incitatus* consul.[5] But regarding the
Senate, what is said to have really happened after all
these threats is that on their manifesting a real desire to
safeguard his life, by granting him a seat not easy of
access, he declared that he laid aside his anger towards all
but a few. But nothing happened even to the few.[6] Our
perplexity increases when we read that this timid, jealous,
irascible, vindictive and savage tyrant passed over with-

---

[1] Josephus, *op. cit.*, XIX, 1, 5, and 13; Dio, LIX, 26; Suet., *Cal.*,
16, 30.

[2] Cass. Dio, LIX, 22. For an act of kindness toward an old
man, *cf.* Sen., *de Brev.*, 20.

[3] *Cf.* Cass. Dio, LIX, 19-20, 27; and for Gaius's lust for
blood, Sen., *de Ben.*, IV, 31.

[4] *Cf.* Suet., *Cal.*, 48-49; Cass. Dio, LIX, 25.

[5] Suet., *Cal.*, 55; Cass. Dio, LIX, 14.

[6] *Cf.* Cass. Dio, LIX, 26.

out punishment the act of a shoemaker in calling some of his freakish conduct a great bit of silliness. Even more extraordinary is it to learn that when he suspected some among his personal attendants and freedmen of complicity in a plot against him, he did not cut them off, but called three of them into his presence and said that he would put an end to himself of his own accord if he seemed to them also to be worthy of death.[1] Such acts as these are not congruous to the character that our authorities are endeavoring to depict.

We return then to the cause for the bitterness between the emperor and Senate which suddenly marred the harmony of their earlier relations; for in this animosity, conjoined to the detestation felt for him by intolerant Jews, we find the key to Gaius's reputation as it has been handed down to posterity. This cause is clearly enough indicated in two of our sources, whose trustworthiness cannot indeed be rated high enough to justify us in relying upon them as authorities for any proposition in itself improbable, or in disharmony with earlier writers. Where, however, as in the present case, what they have to say fits in perfectly well with everything else known about the parties concerned and the general situation, and is not only not improbable but is the only explanation which rationalizes the whole matter, and moreover is in disaccord with their general prepossessions attributing Gaius's conduct to perverse malignity and to causeless enmity towards noble and opulent respectability, then in such a case we may fairly place some confidence in what they have to tell us. To understand how entirely credible their story is, it will be necessary to go back a little in the history of Gaius's family.

Probably as soon as Germanicus died in the Orient

[1] Suet., *Cal.*, 56; Cass. Dio, LIX, 25-26.

(19 A.D.) or at any rate soon after Agrippina reached Rome with his ashes, she was fully convinced that the loss of her husband was due to the machinations of his grandmother, Livia, and his uncle and adoptive father Tiberius; and that she and her children were also marked for destruction.[1] This proposterous idea obsessed her whole subsequent life and led her to a line of conduct disastrous to herself and her two sons. Around her for ten years centered the opposition to Tiberius; and stimulated by interested flattery and sympathy, she manifested an angry apprehension of the emperor by insolence, reproaches, and aspersions, and probably engaged in treasonable plots for the elevation of one of her sons to the throne. It was suggested to her that her only safety lay in taking sanctuary at the statue of Augustus and calling the Senate and people to protect the family of Germanicus, or in flying for refuge to the legions of the Rhine. And similar dangerous ideas were put into her sons' heads. Of all her follies Tiberius was kept informed. Such projects as these in the hands of a woman so determined and reckless and enjoying so much popularity as the widow of the beloved Germanicus, were dangerous and might easily result in civil war. So finally in the year 29 Tiberius felt constrained to complain of her and her two sons before the Senate, and to require their incarceration or relegation to the Ponza Islands.[2] Agrippina subsequently committed suicide and two of her sons perished by execution or suicide. It is charged by Tacitus that these friends who urged her and her sons to injudicious acts were suborned by the crafty Sejanus. Doubtless he had spies who must have been persons of rank sufficient to be on cordial and confidential terms with Agrippina; but it is

[1] See Tac., *Ann.*, II, 71-72, 82; III, 4-5, 15-17.
[2] *Cf.* Tac., IV, 12, 52-54, 59-60, 67; V, 3-5; Suet., *Tib.*, 52-54.

probable that there were others who thought to acquire advantage by acting as volunteer *agents provocateurs,* and who thus coöperated in producing an inadmissable situation and then betrayed their dupe.[1]

Now it was these cases against his mother and brothers which produced in Gaius up to the middle of his reign his feeling against Tiberius and his more than friendly attitude towards the senators, so many of whom had apparently been his mother's and brother's open or secret friends; and it was the papers in these cases against them which he was supposed to have destroyed at the beginning of his principate, undoubtedly to the immense relief of a number of senators who either as tools of Sejanus, or on their own behalf, had been misleading and betraying Agrippina and her sons, and whose double dealing was manifest in these papers.

Such was the situation when the ingenuous young prince in the enthusiasm of commencing his reign burned what were supposed to be these compromising documents, restored those who under Tiberius had been banished, abolished proceedings for lèse-majesté, expressed himself strongly against the harsh rule of his predecessor, called himself the executor of the Senate's desires, and indeed declared that it was as a father to him.[2]

This felicity, as has been said, lasted into the second year of the new reign.[3] But then, about the time of the death of Macro, Gaius appears to have become informed of the contents of the documents which were supposed to have been destroyed. How this came about, whether it had any connection with the death of Macro, who, it is

---

[1] If Suet., *Tib.,* 61, is correct, Tiberius afterwards discovered that Sejanus was assisting to drive Agrippina's family to ruin.
[2] *Cf.* Suet., *Cal.,* 15; Cass. Dio, LIX, 4, 6.
[3] *Cf.* Cass. Dio, LIX, 9.

conceivable, might have preserved them; whether, indeed,
Gaius knew at the time of the bonfire marking the reconciliation between Cæsar and Senate, that the really important documents had been withdrawn from the *dossiers*
for preservation, are matters in which we are without
light. In any case he now knew what these papers contained, and they remained in his archives to be a thorn
in the side of the opposition until finally in the next reign
Claudius, after showing them to those interested, gave
them over genuinely to destruction.[1]

The effect on Gaius of this revelation was very great.
He was still young enough to feel mortified at having
been deceived by men whom he must have seen frequently
at his mother's house, posing as the true friends of his
family against Tiberius. Prosecutions were instituted
against some for special wrongs done to Agrippina or to
her sons or to the real friends who had been concerned in
promoting their cause. Some whom he had amiably re-
leased from punishment as presumably suffering from
the injustice of Tiberius,[2] he now found to have richly
deserved their fate; and he proceeded, possibly stretching
the law, to cancel his pardons and re-inflict the penalty due
them.[3]

As the senators sank in his esteem, Tiberius rose, and
he ceased to blame the man whom he had once thought
harsh, malevolent and unjust.

> He often [says Suetonius] inveighed against all the
> senators alike as clients of Sejanus, as informers against
> his mother and brothers, producing the documents
> which he had pretended to have burned, and justifying

[1] Suet., *Cal.*, 30; Cass. Dio, LIX, 4, 10; LX, 4.
[2] Those, *e.g.*, who had been sentenced under Tiberius on
false charges of delation.
[3] *Cf*. Cass. Dio, LIX, 4, 10, 13; Suet., *Cal.*, 15, 30.

the severity of Tiberius as inevitable in view of the evidence of so many accusers.[1]

With enough additional, but harmonious, details to prove that he is not copying Suetonius, Cassius Dio puts the matter thus:

Up to this time he was always speaking ill of Tiberius and before everyone; and far from reprehending disparagement of him publicly or privately, he even enjoyed it. But now entering the Senate he praised him highly and rebuked the senators and people for their unjust accusations. . . . And then passing in review the case of each man who had lost his life under Tiberius, he showed, to his own satisfaction at least, that the senators were responsible for the deaths of most of them; because they had accused some of them; had borne false testimony against others; and had passed sentence against all. These charges he supported by having freedmen read from the documents which he once said he had burned. Then he added: "if Tiberius acted unjustly, you ought not to have heaped honors upon him when he was alive, nor, by Jupiter, to repudiate what you so often declared and decreed. Not only did you act in a senseless way to him, but you killed Sejanus by corrupting him and filling him with conceit. I can expect nothing good from you." Then proceeding with his speech, he represents Tiberius himself as addressing him and saying: "all that you have said is just and true, so have no friendiness nor compassion for any of them. For all of them hate you, all wish your death: and they will kill you if they can. Do not think of trying to please them by your acts, and do not mind what they say; but consider your own pleasure and safety as indeed the highest justice. Thereby you will escape harm and enjoy all pleasures; and furthermore, whether they like it or not, they will honor you. If you act otherwise, you will get no real benefit of it, and beyond some empty glory will receive

[1] *Cal.*, 30.

no advantage, but will perish ignominiously as the victim of their plots." [1]

It would, of course, be too much to suppose that the foregoing is a transcript of an actual speech. This form of composition was the recognized historiographic way of putting before the reader the author's views either as to the real attitude of a historical character, or as to the attitude which the author, for purposes of his own, chose to ascribe to him. But there is sufficient variance between the sentiments here expressed and the general picture of Gaius which Dio presents, to make it probable that the speech portrays the author's conception of the actual position taken by the emperor. Had Dio introduced it merely as a statement of what might have been said on behalf of the "tyrant" as against the nobility, he would probably, in accord with his practice,[2] have subjoined a reply setting forth the other side. As it is, the matter ends with a publicly announced reëstablishment by the emperor of prosecutions for lèse-majesté, and his departure the same day for some place not far from Rome. No suggestion is made that Gaius's statements and wrath were controverted as untrue, or deprecated as unjust. The senators, now thoroughly alarmed, thanked him for letting them live, and voted and kept on voting extravagant honors and adultations, including a festival and a minor triumph; but Gaius paid no attention to the extravagances decreed by the Senate to soften his resentment.[3]

It is in his manifestations of wrath towards senators

[1] Cass. Dio, LIX, 16.
[2] Cf. XXXVIII (Cicero and Philiscus) 18-30; L, (Antony and Cæsar) 15ff; LII, (Agrippa, Mæcenas, and Octavianus) 1ff; LV (Augustus and Livia) 14ff.
[3] Cf. Cass. Dio, LIX, 16-17.

that students have thought they discovered some of the
strongest indications of his insanity. Some, as has been
said, were prosecuted for offences which now for the
first time came to Gaius's knowledge, and the rest of them
were kept in a state of apprehension by occasional menaces
of vindictive intentions. He is said to have taken a delight
in humiliating them and treating them with insolence,
depriving them of ancient badges of distinction and even
disfiguring them by cruel punishments. We read of his
arrogance towards some who came to pay homage to him,
and some sycophants are said to have gone so far as to
practice the oriental form of prostration before him.[1]

Our authorities also tell us of various exhibitions of
that sardonic banter and cynical humor which became
noticeable in the latter part of his reign. He seems to
have enjoyed bringing to confusion all snobbishness and
hollow pretence.[2] When the rich provincials of Gaul
showed eagerness to acquire *bibelots* with imperial associations, he is said to have sent to Rome for all the old
furniture and trinkets available, and held a sale at Lyons,
himself furnishing to the collectors an abundance of assurance of their authenticity.[3] Religious cant and hypocrisy, however sanctified by age, found in him an acrid
reception, as for instance, in the case of the sycophant
who when the emperor was ill had vowed to devote his

[1] See, *e.g.*, Sen., *de Ben.*, II, 12; *de Const. Sap.*, 18; Josephus,
Ant. Jud., XIX, 1, 8; Suet. *Cal.*, 26-27, 34-35; Cass. Dio, LIX,
18, 27; Philo, 6, 8, 16.

[2] Apropos of his proposal to make his horse Incitatus consul,
Willrich (*op. cit.*, p. 461) remarks: "Wenn er eines Tages
gesagt hat, er werde sein Lieblingspferd, Incitatus, nächstens
zum Konsul ernennen, so mag sein Gedankengang gewesen sein,
dass in Rom so mancher Esel zum Konsulat gelangt sei, warum
also nicht auch einmal ein edles Ross."—*Editor*.

[3] Compare Suet., *Cal.*, 39; Cass. Dio, LIX, 21.

own life for the recovery of the more precious imperial life, and was required to fulfil his vow;[1] or in that of the priest of Arician Diana who held his sinecure on the tenure of fighting any applicant. Gaius saw to it that a competent fighting man applied.[2] His indulgence in this humor was, as we have seen, the immediate cause of his death.[3]

In some cases the tales represent, in all probability, not the reality of Gaius's actions but the reality of the dislike felt for him by those who have supplied history with its material. After a confused account of Gaius's consulships,[4] Dio proceeds to tell how he raised an army with a large camp-following of male and female entertainers and marched to the Rhine frontier and into Germany. Here took place the sham campaigns to which reference has already been made.[5] Next comes the journey south to Lyons, followed by the story of the death of Gætulicus, who had been governor and general in command of the Rhine frontier for ten years.

The rapidity of the marches of considerably over a thousand miles, begun, so Dio indicates, before September and involving a trip across the Alps in autumn, must surprise us when we learn that on October 27, the Arval Brothers met in Rome to hold a service in honor of the downfall of Gætulicus.[6] If the story of the expedition to the north is told with any approach to accuracy, the emperor and his followers, military and festive, must have

---

[1] Suet., *Cal.*, 27; Cass. Dio, LIX, 8.   [2] Suet., *Cal.*, 35.

[3] See Sen., *de Const. Sap.*, 18; Josephus, *Ant. Jud.*, XIX, I, 14; Cass. Dio, LIX, 29.

[4] See Cass. Dio, LIX, 19, 20; *Cf.* LIX, 6, 13, 24; Suet., *Cal.*, 17.

[5] *Cf.* above, p. 396.

[6] *Cf.* Cass. Dio., LIX, 21-23; C.I.L., VI, 2029; Suet., *Cal.*, 43ff; *Claud.*, 9; *Galba*, 6.

left Rome very much earlier in the year than the historian gives us to understand. When Julius Cæsar was hastening with veteran troops to cut off Pompey at Brindisi, the best speed he could make in an easy country for marching was 465 kilometers (about 290 miles) in seventeen days. The distance from Rome to Mainz, where the suspected legate commanded the army of Upper Germany, is three times as far—1,400 kilometers—with the Alps to cross in October. It would clearly be quite impossible for this expedition, starting in September, to reach even the Rhine by the time that the Arval Brothers had received the news in Rome of Gaius's success in ending the conspiracy of Gætulicus.[1] If he departed in the spring or early summer, the story of the consulate becomes even less credible.

Many of the facts related by our biased authorities are out of harmony with their assumption that the emperor was insane. They let it appear too abundantly, for instance, that he did not lose interest in the details of administration; nor neglect the immense burden of work which his position imposed on him; that he found time in his short reign to complete the buildings begun by his predecessor, to project, with expert advice, and begin useful and boldly conceived public works such as harbors for the corn fleet in the Straits of Messina, and the most splendid of all the aqueducts of Rome; as well as to examine carefully a proposal for a canal across the Isthmus of Corinth, and to establish what was probably intended to be a house of refuge in the pass across the Alps.[2] They give

[1] See T. R. Holmes, *Cæsar's Conquest of Gaul* (2nd ed.), p. 635. For the speed of letter carriers, *cf.* Cic. *ad. Fam.*, XIV, 5; XVI, 21; *ad Frat.*, III, 1.

[2] *Cf.* Suet., *Cal.*, 21; Pliny, *N.H.*, IV, 10; XXXVI, 111ff, 122; Frontinus, *de Aq.*, 13, 14; Josephus, *Ant. Jud.*, XIX, 2, 5.

us also to understand that he possessed a well-developed sense of humor, although in the good taste of its manifestation he was not above the level of the ordinary man, and that he could permit himself, without showing any disposition to inflict punishment, to be openly jeered in regard to the matter about which he was supposed to be especially insane.[1]

The reception of the Jewish embassy, if we omit the horror felt by Philo at what he regarded as blasphemy, must strike us as, from the pagan point of view, a distinctly humorous episode enlivened by some wit on the part of Gaius, and terminating in a courteous dismissal quite inexplicable if he were really the madman that Philo supposed him to be.[2] Furthermore, the supposed madman is represented as being led by rational considerations to side with the Jews, towards whom he is said to have felt a frenzy of rage for their refusal to fall in with his delusion, against Flaccus the governor, who had humored his mania but had misgoverned the enemies of the madman.[3] And in the matter of his divinity, the essential point of his madness, he is shown to us as receiving and carefully considering long arguments addressed to his reason, sense of justice and expediency; as admiring the frankness of the petitioner, allowing his own opinions to be changed, and notifying his subordinate of his altered purpose. He manifested complete self-control even when thwarted by an apparent unwillingness to obey his commands, lest a free expression of his opinions might lead to serious results.[4] As to his homicidal activities, it is to be observed that while we are told an abundance of

---

[1] See Cass. Dio, IX, 26.   [2] Cf. Philo, op. cit., 44-46.
[3] Cf. Philo, in Flac. 12-13.
[4] See Philo, Leg. ad Caium, 3, 34, 42; Josephus, Ant. Jud., XVIII, 8, 1-9.

vituperative and minatory language by the emperor, yet
in most of the cases where coherent statements are made
by our authorities and names given, we find that the victim
survived.[1]

These data are inconsistent with the theory of mania.
The maniac does not attend to his day's work, concern
himself with useful things, nor show humor, nor self-
control; nor is he amenable to rational appeal. Furthermore, his mania manifests itself in act as well as thought.
He becomes, as we say, "maniacal," and proceeds to promote his insane ideas by personal violence. There is no
suggestion of this sort in our authorities regarding Gaius.
The maniac is characterized by yet another trait which is
not applicable to Gaius; he is essentially solitary, his abnormal mind makes friendly relations and associations
unattractive and impossible. But Gaius was at all times
sociable and convivial. The rank, manners, and behavior
of his companions during his last two years, are indeed
criticized, but no one suggests that he was at any time
secluded, or avoided social intercourse, or found it difficult.[2] The picture drawn is not that of mania.

Suetonius says that Gaius was epileptic in his boyhood,
and that in later life he was subject to sudden fainting
spells during which he could scarcely walk, stand, or col-
lect himself.[3] Possibly he had epilepsy—no writer speaks
of more serious manifestations—but that would give us
no assistance in explaining the psychological character attributed to him. Mania with epilepsy is very rare.

It is a general habit in seeking to understand historical
matters to overlook the obvious and search for some large
and dignified reason for things. In the period of history

[1] See above, p. 407.
[2] *Cf.* Suet., *Cal.,* 54-55; Cass. Dio, LIX, 5.
[3] *Cf.* Suet., *Cal.,* 50.

under consideration, students have too frequently passed by simple explanations arising out of the common nature of the men of the times and of all times, and have built up imposing structures of conjecture strangely at variance with the facts of human nature as we know it. In the case of Gaius, it is more than probable that the explanation of his behavior lies not in madness but in alcoholic intoxication.

A sketch of his life on this hypothesis will disclose the case of a young man who possessed a bright, active, well-trained mind, and a nervous, affectionate and demonstrative disposition.[1] There had been much tragedy in his life and his mother and brothers had lost their lives in political controversies. He was the youngest boy in the family, and until his seventeenth year it had not been thought that he might become emperor; and even then his chances were not bright. From his seventeenth to his twenty-fifth year he lived a quiet, disciplined, industrious life, the latter part of it on Capri under the strict control of Tiberius who seems to have undertaken to make a man of him.[2] At the age of twenty-five he became emperor and was acclaimed with great and genuine popular enthusiasm. This continued to be felt for him certainly for some time. He should not be regarded as a boy coming awkward and unprepared to his new responsibilities. There can be no reasonable doubt that the astute, intelligent, and patriotic Tiberius gave him a careful training for the position which it seemed now that he must occupy; and indeed his removal to Capri may fairly be connected with that purpose. Once his own master,

[1] See *ibid.*, 55.
[2] *Cf.* Philo, *op. cit.*, 2; Suet., *Cal.*, 10; Josephus, *Ant. Jud.*, XVIII, 6, 4ff; Tac., *Ann.*, VI, 45-46 (doubtless grossly exaggerated).

and with enormous wealth at his disposal, he seems to have given himself over to sensual indulgence and to have discovered in due time, as Philo says, that "the wages of intemperance are weakness and disease which bring a man near to death." [1]

There was about this time, it appears, a marked increase in drunkenness. Pliny informs us that in the reign of Tiberius there began the custom of drinking on an empty stomach—a practice which he strongly deprecated, as he well might if there were many who followed the example of Torquatus. Philo, Seneca, and Plutarch all comment upon and deplore the growing indulgence in wine. [2] Seneca's maturer judgment is at variance with his earlier opinion that by a generous allowance of wine and occasional intoxication the mind might be liberated from the bondage of cares, emancipated, animated, and rendered more daring in all its attempts; but not too often, he adds, lest we cast off a general attachment to the dullness of sobriety. [3]

Both Pliny and Seneca give us careful studies of the physical condition of contemporaries addicted to drunkenness. They emphasize first of all the pallor caused by excessive drinking, the emaciation, and marked distention of the abdomen. The eyes are in a disordered condition; the muscles twitch, and the cheeks, lacking tone, are flaccid. The breath is poisoned by indigestion; dizziness, insomnia, and distressing dreams afflict their victim. To these characterizations, Gaius's appearance seems to have corresponded in a marked degree. He was extremely pale; he had thin legs and a large body; his eyes were

[1] *Op. cit.*, 2-3; *cf.* Suet., *Cal.*, 37.

[2] Pliny, *N.H.*, XIV, 137ff; Philo, *de Ebriet.*, 53; Sen., *Epist.*, CXXII, LXXXIII.

[3] *De Tran. An.*, 17; *cf. Epist.*, LXXXIII.

hollow and his brow wrinkled, and his face often contorted. He suffered from indigestion, insomnia, and strange dreams. Suetonius speaks of occasional faints, which he attributes to epilepsy, and Philo speaks of his dropping off to sleep at entertainments.[1] His serious illness caused no change in his habits. On the day of his death, we are told, he remained in bed until afternoon in consequence of the feast of the previous evening; and according to another account he was preparing to feast again that day.[2]

Viewed in this light many of the stories of his conduct become intelligible: the boastful vainglory which Philo so seriously records;[3] the challenge to Jupiter, which Seneca absurdly declares nerved the assassins to their patriotic task;[4] the intention to make his horse consul;[5] the suppression of Homer and banishing of Virgil and Livy from all libraries; the idea of abolishing the legal profession; sallying forth with jovial companions into the streets and overturning the statues of ancient celebrities;[6] his behavior to the Senate;[7] his actions on the Rhine;[8] and his impudicity of speech.[9] Whatever the defects of Gaius's character, and these were doubtless many and serious, it is important to remember that the story of his short reign has come down to us as written by bitter enemies, exaggerated, distorted, and manifestly absurd.

---

[1] Sen., *de Const. Sap.*, 18; Philo, *op. cit.*, 7; Suet., *Cal.*, 50, 58; Pliny, *N.H.*, XI, 144; XIV, 141ff.

[2] See Suet., *Cal.*, 58, 32, 37; Cass. Dio, LIX, 17, 29; Sen. *Cons. ad Helv.*, 10; Josephus, *Ant. Jud.*, XVIII, 8, 7.

[3] *Op. cit.*, 8, 45; *cf.* Suet., *Cal.*, 22.   [4] Sen., *de Ira*, I, 20.

[5] Suet., *Cal.*, 55; Cass. Dio, LIX, 14, 28.

[6] Suet., *Cal.*, 34.   [7] *Ibid.*, 32, 49.   [8] *Ibid.*, 45.

[9] *Cf. ibid.*, 56; Sen., *de Const. Sap.*, 18; Josephus, *Ant. Jud.* XIX, 1, 5.

CHAPTER XIX

THE PAUCITY OF SOURCE MATERIAL FOR ROMAN HISTORY

THE value of a knowledge of Roman life was considered in an earlier chapter, but we are forced to recognize that however great may be its value, our material for an understanding of it is lamentably defective both in quantity and quality. The ancient writers are few in number; they are often loquacious on trifles but silent on much that a modern student desires to know.[1] Not without reason does the great Mommsen grow exasperated over the defects of our sources, declaring that the literary tradition for the imperial period at least is "not merely without form and colour, but in fact for the most part without substance."[2] The paucity of documents reduces our knowledge to that of the most general outlines; for most of the details, resting on a delicate balancing of meagre evidence, can easily be called into question. The late Mr. W. T. Arnold even went so far as to say that "we in England know absolutely nothing of the history of the Empire."[3]

---

[1] *Cf.* W. T. Arnold, *Studies of Roman Imperialism* (London, 1906), p. 2.
[2] *Provinces of the Roman Empire* (New York, 1887), vol. I, Introd., p. 3.
[3] *Op. cit.,* p. XXXVIII.

Professor West estimated [1] that of the 772 known Latin authors, we have, practically all the books of 37; 43 remain with the greater part of their writings, and of 64 we have a little, while 628 are entirely lost. When we reflect that many of the writers who have survived are very feeble tapers for the illumination of Roman affairs, and that not a few are of the *ignis fatuus* sort, we are bound to feel that this is not very much literary light to dispel the shades of a thousand years.

Few eras in Roman history are more important and more crowded with events whose effects were vital and lasting than the sixty-three years from the tribunate of the elder Gracchus (133-70 B.C.). It covers the various agrarian agitations, the development of class warfare, leading up to the downfall of republican institutions. It includes the scandals of the Jugurthine War and the lasting discredit of the aristocracy; the struggle against the Cimbri and Teutones, who threatened the very life of Rome; various extensive slave insurrections culminating in the revolt of Spartacus; the revolt of the Italian Allies, and the reception into the Roman state of new citizens greater in number than the old, fundamentally altering its composition; the terrible civil war between the popular and reactionary parties under Marius and Sulla; the first proscriptions; numerous massacres, and the attempt to reinstate oligarchic control; the temporarily successful establishment by Sertorius of an independent state in Spain; the spread of Roman dominion throughout the East by Attalus; the wars between Sulla and Lucullus, and the

[1] *Proceedings of the American Philological Association*, 1902, p. xxiff. [The source material for the imperial period has been well treated by E. Kornemann, in *Gercke und Norden's Einleitung in die Altertumswissenschaft*, III Band (Leipzig, 1912), pp. 241-266.—*Editor*].

restoration to control of the leaders of the popular party which Sulla seemed for a time to have definitely excluded from power. Yet for this term of years we have no connected history; it must be pieced out with scraps.[1]

Such literary material as we have is not at all evenly distributed as to time, place, or subject. Most of it relates to the political or social events at Rome, or to the military operations incident to the conquest of the world. The turmoil, gossip, and dissipation of the great city are generously set before us; but apart from the movements of troops, we hear little of what was happening in the rest of the world. Not only the affairs of the provinces, but of Italy itself outside of Rome and the resorts of the aristocracy, would be nearly blank to us were it not for the evidence afforded by archæology. We know almost nothing of the life in the rural homes and in the great provincial cities of the Empire, or, what is of more importance for the study of morals, of the life in the

> quiet country towns in Samnium or Lombardy where character remained untainted in the days of Nero or Domitian, and where the religion of Numa long defied the penal edicts of Theodosius and Honorius.[2]

The memoirs of the most confirmed Parisian boulevardier could hardly be narrower in range than is, for example, Suetonius; and yet throughout Italy, Gaul, Spain, Africa and other provinces the tide of life ran strong. It was the provinces that ultimately emerged and took control while the Senate sank to the level of a town council, and the city of Rome became little more than a symbol of the unity of the world.

[1] An excellent source book for the period is Greenidge and Clay's *Sources of Roman History*, B.C. 133-70 (Oxford, 1903).
[2] Dill, *Rom. Soc. from Nero to M. Aurel.*, p. 529; cf. p. 143ff.

As our landscape is very unequally illuminated, so the chronological panorama unrolls itself in some epochs in almost total darkness. We know very little about the great events which led to the incorporation of the Italians into the Roman body politic, and we have even less information about the reception of all freemen throughout the world into the Roman state. We have most inadequate material for judging why Rome apparently grew in strength during the first century of the Empire when, if reports are true, misgovernment was the rule, but decayed visibly during the ensuing century of peace and prosperity under excellent princes. And the collapse in the third century is nowhere satisfactorily accounted for by our extant sources.

Equally irregular and uneven are our sources for the different aspects of ancient life and conduct. In some cases this is doubtless due to the fact that most of the literature emanated from the small aristocratic class with special and narrow interests, which failed to understand the larger social forces struggling for control. The idea of progress, for instance, as Bury has pointed out,[1] was apparently unknown to the ancient historians. In other cases the character of our sources is due to the ancient aversion from subjects which do not lend themselves easily to dramatic or rhetorical treatment; to the absence of the modern foot-note with its steadying influence; and in part to the selective process of the Middle Ages.[2]

In many cases, furthermore, we are ignorant of an

---

[1] *Ancient Greek Historians*, pp. 199, 255. An exception is made in the case of Polybius, IX, 2.

[2] For the fate of classical books in the early Middle Ages see Sandys, *History of Classical Scholarship* (Cambridge, 2nd ed. 1906), vol. I, p. 362ff; G. H. Putnam, *Authors and Their Public in Ancient Times* (New York, 1894), p. 272ff.

author's identity; sometimes we are at a loss to know the precise period in which he wrote. Authors like Phædrus, Petronius, Longinus, Diogenes Laertius, and the writers of the Augustan Histories are little more than names to us. We have no evidence that will enable us to check or control the bias of some of them. Even when ample information can be obtained concerning the authors and their point of view, we find that we must still reckon with grave defects in the quality of the material. Certain general defects, as we have seen, tend seriously to impair the validity of their testimony. Their blindness to the idea of uniformity in nature, to the idea of causation, to contradictions; their lack of criticism and of pure scholarship created a condition unfavorable to the production of trustworthy historical writings.

In view of the literary remains we have at our disposal for the study of Roman affairs, we may therefore adopt an attitude of scepticism. But scepticism about a matter on which the evidence is insufficient to justify a definite opinion is impossible for the vulgar and appears to be exceedingly difficult for the erudite. The very paucity of material regrading Roman conditions seems often to produce a distinct unwillingness to discard any part of the evidence save where it is manifestly absurd or incredible. Says Ihne:

> We have, moreover, the uneasy feeling that much of what is accepted as true and unimpeachable only appears so because we happen to have no independent contradictory statements, and are therefore not entitled to reject reports, though they may seem from internal evidence to be open to the most serious doubts. This refers to all, and even the best attested facts in the history of Rome.[1]

[1] *History of Rome,* vol. V, pref. pp. v-vi.

If this rule is to be followed even in the face of internal disharmonies which awaken most serious doubts, then indeed is historical criticism badly shackled. A misstatement may be in the guise of the possible as well as the impossible, and where there are but few witnesses for several centuries of a people's life, many statements will be uncontradicted.

It is doubtless owing in part, at least, to the meagreness of the available material that attempts have been made repeatedly to describe one phase of Roman life and history by assembling data that belong to another, widely separated by time and circumstance. It is manifestly absurd to regard Roman life and history as static, and yet there has often been a tendency, particularly among writers on moral conditions, to draw a composite picture by quoting scraps of comedy which reflected Greek rather than Roman life, fragments of Cato and Lucretius, Cicero in forensic and familiar moods, the poets of the Augustan renaissance, Quintilian, Pliny, Tacitus, and Plutarch, as if they were contemporaries and wrote of common things.[1] The result in such cases is merely an *a priori* sketch developed from the author's prepossessions and prejudices, while the data cited as facts supporting the generalizations are merely selected passages chosen to support predetermined assumptions disguised as conclusions.

---

[1] *Cf. e.g.,* C. Schmidt, *Le Société civile dans le monde romain et sa transformation par le Christianisme,* a work which was awarded a prize by the French Academy, and in which the author declares (p. xxxi): "I can say with truth that I have cited no fact which is not supported by positive and authentic testimony." Translated into English under the title *Social Results of Early Christianity* (London, 1885); *cf.* p. 45ff; M. Vanlaer, *La Fin d' un peuple* (Paris, 1895), p. 215ff.

We shall be able to realize more fully the dangers involved in assembling such disparate material if we consider the need of what may be called historical perspective. It is not always easy, even for a student of Roman affairs, without stopping to take thought, to realize adequately and to give due importance to the length of time covered by these scanty historical remains. The latest dates with which we deal are themselves so far from us that a few centuries more or less do not strike our imagination. While we may be able to say offhand that as many years elapsed from Hannibal to Marcus Aurelius as from Columbus to Queen Victoria, we do not often *feel* this; nor do we often consider that there were nearly as great changes in human life and conditions in the one case as in the other. Hence when a writer attempts to draw a picture of Roman life with material extracted from authors ranging from Plautus to Lucian, the case is somewhat akin to an attempt to describe modern English civilization from scraps of early Tudor dramatists who drew from Italian writers; from, say, Clarendon and Hobbes of Stuart times and from the poets of the Restoration; from some moralists of the mid-eighteenth century, to say nothing of later, disparate sources.

We have, so far, been considering the literary productions to which we resort for a knowledge of Roman affairs. But of late years, it need merely be noted, an entirely different sort of evidence has come into prominence, which is free from many of the worst defects of the former class: this we may call in a general way "archæological." It is safe to say that in no field of historical study have results been more conspicuously successful than in the interpretation of the archæological material. The study of the provincial administration is incomparably richer since the publication of the *Corpus Inscriptionum Latinarum* and the Egyptian papyri. From literary sources alone we should have known little of the multitude of *collegia* which played so important a rôle in the life of the common people. The inscriptions have shed new light on the legal constitutions of provincial cities, and the Pompeian *graffiti* have brought before us the actual life of the inhabitants of a small Italian town. But when all is said, the field covered by archæological remains is far narrower than we could wish, and they give but slight information on many of the social subjects which it would be of special utility for us to know. Cumont, who has made such excellent use of archæological evidence in his studies of ancient religions, has well said:

Our position is frequently similar to that of a scholar of the year 4000 who should undertake to write the history of the Passion from the pictures of the fourteen stations, or to study the veneration of the saints from the statues found in the ruins of our cathedrals.[1]

[1] *Les Religions orientales*, pp. 21-22.

INDEX

Accuracy of observation, 39 ff.

Adulation of Senate, 265 ff., 282 ff.

Æsthetics, 93

Agrippa, King, 385

Agrippina, mother of Gaius, 409 f.

America and Rome, 7, 14 ff.

Analogy, historical, 8

Antony, 179, 296

Aqueducts, Frontinus, 94; Claudian aqueduct, 416

Arnold, W. T., on Augustus, 272; on Empire, 422

Arruntius, Lucius, 327 f.

Art, attitude toward, 95

Asceticism, Christian, 109; of later moralists, 111 ff.

Atticus, 161, 224 ff.

Augurs, 187

Augustine, St., on marriage, 112

Augustus, revival of religion, 198 ff.; relations with Senate, 267; Cicero's attitude toward, 297 f.; rule of, 297 ff.

Auspices, 141, 156

Beliefs and acts, 171

Bias, moral, 67

Bibulus, 176

Binet, on testimony, 12; experiments of, 30 f.

Bridge by Gaius, 390 ff.

Bury, J. B., on history, 6

Cæsar, attitude toward religion, 218, 258; his clemency, 219, 288; Epicureanism of, 227; flattery of, 288 f.

Capri, 29, 357

Cassius, 233

Cato, scepticism of, 143

Church, Fathers of, 64

Cicero, use of invective, 56 ff.; on piety, 134; religious doctrines of, 153 ff.; on divination, 157; his trustworthiness, 158; letters of, 160 ff.; his attitude toward Epicureanism, 229 ff.; his veracity, 229; his vituperation of Piso, 236 ff.; his attitude toward Augustus, 297 f.

Claudius, 321, 343, 387

Clodius, 192

Comitia, 260 f.

Conduct, 130

Conspiracies against Augustus, 302

Cotta, doctrines of, 151

Cowper on decadence of England, 117

Credibility of testimony, 27 ff.; 197

Credulity, 43

Criticism, among Romans, 43; of society, 115

Cults, decay of, 190

Cumont, F., on Roman religion, 133; on sources, 429

Defects in sources, 140

Delatio, 270 ff.

Delatores, 337 ff.

Demagogues, 19

Dill, S., on Seneca, 82; on Roman worship, 134; on Roman religion, 138; on Tacitus, 321; on rural life, 424

Diogenes of Oinoanda, 222 f.

Divination, 157, 172 ff.; 205

431

CAPRICORN TITLES

34. *Walter Lord, ed.,* THE FREMANTLE DIARY (THE SOUTH AT WAR). $1.25.
35. *Fowlie,* FOUR MODERN FRENCH COMEDIES. $1.25. (Hardcover $2.50).
36. *Torrey,* LES PHILOSOPHES. $1.65.
    Torrey, LES PHILOSOPHES (Cloth) $3.00.
37. *Ault,* ELIZABETHAN LYRICS. $1.75.
38. *Symonds,* AGE OF THE DESPOTS. $1.65.
39. *White,* MISTRESS MASHAM'S REPOSE. $1.35.
40. *Gilbert,* THE LETTERS OF MACHIAVELLI. $1.65.
41. *Still,* THE WEST. $1.65.
    Still, THE WEST. (Cloth) $2.50.
42. *Myers,* HISTORY OF BIGOTRY IN THE UNITED STATES. $1.65.
43. *Armstrong,* GRAY WOLF. $1.45.
44. *Auerbach,* INTRODUCTION TO ROMANCE LANGUAGES & LITERATURE. $1.65.
    Auerbach, INTRODUCTION TO ROMANCE LANGUAGES & LITERATURE. (Cloth) $2.50.
45. *Viereck,* METAPOLITICS. $1.75.
48. *Symonds,* FINE ARTS. $1.65.
49. *Bemelmans,* SMALL BEER. $.95.
50. *Dangerfield,* STRANGE DEATH. $1.75.
52. *Jaspers,* QUESTION OF GERMAN GUILT. $.95.
53. *Tawney,* EQUALITY. $1.35.
54. *La Guardia,* MAKING OF AN INSURGENT. $1.25.
55. *Cooper,* HOME AS FOUND. $1.35.
56. *Quiller Couch,* ART OF WRITING. $1.35.
57. NEWGATE CALENDAR. $1.45.
58. *Symonds,* LIFE OF MICHELANGELO. $1.75.
59. *Disraeli,* CONINGSBY. $1.75.

CAPRICORN GIANTS

201. *Hauser,* DIET DOES IT. $1.25.
202. *Moscati,* ANCIENT SEMITIC CIVILIZATIONS. $1.65.
203. *Chin P'ing Mei,* HSI MEN AND HIS 6 WIVES. $2.45.
204. *Brockelmann,* ISLAMIC PEOPLE. $1.95.
205. *Salter,* CONDITIONED REFLEX THERAPY. $1.75.
206. *Lissner,* LIVING PAST. $1.95.
207. *Davis,* CORPORATIONS. $2.45.
208. *Rodman,* CONVERSATION WITH ARTISTS. $1.45.
209. *Falls,* GREAT WAR 1914-1918. $1.95.
210. MEMOIRS OF A RENAISSANCE POPE. $1.85.
211. *Schachner,* FOUNDING FATHERS, $2.45.

G. P. PUTNAM'S SONS

210 Madison Avenue ● New York 16, N. Y